JOHN RUSZKIEWICZ
University of Texas at Austin

CHRISTY FRIEND
University of South Carolina

MAXINE HAIRSTON
Late of University of Texas at Austin

second edition

SF COMPACT

Prentice Hall

Upper Saddle River   London   Singapore

Toronto   Tokyo   Sydney   Hong Kong   Mexico City

Editorial Director: Leah Jewell
Editor-in-Chief: Craig Campanella
Executive Editor: Kevin Molloy
Assistant Editor: Melissa Casciano
Editorial Assistant: Megan Dubrowski
Marketing Director: Brandy Dawson
Senior Marketing Manager: Windley Morley
Marketing Assistant: Kimberly Caldwell
Text Permission Specialist: Kathleen Karcher
Editorial Development Editor-in-Chief: Rochelle Diogenes
Development Editors: Laura Olson, Alexis Walker, Veronica Tomaiuolo
VP/Director of Production and Manufacturing: Barbara Kittle
Prepress & Manufacturing Manager: Nick Sklitsis
Prepress & Manufacturing Assistant Manager: Mary Ann Gloriande
Production Liaison: Maureen Benicasa
Creative Design Director: Leslie Osher
Art Directors: Nancy Wells, Anne Bonanno Nieglos

Interior Design Adaptation: Michelle Wiggins
Director, Image Resource Center: Melinda Patelli
Manager, Cover Visual Research and Permissions: Karen Sanatar
Manager, Rights and Permissions: Zina Arabia
Manager, Visual Research: Beth Brenzel
Image Researcher: Robert Farrell
Cover Art Director: Leslie Osher
Cover Art Designer: Ximena Tamvakopoulos, Nancy Wells
Cover Illustration/Photo: Philip Rostron/ Masterfile
Full-Service Project Management: GGS Book Services
Composition: GGS Book Services
Printer/Binder: RR Donnelley & Sons
Cover Printer: Phoenix Color Corp.
Text Typeface: 9/11 New Century Schoolbook

This book includes 2009 MLA guidelines.

Credits and acknowledgments borrowed from other sources and reproduced, with permission, in this textbook appear on appropriate page within text (or on page 538).

Library of Congress Cataloging-in-Publication Data
Hairston, Maxine.
  SF Compact / by Maxine Hairston, John Ruszkiewicz, Christy Friend.—2nd ed.
    p. cm.
  Includes bibliographical references and index.
  ISBN 978-0-205-75119-8 (pbk. alk. paper)   1. English language—Rhetoric—Handbooks, manuals, etc.   2. English language—Grammar—Handbooks, manuals, etc.   3. Report writing—Handbooks, manuals, etc.   I. Ruszkiewicz, John J. 1950–   II. Friend, Christy.   III. Title.
  PE1408.H2965 2007
  808'.042—dc22

                                                     2007005291

10 9 8 7 6 5 4 3 2 1

Prentice Hall
is an imprint of

ISBN 10:   0-205-75119-9
ISBN 13: 978-0-205-75119-8

Writing Processes
Academic Writing
Document Design
Style

part 1

WRITING PROCESSES

part 2

ACADEMIC WRITING

Grammar

Punctuation and Mechanics

*A*fter a hiatus of several editions, Maxine Hairston decided to return to *The Scott Foresman Handbook for Writers* for the eighth edition, coordinating its revision plan and completing a draft of its first chapter before her death on July 22, 2005, at the age of 83. In a remarkable career, Maxine helped to improve the way writing was taught and elevated the status and morale of composition teachers nationally. She retired as professor emerita at the University of Texas at Austin in 1992, but continued to edit her much-admired textbooks, while earning a master's degree in history. Anyone who knew Maxine Hairston appreciated the vitality of her intellect, her absolute delight in learning, and her eternal goodwill and optimism. She was our mentor, colleague, and friend, and we dedicate this edition to her memory.

JR & CF

Preface

As both authors and composition instructors, we recognize that the population of every freshman composition classroom is diverse—from ambitious chemistry majors and aspiring poets to budding entrepreneurs and future teachers. Yet whatever their varied interests, all students want a writing text that is to-the-point, easy to carry, and affordable enough to keep around for future classes and careers. To that end, the second edition of *SF Compact* offers comprehensive, up-to-date coverage of the writing and research processes in a student-friendly package for a lower price than virtually any handbook on the market.

New to This Edition

■ Expanded and revised coverage of research and documentation.

- A revised discussion of finding and evaluating sources (Chapters 40–41) to foreground academic databases.
- New sample citations in MLA, APA, and CMS styles, emphasizing library subscription services and online sources.
- A new MLA sample paper (Chapter 44) that includes visual sources.
- A new APA sample paper (Chapter 45).

■ **Inclusion of image-based exercises**

- New images and captions that incorporate critical thinking questions and brief exercises, so that the visuals not only support the text, but also become part of the learning process and a starting point for class discussion.

■ **New material on paragraphs and transitions**

- Revised chapters on paragraphs (Chapters 12 and 13) that include dozens of examples of effective paragraphs drawn from a variety of sources and disciplines. Chapter 10 also includes a new section on revising paragraphs.
- Chapter 12 now includes multiple examples of weak and strong transitions so that students understand the instruction and see revision in action.

■ **Increased accessibility**

- Tabs now separate major sections of the book, so that students can readily flip to the material they need.
- An alphabetical index of MLA, APA, and CMS citations appears on the back-inside cover, providing students with a quick reference tool for these items.

Proven Features of SF Compact

Academic Writing Part II details for students the nuances of writing in the college environment, including writing arguments (Chapter 8) and writing about literature (Chapter 9).

ESL Material in Chapters 26, 27, and 28 offers advice for negotiating problematic areas of academic English.

Extensive Companion Website at http://www.prenhall.com/sfcompact offers hundreds of interactive, text-tied, and self-graded exercises, as well as additional information on research and documentation.

Student samples throughout the Handbook, including full MLA and APA papers, demonstrate correct documentation style. Also, to reinforce our emphasis on real-world writing we feature several "Going Public" examples showing students engaged in public and community writing.

Serving Students Best

SF Compact presents material from a student's point of view. Therefore each chapter is framed around the questions students commonly ask about writing, rather than around rules and terminology presented out of context. Whether students need step-by-step advice for surviving their first college research paper assignment, tips on preparing a literary analysis for a senior thesis, or formatting guidelines for a business letter, they will find it in *SF Compact*. Our research materials have been carefully refined, and they are clear, easy, and manageable. We tackle thorny issues such as evaluating electronic sources, avoiding plagiarism, and using civil language. Perhaps most important, we address student writers in language that is both personal and encouraging. We recognize that writing is hard work and that this volume only begins to address the complexities writers face in sharing their ideas. We are committed to making students successful writers.

Supplements

■ Resources for Instructors

- **Answer Key** to the exercises within *SF Compact* available online.
- **Companion Website™** at http://www.prenhall.com/sfcompact provides hundreds of **interactive exercises,** text-tied and self-graded; and **research and documentation information**.
- **Evaluating Online Sources with Research Navigator™** helps students make the most of their research time, offering help with the research process and three exclusive databases full of relevant and reliable source material, including EBSCO's *ContentSelect™* Academic Journal Database, *The New York Times* archive, and the *Best of the Web* Link Library. VALUE PACK with *SF Compact*. Visit www.researchnavigator.com to learn more.
- ***The New American Webster Handy College Dictionary*** or ***The New American Roget's College Thesaurus*** in **Dictionary Format** is available in VALUE PACK with *SF Compact*. Contact your Prentice Hall representative for ordering information.

Acknowledgments

For helping us to improve this second edition of *SF Compact*, we are grateful to the talented and professional staff at Prentice Hall. We especially thank Executive Editor Paul Crockett and Developmental Editor Laura Olson for their unfailing support, careful attention and thoughtful advice throughout the revision process; Kelly Keeler and Maureen Benicasa for expertly shepherding the manuscript into print; and Editorial Director Leah Jewell for overseeing the project.

We are also grateful to Brooke Rollins and Brad Stratton for providing research assistance and to student authors Tallon Harding and Jessica Carfolite for sharing their work.

Finally, we wish to thank our reviewers for providing insightful and useful suggestions that guided our revisions: Leigh Edwards, Florida State Univ.; Dr. Bill Clemente, Peru State College; Polly Buckinghamm, Eastern Washington Univ.; Thomas Hemmeter, Arcadia University; Susan Vanderborg, Univ. of South Carolina; Jason Gieger, California State Univ.–Sacramento; Catherine Lally, Brevard Community College; Jennifer Sutter, Pikes Peak Community College; and Susan Rosen, Anne Arundel Community College.

part

Writing
Processes

What D⊙es Writing Involve? **1**

1a Why write?

Writing is not a mysterious activity at which only a talented few can succeed. Nor is it a purely academic skill that you will leave behind at graduation. On the contrary: in our information-based society, almost everyone must write. Through writing, we share what we know, debate issues, promote our beliefs, and advocate change. Whether you are drafting a letter to your senator or posting a message online, writing gives you a voice.

Many people use writing to work through their ideas or to help organize new material in school or on the job. As the novelist E.M. Forster put it, "How do I know what I think until I see what I say?"

The ability to write has become more important with the explosion of electronic media. Today, writers in all fields address wider audiences as part of a typical day's work. You may communicate online with classmates and instructors—in fact, email may be your primary mode of communication. Conferencing software makes it easy to network worldwide. Now, more than ever, writing matters.

To see examples of student writing projects go to <www.prenhall.com/hairston>.

1b What does it take to write well?

First, *see* yourself as a writer. Many people underestimate their potential. Writing is a skill that you can master. Don't let discouraging myths fool you.

- **Myth:** *Good writers are born, not made.*
  Fact: People become good writers by working at it. If you want to write well, you can—if you invest the time.

- **Myth:** *Good writers know what they want to say before they start writing.*
  Fact: Many good writers begin with only a notion of what they want to say. They know that the process of writing can help them generate ideas and rethink what they know.

- **Myth:** *Good writers get it right the first time.*
  Fact: Although experienced writers sometimes produce polished work on the first try, they usually must work through several drafts.

- **Myth:** *Good writers work alone.*
  Fact: Writers often rely on colleagues for ideas and help, even if they do much of the actual composing alone. They may also coauthor articles, reports, or essays.

- **Myth:** *Writing won't be important once you leave school.*
  Fact: Most people write every day, regardless of whether they are in school. Professionals in every field communicate in writing.

- **Myth:** *Writing means putting words on a page—nothing more.*
  Fact: Most writers produce traditional texts such as letters or reports. However, composing such documents as Web sites, brochures, or presentations often also includes working with images, graphics, layouts, and other multimedia elements.

- **Myth:** *Only professional authors publish their work.*
  Fact: Computers make it easy to preserve and distribute documents. The writing you do in school may reach large audiences via the Internet or campus publications.

EXERCISE 1.1 When you hear the term *writer*, what kind of person comes to mind? Many people reserve the terms *author* and *journalist* for those who make their living solely by writing. But can you think of other people who write frequently? What kinds of writing do they do? Discuss your answers with your classmates.

1c How does writing work?

There is no secret formula for writing well, and no quick or foolproof way to turn an initial idea into a polished final text. However, most people, when they write, follow thinking patterns that also occur in other creative activities. Chart 1.1 outlines these patterns as stages of writing.

Remember, though, that this diagram only hints at what writers really do. A chart can't show nuances in the process, nor can it differentiate among individual writers and varied writing situations.

Writers adjust to their purpose, their audience, and the specific demands of the project. Don't think of the writing process as a lockstep march from outlining to proofreading. It's a dynamic, flexible network of choices and skills.

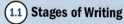

> ### (1.1) Stages of Writing
>
> - **PREPARING:** Read, brainstorm, browse online, and talk to people in order to generate ideas and to decide what you want to write about.
>
> - **RESEARCHING:** Gather facts and examples from your reading, your conversations with others, your field research, or your own experiences.
>
> - **PLANNING:** Organize your ideas and develop them further. Prepare lists, outlines, or note cards and sketch out visual elements.
>
> - **DRAFTING:** Begin to put words (and images or other visual elements, if you're using them) onto a page or screen. Compose one or more drafts. Rethink and reshape your materials as necessary.
>
> - **INCUBATING:** Take time off to let your ideas simmer. New ideas may come after you've taken a break.
>
> - **REVISING:** Review what you have written. Adjust the topic, organization, content, design, and audience as needed.
>
> - **EDITING:** Review and polish your draft for style, clarity, and readability.
>
> - **PROOFREADING:** Read carefully to correct spelling, punctuation, and formatting errors.

EXERCISE 1.2 Think back to a piece of writing you were proud of—perhaps a letter to the editor that was published, a personal statement that won you a scholarship, or an *A* paper in a difficult class—and write a paragraph describing the preparation you put into it, how many times you revised it, and why you think it was successful.

1d How do you define a writing situation?

Writing is a *social activity*, a way of interacting with others. Every time you write, you enter into a *writing situation* in which

- *you*
- say *something*
- to *somebody*
- for *some purpose*.

Every time you write, you should think carefully about your purpose, your audience, and how you want to come across to your readers. Probably no other single habit will do more to help you become a skilled writer.

1e How do you define your purpose(s) for writing?

When you begin a writing project, consider why you are writing in the first place. A general purpose will help you focus and think about the materials you need.

1 Decide what you hope to accomplish. Think about your purpose ahead of time and use it to shape your first draft. Centuries ago, theorists of *rhetoric*, the art of persuasive communication, identified three basic purposes for writing: writing *to inform*, or writing that teaches readers new information; writing *to persuade*, or writing that convinces readers to believe or act in new ways; and writing *to entertain*, or writing that diverts and engages readers. Often you may want to achieve more than one of these goals within a single paper. (See Section 3c for specific methods of organizing projects to suit particular purposes.)

Thinking about these purposes is a practical matter. When you don't know why you're writing, you can't produce a coherent paper.

Sometimes you may not be sure of your purpose until you've written a first draft. You may look into several angles on an idea as you figure out what you want to say. Eventually, though, you must articulate a purpose that satisfies both you and your readers. Use Checklist 1.1 to think about your goals.

checklist 1.1 ┐ Purpose

1. If you are writing a paper for a course, list any description of purpose in the assignment. Target words such as *narrate, explain, argue, and evaluate*.

2. What do you want readers to get from your piece? Do you want to inform, persuade, or entertain? If you have multiple goals, which is the most important?

3. What supporting materials will you draw on to achieve your goals? What research, examples, or personal experiences will you use?

4. How will you present these supporting materials? Will you narrate, define, describe, compare and contrast, explain, or argue?

5. What form will this project take? Will you write a letter, an editorial, a report, a Web page, or a review, for example? Will you incorporate tables, images, or other visual elements?

2 Consider how other elements in the writing situation shape your purpose(s). Although we discuss each aspect of the writing situation separately, in practice it's difficult to consider any of these elements in isolation. For any project, your purpose(s) will help you define your audience, the form in which you present your ideas, and the impression you want to make.

1f   How do you write for an audience?

Each time you write, you have to think carefully about who your audience might be and how they will respond to your material. Sometimes writers have to contend with multiple and possibly conflicting audiences. In other cases, identifying an audience is nearly impossible.

Learning how to appeal to an audience is a skill, and it takes time and practice to master. As you begin to think about your readers, consult Checklist 1.2 on audience. If within a single project you will reach several potential audiences, run through the checklist for each group.

checklist 1.2 ⌐ Audience

1. Does the assignment specify a particular audience? If so, describe that audience. If not, whom do you visualize as the audience(s) for this project?

2. What do they already know about your subject? What kinds of information will they need you to provide?

3. What values and beliefs are important to them? What kinds of examples and arguments are they likely to respond to?

4. What is their attitude about your subject? How will you convince them of the value of your ideas?

5. Will they feel most comfortable with a formal or more casual approach to the topic? What kind of formats, layouts, or visuals will they accept?

EXERCISE 1.3 Briefly analyze what you think readers would want to know if you were writing

1. a personal statement for a scholarship application.

2. a letter disputing a charge on your credit card account.

3. a description of an experiment you carried out for a chemistry class.

4. a flyer advertising a benefit performance by your best friend's blues band.

EXERCISE 1.4 Working with a classmate, look through a magazine—some possibilities are *Sports Illustrated, Spin, The New Yorker, Maxim, Money, Wired, Newsweek,* or *Source*—and study the advertisements and the kinds of articles it carries. Then write a paragraph describing the kinds of people you think the editor and publisher of the magazine assume its readers to be. Use Checklist 1.1 to guide your work.

How Do You Find nd Explore a Topic? 2

2a How do you find a topic?

How do you find a topic that both you and your readers will enjoy?

1 Think beyond broad, traditional topics. Too often, students write about the same issues. Does this list look familiar?

Abortion	Global warming	Euthanasia
Terrorism	Capital punishment	School choice

These issues *are* important, but can you add something current, fresh, or informative to the debate? Because so much has already been written about these issues, you risk bogging down in generalities and clichés.

If you do choose one of these broad topics, make your paper unique by focusing it. Rather than write a general paper, you might concentrate on a recent controversy or a local case. Checklist 2.1 can help you find original angles on a traditional issue.

checklist 2.1

To Find a Topic, Ask Yourself . . .

- **What three subjects do you enjoy reading about most?** What magazines do you pick up? What kinds of books do you browse through? What subjects have you always wanted to learn more about?

- **What three subjects do you know the most about?** What topics could you discuss for half an hour without notes? What problems lead people to seek your advice or expertise? What could you teach someone else to do?

- **What three subjects do you enjoy arguing about most?** On what subjects can you hold your own with just about anyone? What opinions do you advocate most strongly?

- **What three issues in your community do you care about the most?** What issues affect you or people you know? For what causes do you volunteer? What opinions and ideas would you like to communicate to government officials or to the community at large?

2 Consider your interests and strengths. Choose a topic that interests you, preferably one that you already have some knowledge and ideas about. Brainstorm a list of possibilities. Select the idea best suited for the assignment and the amount of time you have. Checklist 2.1 will help you discover topics.

3 Choose a topic in your world. Some of the best issues for writing about are unfolding right in front of you. Even if your instructor has assigned a general topic, try to connect that topic to your own experience in your community.

Such topics connect to your everyday life. You're bound to have a strong interest in finding out more about them. Additionally, you are more likely to do original research; expert sources of information—newspapers, community organizations, government offices, and interested citizens—are close at hand. And should you decide to publish your writing outside the classroom, perhaps as a guest newspaper editorial or as a letter to an elected official, you may even influence public opinion.

4 Browse in the library and online. Look in the library catalog or in the directory of the Library of Congress (better known as the *Subject List*). Just the way a broad subject is broken down into headings and subheadings suggests many topic possibilities. Consult such reference sources as specialized encyclopedias, too.

Even when you don't have a general subject area to direct your library search, try browsing in the new book section or through the op/ed and analysis pages of national publications like the *New York*

@tips

You can usually access newsgroups from your Web browser and explore them with a search engine. To search Usenet groups, try <http://groups.google.com>.

Use a Web search engine, such as *Yahoo!* <www.yahoo.com>, *Google* <www.google.com>, or *Lycos* <www.lycos.com>. The groupings themselves offer a range of general topic areas ("Arts & Humanities," "Health," "Science"), but the topics get more intriguing when you explore them more deeply, especially *Yahoo!'s* "Society and Culture." Check out "Issues and Causes" at <http://dir.yahoo.com/Society_and_Culture/Issues_and_Causes/>.

Times, the *Wall Street Journal*, or *Slate* for current topics that spark your curiosity. You can also use an online search engine such as *Google* or *Yahoo!* to identify possible topics, but be careful. These tools often call up so many information sources that it's easy to become distracted or overwhelmed. A librarian at your campus library can help you direct your online research to reliable, manageable sources.

2b   How do you refine your topic?

Once you have found a promising topic, you'll need to focus your efforts. Problems of focus happen when writers try to cover too much material. This kind of overreaching can result in a project long on generalities but short on lively details and thoroughly developed ideas.

1 Don't try to cover everything. Remember that your time is limited. You can't discover all there is to know about a topic. Even if you could, you wouldn't be able to fit all that into one paper. Narrow your research to something manageable. Any paper you write should contain only a portion of what you know about its subject.

2 Make a tree diagram. To narrow a topic, make a chart on which you divide and subdivide the topic into smaller and smaller parts, each of which branches out like an inverted tree. This tree helps you see many potential areas within each division, as well as the relationships among them.

If you needed to write a five-page paper about an issue in U.S. high schools, what might you choose as your focus and why? How narrow would your topic need to be? Discuss and compare your choice with a group of class-mates, noting the range of possibilities.

Suppose you've become interested in writing about college student debt after watching your roommate run up several thousand dollars in credit-card bills during a single semester. Your tree diagram might look like this:

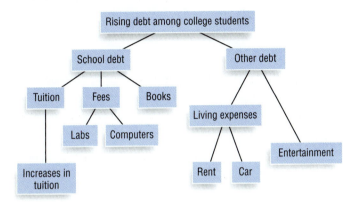

Now select the most promising branch from your first diagram and make a new diagram to refine that idea further.

3 Make an idea map. Another way to narrow a topic is to make an idea map that shows patterns of related ideas worth exploring. In the middle of a blank sheet of paper, write a phrase that describes your general subject. Circle that term—say, *college expenses*—and then, for about 10 minutes, attach every word you can think of either to that original term or to others that you have linked to it. Circle all additional words as you write them, and draw lines connecting them to the words that triggered them.

Your finished map might look like the one on page 12. When you're done, examine the map to see whether any clusters of words suggest topics you might develop. As with tree diagrams, you can use any promising concept from your first idea map as the focal point of a second exercise, starting again with the narrowed subject to develop more ideas.

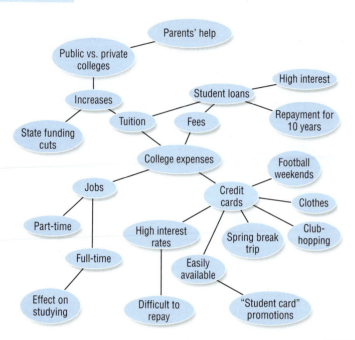

4 Investigate an interesting question or hypothesis. Pursue a problem for which you do not yet have a satisfactory answer—much as investigative reporters look for "leads" that will turn into breaking news stories.

Sometimes a promising issue will take the form of a question: Why is violent crime increasing among juveniles at a time when the overall crime rate is decreasing? Or you might start a project with a *hypothesis,* a statement that makes a claim to be tested. Scientists often begin research projects with these kinds of educated guesses.

A guiding question or hypothesis will help you focus your topic. But at this stage it is probably too early to commit to a definite position. Until the evidence comes in and you have more information, remain flexible in your thinking and be willing to revise your focus and approach.

EXERCISE 2.1 Suppose you want to write a short paper for a composition course on one of the following subjects. Write several promising subtopics that you might focus on; then use a tree diagram or an idea map to generate ideas about the subtopic that you find most interesting.

Crime on college campuses
Illegal drug use
The popularity of MP3 players
Organic foods

2c   How do you explore and develop a topic?

You have a topic. Now you need to explore its implications, find support-ing evidence, and fill in specific details. The term *invention* describes the techniques writers use to generate subject matter for a paper.

Invention techniques help you explore and develop a thesis. You can use any of these techniques at any point in your writing process. Return to them anytime you need to expand and develop your ideas.

1 Freewrite about the topic. Freewriting is writing nonstop for 10 or 15 minutes to explore what you already know and to discover areas you'd like to learn more about. Don't worry about grammar, spelling, or other niceties while you're freewriting—the point of freewriting is to generate ideas. Continue to write as long as ideas come, and don't cross out or reject anything. Be alert for phrases and concepts that extend your thesis in promising directions.

2 Use the journalist's questions. Journalists keep six questions in mind when writing a news story.

Who?	What?	Where?
When?	Why?	How?

These questions help you cover all the bases, especially when writing an informative paper (though not every question will apply to every topic).

3 Look at your topic from different perspectives. Four categories of questions explore topics: questions of *fact, definition, value,* and *policy.* Originally designed to develop speeches for the law courts of ancient Greece and Rome, these questions move from simple to more complex ways of examining an issue.

- Questions of **fact** involve things already known about your topic: What has already happened? What information is already avail-able? What policies are already in place?

- Questions of **definition** interpret these facts and place them in context: What category does your topic fit into? What laws or approaches apply?

- Questions of **value** ask you to make a judgment: Is the idea you're talking about good or bad? Is it ethical or unethical? workable or unworkable?

- Questions of **policy** allow you to consider specific courses of action: What should be done? Are old solutions working, or is a new approach needed?

You won't answer all these questions in a single paper, but they are useful for examining a topic comprehensively. Once you've run through all the questions, decide which one(s) you want to treat in your paper. For more on how these questions can help you construct a thesis statement, see 3a.

4 Write a zero draft.

Just start a draft. The very act of writing will get the creative juices flowing and help you to organize your thoughts. This first try is a "zero draft," a trial run that doesn't really count. Zero drafts are easy to write, and after they're complete, you can select the best material to use in your next draft. Try writing several zero drafts to try out possible approaches.

5 Read up on your topic.

Look up your subject, and read. You'll find detailed instructions on doing library research in Section 39a.

Read to find facts. Read to discover how other writers have treated topics like yours. Seeing others' work will suggest possibilities for your own.

6 Talk to others about your topic.

From the start, invite others to join in your topic. Look for campus events, clubs, or forums. Check the local papers for lectures, films, or community meetings where you might meet people interested in your work.

Online newsgroups and listservs offer access to a wide network of contacts. Post a short description of your project to one of these forums and request input. You may get valuable suggestions from experts in the field. See Section 39c-2 for more on entering online discussions.

Classmates can help each other generate ideas. Talk informally or exchange email with classmates who share an interest in your topic. As you start to explain your ideas to others, more ideas will come to you. You may see arguments you hadn't considered and learn about new sources.

EXERCISE 2.2 Use any two of the techniques described in this section to generate ideas about one of your writing projects in progress. Then discuss your experience with your classmates: Which strategy yielded the best ideas? Which are you likely to use again as a regular part of your writing process?

How Do You Focus and Organize a Writing Project?

3

Now it's time to make some decisions about the direction your paper will take.

This chapter offers strategies to guide you from the invention stage through the planning and organizing stages of a paper, so that you can begin to write with purpose and confidence.

3a   How do you craft a thesis?

As you explore your topic, you will discover one or two issues that will shape your *thesis statement*. A *thesis* is a sentence (or sometimes two or three sentences) that states the point of a paper. Try to construct a thesis statement early in your writing process and use it as a framework for organizing your first draft. By keeping a thesis in mind, you can be sure of covering all the important points.

1 Make a strong point. A thesis statement is more than just an observation; it is a strong, focused statement that might be questioned or challenged. It should offer a clearly stated analysis, critique, or position on your topic that readers will find new and significant.

INSIGNIFICANT	The doughnuts in Jester cafeteria are terrible.
	Even if true, few readers will find this observation substantial enough to support an entire paper.
MORE SIGNIFICANT	University administrators should investigate the impact a Krispy Kreme franchise might have on revenues for the Student Union.
NOT DEBATABLE	Domestic violence harms families.
	Who's going to argue with this claim?
DEBATABLE	The state legislature should pass the current bill mandating harsher penalties for second-offense child abuse and spousal abuse convictions.
TOO GENERAL	Environmental groups and landowners disagree over many issues, including land use, species protection, and pollution regulations.
	You won't be able to research and thoroughly analyze more than one or two specific disagreements in a typical academic paper.

15

MORE SPECIFIC   The debate over whether wolves should still be protected as endangered species, now that wild populations are thriving in the Northwest, raises key questions about how to balance individuals' property rights with the long-term viability of the species.

Once you've written a thesis, ask yourself how a member of your audience might react to it. If you can envision a polite yawn ("So what?") or a blank stare ("What's your point?"), revise your thesis, using the guidelines in Checklist 3.1.

checklist 3.1 — What Makes a Strong Thesis?

- Does it focus on a **substantive issue**, one that deserves readers' attention?
- Is the thesis **debatable**—could reasonable people disagree with it?
- Does it address an issue that affects the public? Is the issue **current**? Will **readers care** about this thesis?
- Is your thesis **clearly stated**? Can readers tell where you stand?
- Can you **support** your thesis adequately, using research or your own experiences? Do you need to narrow or qualify your claim?

2 Preview the direction your paper will take. Write a complete sentence or two that forecasts the ideas you expect to write about, in roughly the same order in which you plan to address them. Be *succinct* yet *comprehensive*—that is, be brief yet indicate the major points you want to make. Your thesis tells readers what to expect.

3 Place your thesis effectively. Don't assume that your thesis must be the first sentence of your paper, although it can be. Your decision about where to put your thesis depends on the writing situation: your audience, your purpose, and the position you want to take on the topic.

When you are presenting information or arguments in a straightforward fashion, you'll state your thesis early. It may even be your first sentence. At other times, you'll provide a context for your thesis by defining key terms or giving background information first. That's why, in academic papers, the thesis statement often appears at the end of the introductory paragraph.

In other situations, you may want to delay your thesis more. You may be writing to explore a question rather than to present a settled opinion. Or, if your thesis is controversial, you may want to present your evidence first. Social science research reports often begin by describing the methods and data and end with larger conclusions. In such cases, your thesis may not be stated until the last paragraph.

However, even if you don't clarify your specific claim until late in the essay, readers should understand what central ideas your paper will address from the beginning.

4 Revise your thesis as your project evolves. If your thesis shifts as you continue to explore, research, and plan your project, then restate it to make it precise and to reflect your changes in direction. This is the right time to be testing your preliminary assumptions and ideas. Learn from every part of the process, and don't be discouraged. Your final thesis may be nothing like what you imagined at the outset—and that's okay.

An Opening Paragraph with Thesis Statement

A thesis statement pulled out of context, like the previous examples in this chapter, can seem pretty bland. Fortunately, in a real paper, a thesis isn't solely responsible for shaping a reader's first impression. Notice how student writer Tallon Harding positions her thesis statement in the opening paragraph from a paper written for a college composition course. The thesis statement is highlighted.

School has just let out but the library is packed with students. Each one of us is studying, working frantically to finish the next day's assignments. The Advanced Placement tests will be given on Monday; the pressure is almost unbearable. A couple of years ago this spectacle would have confounded the average high school librarian, who would have been able to leave as soon as school let out. Recently, however, this scene has become commonplace. Due to a push by school officials looking to receive government grants, students are increasingly pressured to

continued on p. 18

continued from page 17

enroll in college-level courses offered in the high school classroom. As part of a new "Steps to Prosperity" measure recently introduced by the South Carolina state legislature, many districts are even beginning to require students to declare a major as early as their sophomore year in high school (Landrum). Unfortunately, a good, well-rounded high school education involves more than just academic study. It must also include extracurricular activities that help students to grow socially, physically, and emotionally. As schools eliminate these broader elements in the quest to achieve higher and higher academic standards, they leave gaps in students' education and neglect important student needs.

3b   How do you avoid plagiarism?

Early in the writing process, it's important that you understand what constitutes plagiarism, particularly if you're writing papers for an instructor who expects you to use outside sources. Doesn't that require you to use someone else's material and ideas? Well, yes it does. The trick is knowing how to incorporate other people's ideas or research into your work while giving them full credit. Section 42c shows you several strategies for acknowledging someone else's ideas or arguments in a way that gives the original source its due. The point is always to be up front about where you found the idea, quotation, or conclusion that you're incorporating into your work. You should make it possible for anyone who wants to clarify a point or get more information on your topic to go to the source and check it out.

If in previous years you've attended a school in which teachers expected you to memorize large quantities of material and then demonstrate your mastery of that material, it may seem natural to you to simply repeat information that you've gathered from your reading. You're likely to find, however, that in most college writing assignments, instructors want you to go beyond mastery of a body of material to synthesize, respond to, and evaluate its ideas and its arguments.

As a Web-wise student, you know what a wealth of information the Internet can provide on almost any writing topic. You can also find commercial sites that will, for a price, provide you with a finished term paper on just about any topic of your choice. You may have friends who have bought such papers or have done a cut-and-paste job of piecing together a paper from Internet sources. Whatever process they chose, the project they turned in can only be called plagiarism. We want to convince you not to go there, and to show you why.

When you take a process-centered writing course, you have a special opportunity to master a craft essential for doing well in college and, later on, in most professions—certainly in science, law, engineering, college teaching, public relations, and even in medicine and accounting. A skilled writer has an edge in getting what he or she wants in the everyday transactions of life, whether it's to persuade a business to sponsor a charity project, appeal a spike in your property tax, or construct an effective Web site for an organization you support. You don't want to miss an opportunity to acquire such a powerful tool.

3c   How do you organize a writing project?

No matter how good your ideas are, if you don't organize them, readers will get lost and blame you. Coherent organization is the foundation of any writing project.

1 Consider an introduction/body/conclusion structure. This basic pattern works for many kinds of projects. This design suggests logical movement from statement to proof.

- In the **introduction**, you begin by telling your readers clearly and simply what topics your paper will cover.
- In the **body**, of the paper you follow with examples and explanations for each of your main points.
- In your **conclusion**, you tie your points together and leave readers with a sense of closure.

This structure is also called a commitment and response pattern, because in the first section the writer promises to cover certain issues.

The opening commitment can be direct or indirect. In a *direct commitment*, the writer addresses an issue squarely, as if making an announcement. Such an opening obliges the writer to cover every point mentioned.

A commitment can also be made *indirectly* by narrating an anecdote or an incident.

> Did you leave fall registration today with a rearranged schedule because two of the courses you planned to take had been canceled and three others were already full? If so, welcome to the biggest club on campus.

Through indirect commitment, the writer has indicated the subject of the paper without actually saying so.

Papers that result from the basic introduction/body/conclusion pattern will usually take a simple shape.

Basic Introduction/Body/Conclusion Pattern

Introduction *Present thesis . . .*	I. First-year students need a rep. on the board of the student union.

Body ◆ *First argument*
❏ Support: examples, reasons, evidence, etc.
◆ *Second argument*
❏ Support: examples, reasons, evidence, etc.
◆ *Other arguments . . .*
	II. Other years have representation
	   A. All students need a voice
	   B. First-years have special needs
	III. First-years need to be welcomed
	   A. Student union can be friendlier
	   B. Good to socialize outside dorms
	IV. Welcoming campus helps retention

Conclusion *Closing summary . . .*	V. An inviting student union can help first-years join campus communities.

Such papers can also incorporate significant variations. For example, you must usually deal with opposing views; if you don't address them, the paper will seem to evade key questions. Counterarguments—discussions of opposing views—make the structure of the paper more complex. They can be addressed immediately, near the beginning of the paper, or they can be dealt with as they arise in the body of the piece (but don't end with a counterargument, or you'll weaken your own case).

Here's how the basic model might look when counterarguments are added to the mix. (See Section 8d for more on handling different views in a paper.)

Introduction/Body/Conclusion Pattern with Counterarguments

Introduction *Present thesis ...*	I. First-year students need a rep. on the board of the student union.

Body
♦ *First argument*
   □ Support ...
   □ Counterarguments
      addressed by rebuttal
♦ *Second argument*
   □ Support ...
   □ Counterarguments
      addressed by rebuttal
♦ *Other arguments ...*
	II. Other years have representation
	   A. First-years need a voice
	   B. First-years may not understand
	      the system, but can learn it
	III. First-years need to be welcomed
	   A. Student union better than dorms
	   B. Dorm rec-rooms are good, but not
	      for meeting older students
	IV. Welcoming campus helps retention

Conclusion *Closing summary ...*	V. An inviting student union can help first-years join campus communities.

2 Consider a narrative or a process design. When you narrate a story, you usually describe events in the order they occurred. The structure can be quite straightforward.

Narrative Pattern

Introduction *Present thesis ...*	I. Our town's public buildings reflect the architectural styles of several different historical periods.
Body ♦ *First event* ♦ *Second event* ♦ *Third event* ♦ *Other events ...*	II. Colonial town hall (1793) III. Victorian courthouse (1846) and post office (1888) IV. Art-deco library (1932)
Conclusion *Closing summary ...*	V. These buildings tell a story about our town's gradual development.

A narrative can also be more complicated—for instance, by moving back in time with flashbacks.

A process pattern is essentially the same as a narrative pattern, but instead of telling a story you are explaining how something works. You list and describe each step in the process.

Process Pattern

Introduction *Present thesis ...*	I. Winning a reality-TV game show requires patience and cunning.
Body ♦ *First step* ♦ *Second step* ♦ *Third step* ♦ *Other steps ...*	II. First, display trustworthiness. III. Second, form a small coalition. IV. Third, lie low for a while. V. Last, betray coalition members.
Conclusion *Closing summary ...*	VI. To win the big bucks, you need to remember it is only a game.

Be careful to include all the steps in the proper order.

3 Consider a comparison and contrast structure. Sometimes you will have to examine different objects or ideas in relation to each other, especially when you are evaluating or arguing. You can either describe the things you are comparing one at a time (*subject by subject*) or describe them in an alternating sequence (*feature by feature*). The models here are followed by sample outlines.

Comparison and Contrast Pattern: Subject by Subject

Introduction *Present thesis . . .*	I. Sport-utility vehicles, though currently more popular than family sedans, have environmental and safety drawbacks that should make potential buyers beware.

Body
◆ *First subject examined*
❑ First feature
❑ Second feature
❑ Other features . . .
◆ *Second subject*
❑ First feature
❑ Second feature
❑ Other features . . .
	II. Pros and cons of SUVs
	  A. Popularity
	  B. Environmental impact
	  C. Safety
	III. Pros and cons of family sedans
	  A. Popularity
	  B. Environmental impact
	  C. Safety

Conclusion *Closing summary . . .*	IV. Buyers who value safety and the environment over style should bypass sport-utility vehicles in favor of traditional sedans.

SUBJECT BY SUBJECT: SPORT-UTILITY VEHICLES (SUVs)
VS. FAMILY SEDANS

I. **Thesis:** SUVs, while currently more popular than family sedans, have environmental and safety drawbacks that should make potential buyers beware.

II. **Subject 1:** Features of SUVs
   A. *Feature A: Popularity of SUVs*
   B. *Feature B: Environmental impact of SUVs*
   C. *Feature C: Safety of SUVs*

III. **Subject 2:** Features of family sedans
   A. *Feature A: Popularity of family sedans*
   B. *Feature B: Environmental impact of family sedans*
   C. *Feature C: Safety of family sedans*

IV. **Conclusion:** Buyers who value safety and the environment over style should bypass SUVs in favor of a traditional family sedan.

Comparison and Contrast Pattern: Feature by Feature

Introduction *Present thesis . . .*	I.	Sport-utility vehicles, though currently more popular than family sedans, have environmental and safety drawbacks that should make potential buyers beware.
Body ◆ First feature examined ❑ In first subject ❑ In second subject ◆ Second feature ❑ In first subject ❑ In second subject ◆ Other features ❑ In first subject ❑ In second subject	II. III. IV.	Popularity A. Of sport-utility vehicles B. Of family sedans Environmental impact A. Of sport-utility vehicles B. Of family sedans Safety A. Of sport-utility vehicles B. Of family sedans
Conclusion *Closing summary . . .*	V.	Buyers who value safety and the environment over style should bypass sport-utility vehicles in favor of traditional sedans.

FEATURE BY FEATURE: SPORT-UTILITY VEHICLES (SUVS)
VS. FAMILY SEDANS

I. **Thesis:** SUVs, while currently more popular than family sedans, have environmental and safety drawbacks that should make potential buyers beware.

II. **Feature A:** *Popularity*
   A. Popularity of SUVs
   B. Popularity of family sedans

III. **Feature B:** *Environmental impact*
   A. Environmental impact of SUVs
   B. Environmental impact of family sedans

IV. **Feature C:** *Safety*
   A. Safety of SUVs
   B. Safety of family sedans

V. **Conclusion:** Buyers who value safety and the environment over style should bypass SUVs in favor of a traditional family sedan.

The subject-by-subject plan works best in papers involving only a few comparisons; in such pieces readers don't have to recall a large quantity of information to make the necessary comparisons. When you're doing a longer paper, however, use the feature-by-feature pattern; otherwise, readers may lose track of the features you're comparing.

4 Consider a division or classification structure. These two ways of organizing a paper are quite different. A paper organized according to the principle of *division* breaks a topic into its components—its separate parts.

Division Pattern

Introduction *Present thesis...*	I. Candidate Everson's platform is based on four main issues.
Body ◆ First division ◆ Second division ◆ Third division ◆ Other divisions...	II. Crime prevention III. Local tax rates IV. Traffic control V. Environment
Conclusion *Closing summary...*	VI. Everson will devote the most resources to crime prevention.

Classification involves breaking a large subject into categories according to some principle of division. Classification must follow rules that don't apply to division. First, classifications must be *exhaustive:* every member of the class must fit into a category. Any principle of division you use must also be *consistent*. You can't classify by more than one principle at a time. Finally, classes *must not overlap*. That means you should be able to place an object in only one category.

Classification Pattern

Introduction *Present thesis...*	I. This year's most popular bands represent many musical genres.
Body ◆ First classification ◆ Second classification ◆ Third classification ◆ Other classifications...	II. Modern rock III. Reggae and ska IV. Hip-hop and "new soul" V. Folk, bluegrass, and country
Conclusion *Closing summary...*	VI. Young music fans appreciate a variety of musical styles.

Yet most systems of classification break down at one point or another. For example, what do you do with performing acts who play more than one kind of music? Well, you can create yet another class (Latin-pop or folk-rock), or you can classify by the musician's major body of work. But you won't always be able to eliminate every exception.

5 Consider a cause-and-effect design. This design is appropriate when explaining why something has happened. The typical cause-and-effect paper moves from an explanation of some existing condition to an examination of its particular causes. In other words, you see what has happened and you want to know why.

Typically, you'll see more than one explanation for a given event, so a cause-and-effect paper may examine various causes, from the least important to the most important.

Cause-and-Effect Pattern

Introduction *Present thesis . . .*	I. Animated films have succeeded recently due to good writing.
Body ♦ *Effects explained* ♦ *Least important causes* ♦ *More important causes* ♦ *Most important cause*	II. Animated films have made money and gained critical accolades III. Because animation is better IV. Because scripts have broad appeal
Conclusion *Closing summary . . .*	V. Plots and dialogue of new animated films entertain both young & old.

You can begin your essay by identifying an effect and then go on to hypothesize about the causes, or you can start by listing a number of causes and then show how they contribute to a particular effect.

6 Consider a problem-and-solution pattern. Use this pattern to argue for change, to propose an idea, or to settle a problem.

Problem-and-Solution Pattern

Introduction *Present thesis . . .*	I. All business school graduates should be required to take a course on professional ethics.

Body
♦ *Problem and need for solution established*
♦ *Rejected solutions*
  ♦ First rejected solution
    · Advantages
    · Disadvantages
  ♦ Other rejects . . .
♦ *Proposed solution*
  ❑ Feasibility
  ❑ Disadvantages
  ❑ Advantages
  ❑ Implementation
	II. Public distrust following recent scandals is bad for business
	III. Threat of punishment not enough
	  A. May deter some illegal actions
	  B. But damage is done whether or not crime is punished, and
	  C. Unethical actions may be legal
	VI. Ethics class prevents problems
	  A. Easy to add a new requirement
	  B. Some want fewer requirements
	  C. Focus on ethics not legalities
	  D. Principles addressed via debate

Conclusion *Closing summary . . .*	V. A discussion of principles will help graduates balance obligations to public, customers, & investors.

The first part of this pattern says, "We've got a problem and we've got to solve it—now." The second part of the problem-and-solution pattern steers the reader through proposals for solving the problem. Even though most of these ideas will be rejected, each is examined carefully. This section of the essay assures readers that no plausible approach has been ignored.

In the third part of this pattern you propose a solution to the problem. You may then want to discuss the disadvantages and advantages of this proposal, highlighting the advantages. Readers need to feel that nothing is under wraps and that no hidden agendas guide your proposal. You can then conclude by explaining how the change can be put into place.

7 Use formatting and visual elements to reinforce your paper's organization. When the assignment allows it, don't hesitate to use visual devices such as bulleted and numbered lists, headings, color, and images to help readers see how you've organized your project. For detailed advice on incorporating visual elements into a text, see Chapter 10.

EXERCISE 3.1 Working with a group of classmates, consider what patterns you might use for writing about two of the topics listed below. Give reasons why you think those patterns would work well in each case.

Where to eat out near your campus
The popularity of *The Simpsons*
Your experience volunteering at a local agency
Whether the United States should reinstate the military draft

3d How do you outline a paper?

An outline can help you keep a writing project on track. It doesn't have to be a full-sentence outline. No approach to outlining is necessarily "right." Experiment with several techniques until you find what works best for you.

1 Try a working list. The working list is the most flexible of all outlining devices. Start by jotting down the key points you want to make, leaving plenty of room under each major idea. This strategy works best as a preliminary planning technique because it allows you to add examples and points under the main ideas they support as they occur to you.

Working from a brainstorming list or perhaps from freewriting on the subject, select subpoints to fit under these major headings. You might also want to jot "cue notes" in the margin of the working list to remind yourself of anecdotes that illustrate specific points, as in the following example.

Working List: Should people be allowed to own exotic pets?

Why the issue of owning exotic pets is getting attention

- Internet makes it easy to purchase exotic wildlife
- More people interested in owning wild animals *(quote John's roommate?)*
- Few states have strict laws limiting who can own exotic snakes, big cats, tropical birds, and other wildlife as pets *(recent* Times *article: 5000–7000 pet tigers in U.S. alone)*
- Recent safety problems *(give examples: neighbor's escaped boa constrictor, North Carolina case of tiger cubs roaming suburban neighborhood)*
- Animal welfare agencies are calling for stricter rules

Arguments for owning exotic pets

- Many owners responsible, take good care of animals
- Some take homeless or rescued animals that no one else wants *(*Animal Finders Guide *site)*
- Individual property rights

Why stricter limits on ownership should be imposed nationwide

- Would ensure that people don't buy dangerous animals on a whim, then get tired of them
- Could prevent neglect and abuse of pets by requiring owners to educate themselves *(Florida case)*
- Could ensure that pets are safely housed and not dangerous to neighborhood
- Would still allow reputable wildlife preserves and parks to operate

Decide which points you want to treat first and how you can arrange the others. While writing, add and delete items from the list as you need to—nothing in a working list is untouchable.

2 Make an informal (scratch) outline.
The informal or scratch outline arranges points into categories and subcategories. It is considerably fuller than the working list and provides more organizational guidance.

A scratch outline should begin with a thesis that states your claim or main idea. Then decide what major points support that thesis. For each major point you'll need subpoints that support, explain, or illustrate the main point. Your points and subpoints can be quite loose since the conventions of the full-sentence outline need not be followed.

Scratch Outline Format

Working title   Who Should Be Able to Own Exotic Pets?

Working thesis statement   **Thesis:** Lawmakers should pass stricter laws governing who can own exotic wildlife, since the increasing popularity of such pets has created problems with irresponsible owners, neighborhood safety, and unwanted animals.

Main point 1   1. Exotic pets have become increasingly popular in the U.S. during the past few years.

Supporting reasons and evidence for 1
- The Internet has made it easy to buy exotic animals from other nations.
- Few states strictly limit ownership of these pets.
- Ordinary people are increasingly owning such pets: my next-door neighbor, tiger cubs in NC suburbs.

Main point 2   2. Many exotic pet owners endorse lax ownership requirements.

Supporting reasons and evidence for 2	• Most owners are responsible and caring.
	• Many owners are caring for homeless or rescued animals (cite: *Animal Finders Guide site*).
	• Law-abiding citizens should be able to choose their pets.
Main point 3	3. However, stricter ownership requirements are needed to prevent serious problems.
Supporting reasons and evidence for 3	• These can prevent owners from buying exotic wildlife on a whim (give examples of abandoned animals).
	• Requirements can ensure that owners are educated enough to properly care for animals.
	• Requirements can insist on safety precautions so that animals do not become a neighborhood threat.

3 Make a formal (sentence) outline. A formal outline is a fairly complex structure that compels you to think rigorously about how the ideas in a piece of writing will fit together. (That's why instructors sometimes require them.) If your major points really aren't compatible or parallel, a formal outline will expose the problems. When your supporting evidence is thin or inconsistent, those flaws may show up too.

In a formal sentence outline, you state every point in a complete sentence, and you make sentences within each grouping parallel, according to the format in Chart 3.1. As you read through the chart, imagine how you would convert the scratch outline on pages 28–29 into the fuller structure of a formal outline.

(3.1) Framework of a Formal Outline

Title: Start by stating the working title of your paper.

Thesis: State your thesis fully, as a complete sentence.

I.   State the first major point in a complete sentence.

   A. Give the first subpoint for I.

      1. This example, evidence, or subpoint develops subpoint A.

      2. This example, evidence, or subpoint develops subpoint A.

   B. Give the second subpoint for I.

      1. This example, evidence, or subpoint develops subpoint B.

      2. This example, evidence, or subpoint develops subpoint B.

      3. This example, evidence, or subpoint develops subpoint B.

   C. Give the third subpoint for I (and so on).

II. State the second major point in a sentence parallel in structure to the first major point (and so on).

4 Use an outlining program on a computer. An on-screen outline can be expanded, contracted, rearranged, and otherwise altered with ease. A computer outline encourages you to be flexible.

EXERCISE 3.2   Make a working list for a writing project you're currently working on. When you are finished, make a formal outline of the same project. What additions and changes did you make to construct the formal outline? Which outline will you find more helpful when you sit down to begin a draft of the project? Why?

3e   How do you choose a title?

It may seem odd to choose a title while you are still planning and organizing a project. But titles are surprisingly important. Readers want and expect them. In fact, they may be annoyed if they don't find one that helps them anticipate what they will be reading—so craft your title carefully, keeping these tips in mind.

- **Choose a working title early in the process** (one you can change as the work progresses) that will keep you on track as you move through the planning and drafting stages of your project.

Check your working title periodically to be sure it still fits the paper and make adjustments if necessary.

- **Be sure your title accurately reflects the content of your paper.** No cute titles, please. It's essential that your title will let readers know what your paper is really about.

- **Try a two-part title** if you have your heart set on a clever phrase that's not particularly descriptive. Start with the unconventional phrase and follow it with a colon. The second part of the title, after the colon, should clarify exactly what the paper is about, such as in "Short Guy, Big Ego: A Psychological Analysis of Napoleon's Military Strategy."

How Do Yu Write a Draft? 4

4a How do you start a draft?

For many people, getting started is the hardest part of writing. But remember that a first draft doesn't have to be perfect. It's simply a place to start. In this section we offer suggestions to help you through the drafting process—so that you can stop worrying and *start writing*.

1 Find a place to write and gather the things you'll need. If possible, find a spot away from friends, family, and noise, where you won't be distracted. Collect your materials—notes, source materials, and a copy of the assignment—and lay them out where you can see them. In making preparations like these, you're not procrastinating; you're creating a working environment.

2 Keep the ideas coming. Don't agonize over the first few sentences. Treat your first paragraph as a device to get rolling. Write three or four sentences nonstop to build momentum, no matter how imperfect they may be. Words begin to flow once you've warmed up to your topic.

You can always begin with whatever section of the paper seems easiest to write and come back to the introduction later. See Section 13a for more on writing opening paragraphs.

In what writing environments do you produce your best work? What resources and tools help you to write? Make a conscious effort to re-create these conditions each time you begin a draft.

3 Don't criticize yourself or edit your writing prematurely. As you work on a first draft, cut yourself some slack. Good writing develops over time. You can't expect something to be perfectly polished when you first start working on it.

Don't fiddle with problems of mechanics, formatting, or style in your early drafts. Go back and fix difficulties with spelling, punctuation, parallelism, word choice, and the like later. If you bog down in details of form early, you may lose your momentum, letting your brightest ideas fade. Don't play it safe. Push yourself to grapple with difficult ideas. Try out a more interesting style.

4 Set your own pace. Try writing quickly at first. If you hit a snag or can't produce, skip the troublesome spot and move on. Above all, keep writing. A draft in hand, even a sketchy one, will give you a sense of accomplishment and material to develop and refine.

But if you're not comfortable composing quickly, don't feel that you must change. Many skilled writers work slowly. They may take several hours to turn out a few paragraphs, but their first drafts are often quite polished. In the long run, slow writers may spend the same amout of time completing a project as writers who produce material faster but rework that material through more drafts.

5 Get feedback from other writers. Share ideas with other people. Brainstorm for ideas, compare findings, evaluate organizational strategies, and test arguments with your fellow writers. Groups serve as important audiences for drafts and keep writers motivated—after all, no one wants to let colleagues down.

6 Draft on a computer. Use your computer to accumulate and store material for your paper. Keep a file that records your initial impressions about a project. Bookmark online sources. Download copies of relevant articles or images. You'll accumulate a surprising amount of material. (Be sure to keep track of the material in your draft that comes from other sources. See Chapter 39 for more details.)

With a computer you can easily save alternative versions of your draft until you decide which one you want to use.

Finally, computers make it easy to experiment with different formats and to incorporate graphic or multimedia elements. See Chapter 10 for more on visual dimensions of writing.

4b How do you keep a draft on track?

You have a thesis and a general organizational plan. You have gathered resources you plan to use and have even developed an outline. You begin putting words onto the screen. Only now can you see how your plan may have to be altered. Be focused and flexible: focused enough to guide readers through your material and flexible enough to shift strategies when necessary.

1 Highlight key ideas. Keep your main points in mind as you compose the draft. One way to do this is to summarize your thesis in the first paragraph. An opening paragraph can forecast what the rest of the paper will be about.

Even if you open with background information or an anecdote (see Section 13a), keep your main point in mind and don't wander too far astray.

Continue to highlight main ideas throughout the draft. Use phrases such as the following to snap readers to attention.

The main points to consider are . . .

The chief issue, however, is . . .

Now we have come to the crucial question.

Keep readers focused on key points. Express your own thoughts about the topic. Draw attention to contrasting viewpoints.

I believe that . . .

Other researchers say . . .

Critics of this view have argued . . .

Cues as simple as *first, second*, and *third* help structure your paper. For more guidance on using transitional words and phrases, see Section 14b.

2 Keep the amount you write about each point roughly proportionate to its importance in the paper. A lopsided draft misleads readers. Don't let your introduction take up half the paper or promise a solution and then neglect it until the last paragraph. Don't write at length on a minor point or quote at length from one source while neglecting others. Return to your central argument.

Respect the principle of proportion, but be generous with words and ideas in a first draft. You'll discover that it is easier to prune material you don't like than it is to fill in where your ideas are thin. Don't stray too far from your thesis, but do capture any fresh thoughts that emerge as you write. The same is true of examples, illustrations, facts, figures, and details: if they don't work, you can always cut them later or find a better place in the draft to use them.

3 Allow yourself enough time to draw conclusions. Conclusions are important. Don't skimp on the final paragraphs. The ending often determines the impression readers take from your piece.

When you approach the end of a draft, take time to reread what you have written. What are the larger implications of your ideas? What do you want readers to know or believe? What loose ends need to be tied up? Let these concerns shape your conclusion. Try out several endings and choose the one that best fits your audience and purpose. See Section 13b for more on closing paragraphs.

4c How do you know when you have a solid draft?

You'll have a chance to revise and polish later, but don't settle for a draft that's incomplete or rushed.

How do you know when you've made a solid effort? The three standards listed in Checklist 4.1 can assure that your draft is worth reading and responding to.

checklist 4.1 ⌐ Knowing When You Have a Solid Draft

Before you give a draft to your instructor, colleague, or peer reviewer for comments, be sure you've met these standards.

1. **Have you made a good-faith effort?** Be sure you've invested substantial time and thought in your paper. If you haven't, you're passing up the chance to get useful criticism of your paper while it's still in progress.

2. **Is the draft reasonably complete?** Have you stated a thesis, developed it with supporting arguments and examples, and finished with a defensible conclusion? Have you included any charts, tables, or images that will appear in the final project? A few paragraphs don't qualify as a working draft. Nor does a carefully written opening followed by an outline of what the rest of the paper will cover.

3. **Is the draft readable?** You can't expect instructors, classmates, or colleagues to respond to a paper that's hard to read.

   - Double-space your draft, leaving ample margins all the way around the page for comments.
   - Be sure that your printer or photocopier has made dark, legible copies.
   - If you must handwrite a draft, *print* in ink on every other line.
   - Write or print on one side of the paper only, and number your pages.

EXERCISE 4.1 Evaluate a draft you have recently written against the three criteria in Checklist 4.1. Does your paper meet the standards? If not, what changes do you have to make to remedy the problems?

How Do You Revise, Edit, and Proofread?

5

Revising, editing, and proofreading are different phases of the writing process, each of which involves thinking about a different aspect of the paper.

---

chart

5.1 Revising, Editing, and Proofreading

Focus on

Revision
(first draft) — Purpose, audience, content organization

Editing
(later draft) — Style, emphasis, tone

Proofreading
(final draft) — Mechanics, format

When you *revise* your draft, you are *shaping a work in progress.* Review what you have written and look for ways to improve it. You may get new ideas and shift the focus of the paper; you may cut, expand, and reorganize. At this point you are making large-scale changes.

When you *edit* a paper, you turn your attention to clarity, emphasis, and tone. You may rewrite awkward sentences or correct problems with parallelism and repetition. Your goal is to create sentences and paragraphs that present your ideas effectively. These are small-scale changes.

When you *proofread* a paper, you go back over it line by line to correct typographical errors, check for omissions, verify details, eliminate inconsistencies, and remove gaffes. This is the fix-it stage, when you're preparing the paper to appear in public. Postpone proofreading until the end of a project. Otherwise, you could waste time repairing sentences that later might be deleted.

5a   What does revising involve?

When you revise a draft, don't try to work through it paragraph by paragraph, making changes as you go. Large-scale issues of content and rhetorical strategy that affect every paragraph must be addressed before you can polish individual sentences. At this point, reconsider everything you have written. Don't tinker. THINK BIG!

Large-scale changes include revising for focus, purpose, proportion, commitment, adaptation to audience, organization, and content. First, print out a copy of your first draft.

1 Read your draft thoughtfully. Review the assignment and any feedback you have received. How do you feel about the draft? What's good that you definitely want to keep? Where does it seem weak?

Ideally, you should appraise your draft several days (or at a minimum several hours) after you have completed it so that you can read it more objectively.

When you dislike what you've written, when editors have found little to praise, or when you just need a fresh start, consider writing an entirely new draft. Creating a new draft may seem discouraging, but it may be easier than repairing a draft that just won't work. Often, an unsuccessful version points a writer toward what he or she really wanted to write.

2 Refine the focus of the paper. Be sure your draft makes and develops a central point. If the draft makes a lot of general statements without supporting and developing them, you have a problem with focus. Check your examples and supporting material. Your draft may lack the credibility that comes from specific information.

---

checklist 5.1   **Revising for Focus**

- Have you taken on a larger topic than you can handle?
- Are you generalizing instead of stating a specific claim or thesis?
- Have you supported your ideas with sufficient evidence and examples?

See Section 2b for more on focusing a topic and Section 3a for advice on creating and refining a thesis.

3 Consider your purpose. You now need to decide exactly what you want to accomplish. Are your intentions evident to yourself and to your readers?

checklist 5.2 | Revising for Purpose

- Do you clearly state in the first paragraph or two what you plan to do?
- Does the draft develop all the main points you intended to make?
- After reading the draft, will most readers be able to summarize your main idea?

See Section 1e for more on defining your purpose.

4 Examine your paper's proportions. *Proportion* means the distribution and balance of ideas. You should develop your ideas in relation to their importance.

checklist 5.3 | Revising for Proportion

- Are the parts of the paper out of balance? For example, have you gone into too much detail at the beginning and then skimped on the rest?
- Can your readers tell what points are most important by the amount of attention you've given to them?
- Does the conclusion do justice to the ideas it summarizes?

5 Check for adaptation to audience. Sometimes a first draft is *writer centered;* that is, the writer has concentrated on expressing his or her ideas without thinking much about the audience. Such an approach can be productive in a first draft, but a major goal of revising should be to change *writer-centered* writing to *reader-centered* writing. Put yourself in the place of your readers.

checklist 5.4   Revising for Audience

- Do you spend too much time discussing material that most of your readers already know?
- Do you answer important questions that readers might have about your topic?
- Do you define all the concepts and terms your readers need to know?
- Do you use language your readers will understand?

See Checklist 1.2 on audience (p. 6) for more advice.

6 Check the organization. A well-organized project has a plan and direction. It moves from beginning to end without getting lost.

checklist 5.5   Revising for Organization

- Does your paper state a clear thesis or claim? Does it then develop key points related to that thesis?
- Does the development of your points follow a pattern readers will recognize?
- Do the transitions move readers sensibly from point to point?
- Would the paper work better if you moved some paragraphs around?

See Section 3c for more detailed tips on organization and Section 14b for more on making smooth transitions between ideas.

7 Evaluate your design and check images and graphics. Now that you have a complete draft, you can assess how well the document is working visually: Have you used an appropriate format? Are the pages readable? Are sections logically arranged? Check any tables, charts, and images. Are they substantive, accurate, and legible? For more information about revising design elements, consult Chapter 10.

8 Check the content of the paper. When you revise, you may need to add information to give a paper more substance.

checklist 5.6 ⌐ **Revising for Content**

- Do you fully develop and support each main idea?
- Do you need to add specific information and concrete examples that will make your case stronger? Do you need to do more research?
- Do you cite reliable, credible sources to back up your ideas?
- Does the title of your paper reflect its content?

If the content of your draft seems thin, return to the library or to other sources. See Chapter 39 for more on doing research.

9 Revise from a printed copy, not from a computer screen. Revising, editing, and proofreading work best from hard copy. Weak organization, sprawling paragraphs, poor transitions, and repeated words show up more clearly in print than on the screen.

Afterwards, transfer the corrections you made on the printed version to the computer file.

EXERCISE 5.1 Apply the criteria for large-scale revision described above to a draft you have written.

5b   What does editing involve?

Revision should have given you a better-focused, better-organized, more interesting draft. Now you're ready to *edit*, that is, to make the small-scale changes that you put on hold while you were revising.

Now is the time to use the handbook to check on style (Part 4), grammar and usage (Part 5), and mechanics (Part 6).

1 Make your language concrete and specific. *Concrete* language describes things as they are perceived by the senses: colors, textures, sizes, sounds, actions. *Specific* language names particular people, places, and things.

Readers need vivid descriptions that bring concepts to life. As you edit, add people to your discussions, illustrate generalizations with examples, and supply your readers with facts and images. Give your writing texture. See Chapter 16 for more on adding detail and variety to your writing.

The "deleted scenes" included in DVD versions of most popular movies—such as the scene represented in this still from *Pirates of the Carribean* (Dir. Gore Verbinski, 2003)—give us clues about how filmmakers approach editing choices in their work. View the deleted scenes from a movie you like. What can you infer about why this material was cut? Do the director's choices suggest strategies that you might apply to your writing?

2 Strive for a readable style. Look at your word choices. Do you achieve the right level of formality? Do you balance technical terms with everyday language? Are your subjects specific? Do your verbs express actions? Are your words vivid and accurate?

Different writing styles are appropriate in different settings. When in doubt about what kind of language you should use, take a look at similar pieces others have written.

Finally, check every word you're not sure of in a dictionary or thesaurus. See Chapter 16 for more detailed suggestions on style.

3 Be sure that your tone is appropriate. Avoid polarizing or hostile language. Replace any name-calling (such as "traitor" to refer to anyone who disagrees with the president), stereotypes (such as "religious right fanatic" for anyone who attends an evangelical church), or unduly extreme descriptions with more moderate references.

Reasoned arguments cannot rely on emotional language ("I am disgusted by the tobacco industry's greed because . . . "). Your expressions of feeling shouldn't become the focus of an argument.

For more information about tone, consult Section 8c.

4 Cut wordiness. Generating ideas produces wordy first drafts. In subsequent drafts, cut. Go after sprawling verb phrases, redundancies, and strings of prepositional phrases. Be ruthless. You can almost always cut your prose without losing anything (see Section 16b).

5 Test your transitions. *Transitions* are words and phrases that connect sentences, paragraphs, and whole passages of writing. When transitions are faulty, a paper will seem choppy and disconnected. Read your draft aloud. Improve the places where you pause, stumble, or detect gaps. Often you just need to add a word or phrase, such as *on the other hand, however,* or *finally.* In some cases, however, you'll have to rearrange whole sections in a more coherent order. See Chapters 12 and 14 for additional suggestions.

6 Polish the introduction and the conclusion.   The introduction of a draft merits special attention, but don't edit it until you know precisely how your paper is going to come out. Make sure the introduction is accurate and interesting.

The conclusion also warrants care; but don't fuss with it until you have the main part of the paper under control. A strong ending pulls the paper together and leaves your readers satisfied.

For more specific suggestions on how to improve introductory and concluding paragraphs, see Chapter 13.

7 Use a computer style checker—carefully.   Style checkers and editing programs have various functions: they may locate expletive constructions, spot clichés, detect repetitions, and so on. But for all their cleverness, such programs can't assess context. If you use a style checker, don't assume that it can polish a paper *for* you.

8 Refine your layout and design.   Now is the time to fine-tune and polish your document's design. See Chapter 10 for more detailed advice on design issues.

checklist 5.7 — When Editing

- Sharpen your language—make it concrete and specific.
- Check your word choice—make it readable and clear.
- Lop out wordiness.
- Be sure your tone is appropriate.
- Test your transitions.
- Polish your opening and closing.
- Use a style checker if you find it helpful.
- Fine-tune design and layout.

hi**g**hlight | *Edited Sentences from Student Papers*

Here are some sentences from student papers that have been improved by judicious editing. Notice that the changes do not greatly alter the sentences' meaning.

ORIGINAL At some point or another, the experience of peers pressuring one to engage in binge drinking is a dilemma that most college students will have to face.

EDITED At some point, most college students face peer pressure to engage in binge drinking.

ORIGINAL The companies and products that advertise in women's fashion magazines know that most young women in the U.S. want to be beautiful and alluring and design their ads to reflect this.

EDITED The companies that advertise in fashion magazines know that young women in the U.S. want to be beautiful and alluring, so they design their advertisements to appeal to these desires.

5c What does proofreading involve?

When you are satisfied with the content, organization, and style of your paper, you're ready to put it in final form. Like checking your appearance in the mirror before an important meeting, *proofreading* provides a final measure of quality control.

Use Parts 4, 5, and 6 of the handbook to check punctuation, usage, and the conventions of edited American English.

1 Check your weakest areas. If you are a poor speller, consult the dictionary. If you are inclined to put commas where they're not needed, check your commas. Double-check troublesome words such as *its/it's, your/you're,* and *there/their/they're.*

2 Check for inconsistencies. Have you switched your point of view in ways that might be confusing? Do you use contractions in some parts of the paper but avoid them in others? Are headings in boldface on some pages and italics on other pages? Is the tone appropriate throughout?

3 Check punctuation. Look for comma splices. Review all semicolons. See that proper nouns and adjectives and *I* are capitalized. Check that quotation marks and parentheses are in pairs. (See Chapters 29–37.)

4 Run your computer's spellcheck. A spellchecker won't catch every misspelling. Follow up with a final check of your own.

5 Check for typographical errors. Look for transposed letters, dropped endings, faulty word division, and omitted apostrophes.

6 Check the format of your paper. Number your pages. Italicize or underline titles of sources as needed. Put other titles between quotation marks (see Chapters 33 and 36). Cite outside sources appropriately and list them in your bibliography (see Chapters 41 and 44–46). Set the margins correctly and review the page breaks. Finally, staple or clip your pages together.

EXERCISE 5.2 Proofread a writing project you've recently completed, looking at all the areas discussed in Section 5c. Which problems do you spot most often? How do you think you might avoid them in future projects?

part

2

Academic Writing

How Do You Write in College?

6

6a How do you write a successful academic paper?

While expectations in college vary from course to course, most instructors will require you to approach topics with a critical eye, to justify your ideas with logical reasons and evidence, and to cite the sources of your information. These expectations are not optional; they are your *responsibilities* as a college writer. When you understand these responsibilities, you can address academic audiences with confidence.

1 Review the assignment. Before you get too far into a topic, assess the requirements and think ahead. How much research will you have to do? What special materials will you need? How much time do you have?

2 Don't take on too much. When you make a claim in a paper, assert what you believe. Establish your position and defend it. Don't overextend; stake out a topic that you can manage. Then you'll have a chance to think and write about it in detail. See Section 2b for advice on how to narrow a topic.

3 Support your claims with reasons and evidence. If one word could describe college instructors and professors, it would be *skeptical*. They want reasons and evidence. It's usually not enough to claim on the basis of personal opinion or feelings that something is true or that something should be done. Generally, the best topics for academic assignments are amenable to factual evidence and research.

4 Understand what constitutes good reasons and acceptable evidence in academic writing. Academic writing has standards of argument and proof that are more rigorous than what's expected in many other kinds of writing.

Support your arguments with logical reasons and sufficient evidence. Your supporting materials should come from reliable, recent sources. You should produce enough supporting materials to show that you're knowledgeable about the topic. This means doing research.

Writing an Annotated Bibliography

An instructor may ask you to turn in an *annotated bibliography* that briefly describes and evaluates the sources you plan to use in a paper. This excerpt from college student Matt Valentine's annotated bibliography details some of the materials he eventually included in a term paper about the Holocaust. Note the breadth and variety of his sources. Do you think he's chosen materials that his instructor will find valid and reliable? Are they the right kinds of evidence for an academic paper?

Working Bibliography for "The Rhetoric of Atrocity:

How People Write and Talk About the Holocaust"

American Jewish Committee. *The Jews in Nazi*

Germany: A Handbook of Facts Regarding Their

Present Situation. 1935. New York: Fertig,

1982. Print. This republished book gives

perspectives held by American Jews in the

years preceding the Holocaust.

Keegan, John. "Code of Silence." *New York Times* 25

Nov. 1996: A13. Print. This news article

reports on the release of government records

suggesting that officials of the Allied forces

were aware of the Holocaust death camps but

chose to keep the information away from the

public and not to act upon it.

Be aware that some instructors will ask for bibliographic entries that are longer and more in-depth than the ones Matt composed. Check with your instructor if you have questions about the length and content of your annotations.

5 Document your sources. When you cite statistics or research, your teacher will want to know where you got your data. If you use *any* material that someone else thought of or wrote first, you're obligated to give that source credit. If you don't, you're committing plagiarism, a serious offense. (See Section 41d for more about plagiarism.)

Documenting sources is an essential part of college writing. It's not difficult to do once you know the guidelines. Sections 41a and 41c offer comprehensive information on documenting sources.

6 Follow research and writing conventions appropriate to your subject area. Be aware that expectations differ from subject area to subject area. These differences grow out of the different *goals* and *approaches* valued in the various disciplines of the humanities, social sciences, and natural sciences.

- **Goals:** What kinds of questions interest scholars in this discipline? What do they want to find out? Do they want to know how physical objects and processes work? Are they interested in discovering how people have interpreted the world at different times or in different cultures?

- **Methods:** How do scholars in a particular discipline go about finding out what they want to know? Do they test hypotheses systematically and empirically? Do they critically interpret texts and other artifacts?

- **Evidence:** What kinds of materials do scholars in a subject area typically use to support their arguments—numerical data, historical artifacts, quotations from literary or philosophical texts?

- **Genres:** What kinds of documents do scholars in a field typically produce—lab reports, critical analyses, case studies, personal commentaries? What organizational and stylistic conventions are typical?

- **Documentation:** What system do scholars in the field use for citing and documenting sources?

hi**g**hlight | *Writing in Different Academic Disciplines*

 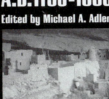 

HUMANITIES	SOCIAL SCIENCES	NATURAL SCIENCES
Subject areas		
Literature,philosophy, history, classics work, education	Sociology, psychology, anthropology, social zoology	Astronomy, botany, chemistry, physics,
Purposes		
To study how people uselanguage or other symbols to interpret experience	To study how people create and live within social systems	To study the structure and workings of the physical world
Methods		
Close reading and analysis of texts	Fieldwork and other observational research statistical analysis of data	The scientific method, experimental testing of hypotheses
Sources		
Literary, philosophical, and historical works and critical commentaries on them	Data collected from interviews, surveys, field observations; previous research by other scholars	Data collected through systematic observation in controlled settings
Genres		
Critical and interpretive essays, book reviews, personal and of reflective pieces, creative writing	Field notes, case studies, research reports, reviews research	Lab reports, research reports, summaries of research, process analyses
Documentation		
Usually MLA	Usually APA	Often CSE

7 Remember that college instructors expect professional-looking work. Before you submit an essay for a grade, proofread for faulty punctuation, agreement errors, and spelling. Get a second opinion from a friend. Consult the grammar and usage portions of this book. Run your computer's spellchecker. Check that your paper complies with any formatting instructions included in the assignment: Has the instructor specified MLA or APA style? a particular font size? single or double spacing? See Section 5c for advice on proofreading and Chapters 44 through 46 for help with particular formats.

Instructors don't like to get papers they can barely read. Word-process all writing projects, double spaced, with numbered pages. Be sure your printer produces quality output. Fasten with a staple or paper clips.

checklist 6.1 ⌐ Writing for College Assignments

When you write in college, remember to

- Assess the assignment and plan to meet its requirements.
- Limit your thesis to one that you can adequately cover and support.
- Support your claims with reasons and evidence.
- Keep in mind what constitutes acceptable evidence in academic writing.
- Follow conventions appropriate for the subject area.
- Document your sources.
- Hand in only carefully edited, proofread, professional-looking papers.

EXERCISE 6.1 From a popular magazine, select an article on a current topic. Then find a scholarly journal article on the same topic. Compare and contrast the kinds of evidence used in the two pieces: How much evidence does each writer cite? What kinds of sources does each draw on? Which piece do you find more interesting? more convincing?

6b How do you write on essay examinations?

Every writer should know how to compose under pressure. Researchers estimate that up to half the writing you do during college will occur on exams. After you leave school, you'll find that many jobs require the ability to write quickly and efficiently. Unfortunately, many writers resign themselves to failure at this kind of writing, believing, "I freeze under pressure."

Don't give up before you start. You *can* write well in an exam setting if you understand the unique skills involved and work to master them.

1 Know the material. Preparation is half the battle. Lay the foundation for success in advance. Attend class regularly. Keep up with required readings. Participate actively in class.

Absorbing the material is not enough. You need to organize and think critically about what you know. As you read, summarize important ideas in your own words to be sure that you understand them. Review your notes periodically and ask yourself how new material fits with the old. When you have questions, speak up.

To practice applying your knowledge, imagine how the material you're studying might relate to a current event or controversy. See Chapter 7 for detailed advice on getting the most out of your reading.

2 Find out as much as you can about the exam. As the exam date approaches, ask your instructor for details: How many questions will the test include? What kinds of questions? What topics will be emphasized? Will you get to choose from several questions? Knowing some parameters will help guide your study.

3 Use your study time intelligently. You need to be in top form to write well on an exam. Forgo extreme studying techniques, such as cramming or pulling all-nighters, that leave you exhausted. Don't try to learn every piece of information covered in class; you'll only feel overwhelmed.

Spend your time practicing the thinking and writing skills that exam essays require. Make scratch outlines of important theories or arguments you think are likely to be covered, with one or two key examples or details, and use these as the basis for your review. Once you have command of the material, devise questions similar to those you think might appear on the exam and practice answering them. Use a timer to accustom yourself to thinking under pressure.

Try forming a study group with colleagues. Meet once or twice before the exam to compare notes, puzzle out gaps in your knowledge, and practice explaining key points to each other.

4 Devise strategies for coping with pressure. Anticipate difficulties and decide beforehand how you will deal with them.

First, eliminate unnecessary stress. Get a good night's sleep, eat a healthful meal, and keep anxiety-producing cramming to a minimum before the exam. Gather all your materials—examination booklets, pens, calculator, and notes or books if the instructor allows them— well in advance. Arrive a few minutes early, but not too early; sitting in an empty classroom for too long may make you nervous.

You can head off specific problems that happen during exams. If you tend to panic when you see an unfamiliar question, plan to work on the easiest items first, then come back to the more challenging ones. If you fall apart when time runs short, give yourself a safety net by outlining each response before you start writing, so you can attach the outline to any unfinished response. This kind of planning will free you to focus on the actual writing.

5 Figure out what the question is asking you to do. Analyze each exam question carefully before you begin writing.

Start by locating the key terms—nouns or noun phrases—that *identify* or *limit* the subject: "Discuss the *major components* of *Plato's educational ideal* as elaborated in *The Republic*"; "Explain *four kinds of confounding* that can occur in *observational research*." Next, underline key verbs that tell you what to do with the topic: *analyze, compare, discuss, explain, trace*. See Chart 6.1.

Finally, delete material that does not seem relevant to the question. In this example from a British literature course, for instance, the core question is stated only in the last sentence.

> Since the beginning of the semester, we have seen thinkers such as Freud, Marx, and Nietzsche describe the philosophical contradictions that inhabit the twentieth century. *Choose one major text we have read this semester and trace the ways in which that work describes contradictions in private, public, or intellectual activities.*

Here the references to Freud, Marx, and Nietzsche only introduce the idea of "contradiction," the focus of the main question. To answer this question, you don't need to comment on any of these thinkers; you just have to explain how contradiction shows up in one of the literary texts you studied for the class.

---

chart

(6.1) Common Exam Terms

- **ANALYZE:** Break an argument or a concept into parts and explain the relationships among them; evaluate or explain your interpretation or judgment.
- **APPLY:** Take a concept, formula, or theory and adapt it to another situation.
- **ARGUE, PROVE:** Take a position on an issue and provide reasons and evidence to support that position.
- **COMPARE:** Point out similarities between two or more concepts, theories, or situations.

- **CONTRAST:** Point out differences between two or more concepts, theories, or situations.
- **CRITIQUE, EVALUATE:** Make and support a judgment about the worth of an idea, theory, or proposal, accounting for both strengths and weaknesses.
- **DEFINE:** State a clear, precise meaning for a concept or object, and perhaps give an illustrative example.
- **DISCUSS, EXPLAIN:** Offer a comprehensive presentation and analysis of important ideas relating to a topic, supported with examples and evidence. These questions usually require detailed responses.
- **ENUMERATE, LIST:** Name a series of ideas, elements, or related objects one by one, perhaps giving a brief explanation of each.
- **REVIEW, SUMMARIZE:** Briefly lay out the main points of a larger theory or argument.
- **TRACE:** Explain chronologically a series of events or the development of a trend or idea.

EXERCISE 6.2 Identify key terms in an examination question from another course or from a standardized test for college admission, job certification, or another purpose. What specific topics does the question stake out? Which verbs tell you what to do with those topics? If you have a copy of your response, analyze how well you fulfilled these instructions.

6 Budget your time. Keep the amount of time you spend on each question proportionate to its importance. Here is a simple way to figure out how to allocate your time: Divide the number of points each question is worth by the number of points on the whole exam. The result equals the percentage of time you should devote to that question.

If you run out of time in the middle of a response, resist the temptation to steal time set aside for other questions. Instead, jot a note to your instructor explaining that you ran out of time, and attach your outline. Many instructors will give partial credit for outlined responses.

7 Make a plan. To pack as much writing as possible into the allocated time, take five minutes or so to map out your answer. If the question asks for independent argument or analysis, consider brainstorming or freewriting to generate ideas. If the question asks you to synthesize course material, try an idea map that organizes information under key categories. (See Section 2b for more on prewriting techniques.)

Use these initial ideas as the foundation for a list or scratch outline of the full response. Whatever format you choose, it should include your thesis, main supporting ideas, and important examples. Once your outline is in place, you are ready to begin the actual writing. See Sections 3c and 3d for more on organizing and outlining an essay.

8 Understand what a good response looks like. Most instructors want a tightly organized response that contains the following elements.

- **A clear thesis statement** in the first paragraph or, better yet, in the first sentence.
- **Logical organization** with a single key idea developed in each paragraph and with clear transitions between points.
- **Adequate support and evidence** for each point, drawn from course readings and lectures.
- **Your own views or analysis** when the question asks for them. Remember, though, to justify your ideas with evidence and support.
- **A conclusion** that ties together main points and summarizes their importance, even if you have time for only a sentence or two.
- **Clear prose** free of major grammatical and mechanical errors.

Finally, before you set aside a lot of time for editing and proofreading, ask your instructor how he or she deals with grammatical and mechanical problems. Many teachers don't penalize minor mistakes, but others are sticklers for correctness.

How D You Read and Think Critically?

7

Each day you are bombarded with messages that try to influence you. Dealing with these competing messages requires that you examine ideas, ask questions, challenge arguments, and decide which viewpoints are worth accepting—in other words, that you think *critically*. The critical and analytical skills you develop now will serve you for the rest of your life.

In college, a crucial element of critical thinking involves learning to read critically, because much of what you write and think about is in response to what you read.

7a How do you read to understand complex material?

College reading assignments pose special challenges. In high school, teachers may cover a textbook chapter in a week; in college, instructors often assign several chapters in the same amount of time, along with supplementary readings from scholarly journals, literary texts, and other sources. College assignments may also address more abstract ideas and use more complicated language. Whereas you may be accomplished at reading sources that summarize and analyze issues *for* you, in college you'll have to weigh issues and interpret findings on your own.

You'll need to develop specialized skills that help you become an active, engaged reader.

1 Preview the text. You'll find it easier to read an unfamiliar text if you first preview its important features.

- **Genre.** What kind of document is it? Different genres have different purposes and audiences, which you should keep in mind as you read.
- **Title and table of contents.** What do the title and table of contents tell you about the piece's content and purpose?
- **Organization.** If you're reading a printed text, are there headings or subheadings? If you're reading a Web site online, are major sections listed in the left-hand frame or on a home page? What do these divisions suggest about the text?

- **Sources.** Inspect the bibliography and index. What do the sources listed there tell you about the kinds of information the writer will draw on?
- **Point of view.** Is the author's point of view known and relevant? What are the interests and biases of the publisher or the sponsoring institution? Does the text purport to be objective, or does it present itself as subjective and personal?

Before reading a piece, determine your goals: Are you skimming the piece to see if it's relevant to a paper you're writing? Are you mainly interested in major concepts and arguments, or do you need to know details? Do you want to develop your own opinions on the subject? These goals should influence how much time you spend reading and which of the strategies discussed in the following sections you decide to use.

2 Look up unfamiliar terms and concepts. It's easier to understand difficult material if you have the relevant background knowledge. When you preview a text, circle major terms, concepts, or topics that sound unfamiliar. A look at the dictionary or an encyclopedia entry will put you on solid ground. Keep a dictionary at hand while you read so that you can clarify confusing references as they crop up.

3 Slow down. Read slowly and reread two or three times to develop a thorough understanding of a text. Many experts read things twice: the first time just to understand what the writer is saying, the second to focus on their own reactions and opinions. Whatever your strategy, don't rush.

4 Annotate the text to clarify and respond to its content. Critical reading involves more than absorbing words on a page. It's an active process.

If you're not accustomed to taking notes on your reading, here are some useful strategies.

- **Content notes.** Highlight key passages. When you arrive at an important point or get tangled in a difficult passage, translate it into your own words to clarify its meaning.
- **Context notes.** To follow a text's structure, jot down key words that explain where the argument is going or how a new point fits in.
- **Response notes.** Don't just accept what a reading says. When the text raises questions in your mind, write them down. Carry on a dialogue with your reading to develop your own perspective on the issues being raised.

hihlight | Sample Annotations

Caryl Rivers

The Persistence of Gender Myths in Math

by Rosalind Chait Barnett and Caryl Rivers

(*Education Week*, October 13, 2004)

Should we be worried that young girls are not pursuing math-related careers at the same rate as young men? After all, in our technological era, many of tomorrow's well-paying jobs will require competence at mathematics. But today, women make up only 19 percent of the science, engineering, and technology workforce. In 1998, only 16 percent of computer science degrees were awarded to women, down from nearly 40 percent in 1984, and the downward trend continued in 2003.

look up

Can teachers have a role in changing this picture? Or would they just be going up against innate biological differences in a (futile) attempt at social engineering?

# of women in science is decreasing— they are asking whether teachers can help reverse this trend

Some argue that girls don't have the right brain structures to be good at math. Cambridge University Psychologist Simon Baron-Cohen, the author of *The Essential Difference*, goes so far as to say that men have "systematizing brains" well-suited for the hard sciences. Women, in contrast, have "empathizing brains," designed for caretaking and mothering. And the best-selling author Michael Gurian (*The Wonder of Boys*) says that only 20 percent of girls have the right brain structure for performing well at math.

fact or his opinion? When published?

Possible cause #1: girls' brains not suited for math

It is indeed the case that men far outnumber women in math-related fields. But is this evidence for innate male superiority? The answer is no. New research finds few sex differences in the math abilities of boys and girls. In 2001, sociologists Erin Leahey and Guang Guo of the University of North Carolina at Chapel Hill looked at some

new study w/opposite finding

continued on next page

continued from page 57

20,000 math scores of students between the ages of 4 and 18 and found <u>no differences of any magnitude</u>, even in areas that are supposedly male domains, such as reasoning skills and geometry. The finding astonished the researchers, who said, "Based on prior literature . . . we expected large gender differences to emerge as early as junior high school, but our results do not confirm this." And a meta-analysis of SAT scores for some 3 million students found that girls and boys performed virtually identically in math.

found no differences

When you're working on a project that involves research, it's especially important to take notes. Your annotations identify ideas and information worth returning to, highlight passages you want to quote, and help you synthesize and engage in dialogue with the authors and texts you are encountering. See Chapters 41 and 42 for more on incorporating material you've read into a research paper.

5 Adapt your reading process to online settings. Electronic texts pose special challenges. Experts on reading have coined a new term—*screen literacy*—to describe the skills readers need to navigate online texts.

Online texts are less stable and more loosely structured than printed texts, and the boundaries that separate one online text from another are blurred. These features can make it hard to find your place within a text, to return to important material, or to figure out how the pieces of a text fit together.

When you go online, you have to adjust your reading process. Here are some strategies that experts recommend:

- Be selective about what you read. Skim and peck to find the most relevant items.

- Approach online reading with your own agenda rather than following the author's preferred path through the text.

- Pay as much attention to visual elements as to the words in a text.

You'll also need to develop strategies for keeping track of the material you read online. When you want to read an online text carefully or return to it later, download and print it. (Be sure to record the date you found the text; if you use the source in your paper, you'll need the date for the "Works Cited" page.) Use your browser's "bookmark" feature to mark sites so that you don't lose them. Arrange your bookmarks in folders that reflect each major section or theme of your project. If a site is likely to change, download and save the material that you want.

Use the annotation features of your word-processing program to record your reactions to files you download (but be careful to clearly separate your comments from the original text). Annotate your bookmarks to remind yourself why a particular site or page is important. (See Section 38b for more advice on organizing research materials and Sections 41b and 42c for advice on incorporating research into a writing project.)

EXERCISE 7.1 Use the three note-taking strategies described in Section 7a-4 to annotate a reading assignment in one of your other courses. How do these strategies compare to your typical approach to reading? Which strategy did you find the most helpful, and why?

7b How do you think critically about your reading?

Critical thinking is an extended and focused version of the kind of thinking we all do every day when we gather evidence, examine options, look at advantages and disadvantages, and weigh others' opinions.

1 Read as a believer and as a doubter. Approach your reading with an open mind. Learn, even from perspectives contrary to your own. An excellent way to engage with your readings is to play what the writing expert Peter Elbow calls the "believing and doubting game." This approach asks you to read and respond to a piece twice, each time adopting a dramatically different attitude.

First, read the piece with generosity. What makes the argument so compelling to the writer? What claims, examples, or beliefs seem reasonable or persuasive? Write a paragraph exploring whatever seems most worth believing in the piece. Keying in on strengths will guard against rejecting the argument too readily.

Then read the piece a second time as a "doubter." What are the gaps, exaggerations, errors, and faulty reasoning? What are the problems in the writer's perspective? Again, summarize your conclusions in a paragraph. Keying in on weaknesses will guard against accepting the argument too readily.

2 Assess the writer's qualifications. Check the author's qualifications for everything you read. Does the writer have expertise, personal experience, academic training, or adequate knowledge? A lack of expert qualifications doesn't necessarily invalidate a writer's arguments, but it should make you examine them with extra care. See Section 40a-3 for more on evaluating a writer's credentials. Section 40a-2 tells how to evaluate the credibility of different kinds of publications.

3 Look carefully at the evidence presented. A strong argument must back up its claims. When you read an argument, size up the evidence.

- **How much evidence does the writer present?** Does the amount of support seem substantial enough, or does the writer rely on just one or two examples?
- **Where does the evidence come from?** Is it recent, or is it so old that it may no longer be accurate? Does it seem trustworthy, or does the writer rely on dubious sources?
- **Is the evidence fairly and fully presented?** Do you suspect that the writer has manipulated the information?

Guard against gravitating toward arguments that confirm your own beliefs and avoiding those that don't. Seek out different perspectives. See Section 8b-3 for more on evaluating the evidence presented in an argument.

4 Assess whether the writer's claims go beyond what the evidence actually supports. Does the writer draw conclusions that go beyond what his or her support warrants? Question any argument that stretches its conclusions too far.

5 Look for what's *not* there: the unstated assumptions, beliefs, and values that underlie the argument. Does the writer take for granted certain knowledge or beliefs? Often, what someone takes for granted in an argument should be disputed. Examine the author's untested claims.

See Sections 8a-3 and 8b-4 for how to spot and evaluate hidden assumptions in an argument.

6 Note any contradictions. Where pieces of an argument don't fit together, question why.

7 Examine the writer's word choices to identify underlying biases. Everyone has biases. Be sensitive to bias so that you aren't swayed unwittingly.

You don't have to distrust everything you read, but be alert when writers overload their prose with highly positive or extremely negative adjectives.

8 Be skeptical of simple solutions to complex problems, and resist black-and-white thinking. Be wary of quick, easy answers to difficult problems. Most problems are complex. There is seldom one "right solution."

Every solution to a problem has extra consequences. As you read an argument, look for the long-term implications of the writer's position. Don't settle for easy answers.

EXERCISE 7.2 Read an editorial in today's news twice, playing the "believing and doubting game" described in Section 7b-1. Which did you find more challenging, reading as a believer or reading as a doubter? Why? Did you notice anything using this method that you might not have noticed if you had read the piece just once?

How Do You Write Pwerful Arguments?

8

8a What does argument involve?

Many writing projects you undertake will try to persuade a particular audience to accept a claim, using *logical reasoning* supported by facts, examples, statistics, or other kinds of *evidence*. The ability to construct an argument is an essential skill.

1 Know the difference between genuine arguments and other kinds of disagreements. Rhetoricians use the term *argument* in a specialized way. When we talk about *argument*, we mean a discussion of an issue with two qualities:

1. People might reasonably disagree about it.
2. There are *reasonable* grounds for supporting one viewpoint over another.

An assertion that no one would dispute is not an argument.

Disputes about subjective tastes aren't true arguments either, because it's impossible to prove that one opinion is more valid than the other.

A statement also is not an argument when it seeks to persuade with threats, emotional manipulation, or trickery rather than with reasoning. Although writers use these techniques as though they were arguments, don't be fooled. Arguments draw on different strategies entirely.

EXERCISE 8.1 Though the t-shirt slogans pictured on page 62 seem to threaten readers, both address serious public issues. The "Vote or Die!" shirt was part of a larger public relations campaign spearheaded by Sean "P. Diddy" Combs to encourage citizens aged 18–30 to vote in the 2004 presidential election. The shirt on the right is available on <www.thoseshirts.com>, a Web site that caters to politically conservative tastes. Look closely at each shirt, then answer these questions: Do you think either of these images implies a reasoned argument? If so, what is being argued? If not, what would need to be added for you to consider the slogan an argument? Discuss your responses with a group of classmates.

2 Understand an argument as a claim supported by reasons and evidence. British logician and philosopher Stephen Toulmin has developed a useful model for understanding how arguments are structured. The Toulmin model says that in every argument, a writer begins by making a general assertion—a *claim*—and then produces one or more grounds for supporting that claim. Support for a claim may include *reasons* (smaller assertions that often begin with the word *because*) and *evidence* (relevant examples, facts, statistics, or experts' statements).

Here's a simple way of outlining how an argument is put together.

Argument = Claim + Reason(s) and Evidence

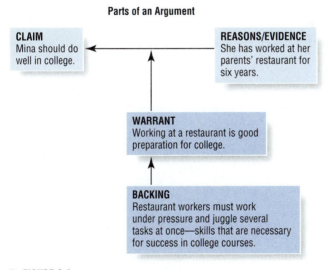

Parts of an Argument

CLAIM
Mina should do well in college.

REASONS/EVIDENCE
She has worked at her parents' restaurant for six years.

WARRANT
Working at a restaurant is good preparation for college.

BACKING
Restaurant workers must work under pressure and juggle several tasks at once—skills that are necessary for success in college courses.

■ **FIGURE 8.1**

3 Recognize that arguments rest on unstated beliefs, or warrants.

Simply laying out a claim and some kind of support isn't enough to make a solid argument. Some ways of connecting claims with reasons and evidence are more persuasive than others.

Toulmin's model uses the term *warrant* to describe the justification—a general belief, rule, or principle—that links the claim and its support in an argument. A persuasive argument must rest on warrants that readers find satisfactory, or readers will reject it.

Sometimes a warrant is so self-evident that it's left unstated. The writer assumes that once the claim and its support are presented, readers will supply and accept the warrant on their own.

But sometimes an argument rests on a warrant that may seem reasonable to some readers, but not to others. The writer needs to state the warrant and provide some explanation and support for it. Reasons and evidence used to support the warrant in an argument are called *backing*. Figure 8.1 shows an example of an argument; the claim, reasons and evidence, warrant, and backing are labeled.

EXERCISE 8.2 Each argument below contains a claim and supporting reasons or evidence. Supply the unstated warrant(s) that link each claim to its data, and then evaluate the warrant. Do you find the warrant convincing? Why or why not? We've done the first one for you.

ARGUMENT *Claim:* The federal government should spend more money on cutting-edge cancer research.

Reason / evidence: Studies show that the treatments developed in this kind of research save lives.

RESPONSE *Warrant:* The government should fund programs that save lives.

Analysis: This warrant is fairly convincing. However, it's possible that the government doesn't have enough money to fund *every* program that might save lives. What if a program is very expensive but will save only a few lives? This argument needs some support to show that cancer research saves more lives than other kinds of programs.

1. *Claim:* Dr. Olson is an excellent literature professor.
   Reason / evidence: She truly knows her subject matter. She has published nine books on British poetry and is recognized as a leading expert on William Wordsworth.

2. *Claim:* Local governments should not use tax money to subsidize the construction of professional sports stadiums.

Reason / evidence: Only a small portion of the population attends professional sporting events. Some people simply don't like sports, others don't have the time to attend games regularly, and many simply can't afford to pay $30–50 for a single ticket.

4 Recognize that many claims include a qualifier that clarifies the limited circumstances in which that claim holds true. Because most claims aren't true in every single case, many arguments include a limiting phrase or statement called a *qualifier—probably, in most cases, primarily, except*, for example.

8b How do you construct a solid written argument?

Making a claim and supporting it with reasons and evidence seems like a natural process, since most of us engage in informal arguments nearly every day. But it is not a process to take for granted, especially when you're asked to prepare a formal written argument in school or for a job. In college, you'll be asked to write persuasive papers that include strong theses and carefully chosen support, and this writing will have to take your purpose into account even as it appeals to a specific audience.

Being able to engage in a formal argument is essential because it allows you not only to develop but also to demonstrate your knowledge of the topics you study. In fact, formal argument is one of the most important elements that distinguishes college-level writing from the high school essays that merely summarize existing research. Because of the importance of argument in educational and professional settings, you'll want to know how to present your cases effectively and memorably.

1 Clarify your claim. What do you want readers to take from your piece? Your answer is your claim. In many academic papers, your claim will be stated early, as a thesis statement.

For detailed advice about discovering and narrowing a topic and developing a thesis, see Chapter 2 and Section 3a. For more on building a research project around a particular claim, see Chapter 38.

2 Gather reasons and evidence to support your claim. What material can you find to develop and strengthen your claim? Check the library for books, periodical articles, research reports, and government documents. Conduct a search on the Internet. For expert testimony, interview an expert.

Depending on your audience, you might also explore more personal and anecdotal kinds of support, such as memories or firsthand experience.

Cast a wide net. You may not include everything you find in the finished paper, but new evidence may help you adjust claims that have been overstated or misguided. Evidence can also suggest supporting reasons that hadn't initially occurred to you.

For more information about finding sources, see Chapter 39.

3 Evaluate your evidence. Select the supporting materials most appropriate to the writing situation. No matter the source of your evidence, be sure that it meets certain basic requirements.

- **Timeliness.** Are the statistics, information, and examples you use recent, or are they so old that they may no longer be accurate?
- **Comprehensiveness.** Do you have enough support for your claim, or are you generalizing from only one or two examples?
- **Credibility.** Do you draw your evidence from sources that both you and your readers trust?

For detailed discussions of how to evaluate evidence, see Sections 7b and 40a.

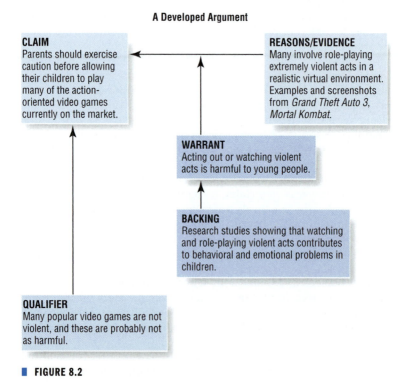

A Developed Argument

CLAIM
Parents should exercise caution before allowing their children to play many of the action-oriented video games currently on the market.

REASONS/EVIDENCE
Many involve role-playing extremely violent acts in a realistic virtual environment. Examples and screenshots from *Grand Theft Auto 3*, *Mortal Kombat*.

WARRANT
Acting out or watching violent acts is harmful to young people.

BACKING
Research studies showing that watching and role-playing violent acts contributes to behavioral and emotional problems in children.

QUALIFIER
Many popular video games are not violent, and these are probably not as harmful.

■ **FIGURE 8.2**

4 Identify the warrants, or beliefs, that underlie your argument and consider whether readers will accept them. If you suspect that readers may doubt or disagree with your assumptions, explain and support them. This step is especially important when you're writing for a hostile or unfamiliar audience. Cite *backing* for your warrant.

Figure 8.2 shows how a fully developed argument on the topic of violence in video games might look.

EXERCISE 8.3 Construct a diagram similar to the one shown in Figure 8.2 to outline a claim, reasons, evidence, warrant, backing, and qualifier for a course paper you are working on.

8c How do you write an argument that appeals to readers?

Some people see an argument as a war of words in which enemies line up on opposing sides of an issue, each with the goal of demolishing the other side. Competitive, winner-take-all arguments have their place in settings where compromise is impossible or undesirable, but they're not appropriate for much of the writing you'll do.

You won't persuade people by making them angry. You'll only make them stick to their positions more stubbornly. Think of argument not as a battle, but a dialogue. In a dialogue, both sides exchange ideas as they search for a solution. The following section explores strategies for working with readers who disagree with you.

1 Be credible. Be certain that the way you present yourself in your project—your *ethos*—is that of a person readers can respect and trust. People are more likely to listen to what you have to say if you present yourself as believable, knowledgeable, thoughtful, and fair. If you treat your readers as informed equals who are open to rational persuasion, they'll be more likely to listen sympathetically. You don't persuade people by making them angry.

To this end, you'll want to use civil and inclusive language. Slurs, name-calling, and negative stereotyping may impress a small audience that already shares your feelings. But the wider audience of people you don't know will probably think you simplistic and small-minded if you use terms like *bleeding-heart liberal* or *right-wing nut case* in an argument.

You'll also want to be sure that your language is directed at your actual audience, not above them or below them. You want readers to identify with you, and they won't do that if you are either too technical for them to understand or too simplistic to be taken seriously.

2 Draw on shared beliefs and values. Even when you're addressing readers whose position is completely opposed to your own, search for common ground. Any shared belief or value, no matter how general, may serve as a warrant on which you can build an argument those readers will find reasonable. An argument that begins from common beliefs might not change anyone's mind immediately, but it probably will get a fair hearing, and it may initiate a civil exchange of ideas. That's what argument is all about.

3 Handle information honestly. It may be tempting to construct an argument by using only sources that favor your argument or information selectively—leaving out data or trends or incidents that don't support your case. In the long run, such an argument won't go down well with critical readers. They'll ask just the sorts of questions about your claims and supporting evidence that may undermine your work:

- Are the claims supported by evidence from reliable and authoritative sources?
- Are the claims supported by evidence from a variety of sources?
- Has evidence been fairly—not selectively—reported?
- Is the evidence presented enough to support the claims?
- Has evidence been accurately documented?

You should be able to answer *yes* to every question.

4 Quote fairly from your sources. Citing authorities is a powerful way of supporting an argument. But you must quote responsibly and fairly, presenting the words of any source just as the author intended them, so far as you can tell. You shouldn't trim or embellish a quotation to make it sound more in accord with your positions. Nor should you unfairly quote those who disagree with you, leaving out words or contextual information that might make a difference in the sense. See Chapter 42 for detailed advice on quoting from sources.

5 Use emotional appeals sparingly. Just as your credibility or personal *ethos* plays a role in making an argument work, your ability to generate emotions in your readers can also play a part. In many academic and public forums, overtly emotional arguments don't play well. They are seen as sentimental or manipulative. So you need to deal with emotions carefully, understanding that many arguments do generate feelings such as anger, fear, sympathy, envy, or jealousy. You can raise such feelings with just a few hot-button phrases.

There is a role for feelings in arguments, but an emotion should not be evoked as a substitute for reasonable claims or a preponderance of evidence. Rather, emotions should complement a case supported by good reasons and solid evidence.

8d　How do you effectively address other viewpoints?

If you're going to write about controversial issues, you can't simply pretend that your position is the only one. You'll need to acknowledge that other arguments exist and address them effectively, or readers will think that you haven't done your homework.

1 Present opposing arguments fairly. Logicians use the term *straw man fallacy* to describe the misleading practice of summarizing another position in an oversimplified way that makes it easy to knock down. When you compose an argument, summarize opponents' reasoning fully and generously, or readers will perceive you as unfair.

2 Consider refuting an opposing argument. Once you've acknowledged other viewpoints, what do you do with them? Readers want to know how they affect the strength of your argument. One option is to *refute* an opposing position—that is, to disprove the argument by pointing out its weaknesses or fallacies. It's possible to critique an argument on several grounds.

- **Question the claim.** Is it overstated? Is it insufficiently supported? (See Section 7b for more on how to spot a flawed claim.)
- **Question the evidence.** Does the evidence come from reliable sources? Is there enough of it? Is it recent enough to be accurate? (Sections 7b and 40b contain guidelines for evaluating evidence.)
- **Question the warrants and backing.** Does the argument rest on beliefs, values, or assumptions that you think are invalid? Does the writer need to justify and support those assumptions? (See Section 7b for more on critiquing warrants and backing.)

When you've identified problems in one or more of these areas, point them out and call on readers to reject the argument.

3 Consider making concessions to another position. Often you won't be able to reject an opposing argument completely; most reasoned arguments do have some merit. In such cases you'll do well to concede that some of your opponent's points are valid and then argue that under the circumstances you believe yours are stronger. When you do this, you not only seem fair-minded, but you avoid backing yourself into an untenable position.

8e How can you recognize and avoid fallacies?

Fallacies are shoddy imitations of well-reasoned arguments. Most fallacies look good at first but turn out to be based on dubious assumptions and careless generalizations. Here are 10 kinds of fallacy you're likely to encounter. Detecting and debunking fallacies is an important part of agile thinking.

1 Avoid argument to the person (in Latin, *ad hominem*). This fallacy makes a personal attack on an opponent rather than focusing on the issue under discussion. *Ad hominem* arguments become smear tactics when a speaker or a writer attacks an opponent's personality or personal life.

A speaker who resorts to abusive rhetoric is avoiding the real issues. But don't confuse the *ad hominem* fallacy with relevant questions about credibility. It's legitimate to question a writer's qualifications or motives, as long as those considerations are relevant to the issues being discussed.

2 Avoid circular reasoning. This fallacy—also called *begging the question*—happens when instead of supporting a claim, the writer simply restates the claim in different words. Here's an example: "The death penalty is wrong because the state should not have the power to end a criminal's life." Unless the writer goes on to explain *why* it's wrong and provides supporting data, this claim begs the question. An unsubstantiated claim is not a reasoned argument.

3 Avoid hasty generalization. This fallacy involves drawing conclusions from too little evidence. Be careful about making claims that use absolute terms such as *always, never, everyone, no one, all*, and *none*. Absolutes are seldom accurate, so cover yourself by using qualifiers like *some, in most cases*, and *many*. Be skeptical of arguments that overstate their claims. (See Section 8a-4 for more about using qualifiers in an argument.)

4 Avoid false cause arguments (in Latin, *post hoc, ergo propter hoc*, or "after this, therefore because of this"). These arguments incorporate the faulty assumption that because one event follows another, the first event caused the second. Setting up false cause arguments is a form of oversimplification that grows out of the desire to believe in easy answers rather than wrestle with complex questions about who caused what and why.

False cause arguments about social and political issues can be harder to spot. Consider this statement:

> In the years since the highway speed limit was raised to 70 miles per hour, the annual number of traffic fatalities in our state has doubled. Clearly, the new speed limit is causing unnecessary deaths.

Can one reasonably infer this causal relationship without evidence of direct links?

5 Avoid either/or arguments (also called *false dilemma* or the *fallacy of insufficient options*). This type of faulty reasoning states an argument in terms that imply that one must choose between only two options—right/wrong, good/bad, moral/immoral, and so forth. This is another form of simplistic reasoning that glosses over complex issues and instead attacks the opposition.

The loaded rhetorical question that allows for only one acceptable answer is another form of the either/or argument.

> Are we going to increase the number of police officers in this city, or are we going to abandon it to thugs, gangs, and drug dealers?

Resist polarized thinking. It is at best, naive and at worst, fanatical.

6 Avoid red herrings. This tactic involves diverting the audience's attention from the main issue by bringing up an irrelevant point. (The phrase refers to the practice of dragging strong-smelling smoked fish across a trail in order to confuse hunting dogs and send them in the wrong direction.) Arguers of a weak case employ a *red herring* by bringing in some emotionally charged but irrelevant point to distract their audience from focusing on the real issue.

7 Avoid slippery slopes. This fallacy occurs when a writer assumes that an initial action will automatically set in motion an unstoppable chain of events. For example:

> If I allow you to stay out until 2 a.m. this weekend, you'll want to stay out until 3 a.m. next time, and pretty soon you'll be staying out all night every weekend.

You'll encounter slippery slopes most often when writers are promoting or opposing a particular course of action. Be wary of predictions that lack explanation and argument to support each link in a chain of events.

8 Avoid false analogies. These are comparisons that do not hold true or prove misleading. Analogies can be invaluable in helping readers understand abstract or elusive ideas and concepts. Sometimes, however, in trying to make an argument more attractive to readers, writers create a false analogy in which the comparison drawn simply won't hold up. For example:

> A corporation couldn't operate without the leadership of a CEO to set priorities and make the big decisions. A family operates the same way: one spouse must be the head of the household, or chaos will result.

Ask yourself this: Are the similarities between the things being compared strong enough to warrant the conclusions being drawn? If they're not, reject the analogy.

9 Avoid *non sequitur*. Latin for "it does not follow," *non sequitur* is similar to the red herring fallacy, but whereas red herrings are designed to distract a reader from the central argument, *non sequitur* asks readers to accept the irrelevant material as proof. Here's an example.

> That candidate would be an excellent mayor—after all, he was a successful businessman for years.

10 Avoid bandwagon appeal. This tactic argues that an activity or a product must be worthwhile because it is popular or that an idea must be true because "everyone" believes it.

---

summary **Ten Common Fallacies**

1. **Argument to the person (*ad hominem*):** attacking the person instead of focusing on the issues involved.
2. **Circular reasoning:** restating instead of proving a claim.
3. **Hasty generalization:** drawing conclusions from scanty evidence.
4. **False cause:** presuming that if *B* follows *A*, *A* caused *B*.
5. **Either/or:** suggesting that only two choices are possible when in fact there may be several.
6. **Red herring:** bringing in an irrelevant issue to deflect attention from the main point.
7. **Slippery slope:** assuming that one event will set off an unstoppable chain reaction.
8. **False analogy:** making a comparison between things that are too dissimilar for the comparison to be useful.
9. ***Non sequitur:*** drawing a conclusion from irrelevant data.
10. **Bandwagon:** claiming that widespread popularity makes an object valuable or idea true.

EXERCISE 8.4 Work with other students in a group to spot the fallacies in these arguments. In some instances you may find more than one.

1. Everyone knows that the next decade will be a poor time to go into medicine because government regulation is ruining the profession.

2. The great peasant rebellions in the Middle Ages happened because the rulers taxed the peasants to the limit to pay for foreign wars and neglected conditions in their own country; the United States can expect similar uprisings if it doesn't drastically cut its defense budget and invest in domestic social programs.

3. As a legislator, I can't get too upset about the proposed tuition raise when every time I drive by our state university I get caught in a traffic jam of students in their new four-wheel-drive vehicles and pricey convertibles.

How Do You Write bout Literature?

9

A literary analysis is a common assignment in English courses. But requirements and approaches vary from teacher to teacher and course to course. Instructors think in different ways, depending on their background, training, inclinations, and familiarity with literary theory. Critical approaches to literature today can range from close readings of individual texts to wide-ranging confrontations with issues of politics, gender, and culture. In nearly all cases, however, writing a literary analysis means going beyond a simple summary of or initial reaction to text.

What is the point of writing about literature? It can be to heighten your appreciation for literary work, to demonstrate your ability to support a thesis about a piece of literature, to explore how readers respond to texts, to enhance your skill at interpretation, to expand your knowledge of a particular era or literary movement, or to heighten your sensitivity to other cultures. It can also be a creative activity—a way to go public with your writing.

9a What elements should you look for when you read literature?

You should become familiar with the elements that are integral to literary works. Recognizing these elements and devices can help you formulate and refine a topic, develop a thesis statement, and provide evidence for a writing project. Checklist 9.1 describes some of these basic elements.

checklist 9.1      Basic Literary Elements

- **PLOT:** Plot refers to the writer's arrangement of events in a story and the reasons behind that arrangement. Plot can be presented in a number of ways, including chronologically and by using flashbacks.
- **SETTING:** The setting establishes the world in which the characters live and act, including time, place, and social and cultural contexts.

- **CHARACTER:** Writers create characters to make the reader care about what is happening or to reinforce symbols or themes in a text.

- **THEME:** The theme of the work is, to put it simply, what the work is *about* (its main concept), as opposed to what *happens* in it (see the discussion of plot, above). A writer will often use a theme to pull together several other elements of the work. Some common themes are *jealousy, ambition, hypocrisy*, and *prejudice*.

- **POINT OF VIEW:** Point of view focuses on who is telling the story (the narrator or speaker) and how it is told. Narrators can speak in the first, second (rarely), or third person. Some narrators are *omniscient* (able to tell us what is going on in the minds of characters), while others are *objective* (able to tell us only what the characters say and do). Some are involved in the plot, and others are mere observers.

- **DICTION (WORD CHOICES):** As you read, assume that every word was chosen carefully. Look up any words you don't understand. Dictionaries provide the literal meanings of words, their *denotations*; also be aware of possible *connotations*, or emotional associations and meanings. In addition, look for *ambiguity*, the possibility of two or more meanings, in a writer's diction.

- **FIGURATIVE LANGUAGE:** A figure of speech is a deviation from the literal meaning of a word or phrase. Writers use figurative language to challenge, inspire, or connect with readers; to bring linguistic vitality to a work; or simply to stretch their creative wings. *Metaphor* and *simile* are probably the most common figures of speech; others include *oxymoron, personification, hyperbole, synecdoche*, and *metonymy*. (Explanations of these terms and other figures of speech usually can be found in the glossaries at the back of literature textbooks.)

- **IMAGERY:** Writers use concrete language to make readers understand what they are seeing, hearing, smelling, tasting, and feeling. As you read, be aware of how the writer uses words to speak to your senses.

- **SYMBOLS:** It can be easy to confuse symbols with metaphors. While a metaphor is a comparison of two unlike objects or concepts, a symbol is one thing that stands for another. The dove, for example, can be a symbol for peace, just as the heart is a common symbol for love. A symbol's context will often suggest its meaning.

- **SOUND AND RHYTHM:** Because of the musical nature of their work, poets are especially concerned with the sound and rhythm, or *meter*, of words in a text. Common devices that involve sound include *onomatopoeia* (the sound of the word suggesting its meaning) and *alliteration* (the repetition of the same consonant sounds at the start of words near each other in a text).

- **TONE:** Tone is the mood or feeling the writer creates about the subject matter of a text. The tone might be serious or comical, angry or sad, optimistic

continued on next page

continued from page 75

or pessimistic, for example. Once you have an idea about the tone of a piece, ask yourself how the writer achieves it—through imagery, descriptive details, diction, or symbols, for instance.

- **VISUAL, DRAMATIC, OR CINEMATIC ELEMENTS:** Media such as film and television are primarily visual and thus involve specialized technical elements—shots, scenes, camera angles, lighting, and so on. When you undertake a writing project that focuses on a visual or multimedia text, your instructor may explain relevant terminology and elements in class. If you're unsure, ask which devices he or she expects you to be familiar with.

The etching of Charles Dickens' young Oliver Twist asking for more gruel in the orphanage illustrates the novel's grim setting. The illustration is by George Cruickshank.

A good introductory source on writing about film is the Dartmouth University Composition Center's *Writing About Film* Web page at <http://www.dartmouth.edu~writing/materials/student/humanities/film.shtml>.

9b   What approaches can you use to write about literature?

When you begin a literary analysis paper, have a general strategy in mind. When you write about a piece of literature or a film, you will usually use one or two of the following approaches. (Again, we use *text* to mean written work and film.)

1 Perform a close reading. A "close reading" of a text uncovers the meaning and possible interpretations of a passage, sometimes line by line (or, in the case of film, shot by shot or scene by scene). A close reading considers how the work makes readers entertain specific ideas and images. If a work includes visual images, a close reading examines how

they interact with elements of a written text. (Also see Section 7b on how to read critically.)

EXERCISE 9.1 As this still from *The Return of the King* (2003) illustrates, cinematographic elements such as camera angles, set design, and lighting often help to establish setting, tone, and theme in a film. If you have seen this film (or one of the others in the *Lord of the Rings* trilogy), what literary elements did you find most striking or effective? If you haven't seen the film, can you think of another film you've seen that made effective use of literary elements? Discuss your answers with a group of classmates.

2 Analyze key themes in a work. When you discover key themes, examine them to show how the parts of the work convey their meanings to readers.

3 Analyze plot or structure. Study the way a work of literature is put together. Why did the writer choose this particular arrangement?

4 Analyze character and setting. Study the behavior of characters to understand their motivations and the ways they relate to each other. How does the writer create characters through description, action, reaction, and dialogue so that they embody themes and ideas?

Study the setting to determine how the environment of a work (where things happen in a novel, short story, or play) affects what happens to the characters. How does the setting represent the characters' inner being and manifest cultural values?

5 Analyze the text as an example of a particular genre. You can study a particular work by evaluating its form—tragedy, comic novel, sonnet, detective story, epic, situation comedy, film noir, and so on. How does the work compare to other examples of that genre?

6 Explore a historical or cultural analysis. A literary work reflects the society that produced it. Similarly, historical events may change the context in which we read a text.

You can also explore how a work of art embodies culture. What assumptions, beliefs, and values can be found in the literary work?

7 Analyze a work from the perspective of gender. Literary works portray women and men in roles in society. How do literary works embody relationships of power between men and women?

8 Examine the biography of the author or the author's creative process. A writer's life is expressed in and through literary work. Similarly, you might learn all you can about the way a particular work was created. What do the sources, notes, influences, manuscripts, and revised texts behind a finished book, poem, or film tell about the way a particular work was created?

9 Edit a text or produce a literary Web site. The production of literary journals or, more recently, Web sites that focus on cultural ideas and themes are creative ways of going public with writing. You can select and comment on new works or edit older, neglected texts in the public domain.

9c   What sources can you use in writing essays about literature?

The research resources available for your literary analysis will make your work easier, more authoritative, and more interesting.

1 Understand the primary texts you are reading. In working with literary and cultural texts, you need to establish certain basic facts. Are you reading (or viewing) a first edition of a work or a revised version, an edited version, a translation, or, in the case of a film, a later "director's cut" that differs from the version shown in theaters? These considerations help define the subject of your subsequent analysis precisely. Evaluate the preface or front matter of works of literature to discover when they were written, by whom they were published, how they have been transmitted, and how they may have changed over the years.

2 Consult secondary sources on literary subjects. To locate secondary sources on literary topics, begin with the following indexes and bibliographies available in a library reference room.

Essay and General Literature Index

MLA International Bibliography

New Cambridge Bibliography of English Literature

Year's Work in English Studies

Many useful Web sites are available as well. Check out the following:

The E Server. <http://eserver.org>

Literary Resources on the Net.
<http://andromeda.rutgers.edu/~jlynch/Lit>

The Online Books Page. <http://digital.library.upenn.edu/books>

University of Virginia Library Electronic Text Center.
<http:// etext.lib.virginia.edu>

9d   How do you develop a literary project?

When you develop a literary paper or project, you need to read carefully, formulate clear ideas about your subjects, report information accurately, and design a project that will be interesting and enlightening to others.

1 Begin by reading carefully. The evidence you'll need to write a thoughtful, well-organized analysis may come from within the literary work itself and from outside readings and secondary sources. Your initial goal is to find a point worth making, an assertion you can prove with convincing evidence.

To find your point, begin by *positioning* the work (or works) and then reading and *annotating* them carefully (see Sections 7a and 41a).

You can position works in many ways. Yet you should also read with an open mind, to savor the literary experience. While reading, take notes to record your immediate responses. Ask yourself questions.

- What engages me as I read the work?
- What puzzles or surprises me?
- What characters or literary devices seem most striking or original?
- What upsets me or seems most contrary to my own values and traditions?

Make a list of such queries as you read, and reexamine them when you have finished. To stimulate more questions, compare and contrast the work(s) you have read with other similar works. To further stimulate your thinking, consider specific ways of approaching a literary text (see Sections 9b-9c) and try using brainstorming and idea mapping (see Sections 2a-2b).

2 Develop a thesis about the literary work(s) you are studying. Begin with a question you are eager to explore in depth, a research query or hypothesis generated by reading secondary sources or by discussions with other readers.

When you've put your question into words, test its energy. If the answer to your inquiry is too obvious, discard it and try another. Look for a surprising, even startling question—one whose answer you don't know. Test that question on classmates or your instructor.

When you have found your question, turn it into an assertion—your preliminary thesis statement.

Is this an assertion you are interested in proving? Is it a statement other readers might challenge? If so, write it down and continue. If not, modify it or explore another issue.

3 Read the work(s) again with your thesis firmly in mind. Read slowly and critically this time. Look for characters, incidents, descriptions, speeches, dialogue, or images that support or refute your thesis. Take careful notes. If you are using your own text, highlight significant passages in the work.

When you are done, evaluate the evidence you have gathered from a close reading. Then modify or qualify your thesis to reflect what you have learned or discovered.

If necessary, return to secondary sources or other literary works to supplement and extend your analysis. Play with ideas, relationships, implications, and possibilities. Don't hesitate to question conventional views or to bring your own experiences to bear.

Begin drafting your paper, drawing together your specific observations into full paragraphs. Weave your analysis and the evidence together neatly.

If you consult secondary sources while writing the paper, take careful notes from the books and articles you read. Be sure also to prepare accurate bibliography cards for your Works Cited page. (See Chapter 38 on planning a research project.)

4 Use scratch outlines to guide the first draft. Try out several organization plans for the paper (see Section 3b), and then choose the one you think is best.

When you have a structure, write a complete first draft. Stay open to new ideas and refinements of your original thesis, but try not to wander unless such material relates directly to your thesis. If you do wander, consider whether this digression might be the topic you *really* want to write about.

Avoid the draft that simply paraphrases the plot. Equally ineffective is a paper that merely praises the author. Avoid impressionistic judgments. Don't expect to find a moral in every literary work, or turn your analysis into a search for "hidden meanings." Respond honestly to what you are reading. You may want to follow the conventions of the MLA research paper or the *Chicago Manual of Style* paper (see Chapters 44 and 46). Checklist 9.2 covers a few basic conventions of literary analysis.

checklist 9.2

Conventions in a Literary Paper

- **USE THE PRESENT TENSE TO REFER TO EVENTS OCCURRING IN A LITERARY WORK:** Hester Prynne *wears* a scarlet letter; Hamlet *kills* Polonius. Think of a literary work as an ongoing performance.

- **IDENTIFY PASSAGES OF SHORT POEMS BY LINE NUMBERS:** (*"Journey of the Magi,"* lines 21–31). Avoid the abbreviations *l* or *ll* for *line* or *lines*, because they are sometimes confused with Roman numerals; spell out the words. See Section 35c for advice on punctuating lines of poetry that appear within a paper.

- **PROVIDE ACT AND SCENE DIVISIONS (AND LINE NUMBERS AS NECESSARY) FOR PASSAGES FROM PLAYS.** Act and scene numbers are now usually given in Arabic numbers, although Roman numbers are still common and acceptable: *Ham.* 4.5.179–85 or *Ham.* IV.v.179–85. The titles of Shakespeare's works are commonly abbreviated in citations: *Mac.* 1.2; *Oth.* 2.2. Check to see which form your instructor prefers.

- **PROVIDE A DATE OF PUBLICATION IN PARENTHESES AFTER YOUR FIRST MENTION OF A LITERARY WORK:** Before publishing *Beloved* (1987), Toni Morrison had written. . . .

- **USE TECHNICAL TERMS ACCURATELY.** Spell the names of characters correctly. Take special care with matters of grammar and mechanics.

- **FOLLOW THE CONVENTIONS OF LITERARY ANALYSIS.** When inserting a quotation from a literary work or a critic into your paper, identify it and explain its significance. Be sure quotations fit into the grammar of your sentences.

hi🌀hlight | A Literary Analysis Paper

 In the following literary analysis, "Queen Jane Approximately" (a clever allusion to a song by Bob Dylan), student Sally Shelton from the University of South Carolina does a close reading of a poem by Sharon Olds, "The One Girl at the Boys' Party." She approaches the work from a feminist perspective, examining the interplay of gender roles between one young girl and a group of boys. Shelton supports her analysis by carefully citing passages from the poem, which we have reprinted in its entirety. *continued on next page*

continued from page 81

The One Girl at the Boys' Party
By Sharon Olds

When I take my girl to the swimming party	1
I set her down among the boys. They tower and	2
bristle, she stands there smooth and sleek,	3
her math scores unfolding in the air around her.	4
They will strip to their suits, her body hard and	5
indivisible as a prime number,	6
they'll plunge in the deep end, she'll subtract	7
her height from ten feet, divide it into	8
hundreds of gallons of water, the numbers	9
bouncing in her mind like molecules of chlorine	10
in the bright blue pool. When they climb out,	11
her ponytail will hang its pencil lead	12
down her back, her narrow silk suit	13
with hamburgers and french fries printed on it	14
will glisten in the brilliant air, and they will	15
see her sweet face, solemn and	16
sealed, a factor of one, and she will	17
see their eyes, two each,	18
their legs, two each, and the curves of their sexes,	19
one each, and in her head she'll be doing her	20
wild multiplying, as the drops	21
sparkle and fall to the power of a thousand from her body.	22

Sally Shelton

Professor Moore

English 102

21 April 2006

Queen Jane Approximately

Sharon Olds' "The One Girl at the Boys' Party" examines the tense competition between the sexes. The poem illustrates the innate vulnerability of men while portraying females as winning the attention and respect they rightfully deserve. Olds achieves these insights by examining the isolation of a young girl at a party of boys. She infuses the situation with ironies and repeated images that probe themes of gender, sexuality, and domination.

The poem deceives the reader initially by putting the youths in typical gender roles. The speaker takes her daughter (1) to a party where she "set[s] her down among the boys" (2) like a toy or doll for their amusement. She is placed within a situation where she must prove herself. The boys, in turn, "tower and/bristle" (2-3) at the intrusion. While she is being "set down," the boys move like a gang, intimidating and, perhaps, angry. Yet suddenly, the attention of the poem shifts from the girl to the boys as the young woman quickly and nonchalantly asserts her dominance over the unwitting youths.

The contrast between the girl and the group of boys is established early in the poem. While the boys "tower and bristle," the lone girl "stands there smooth and sleek" (3), firmly placed, establishing her ground, unabated in her delicate sensuality, and controlling the air about her. It is in this "brilliant air" (15) that her "math scores" (4) begin to unfold. References to mathematics throughout the poem illustrate how the young girl, and perhaps the speaker of the poem, have conquered the situation already. They have figured the boys out through methodical and meticulous calculations.

To complete the reversal of gender roles, the boys, who were the first to dominate in the poem, assume a subordinate and effeminate role. As if to expose themselves as sensual and enticing beings, "[t]hey will strip to their suits" (5), leaving themselves vulnerable (she can count the "curves of their sexes") (19) and hoping that the girl will "strip" to her vulnerability as well. The girl,

continued on next page

continued from page 83

however, remains in control, "her body hard
and/indivisible as a prime number" (5-6). The pool of
males will forever attempt to figure her out, but she
has solved them. She stands before the boys in the
pool, with "the numbers/bouncing in her mind" (9-10),
her calculations racing. She, who was initially
perceived as an intrusion, a toy to be discarded, has
now silently attracted the curiosity of the boys.

   Now that the girl's presence has consumed the
scene, the boys become enchanted by her sensuality.
The infinite "molecules of chlorine" (10) that
comprise the girl's intelligence intoxicate the boys,
who have by now succumbed to the innocent appeal of
"the bright blue pool" (11). Sexual desires come into
play: her tomboyish ponytail catches their gaze.
Although it "hang[s] its pencil lead" (12), a phallic
symbol with piercing connotations, the boys still
allow their gaze to follow the ponytail "down her
back" (13). Then they notice the girl's figure, more
"smooth and sleek" (3) than before, in "her narrow
silk suit" (13) with the mouth-watering "hamburgers
and french fries printed on it" (14) that "glisten in
the brilliant air" (15). Lastly, they notice her face,
"sweet," "solemn," and "sealed" (16-17). No longer an
object to discard, the girl becomes for the boys an
embodiment of a desire that will never be satiated.

   Again, the speaker widens the schism between the
girl and the youths. It began with the girl doing all
the observing and calculating, but soon the boys catch
on. Threatened by her ability to strip them, they
"plunge in the deep end" (7), hoping to hide their

vulnerability while attempting to entice the girl. The act of plunging is risky and the boys nearly drown in their attempts to impress her. Defeated and weakened, they have to "climb out" (11), still fragile and susceptible, and, moreover, they discover how badly they are getting beaten. Then they enter the game, the observed becoming the observers. While the boys "see her sweet face . . . a factor of one" (16–17), the girl outnumbers them when she "see[s] their eyes, two each,/their legs, two each, and the curves of their sexes,/one each" (18–20). She sheds some power when she lets her "drops/sparkle and fall" (21–22), but they will never gain a hold on her because she will forever "be doing her wild multiplying" (20–21). The boys cannot enumerate her "to the power of a thousand" (22), so her "power" controls them and overwhelms them. She has reduced these once towering and bristling boys to vulnerable, starstruck, and curvy subordinates by daring them to plunge into the deep end of womanhood.

Through the character of the girl, the speaker offers insight into how women encompass an infinite power and elegance that men miscalculate and misunderstand. The girl triumphs while the boys sink into her deep intelligence, stamina, and sensuality. In the game of relationships, here staged as a pool party, there are those who tower, those who plunge, and those who calculate.

Work Cited

Olds, Sharon. "The One Girl at the Boys' Party." *The Dead and the Living*. New York: Knopf, 1984. Print.

part

3

Document Design

How Do You Design Documents?

Writing has always been influenced by visual and tactile elements. Arguably, the earliest writing arose from crude marks on bones, and developed into symbolic hieroglyphs and pictographs on stone and bronze. As time passed, written communications evolved in a range of materials (clay, papyrus, parchment, paper) and instruments (stylus, quill, pen, typewriter). Early books, especially Bibles, were often so vibrantly illustrated that we describe them as *illuminated*. The era of print introduced new ways of conveying messages, both visual and verbal.

Today, computers and digital media are influencing the style of writing by handing the tools of design and production directly to the author. With computers, you have previously unimaginable powers to change the look of your writing.

The contrasts between different wars (World War II and Vietnam) in different eras are evident in the visual styles of famous posters from those periods. During World War II, Rosie the Riveter symbolized civilian support for the war effort. The Vietnam-era poster sends a contrary message. How do the visual elements—the images, layout, typefaces—of the two posters work to convey these different messages? Discuss the differences with a group of classmates.

If you want your work to reach an audience, you have to think about not just what it says, but how it looks. Readers today expect writing to be visually inviting and easy to navigate—otherwise they may not bother to read it. You need to know the basics of *visual style* and *document design*.

Creating documents involves decisions about a document's format and style: Should you send an email, a letter, or a memo? Would your audience prefer a printed brochure or a Web site? Should you use a playful or a serious font for the main text? Are colors and graphics appropriate? These are just a few of the questions you'll resolve as you turn working drafts into finished documents.

Even when you know how you want a document to look, creating that look—usually with a computer—is a separate matter. Fortunately, most word-processing and design programs share a standard language for document design. This chapter will help you build a basic design vocabulary, and it offers pointers for working with specific design elements and avoiding common pitfalls.

10a How do you design documents with a computer?

Most writers use computers, but few use them to their full advantage. Familiarize yourself with your computer's capabilities to make the design process easier and improve the quality of your product.

Begin by exploring the design features of your word processor, either through the user's manual or by hands-on experimentation (see Figure 10.1).

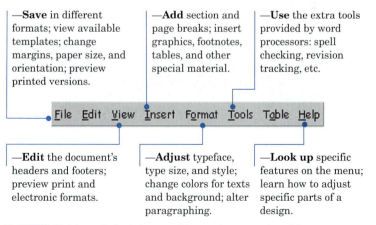

—**Save** in different formats; view available templates; change margins, paper size, and orientation; preview printed versions.

—**Add** section and page breaks; insert graphics, footnotes, tables, and other special material.

—**Use** the extra tools provided by word processors: spell checking, revision tracking, etc.

File Edit View Insert Format Tools Table Help

—**Edit** the document's headers and footers; preview print and electronic formats.

—**Adjust** typeface, type size, and style; change colors for texts and background; alter paragraphing.

—**Look up** specific features on the menu; learn how to adjust specific parts of a design.

■ **FIGURE 10.1** Learn the basic features of your word processor through its menu.

10b   How do you lay out pages?

When format specifications are rigid, follow them to the letter. When you have flexibility, take advantage of it. Below you'll find a list of page features you can use to achieve specific effects.

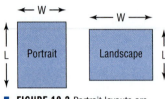

FIGURE 10.2 Portrait layouts are longer than they are wide. In landscape layouts, width is greater than length.

1 Choose a manageable size and orientation. Large pages give you more surface area, but they can be difficult to design effectively. Large electronic pages may require too much scrolling.

Portrait orientation works well with most formats because it presents the main text in one midsize column. *Landscape* orientation is generally reserved for graphic material too wide for portfolio orientation (see Figure 10.2).

2 Break material into units. Decide on a paragraph format. *Block paragraphs* have no indentation on their first lines but are separated by extra spacing between each paragraph. Standard *indented paragraphs*, on the other hand, need no extra spacing. Besides paragraph format, you must determine line spacing. Print formats often use indented paragraphs with more than single spacing between lines of type. Web pages and email, on the other hand, are easier to read when they are single-spaced. Not only does the type look lighter on a screen, but single spacing means that readers need not do extra scrolling to get through the document.

In some kinds of documents—such as pamphlets and newsletters, you might use columns, boxes, or background shading to chunk information to make it more readable. In others—such as research papers or résumés—use headings to break the information into helpful sections.

3 Arrange material according to relevance. Readers of English tend to move from the upper left corner of a page to the lower right. Put leading material at the top of a page and less interesting but necessary material toward the bottom.

- Place the most important material in columns spanning the body of the page.
- Move supplementary material toward the side and bottom margins.
- Group related pieces of material near each other.

- Distinguish special material by indenting or framing it.
- In headers, add navigational details such as current section titles (also called *running heads*), page numbers, and information about the writer.
- In footers, place routine but necessary information such as contact addresses, page numbers, organizational information, and credits.

4 Align material to direct readers' eyes down and across the page.

Left alignment is the most readable layout for text, but images and graphics often work well with center or right alignment. Right-aligned images are effective when they are "wrapped" by left-aligned text—that is, when the lines of text appear on the same horizontal lines used by the image (see page 97). Center alignment is better for images not wrapped by text, since left or right alignment leaves too much white space in the body of the page.

Subsections. Subsections, groups of related paragraphs under a heading, are just a step up from plain paragraphs. By highlighting topics within a larger section, subsections help readers follow your discussion.

Reviews from Center Stage

Lame indeed.

The recent popularity of boy-band parody Wounded Duck isn't all that surprising. What is surprising is the ability of surly fans to endure the tiresome antics for an hour-long set. How many times can you watch the elaborately choreographed dancers flub their moves before it gets old?

Okay, I'll admit to guffawing through the first three songs—but once you get the gist of the show, there isn't much more to see. My advice—should the Duck fly into town opening for another band—show up ten minutes before the headliners, get a few laughs, and then listen to some real music.

How old school is too old school?

Before Friday, I thought I had an answer to this question. DJ Crusty's energetic set showed that digging up musical fossils isn't all about giving rock legends cameos in your music video. There are still treasures to be found—treasures encased in wax. Crusty's ability to synthesize diverse flavors of vinyl into addictive compounds explains why he has crossed over from the club set into the mainstream.

Lists. It's often awkward to form a series of regular, repetitive statements into a paragraph. Try a list instead. Use numbered lists when information needs to be presented in a strict order.

Festival 2007: Survivor's Guide

The spring rains and crowds can sometimes put a damper on your ability to enjoy the music. Never fear! We've provided a list of suggestions to make the best of your aural outing.

♪ Take your own water bottles. You'll have to wait in line for even the basics once inside.

♪ A waterproof mat is also a good idea. The ground gets pretty muddy, especially by the final days.

♪ Bring plenty of your own toilet tissue. Supplies in the portable facilities run low after just a few hours.

♪ If you're planning on attending more than one day, earplugs will keep your hearing from going dull.

♪ A hooded raincoat can keep you dry during the early afternoon showers.

♪ If you plan on heading for the mosh pit, ignore all of the above and just bring elbow pads.

Tables. Tables work well for presenting structured information, especially (but not exclusively) statistical data, which can also be turned into graphs (see Section 10d-1). You can also use tables to display categories of information and complicated lists.

Festival 2007: Daily Venue Schedules				
	Center Stage	East Stage	West Stage	Welcome Stage
Wed.	Classic Rock	World Beat	Punk	Polka
Th.	Funk and Soul	Swing	Reggae and Ska	Metal Mania
Fri.	Rock and Pop	Blues	Hip-hop and R & B	Local Grab Bag
Sat.	Rock and Pop	Jazz	Country	DJ Showcase
Sun.	International Folk	Classical	Gospel	Amateur Contest

Frames. When you want to set material apart from the main text, place it in a *frame* or a box, which you can create with lines and/or changes in background color.

About the Festival (cont.)

The annual festival began in 1982 as a relatively small, "y'all come" event. There was only one stage in the town square at that time. Those first few years didn't attract much national attention, but the music was rich with a variety of local flavors—from rock to jazz to punk to (we're not ashamed to admit) disco.

1987: Going National
A big break came for the festival in 1987, when national, independent label Snub Pop agreed to host a second stage. Before long, other national labels were seeing the festival as an opportunity to promote otherwise unknown bands.

The menu of bands was interesting enough to attract music lovers from all over the state. Eventually, the small festival grew to include most types of American music, until, last year, we finally added a fourth venue, allowing us to accommodate more and more international genres as well.

5 Use white space to avoid clutter. White space reduces clutter.

- Leave ample margins at the top and sides of your pages.
- Surround titles, graphics, and frames with unused space.
- Double-space between paragraphs.
- Indent special blocks of material.
- Allow adequate space between columns in multicolumn documents.

10c How do you choose type?

Typefaces (or *fonts*) and *type styles* have personalities; they convey mood, attitude, and tone; and they affect readability.

1 Select a suitable typeface. Knowing the general characteristics of each family of fonts will help you make appropriate choices.

- **Serif fonts.** Serifs are the little lines, or "feet," that appear at the bottom or top of the main strokes in a letter. Two common serif fonts are Courier and Bookman. Serif fonts are highly readable.

- **Sans serif fonts.** Sans serif fonts—letters without the little feet—have a clean, modern look. Two common sans serif fonts are Arial and Helvetica. Sans serif fonts are good choices for display type and material to be read on an electronic, faxed, or photocopied page.

- **Decorative or ornamental fonts.** Decorative fonts have personality, but they aren't always easy to read, which makes them poor choices for long passages of text. Save these fonts for a special effect.

- **Symbol fonts.** *Dingbats* allow you to add special characters. See Chart 10.1.

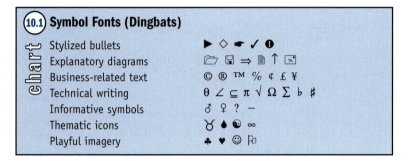

10.1 Symbol Fonts (Dingbats)

Stylized bullets	▶ ◇ ☛ ✓ ❶
Explanatory diagrams	🗁 🖫 ⇒ 🖹 ↑ 🔲
Business-related text	© ® ™ % ¢ £ ¥
Technical writing	θ ∠ ⊆ π √ Ω Σ ♭ ♯
Informative symbols	♂ ♀ ? —
Thematic icons	♉ ♦ 🌐 ∞
Playful imagery	♣ ♥ ☺ 🎵

2 Use type styles strategically. Type styles that differ from plain text will draw readers' attention. Use them sparingly, however, to avoid loss of impact. See Chart 10.2.

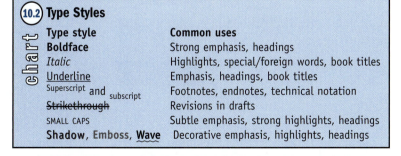

10.2 Type Styles

Type style	Common uses
Boldface	Strong emphasis, headings
Italic	Highlights, special/foreign words, book titles
<u>Underline</u>	Emphasis, headings, book titles
Superscript and subscript	Footnotes, endnotes, technical notation
~~Strikethrough~~	Revisions in drafts
SMALL CAPS	Subtle emphasis, strong highlights, headings
Shadow, Emboss, <u>Wave</u>	Decorative emphasis, highlights, headings

3 Adjust type size for readability. Medium type sizes (usually 10 or 12 points) work best for the main body of text. Use larger type to emphasize headings and titles. Use smaller type to downplay less important material in margins, headers, and footers. Draw readers' eyes toward the body of a page rather than toward running titles, contact information, or supplementary comments.

Remember the following:

- Electronic documents will look strange if the fonts you use aren't installed on your readers' computers.
- Changing the font face may change the height and length of lines.
- Serif fonts can be difficult to read on computer screens.
- Certain font styles and colors (such as blue underlining) may have special meaning in Web pages and other hyperlinked documents.

10d   How do you use graphics and images?

Use graphics and images to enhance and complement the text of your document.

1 Present numerical data with graphs.

Graphs help readers visualize the significance of statistical information.

Bar graphs show comparative values.

Line graphs show trends and changes across time.

Area graphs show portions of a whole as comparative trends.

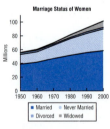

2 Clarify details through charts and diagrams.

Use a chart or diagram to give readers details about your topic that are difficult to explain in words.

Whereas charts show connections among related things, diagrams supplement verbal descriptions with instructive images. See page 95 for examples of common types of charts and diagrams.

Pie charts show portions of a whole.

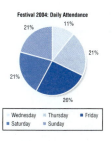

Organizational charts show hierarchical relationships.

Flow charts show procedural relationships.

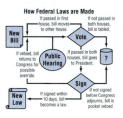

Timelines show sequential relationships.

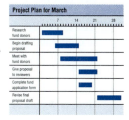

Diagrams illustrate textual descriptions.

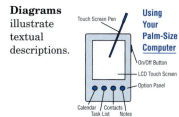

3 Enliven writing with photos and illustrations.

Photos and illustrations (cartoons, drawings, engravings) let you show readers—at a glance—aspects of your subject that would otherwise need lengthy description. Be sure that they reinforce important points and do not distract or mislead readers.

Many options exist for acquiring photos and illustrations. You can purchase digitized photos on the Web (some are even free) or on CDs. You can create your own with a digital camera. You can translate existing photos or illustrations into electronic formats with a scanner or camera.

For a minimal cost, you can buy clip art images. Clip art collections are not sophisticated, but they can be useful for posters, brochures, newsletters, and other low-cost publications.

4 Edit your images.

In most projects today, you'll likely use digital images and photographs, which can be easily cropped, edited, and improved to look good on a page or screen. You can edit images you download or take yourself in software as sophisticated as *Adobe Photoshop* or in tools usually included with your computer, such as *iPhoto* or *Picture Man*. Even word processors enable you to resize and position images you import into documents. Check out the software available to you and then explore how it works. You'll master the basic features quickly:

- **Sizing images.** After you import an image into a document, you can change its size, usually just by pulling a corner or typing a size in a control box. In reports and research papers, an image should be no larger than it needs to be to be effective and "readable." In electronic projects, smaller images are also quicker to download than larger ones and take up less digital space. Use bigger images in those projects that need their impact—such as brochures or posters. Note that changing the size of an image can affect its quality and sharpness.

- **Cropping images.** Use editing tools to focus on those parts of an image your project needs. Simple cropping tools allow you to select exactly which part of a digital image to use. See Figure 10.3.

- **Placing images.** Software tools ordinarily allow you not only to place an image where you want it on a page (left, right, center), but to wrap text around it in various ways. Where you place an image will affect the way readers consider it. See Figure 10.4.

- **Coloring images.** You can usually choose to display an image in color, black/white, or sepia tone (a reddish-brown tone), or with various special effects that change its texture. You can also use the available editing tools to improve the color balance (to get flesh tones right, for example), to add or flatten contrast, to brighten or darken the image, to deepen or moderate the color (called "saturation"), and so on. Tinker with these tools until you get an image you feel is "right." But when you'll be making major changes, work with a *duplicate* of your original image just in case you want to return to the original.

FIGURE 10.3 A cropping tool is used to select one part of a photograph and to reshape its proportions from rectangular to square. One caution: the image of the squirrel here would lose sharpness as it is enlarged.

FIGURE 10.4 A format box in a word processor will enable you not only to place a photograph exactly where you need it, but to wrap text around it in a variety of ways.

5 Separate material with borders and rules. Borders and rules—horizontal or vertical lines between units of material—provide visual guides to how you have divided material in a document.

Horizontal lines or rules often mark the beginning of new sections. You'll often see rules separating footnotes or running heads from the main text. You might see a vertical rule when marginal comments or graphics appear in a sidebar.

10e How do you work with color?

Match your use of color to your writing situation. Color is not always appropriate in academic papers, but it may be necessary to attract attention to brochures, newsletters, and Web pages.

1 Select a readable color scheme. Color schemes assign colors to various elements on a page (headings, rules, frames, borders, graphics). To be readable, background and type colors must contrast but not clash. Bright colors must be used sparingly, as they can tire the eyes.

2 Create a mood for your document. Bright colors have a bold effect, even when applied sparingly. Soft colors, on the other hand, may need to cover an entire page to have a noticeable impact. Some color combinations—for example, purple and orange or yellow and black—are bold; they shout for attention. Others—shades of blue combined with ivory—are subtle. Some colors just seem to clash—pink and bright green, for instance, and purple and yellow—but one can't say flatly that certain colors should never be combined.

3 Use color to highlight or soften elements of your layout. A bold heading can be made less striking by changing the color from black to a softer blue or gray. Plain text in the body of a paragraph can be made more striking by changing it to red.

Mdel Documents 11

In this chapter you'll find model documents illustrating a variety of print and electronic formats. Where print formats have corresponding electronic formats, we show examples in both media.

11a How do you write email?

Over the last few years, instructors and employers have come to expect students and workers to conduct business through email. In writing class, you may be asked to submit assignments as file attachments or to collaborate with fellow students through online messages. In workplaces, email has replaced printed memos (see Section 11e) for everyday correspondence, and it has become an important means of communicating cheaply across long distances.

checklist 11.1 — Email

- Use short block paragraphs; long paragraphs are difficult to read on screen. Double-space between paragraphs, but don't indent.
- Avoid "Reply to All" when responding to messages received. Respond to everyone on an email list only when you think all will be interested in your comments.
- Make sure attached files are in a format your audience can view and that you have scanned them for viruses.
- If you use a common signature for all your messages, make sure the text of the signature is suitable for both professional and personal audiences; otherwise, edit the signature when the occasion calls for it.
- Avoid lengthy emails in business situations. Keep the message focused.

checklist 11.2 — Typical Print Documents

- Use standard letterhead paper (8½ by 11 inch).
- Use portrait orientation unless you plan to fold the document or you need extra room for graphics and images.

continued on page 100

EMAIL MESSAGE

The **message header** includes all necessary delivery information. (See below.)

A **salutation** is often optional; use one when addressing an audience you don't know.

The **body** can include block paragraphs, lists, and subsections set off by dashed lines or extra spacing.

The **closing** and **signature** will depend on the formality of the message. For professional messages, include your title and organization.

EMAIL HEADER

The **To** line includes one or more email addresses for recipients. Remember that addresses must be completely accurate.

The **From** line will usually be filled out by your email program with your name and address. If you have more than one email account, you may be asked to specify which one will be used to send the message.

```
      To: emilyjackson@mail.um.net
    From: Arnold Peale <apeale@mail.um.net>
 Subject: Web project requirements
      Cc: jasonc@mail.um.net; betho@mail.um.net
     Bcc:
X-Attachments:
```

The **Attachments** line will include the file names of electronic documents you would like to send along with your message. Email clients vary in how they ask you to specify attachments.

The **Subject** line includes a short phrase about the topic of your message—make sure it is relevant to your recipients.

Cc lines can be used to send other individuals copies of the message. (See also Section 11e.)

continued from page 98

- Leave at least a one-inch margin on all sides. If you plan to bind the document, add more space on the bound edge.
- Use double or single-and-a-half spacing unless otherwise specified, especially with small type. Single spacing is used in letters or sometimes in long documents to cut printing costs.
- Use headers and/or footers with running titles and page numbers for multipage documents.

checklist 11.3 — Typical Onscreen Documents

- Make sure your audience has the right software to view the document format you're using.
- Short, single-spaced block paragraphs are most common for onscreen documents.
- Use sans serif typefaces and avoid long stretches of bold, underlined, or italicized text.
- If you have hypertext links, test them to make sure they work.

11b   How do you write business letters?

When you write a business letter, remember that it may become part of a permanent file. Make the letter as complete and accurate as possible so that the recipient(s) can act on it.

checklist 11.4 — Business Letters

- Choose a *block, modified block*, or *indented* letter format.
- Single-space paragraphs and addresses in the letter; double-space between the return address, date, inside address, salutations, body paragraphs, and closing.
- Use one-inch margins on all sides.
- When using letterhead paper, you don't need to repeat the return address as long as it includes all necessary contact information.
- Make the inside address as specific as possible so that the letter will go directly to its intended audience.

continued on page 102

BUSINESS LETTER IN BLOCK FORMAT

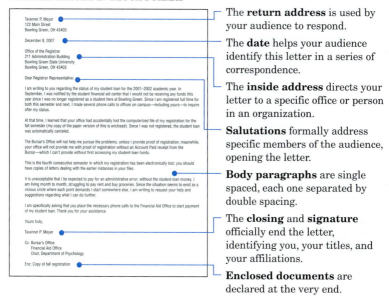

The **return address** is used by your audience to respond.

The **date** helps your audience identify this letter in a series of correspondence.

The **inside address** directs your letter to a specific office or person in an organization.

Salutations formally address specific members of the audience, opening the letter.

Body paragraphs are single spaced, each one separated by double spacing.

The **closing** and **signature** officially end the letter, identifying you, your titles, and your affiliations.

Enclosed documents are declared at the very end.

BUSINESS LETTER IN MODIFIED BLOCK FORMAT

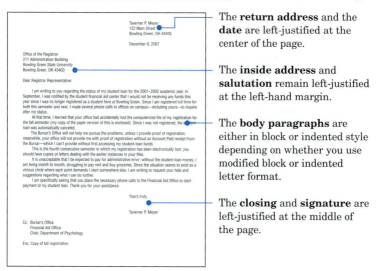

The **return address** and the **date** are left-justified at the center of the page.

The **inside address** and **salutation** remain left-justified at the left-hand margin.

The **body paragraphs** are either in block or indented style depending on whether you use modified block or indented letter format.

The **closing** and **signature** are left-justified at the middle of the page.

continued from page 100

- Place a colon after the salutation.
- In the body, be brief but state all pertinent facts, including names and dates. Keep your letter to one page if you can.
- Make your diction and style fairly formal, unless you already have established a casual tone with the addressee.
- Follow your closing with a comma, four blank lines, your name, and your professional title; sign in the space created by the blank lines.
- After the closing and signature, note any copies of the letter you have sent and any attached documents you have enclosed with the letter.
- Proofread your letter carefully and keep a copy for your records.

11c   How do you write letters of application?

A letter of application is an especially important form of business communication. The same advice and guidelines apply to it as to a business letter. In a letter of application, however, you have the extra challenge of presenting yourself favorably without seeming to brag. Use the application letter to draw attention to the reasons an employer should consider you for a job or an interview.

checklist 11.5

Letter of Application

- Follow the basic formatting guidelines for a business letter (see Checklist 11.4) or email (see Checklist 11.3), depending on the medium you use to correspond.
- State the position for which you are applying. Follow up with a summary of your qualifications for the position. Focus on those qualifications that best suit the job in question; the résumé will cover the rest.
- Focus on how you might meet the organization's needs and on what you could accomplish *for the organization*—not on what you hope to get from the position.
- Show some knowledge about the organization or company to which you are applying, but offer praise only in order to show why you're interested in working for that employer.
- Maintain a polite and respectful—but confident—tone.
- Remember that your letter of application may have a long life. If you're hired, it will become part of your personnel record. If you're not hired, it may go into a file of applicants for later consideration.

LETTER OF APPLICATION IN BLOCK FORMAT

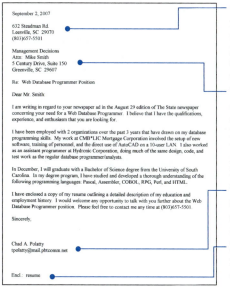

The **return address** should include a telephone number so the recruiter can contact you immediately if more information is needed or an interview is requested.

The **inside address** and **salutation** will match the contact name given in the job listing. When not responding to a listing, locate a contact name at the company's hiring office.

The **closing** and **signature** in a letter of application do not differ from those in standard business letters.

Enclosures will often include a printed résumé and a list of references.

LETTER OF APPLICATION IN EMAIL FORMAT

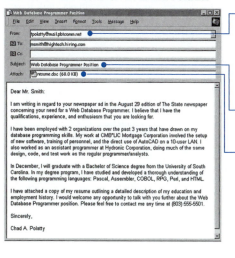

Email addresses replace postal addresses in the heading of the message. Postal addresses and telephone numbers can appear in the body of the letter if needed.

The **subject line** should announce the position for which you are applying.

File attachments are used instead of enclosures. Make sure to use common or requested electronic formats.

11d How do you write résumés?

Your résumé is a concise outline of your academic and employment history, designed to give a prospective employer a quick but thorough overview of your qualifications. Take great care in preparing your résumé. Once in the hands of a recruiter, your list of achievements and skills will be used to decide whether an employer will contact you for an interview.

checklist 11.6 ┐ Résumés

- At the top of your résumé give your name as you would like to be recognized in a professional setting.
- Provide up-to-date contact information so that a prospective employer can reach you for interviews.
- Before you list your skills, state your objective. This section may be omitted when your employment goals are explained in an accompanying cover letter. Some résumé guides now consider the objective line optional.
- Create a categorized list of your academic degrees and awards, professional certifications, previous jobs, technical skills, and relevant course work.
- Arrange this list according to how effective the categories and qualifications you have listed will be for attaining the desired job.
- Educational achievements usually go first. List year, degree, and institution, as well as scholastic honors won.
- If the prospective job requires specialized skills (computer skills, technical procedures), list those with which you have the most familiarity.
- List your work experience. Besides mentioning employers and time periods, state your responsibilities and achievements in succinct but specific terms. Account for all periods longer than a few months.
- List course work only when it explains how you attained skills outside your work experience. List nonwork, nonacademic activities and achievements only if you think an employer might consider them relevant assets.
- You cannot be required to mention age, gender, race, religious or sexual preference, political affiliation, or marital status.
- When requested, include a list of references (all of whom you have checked with beforehand) or indicate a placement service with your complete dossier. This list can usually be submitted as a separate, attached document.

PRINT RÉSUMÉ EMPHASIZING EDUCATION AND EXPERIENCE

The **header** includes your name and contact information. Most students include a **local address** where they can be contacted at school, as well as a **permanent address**.

The **body** includes a list of your qualifications divided into categories. Use different type styles to highlight information that employers might find most interesting, such as the names of companies you've worked for or your school.

The **footer** will often include the phrase "References available on request."

RÉSUMÉ FORMATTED AS TEXT-ONLY EMAIL MESSAGE

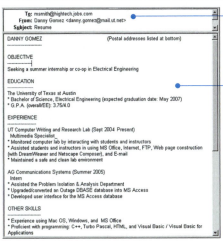

The **email header** will include the recipient's address, your return address, and a subject line indicating that the message is a résumé.

The **body** of a text-only email does not accept most types of visual formatting. Use asterisks, dashed lines, all caps, and underscores to replace the special type styles and graphics used in print or Web résumés.

ONLINE RÉSUMÉ

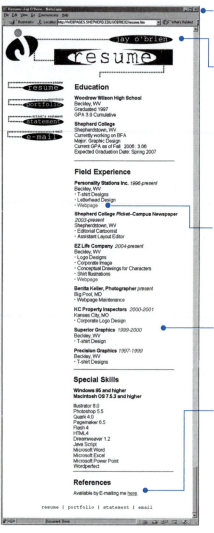

The **page title** includes your name and the word *résumé*, so that the page can be found by Web search engines.

Jay O'Brien omits conventional **contact information** such as his postal address and current phone numbers on his Web résumé. He expects employers to reach him via an email link. However, it might be wise to offer a postal address, phone number, and full email address so employers who print out your résumé will still be able to reach you.

Links to other Web pages can help you better demonstrate your goals and qualifications. Jay O'Brien provides a link to an online portfolio of his work—something a print résumé doesn't accommodate.

The **body** can go beyond a single page—but make sure headings are easy to read, so someone browsing your résumé can quickly identify the highlights of your qualifications.

Your **list of references** should never be posted on the Web. Instead, ask interested employers to request references by email.

11e How do you write professional memos?

Memorandums are used within organizations as a means of communication between members. As a result, memos omit some of the formalities used in business letters to be sent outside the organization: formal salutations and closings, for example, aren't usually required. But memos do maintain a professional tone, and they contain information needed for keeping records of business interactions.

checklist 11.7 — **Memos and Professional Email**

- Follow your organization's standard layout, which will usually include a date, a "To" section, a "From" section, and a subject line.
- Use block paragraphing and a one-inch margin (for print memos).
- In the subject line, enter a phrase that will make clear to your recipients the relevance and importance of your message.
- Most printed memos don't have salutations, because the intended audience is named in the "To" section. An email message sent to more than one person, however, might require a group salutation.

PRINTED MEMO

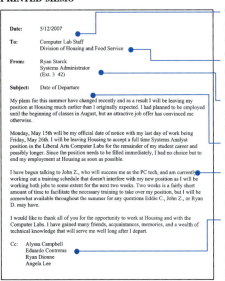

The **date** may be used to refer to the memo in future correspondence.

The **To** section names an individual or group in the organization.

The **From** section should list your name, title, department, and contact information.

The **Subject** line is brief and to the point.

The **body paragraphs** state your business clearly and succinctly.

The **Cc** section lists names of individuals who should receive copies of the memo. This list often includes coworkers who are indirectly involved in the business being discussed.

EMAIL MEMO

Email addresses replace names and departments in the **To** and **Cc** lines.

A **salutation** is often used in email; when you email a group of people, you may need to state the name of the group, so people will know why they have been copied on the message.

An **email signature** closes the message, providing your name and title (what's in the **From** lines of print memos).

11f How do you write messages to online forums?

Besides email, other forms of online communication have recently evolved. Online forums generally consist of dated postings (messages submitted by discussion participants) and threads (lines of discussion focused on a particular topic). Web forums and newsgroups are two formats of online discussion that display threads and postings hierarchically, according to topic. The sample Web forum on the facing page shows a series of threads about an article read for a University of Texas composition class. Email lists, or listservs, are another common type of online forum. Readers and writers participate by subscribing to a listserv, which allows them to receive new postings in their email inbox, and by sending messages to the list's email address. Whichever format you use, keep in mind the common conventions for participating in online discussions—conventions often referred to as "netiquette."

checklist 11.8

Messages to Online Forums

- Read a number of messages in the forum before you send your own. Try to get a feel for the tone and interests of other participants.
- Avoid posting personal attacks, or *flames,* to authors of messages disagreeing with you. Flame wars make forum participants uneasy, and productive discussion nearly impossible.

- Avoid starting off-topic threads—sometimes called *spamming*. Forums differ in how they treat online spam and what members believe constitutes a useless message, but expect some people to become annoyed if you regularly send messages irrelevant to them.

- Don't respond to the entire forum when you really want to respond to just one participant. Avoid this problem by making sure your "To" address doesn't match the address of the forum itself.

- When replying to a thread, remove all text from the previous message that doesn't relate to your response. Don't expect readers to scroll through screens of other people's writing to find your 10-line response.

WEB MESSAGE FORUM

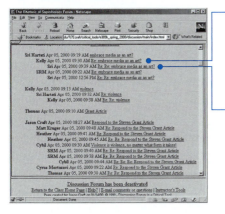

Threads appear as an initial message (starting at the left-hand margin) followed by a series of responses. Each response is attached to the message it most immediately addresses.

Responses are listed as linked text indicated by "Re:" and followed by the subject line of the initial message in the thread. Click on the link to read the message. Some forums allow respondents to create their own subject lines.

WEB FORUM RESPONSE FORM

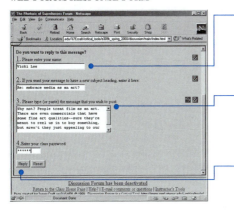

Enter the **name** you would like to appear with your posting. Some forums allow anonymous postings; others, such as class forums, require your real name.

Enter your **message** in plain text format. Some forums allow you to use HTML codes to enhance the appearance of the message.

Click the " **Reply** " button (or "Submit") to add your message to the thread. This forum happens to require a password to participate.

11g How do you write newsletters?

A newsletter gives an organization an excellent way to keep in touch with its members. With desktop publishing, newsletters are easy to create.

checklist 11.9 — **Newsletters**

- Select the size of paper and the method of binding, and plan the number of pages you will use. Choose a margin width that allows for binding or folding.
- Determine whether you'll use images and how many colors you want to show. Colorful designs are more costly.
- Decide whether you'll use multicolumn pages. More columns usually mean more planning, but when formatted carefully, multiple columns make more efficient use of space.
- Map out each page with two goals in mind: (1) showcasing the most important articles and (2) preventing your reader from having to jump from page to page to read a single article.
- For your masthead, use a distinctive font that reflects the spirit of the organization represented by the newsletter.
- Adjust headlines according to their importance, but maintain a consistent font size and style throughout the body of the articles.
- Write short paragraphs to avoid long, unbroken stretches of print, especially when you're using narrow columns.

FRONT PAGE OF A NEWSLETTER

The **masthead** identifies a newsletter with a specific organization, often showing logos or catchphrases members recognize immediately. Mastheads also include publication date and issue number.

Lead articles appear on the front pages of newsletters—they reflect the most important recent events appearing in the issue.

Images are "wrapped" by text so that the space on each page is used efficiently, and related material is closely grouped.

Borders are sometimes used to frame text or decorate the margins.

PAGE 3 OF A NEWSLETTER

Running heads often include the same information appearing in the masthead, sometimes with page numbering.

Standard articles are introduced with enhanced headlines. This example uses a left-justified block style of paragraphing.

Regular features are columns that appear in each issue; they are often framed or otherwise distinguished from standard articles so they can be easily recognized.

Footers can include page numbering and information appearing in the masthead.

11h How do you write brochures?

Brochures can provide information about an organization and its activities easily and, depending upon the elaborateness of your design, inexpensively. Brochures generally answer a few basic questions—who? what? why? when? where?—and they share the common goal of stimulating interest. Ideally, a brochure you create will provide enough information to capture your audience's attention and show readers where to find further details.

checklist 11.10 — Brochures

- Decide on the purpose of the brochure. Is it to introduce your organization? to talk about events or activities? Think about how you want your audience to respond to the brochure, and choose content accordingly.
- Plan the layout of the brochure carefully, keeping in mind how it will fold and how both sides will look. If the brochure is to be mailed, leave one panel blank for the address.
- Sketch out, or storyboard, each panel to visualize how you'll lay out information in the brochure.
- If possible, make each panel of the brochure a self-contained unit so that each section will still make sense when read in its folded state.
- Limit the amount of information to what readers can absorb in a few minutes, but tell them how they can learn more.

FRONT PANEL OF A BROCHURE

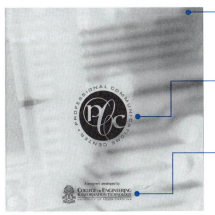

Use **graphics** and **colors** to attract the eyes of readers. Keep in mind that most brochures must compete for attention.

The **logo** for the organization should appear on the front panel. This logo begins building a persona that the following panels will develop.

Show **addresses** and **contact** information so that readers get a clear idea of the organization's affiliations and institutional relationships.

INSIDE PANELS OF A BROCHURE

Each **panel** includes a main heading with related passages of text. Panels have consistent layouts so readers can easily see the central points.

Headings are set apart from other text using inverted background and foreground colors. Provocative, eye-catching phrases draw readers in.

Contact information and the organizational **logo** reappear on the end panel, reminding readers that further details are available if they are interested.

Images have been carefully selected to portray themes and activities related to the organization. Here the images form a collage extending across all panels.

Paragraphs focus on the highlights of the organization, especially those that will seem most intriguing to the target audience.

part

4

Style

What Makes Paragraphs Work?

12

When writers organize material into paragraph form, treating a single idea in each paragraph and connecting the paragraphs to each other, readers can follow the material more easily. Paragraphing also makes a text look visually inviting, drawing readers in and encouraging them to read on.

12a How do you construct unified paragraphs?

A *unified* paragraph makes a single point and develops it, without detours into irrelevant or tangential information. When you begin a paragraph, first ask yourself, "What point am I trying to make?" and then check your draft periodically to be sure you haven't strayed from your purpose.

1 Anchor your paragraph with a topic sentence. One way to keep a paragraph focused is to use a **topic sentence** that states your main idea clearly and directly. The topic sentence doesn't have to be the first one in the paragraph, although it often is.

> **Sleep has become another casualty of modern life.**
> According to sleep researchers, studies point to a "sleep deficit" among Americans, a majority of whom are currently getting between 60 and 90 minutes less a night than they should for optimum health and performance. The number of people showing up at sleep disorder clinics with serious problems has skyrocketed in the last decade. Shift work, long working hours, the growth of a global economy (with its attendant continent-hopping and twenty-four-hour business culture), and the accelerating pace of life have all contributed to sleep deprivation. If you need an alarm clock, the experts warn, you're probably sleeping too little.
> —JULIET SCHOR, "The Overworked American"

A writer can also lead up to a topic sentence (or topic sentences), first giving readers details that build their interest and then summarizing the content in one sentence.

> In 1938, near the end of a decade of monumental turmoil, the year's number-one newsmaker was not Franklin Delano

Roosevelt, Hitler, or Mussolini. It wasn't Pope Pius XI, nor was it Lou Gehrig, Howard Hughes, or Clark Gable. **The subject of the most newspaper column inches in 1938 wasn't even a person. It was an undersized, crooked-legged racehorse named Seabiscuit.**

—LAURA HILLENBRAND, *Seabiscuit: An American Legend*

Not all paragraphs have topic sentences, nor do they need them, since writers can unify paragraphs in a number of ways. But they work especially well to anchor and control the flow of ideas in academic writing. By reading from one topic sentence to the next in the paragraphs that make up your paper, you can usually tell if you're developing your thesis as you have planned. For more on organizing a draft around a thesis, see Section 3c.

2 Use internal transitions to unify your paragraphs. Even when you have a clear focus, the connections among sentences or ideas in a paragraph may not always be immediately apparent to readers. In such cases, you'll need to incorporate *internal transitions*—words and phrases that act like traffic signals to move readers from one point in an argument or explanation to another.

Consider this paragraph from a student draft. It is focused on a single issue—the rise of cheating on campus—but the first version seems choppy because it lacks internal transitions.

WEAK TRANSITIONS

Cheating has become frighteningly common. My roommate brought her mother to campus to complain when she failed Spanish for copying her term paper from a Web site. My English professor reported two students in my English literature class to the dean for allowing a high school teacher to write a paper for them. The Academic Affairs office reported that academic misconduct is up by 20 percent over last year. What is happening on our campus? Parents and teachers once instilled in students the value of doing one's own work instead of cheating.

INTERNAL TRANSITIONS ADDED

Cheating is becoming frighteningly common **on our campus. Last week** my roommate brought her mother to campus to complain when she failed Spanish for copying her term paper from a Web site. **Earlier this semester**, my English literature professor reported two students to the dean for allowing a high school teacher to write a paper for them. **These cases are not unusual, campus officials say.** The Academic Affairs office reported **last week** that academic dishonesty cases are up by 30 percent over last year. What is happening on our campus? Parents and teachers **used to** instill in students the value of work; **now** many are encouraging them to **cheat.**

To incorporate internal transitions into a paragraph you've written, try these strategies:

- **Use transition words** such as *first, next, however*, and *in addition* to show the relationships among sentences and ideas. See Section 14b-1 for a list of such words.

- **Repeat key words or phrases** to tie related sentences together. The paragraph above, for example, repeats terms like *dishonesty* and *cheating* to connect the examples of cheating on campus. See Section 14b-2 for more on using repetition.

- **Use parallel phrases**—phrases that begin with the same word or that share the same grammatical structure—to emphasize connections among similar examples or related pieces of information. For more on using parallel structure to unify a paragraph, see Section 14b-5.

See Chapter 14 for a detailed discussion of transitions.

EXERCISE 12.1 Examine critically one or two paragraphs of a draft you're currently working on: Do the paragraphs seem adequately unified? What unifying strategies have you used? Can you think of others that might be useful?

12b How can you organize paragraphs?

Why do specific organizational patterns recur in writing? Perhaps these patterns emerge because they resemble typical ways of thinking. Whatever their origins, the paragraph patterns discussed in this section are common, and writers looking for a way to begin a draft can profit by trying them.

1 Illustration. A paragraph of illustration begins with a general statement or claim and develops it with supporting details, evidence, or examples. In an argument paper, writers often follow a general claim with one or more pieces of supporting evidence.

> For more than 40 states, the days of traditional multiple-choice tests that required teachers to set aside real learning and teach test-taking skills are fading. Today's tests often include open-ended questions, demand writing samples, and require students to show, honestly and accurately, what they know. The new tests ask students to solve complex mathematics problems and explain solutions, to critically examine literary techniques and articulate their thinking in written essays. That's a far cry from drills in

information regurgitation. On the recent New York state test for 11th-graders, 92 percent passed the new, tougher test in English language arts. This kind of testing leads to better teaching. It also tells elected officials and educators where they ought to direct resources and efforts.

—Louis V. Gerstner, Jr., "High Marks for Standardized Tests"

2 Question and answer. Asking and answering a question is another way to organize a paragraph.

How good are graphic novels, really? Are these truly what our great-grandchildren will be reading, instead of books without pictures? Hard to say. Some of them are much better than others, obviously, but this is true of books of any kind. And the form is better suited to certain themes and kinds of expression than others. One thing the graphic novel can do particularly well, for example, is depict the passage of time, slow or fast or both at once—something the traditional novel can approximate only with empty space. The graphic novel can make the familiar look new. The autobiographical hero of Craig Thompson's *Blankets*, a guilt-ridden teenager falling in love for the first time, would be insufferably predictable in a prose narrative; here, he has an innocent sweetness.

—Charles McGrath, "Not Funnies"

3 Narration or process. One way to develop a paragraph is to relate events or the steps of a process in chronological order. This pattern is obviously appropriate for writing personal or historical accounts, but you can also use it effectively to describe a scientific or technical process.

The clanking from within the giant white magnetic resonance imaging (MRI) scanner sounds like somebody banging a wrench on a radiator. "Tommy," a healthy 8-year-old, is halfway inside the machine's round chamber, and his little white-sweat-socked feet keep time with the noise. A mirror on a plastic cage around his head will allow him to see images and video. During the next 45 minutes, Dr. Golijeh Golarai, a researcher at Stanford University, will ask Tommy to hold his feet still as she directs a computer to flash pictures at him, including faces of African American men, landscapes, faces of white men, then scrambled faces in a cubist redux. When the boy thinks he sees the same image twice, he pushes a button. The machine is tracking the blood in his brain as it flows to the neurons he is using to perform the assigned task.

—Joan O'C. Hamilton, "Journey to the Center of the Mind"

4 Definition. Paragraphs of definition often work well in the first part of a report or article that explains or argues. They help to establish the meaning of important terms the author is going to use.

> From kids and people my own age I picked up *Pachuco*. **Pachuco (the language of the zoot suiters) is a language of rebellion, both against Standard Spanish and Standard English.** It is a secret language. Adults of the culture and outsiders cannot understand it. It is made up of slang words from both English and Spanish. *Ruca* means girl or woman, *vato* means guy or dude, *chale* means no, *simon* means yes, *churro* is sure, talk is *periquar,* *pignionear* means petting, *que gacho* means how nerdy, *ponte aguila* means watch out, death is called *la pelona*. Through lack of practice and not having others who can speak it, I've lost most of the *Pachuco* tongue.
>
> —**Gloria Anzaldúa**, "How to Tame a Wild Tongue"

5 Classification. A classification paragraph that divides a subject into the categories to be discussed can work well as the opening paragraph of a paper or a section of a paper. Used this way, it helps to unify the essay by forecasting its organization.

> **In fact, over the past two decades, there have been essentially two forces contributing new words to the language: rap music and business consultants.** One gave us "dis," "props," and "for shizzle"; the other gave us "proactive," "synergy" and "agent of change."
>
> —**Adam Sternbergh**, "Got Bub All Up in the Hizzle, Yo!"

6 Comparison and contrast. A paragraph can also be built on a comparison-and-contrast pattern. The following example, taken from a report on homeless youth in New York City, sets up a contrast in the first sentence.

> **While urban nomads and the city's traditional homeless youth often share a history of physical or sexual abuse, the two groups differ in many respects.** Typically, New York's population of runaways and homeless youths is heavily minority and includes both girls and boys. By contrast, urban nomads tend to be white and largely male, with backgrounds that are typically working-class and occasionally middle-class. Many are children from homes where a parent's remarriage has produced family conflicts. Others are simply bored.
>
> —**Alison Stateman**, "Postcards from the Edge"

7 Cause and effect. Cause-and-effect paragraphs can proceed in two ways: they can mention the effect first and then describe the causes, or they can start by giving causes and close with the effect. We illustrate both patterns here.

CAUSE TO EFFECT

Once overhunted, white-tailed deer have returned in such explosive numbers that they're ravaging forestland and besieging rural and even suburban communities. The animals cause car accidents, carry ticks that can transmit infectious diseases to people, chew up landscaping, and otherwise make pests of themselves, albeit sometimes strikingly graceful ones.

—ANNE BROACHE, "Oh Deer!"

EFFECT TO CAUSE

Why do so many citizens of the world's oldest democracy not vote when they can, at a time when the struggle for democracy in Europe and throughout the rest of the world has reached its most crucial and inspiring level since 1848? Partly, it's an administrative problem—the disappearance of the old party-machine and ward system, whose last vestige was Mayor Daley. Whatever its abuses, it got people street by street, household by household, to the ballot boxes. Its patronage system did help tie American people, especially blue-collar and lower middle-class ones, to the belief that they as citizens had some role to play in the running of their country from the bottom up, ward by ward. It reinforced the sense of participatory democracy.

—ROBERT HUGHES, *The Culture of Complaint*

8 Analogy. An **analogy** is an extended comparison. One especially good use of analogy is to help readers understand a concept by showing a resemblance between a familiar idea and an unfamiliar one.

Short-order cooking is like driving a car: anyone can do it up to a certain speed. The difference between an amateur and a crack professional isn't so much a matter of specific skills as of consistency and timing. Most diner kitchens are fairly forgiving places. You can break a yolk or two, lose track of an order, or overcook an omelette and start again without getting swamped. But as the pace increases those tolerances disappear. At the Tropical Breeze, a single mistake can throw an entire sequence out of kilter, so that every dish is either cold or overdone. A cook of robotic efficiency, moving steadily from task to task, suddenly slips a cog and becomes Lucy in the chocolate factory, stuffing candies into her mouth as they pile up on the assembly line.

—BURKHARD BILGER, "The Egg Men"

EXERCISE 12.2 Use the paragraph patterns discussed and illustrated in Section 12b to write paragraphs for two of the following situations.

1. Summarize the arguments on one side of a local controversy you feel strongly about—for example, a new city ordinance, an upcoming election, or a controversial public event or program.

2. Explain how to operate a machine you use regularly—for instance, a laptop, a jet ski, a cell phone, or a coffeemaker.

3. Set up a classification of your relatives at a family get-together, the students in your major, the music in your personal collection, or the passengers you encounter every day on a bus or subway.

12c   How can you create polished paragraphs?

A paragraph that's merely focused and well organized is like a family sedan: it gets your readers where they need to go, but the ride may lack pizazz. If you want readers to respond strongly to your writing, then craft paragraphs that are stylish and engaging as well as clear.

1 Revise for variety. Good paragraphs offer readers a mix of general statements and vivid details. This sort of variety keeps readers interested. Variety also helps to communicate your ideas: details help to illustrate abstract concepts that readers might otherwise find difficult, and general statements tie together details that might initially seem unrelated. Here is a writer clarifying a hard-to-grasp, abstract concept using an analogy that helps us to picture it very specifically.

> The distinction between Newton and Einstein's ideas about gravitation has sometimes been illustrated by picturing **a little boy playing marbles in a city lot. The ground is very uneven, ridged with bumps and hollows. An observer in an office ten stories above the street would not be able to see these irregularities in the ground. Noticing that the marbles appear to avoid some sections of the ground and move toward other sections**, he might assume a "force" is operating which repels the marbles from certain spots and attracts them toward others. But **another observer on the ground would instantly perceive that the path of the marbles is simply governed by the curvature of the field.**
> —LINCOLN BARNETT, *The Universe and Dr. Einstein*

2 Revise for economy. Well-crafted paragraphs move readers smoothly from point to point without bogging down in unnecessary verbiage or repetition. When you revise a paragraph, you'll often have to gut whole phrases or sentences when they contribute little to your meaning. (See Section 16c for more advice on streamlining sentences.)

INFLATED FIRST DRAFT

Bicycles are a major form of transportation in many Third World countries because they are inexpensive and easy to maintain. Nowhere are they more important than they are in China, where one can see masses of them on the streets in every city. ~~Probably no one knows how many bicycles there are in China, nor does there seem to be any way of finding out~~. Virtually everyone seems to ride them—well-dressed businessmen with their briefcases strapped to the frame; a husband with his wife riding behind him and their child on the handlebars; women of all ages, some even in long dresses; and college students carrying their schoolbooks on their backs. The newly arrived American cyclist ~~in Beijing or Shanghai~~, however, would be astonished ~~not only~~ to see ~~the great numbers of bicycles, but to see what kinds of bicycles the Chinese ride and~~ how many other uses, besides simply riding, the Chinese have been able to figure out for bicycles.

REVISED FOR ECONOMY

Although bicycles are a major form of transportation in all Asian countries, nowhere are they more important than in China, where one can see masses of them on the streets in every city. Virtually everyone seems to ride—well-dressed businessmen with their briefcases strapped to the frame; a husband with his wife behind him and their child on the handlebars; women of all ages, some even in long, narrow dresses; and college students carrying their books on their backs. The newly arrived American cyclist, however, would be astonished to see how many other uses, besides simply riding, the Chinese have for their bicycles.

EXERCISE 12.3 Streamline and strengthen this paragraph from a student's first draft by trimming in places that seem wordy. You may need to cut or revise words, phrases, or whole sentences. Compare and contrast your revised version with a classmate's version.

    There are many different scholarly views concerning
    Alexander the Great's ultimate goal in relation to his
    military pursuits. Some historians consider Alexander to
    have been a power-hungry tyrant without whom the world
    would have been better off. Others see Alexander as the
    great unifier of humankind, one who attempted to bring
    together many cultures in one coherent empire. Others view

him as the ultimate pragmatist—not necessarily having any preplanned goals and aspirations of conquering the world, but merely a king who made the very best of his existing circumstances. Some believe that Alexander's accomplishments were not great at all, but that most of what was written concerning Alexander is basically just a mixture of legend and myth. Others feel his achievements stand as monuments in human history to the enormous capability of the human spirit and will.

12d How can you improve paragraph appearance?

Writers need to think about how their work is going to look in print. If readers see a long stretch of text unbroken by paragraphs, white space, headings, or images, most assume that the material will be hard to read. Your readers are much more likely to take a friendly attitude toward a piece when they can see that your paragraphs are fairly short. How short is a "fairly short" paragraph? Probably no more than seven or eight sentences—and in many cases, even fewer.

1 Break up long paragraphs that look hard to read. You shouldn't chop up paragraphs arbitrarily just to make your paper look inviting; a paragraph is supposed to develop an idea, and it usually takes several sentences to do that. After you write a paragraph, reread it. Checklist 12.1 can help you spot places to divide it.

checklist 12.1  **Places to Break Up a Long Paragraph**

- **SHIFTS IN TIME.** Look for spots where you have written words such as *at that time, then,* or *afterward,* or have given other time signals.
- **SHIFTS IN PLACE.** Look for spots where you have written *another place* or *on the other side,* or have used words that point to places.
- **SHIFTS IN DIRECTION.** Look for spots where you have written *on the other hand, nevertheless,* or *however,* or have otherwise indicated contrast.
- **SHIFTS IN EMPHASIS OR FOCUS.** Look for spots where you have shifted to a new point, perhaps using words such as *another, in addition,* or *not only.*

But don't break an entire paper into one- or two-sentence paragraphs. It's true that long paragraphs intimidate readers; however, too many short ones can distract them or make them feel the material is trivial. Extremely short paragraphs are best saved for special effects.

2 Use short paragraphs for effect. Don't be afraid to use one- or two-sentence paragraphs occasionally, but do so deliberately and to achieve a specific effect. Sometimes you may want to insert a very short paragraph to make a transition between two longer paragraphs. At other times you can use brevity for dramatic emphasis, as Angier does in the following passage.

> Ah, romance. Can any sight be as sweet as a pair of mallard ducks gliding gracefully across a pond, male by female, seemingly inseparable? Or, better yet, two trumpeter swans, the legendary symbols of eternal love, each ivory neck one half of a single heart, souls of a feather staying coupled together for life?
>
> **Coupled for life—with just a bit of adultery, cuckoldry, and gang rape on the side.**
>
> Alas for sentiment and the greeting card industry, it turns out that, in the animal kingdom, there is almost no such thing as monogamy. As a wealth of recent findings makes clear as a crocodile tear, even creatures long assumed to have faithful tendencies and to need a strong pair bond to rear their young are in fact perfidious brutes.
>
> —**NATALIE ANGIER**, "Mating for Life?"

3 Adapt paragraph length to your writing situation. Finally, then, how long should a paragraph be? The answer, as you might expect, depends on your writing situation—your purpose, your audience, and your medium.

Consider long paragraphs when

- you are developing complex ideas in detail.
- your audience is experienced and skillful.
- you are writing in a genre, such as the academic essay, in which longer paragraphs are the norm.
- readers are patient and seeking information.

Consider short paragraphs when

- readers are impatient or are skimming for content.
- readers are inexperienced or unfamiliar with the topic.
- you are writing in a genre, such as a newspaper editorial, in which short paragraphs are the norm.
- readers are reading online.

EXERCISE 12.4 Analyze the writing situation for the scientific article excerpt and the "Mosquito-Pro" Web page pictured above. Who is the intended audience and what might their expectations be? What can you deduce about the writer's purpose?

EXERCISE 12.5 Review a paper draft you're currently working on, paying attention to paragraph lengths. Do you see places where paragraphs could be combined, divided, or reorganized to better fit the writing situation? If so, make the changes.

How Do You Craft Opening And Closing Paragraphs? 13

13a What makes an opening paragraph effective?

Like the lead of a front-page newspaper story, the first paragraph of any document you write must do several things:

- Get your readers' attention and interest them in reading more.
- Introduce your main idea.
- Signal to readers what direction your paper will take.
- Set the tone of your project.

Different kinds of writing call for different opening paragraphs. For certain kinds of writing—laboratory reports, grant proposals, business letters—readers expect specific kinds of opening paragraphs. In such

Almost everyone in the United States can recite the opening lines from *Star Wars* ("A long, time ago, in a galaxy far, far away . . . ") and Abraham Lincoln's "Gettysburg Address" ("Four score and seven years ago, our forefathers brought forth on this continent a new nation . . . "). Why do you think these introductions are so memorable? How does each catch attention, suggest content, and set a particular tone? Which of the strategies used in these opening lines, or in other memorable opening lines you can think of, might you try in writing a paper?

cases, find out what the typical pattern is and use it. In other kinds of writing, such as newspaper articles, critical analyses, personal experience papers, and opinion pieces, you have more freedom and can try various approaches.

1 Begin with a narrative. A narrative or anecdote catches readers' attention and sparks their interest in the topic, as the following opening paragraph from a magazine article illustrates.

> Like most Peace Corps volunteers, Martin Giannini embarked on his mission full of high hopes and enthusiasm. His assignment in Togo promised to be the adventure of a lifetime. It certainly was—but not the kind he expected. Giannini's African adventure ended in a padded room in a Chicago psych ward. "I was totally loony," admits Giannini. "It felt like I was in some 'X-Files' episode with instructions being planted in my brain. I tried to escape, but couldn't get past the four guards." What led Giannini, a healthy young man with no history of mental illness, to take on a battalion of guards in a psychiatric hospital? A drug, say his doctors. An antimalaria drug the Peace Corps recommended.
>
> —Dennis Lewon, "Malaria's Not-So-Magic Bullet"

2 Begin with a description. An opening description creates a vivid picture and sets a tone, as this example from an article on exotic Southern cuisine demonstrates.

> It's just past four on a Thursday afternoon in June at Jesse's Place, a country juke seventeen miles south of the Mississippi line and three miles west of Amite, Louisiana. The air conditioner hacks and spits forth torrents of arctic air, but the heat of summer can't be kept at bay. It seeps around the splintered doorjambs and settles in, transforming the squat particleboard-plastered roadhouse into a sauna. Slowly, the dank barroom fills with grease-smeared mechanics from the truck stop up the road and farmers straight from the fields, the soles of their brogans thick with dirt clods. A few weary souls make their way over from the nearby sawmill, the kind of place where more than one worker has muscled a log into the chipper and drawn back a nub. I sit alone at the bar, one empty bottle of Bud in front of me, a second bottle in my hand. I drain the beer, order a third, and stare down at the pink juice spreading outward from a crumpled foil pouch and onto the dull, black vinyl bar.
>
> —John T. Edge, "I'm Not Leaving Until I Eat This Thing"

3 Begin with a question or a series of questions. Opening questions provoke readers' curiosity.

> Should we be worried that young girls are not pursuing math-related careers at the same rate as young men? After all, in our technological era, many of tomorrow's well-paying jobs will require competence at mathematics. But today, women make up only 19 percent of the science, engineering, and technology workforce. In 1998, only 16 percent of computer science degrees were awarded to women, down from nearly 40 percent in 1984, and the downward trend continued in 2003.
>
> —ROSALIND CHAIT BARNETT AND CARYL RIVERS,
"The Persistence of Gender Myths in Math"

4 Start with your thesis. Sometimes you will do best to open your essay by simply telling your readers exactly what you are going to write about. Such openings work well for many papers you write in college courses, for reports you might have to write on the job, and for many other kinds of factual, informative prose. Here's a good example from a student essay that evaluates the effectiveness of spanking.

```
     It is unfortunate that the new spanking advocates get

so much attention in the popular press, since their

arguments are so poorly supported. These crusaders draw on

personal anecdotes and "experts" of dubious credibility to

glorify physical punishment and to blame non-spanking

parents for everything from school shootings to violent

rap lyrics. Yet even a cursory look at the scientific

research in this area confirms that kids who are spanked

are more—not less—likely to misbehave or suffer from

mental problems. How we choose to treat our nation's

children is a serious matter. We must make these decisions

based on the best information available—not on the dire

predictions of a few extremists.
```

See Section 3a for more on constructing a thesis statement and incorporating it into a writing project.

EXERCISE 13.1 Choose from the strategies discussed above and write two versions of an opening paragraph for one of the following essay titles. Then join with classmates who have chosen to write on the same title and read your paragraphs aloud. Discuss which ones seem to work well and why.

1. The American Medical Establishment as Seen Through *Scrubs, Grey's Anatomy*, and *House*

2. What It Means to Live on Minimum Wage: A Case Study

3. Why You Should Vote in the Next Election

4. Is Steroid Use a Major Problem in Professional Sports?

13b   What makes a closing paragraph effective?

Your closing paragraph should wind up your paper in a way that makes readers feel that you have tied up the loose ends—that you have fulfilled the commitment you made in the opening paragraph. You don't want your readers asking "And so?" when they finish, or looking on the back of the page for something they may have missed.

There are no simple prescriptions for achieving that important goal. However, we suggest five general strategies you can use, alone or in combination.

1 Summarize the main points you have made. Often you'll want to bring your paper to a close by reemphasizing your main points. (But don't repeat the very same words you have already used, or your ending may sound redundant or forced.) In this example, student writer Jeremy Christiansen reviews key points about school resegregation.

America continues to see a growing trend towards public-school resegregation, a problem that was not discovered until recent studies were conducted to test the successes of *Brown v. the Board of Education* after 50 years. The findings were startling, since they suggest that what was once known as the most important court decision of the 20th century may have been a failure. American ideals espouse diversity and equal opportunities for all. School resegregation not only discourages diversity but limits opportunities for minorities and whites alike. We will not have true equality in educational opportunities until we find a way to create

racially, ethnically, and economically integrated public
schools. Unfortunately, further attempts to desegregate,
though necessary, will likely spark even more controversy,
which may last 50 more years.

2 Make a recommendation when one is appropriate. This strategy
brings a paper to a positive ending. Here is a conclusion from a piece
that explores the cognitive benefits of watching television.

> Kids and grown-ups each can learn from their increasingly
> shared obsessions. Too often we imagine the blurring of kid and
> grown-up cultures as a series of violations: the 9-year-olds who
> have to have nipple brooches explained to them thanks to Janet
> Jackson; the middle-aged guy who can't wait to get home to his
> Xbox. But this demographic blur has a commendable side that we
> don't acknowledge enough. The kids are forced to think like
> grown-ups: analyzing complex social networks, managing
> resources, tracking subtle narrative intertwinings, recognizing
> long-term patterns. The grown-ups, in turn, get to learn from the
> kids: decoding each new technological wave, parsing the
> interfaces and discovering the intellectual rewards of play.
> **Parents should see this as an opportunity, not a crisis.**
> **Smart culture is no longer something you force your kids**
> **to ingest, like green vegetables. It's something you share.**
>   —STEVEN JOHNSON, "Watching TV Makes You Smarter"

3 Link the end to the beginning. One excellent way to end a writing
project is to tie your conclusion back to your beginning, framing and unifying your paper. Notice how skillfully Gary Engel uses this strategy in
an article analyzing the cultural significance of Superman.

> OPENING PARAGRAPH
>
> When I was young I spent a lot of time arguing with myself
> about who would win in a fight between John Wayne and
> Superman. On days when I wore my cowboy hat and cap guns, I
> knew the Duke would win because of his pronounced superiority
> in the all-important matter of swagger. There were days, though,
> when a frayed army blanket tied cape-fashion around my neck
> signaled a young man's need to believe there could be no end to
> the potency of his being. Then the Man of Steel was the odds-on
> favorite to knock the Duke for a cosmic loop. My greatest
> childhood problem was that the question could never be resolved
> because no such battle could ever take place. I mean, how would
> a fight start between the only two Americans who never started

anything, who always fought only to defend their rights and the American way?

CLOSING PARAGRAPH

In the last analysis, Superman is like nothing so much as an American boy's fantasy of a messiah. He is the male, heroic match for the Statue of Liberty, come like an immigrant from heaven to deliver humankind by sacrificing himself in the service of others. He protects the weak and defends truth and justice and all the other moral virtues inherent in the Judeo-Christian tradition, remaining ever vigilant and ever chaste. What purer or stronger vision could there possibly be for a child? Now that I put my mind to it, I see that John Wayne never had a chance.
>   —GARY ENGEL, "What Makes Superman So Darned American?"

4 Point to directions for future research or action, or identify unresolved questions. Concluding paragraphs that suggest these sorts of connections are especially common in academic research projects.

Reading the arguments about assisted suicide reminded me of a line from Bertolt Brecht's *The Three-Penny Opera*: "First feed the face, and then talk right and wrong." As a general rule, that statement itself is wrong, of course, but it can serve as a salutary warning. First, provide decent health care for the living; then, we can have a proper debate about the moral problems of death and dying.
>   —MICHAEL WALZER, "Feed the Face"

5 Stop when you're finished. Probably the most important thing to remember about closing a paper or essay is not to overdo your conclusion. If you have covered all your points and are reasonably satisfied with what you've said, quit. Don't bore your reader by tacking on a needless recapitulation or adding a paragraph of platitudes.

EXERCISE 13.2 Exchange drafts with two or three other students who are working on the same assignment. Each person should read the closing paragraphs of the other papers. Working in a group, identify the strategies each writer has used to bring his or her paper to a conclusion; discuss how well they work, and suggest alternative possibilities.

How Do You Manage Transitions?

14

Skilled writers work hard to help their readers move easily through a piece of writing. Readers won't stick around long if they have trouble following an argument or the thread of a narrative. The best unifying device for any piece of writing is *organizational*; that is, it comes from an underlying pattern that moves the reader along smoothly. You'll find examples of such patterns in Section 3c (for whole papers) and Section 12b (for paragraphs).

But even when your paper follows a clear pattern, you sometimes need to tighten your writing by using *transitions*, those words and phrases that act like hooks, links, and directional signals to keep readers moving from point to point within a paragraph, and from one paragraph to another.

14a How do you spot problems with transitions?

When you're revising, check for places where your readers might find your writing choppy or abrupt, and revise accordingly. Look for these trouble spots.

1 Check for paragraphs made up of short, simple sentences that seem disconnected. Effective paragraphs follow what writing experts call the "old-new contract"—they advance an argument or idea by linking each piece of new information to something that's gone before, so that the connections are immediately clear to readers. When a writer neglects to link old and new information, a paragraph may read more like a random series of observations than a coherent discussion.

WEAK TRANSITIONS

Some Americans live in affluent suburbs or university communities. It's easy to get the impression that the American population is healthy. Joggers and bicycle riders are everywhere. Many restaurants feature low-fat entrees. Many Americans are unhealthy. Thirty percent are seriously overweight. Alcoholism is a problem and many teenagers smoke. Obesity among children is increasing.

133

Here is a revised version, with some sentences combined and others connected (transitional words are boldfaced).

BETTER

If one lives in an affluent suburb or near a university, it's easy to get the impression that the American population is healthy. In **such** places, joggers **and** bicycle riders are everywhere, and restaurants feature low-fat entrees. The truth is, **however**, that many Americans are not healthy. Thirty percent are seriously overweight, alcoholism is a problem, **and** an increasing number of teenagers smoke. **Moreover**, obesity among children is increasing.

2 Check for sentences that begin with vague references like *it is, there are,* and *there is.* Often sentences that begin with these phrases (called *expletives*) are poorly connected to each other because it's hard to tell who or what the subject is. For example:

WEAK TRANSITIONS

It is a truism that good manners are like skeleton keys. There are few doors they will not open. Some people think that good manners are pretentious. They are a way of condescending to people. That is a misunderstanding. The real purpose of manners is to make social situations comfortable and to put the people you are with at ease. Manners are also practical to have. There are many companies that insist that their executives have good manners. Some business schools include a course on manners in their curricula.

Here is the paragraph reworked with better sentence openings and stronger connections. Transitional terms are boldfaced.

BETTER

Good manners, like skeleton keys, will open almost any door. **While** some people think that good manners are pretentious and condescending, that's a misunderstanding. **On the contrary**, manners exist to make social situations comfortable by putting everyone at ease. **Moreover**, manners are a practical asset in the job market. Many companies insist on well-mannered executives, **which** has prompted some business schools to include a course on manners in their curricula.

For suggestions on revising to eliminate expletive phrases, see Section 16c-6.

3 Check for gaps between paragraphs. Sometimes major gaps appear between paragraphs, and readers get temporarily lost. Suppose that you encountered the following two paragraphs in a personal essay. You'd probably have trouble figuring out how the second paragraph relates to the first.

> When I arrived here four years ago, I found that the skills I had learned in order to survive in Sudan were useless. I knew how to catch a rabbit, challenge a hyena or climb a coconut palm, but I had never turned on a light, used a telephone or driven a car.
>
> Within a month I understood how to work most modern conveniences and started my first job as a courtesy clerk and stocker at Ralph's grocery store in San Diego. Things like mangoes, chard and yams were familiar, but when customers asked about Cheerios or Ajax, it was as though my years of learning English in the refugee camp were worthless.

Here's the original passage as it appeared in Alephonsion Deng's essay, which appeared in *Newsweek* magazine. The linking sentence is boldfaced.

> When I arrived here four years ago, I found that the skills I had learned in order to survive in Sudan were useless. I knew how to catch a rabbit, challenge a hyena or climb a coconut palm, but I had never turned on a light, used a telephone or driven a car.
>
> **Luckily, the International Rescue Committee provided us with classes and mentors to teach us basics about computers, job interviews and Western social customs**. Within a month I understood how to work most modern conveniences and started my first job as a courtesy clerk and stocker at Ralph's grocery store in San Diego. Things like mangoes, chard and yams were familiar, but when customers asked about Cheerios or Ajax, it was as though my years of learning English in the refugee camp were worthless.
>
> —ALEPHONSION DENG, "I Have Had to Learn to Live with Peace"

Links between paragraphs can take several forms; Section 14b explains these in more detail.

14b How can you strengthen transitions?

If you want to use transitions successfully, remember the old-new contract: Each sentence or paragraph should contain a seed out of which the next sentence or paragraph can grow. Always include a hint, a reference, a hook, or a repetition that helps the reader link what you're saying with what has come before and what lies ahead.

1 Use common transition words to connect ideas. You can make your paragraphs tighter and more focused by using transition words to tie sentences together. Transition words are not neutral; each one gives readers a different signal about where your argument is going. When you're in doubt about which term to choose, check Chart 14.1 below.

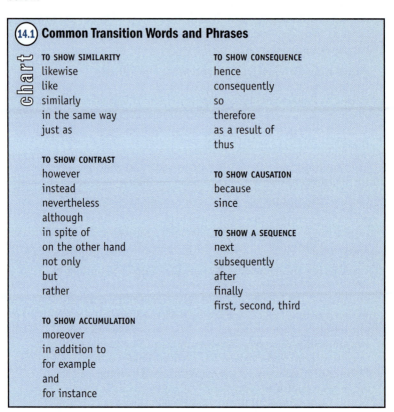

14.1 Common Transition Words and Phrases

TO SHOW SIMILARITY
likewise
like
similarly
in the same way
just as

TO SHOW CONTRAST
however
instead
nevertheless
although
in spite of
on the other hand
not only
but
rather

TO SHOW ACCUMULATION
moreover
in addition to
for example
and
for instance

TO SHOW CONSEQUENCE
hence
consequently
so
therefore
as a result of
thus

TO SHOW CAUSATION
because
since

TO SHOW A SEQUENCE
next
subsequently
after
finally
first, second, third

2 Repeat a key term throughout a paragraph to establish a central idea. Using one or two key words or phrases several times in a paragraph can tie it together effectively.

REPEATED WORDS BOLDFACED

The new black middle class came of age in the 1960s during an unprecedented American **economic boom** and in the hub of a thriving **mass culture**. The **economic boom** made luxury goods and convenient services available to large numbers of hard-working Americans for the first time. American **mass culture** presented models of the good life principally in terms of conspicuous consumption and hedonistic indulgence. It is important to note that even the intensely political struggles of the sixties presupposed a perennial **economic boom** and posited models of the good life projected by U.S. **mass culture**. Long-term financial self-denial and sexual asceticism was never at the center of a political agenda in the sixties.

—CORNEL WEST, *Race Matters*

3 Use the demonstrative pronouns *this, that, these, those,* and *such* to tie ideas together. Each boldfaced word in the following example hooks directly into the previous sentence.

DEMONSTRATIVE TERMS BOLDFACED

Making a movie is a collaborative endeavor, and scriptwriters point **this** out frequently. Occasionally a screenplay will survive the transfer from paper to film intact, but **that** is the exception rather than the rule. Typically, producers, directors, actors, and agents all have a say in the final product. Coping with **such** high-handed meddling is often difficult for young writers, and **those** who cannot compromise rarely stay in the business for long.

4 Use relative pronouns to show links between ideas. *Who, which, where*, and *that* are powerful words that link a descriptive or informative statement to something that has preceded it. Relative pronouns can be especially helpful when you need to combine several short, choppy sentences into one.

RELATIVE PRONOUNS BOLDFACED

Emma's first few weeks at the conservatory were exhausting but exhilarating. It was a place **that** challenged her, one **where** she could meet talented people **who** shared her passion for dance. The competition among the students was friendly but intense, **which** only increased her determination to practice and learn.

5 Use parallelism to link ideas. You can create tightly focused paragraphs by writing a series of sentences that incorporate parallel phrases.

PARALLEL PHRASES BOLDFACED

I spent my two days at Disneyland taking rides. **I took** a bobsled through the Matterhorn and a submarine under the Polar Ice Cap and a rocket jet to the Cosmic Vapor Curtain. **I took** Peter Pan's Flight, Mr. Toad's Wild Ride, Alice's Scary Adventures, and Pinocchio's Daring Journey. **I took** a steamboat and a jungle boat. **I took** the Big Thunder Mountain Railroad to coyote country and the Splash Mountain roller coaster to Critter Country. **I took** a

"Pirates of the Caribbean" ride (black cats and buried treasure) and a "Haunted Mansion" ride (creaking hinges and ghostly laughter). **I took** monorails and Skyways and Autopias and People Movers. More precisely, those rides **took** me: up and down and around sudden corners and over rooftops, and all I had to do was sit back and let whatever conveyance I was sitting in do the driving.

—WILLIAM ZINSSER, *American Places*

6 Consider using headings or other visual markers as transitions. In some kinds of documents, writers may use visual signals as well as—or sometimes instead of—words to help readers follow an argument.

Business and technical writers commonly use headings and subheadings to separate sections of a document so that readers can see where one idea ends and another begins. Résumés often use headings such as "Education," "Experience," "Awards," and "References" so that readers can locate relevant information. Brochures, flyers, and instructional manuals employ graphics, images, and color to mark divisions or to tie together related material. On the Web, writers create hyperlinks to connect documents.

When you incorporate visual transitions into a writing project, ask whether the particular strategy is appropriate for the situation. If you're not sure, look at models to see the kinds of transitions other writers have used in similar situations.

What is an orphan film?

Narrowly defined, it's a motion picture abandoned by its owner or caretaker. More generally, the term refers to all manner of films outside of the commercial mainstream: public domain materials, home movies, outtakes, unreleased films, industrial and educational movies, independent documentaries, ethnographic films, newsreels, censored material, underground works, experimental pieces, silent-era productions, stock footage, found footage, medical films, kinescopes, small- and unusual-gauge films, amateur productions, surveillance footage, test reels, government films, advertisements, sponsored films, student works, and sundry other ephemeral products of celluloid (or paper or glass or tape or . . .).

Examine this Web page designed by Laura Kissel and Dan Streible for an annual film festival at the University of South Carolina. How do the designers use fonts, headings, lists, hyperlinks, or other visual elements to help readers navigate the information on this page? What elements link similar ideas? Which elements show relationships among ideas? How effectively do you think these visual elements work? What changes might you suggest?

Also be sure that a particular transition gives readers the right signal. For example, a heading indicates a new topic, but it doesn't necessarily show readers how one topic relates to another. You'll often need to supplement visual devices with traditional linking words and phrases.

For more information about integrating visual elements into a text, see Chapter 10. For examples of documents that incorporate visual elements, see the model documents in Chapter 11.

EXERCISE 14.1 Read the following two paragraphs and diagnose the transition problems you find between the paragraphs and within each one. Then revise the paragraphs to improve the transitions, drawing on at least two of the strategies described in this section.

> There is nowhere to park on campus. The parking situation is impossible for first-year students. My roommate missed her first college class because she could not find a parking spot. Some people say that freshmen should not be allowed to drive to campus. First-year students are required to live in the dorms. The dorm I live in is 15 minutes away from all my classes. I have to drive.
>
> There are only a few parking garages and many under-utilized grassy areas on campus. There is a large green space on either side of the engineering complex that is not being used. The courtyard in front of the library is always empty. The fountain attracts litter. Why can't the university use some grassy areas for parking garages? The university could use some money from parking tickets to pay for new parking. The shuttle bus system could be used to transport students from remote parking areas onto campus.

EXERCISE 14.2 Use one or more of the transitional devices discussed in this section to strengthen connections between new and old information in a writing project you're currently working on.

How Do You Construct Effective Sentences?

15

15a How are sentences structured?

Traditional terms used to describe the architecture of sentences—*clauses, phrases, subordination, coordination, parallelism*—can make writing sentences seem complicated. But even the most complex sentences are based on a few comprehensible structures and principles.

1 Understand sentence patterns.

A **sentence** can be described as a group of words that expresses an idea and that is punctuated as an independent unit. All sentences have a **subject** (the doer of an action) and a **predicate** (the action done). Beginning with this assumption, just five patterns can describe the framework of many sentences you write.

1. **Subject + verb (intransitive).** This is the simplest sentence pattern, the one with the fewest parts. Like all sentences, it includes a *subject*, the doer of an action; and a *verb*, the action performed. When the verb is *intransitive*, it doesn't need an object to complete its meaning.

Subject	Verb (intransitive)
The lawyer	fainted.
The floodwaters	receded.
All the children	smiled at once.

EXERCISE 15.1 Compose three sentences that follow the subject–intransitive verb pattern. Underline the intransitive verb in each sentence.

2. **Subject + verb (transitive) + direct object.** This sentence pattern adds a third element to the subject and verb: an *object*, which identifies to what or to whom an action has been done. Objects can be words, phrases, or clauses. The pattern requires a transitive verb that conveys its action to an object.

Subject	Verb (transitive)	Object
The lawyer	accepted	the case.
The heavy rains	destroyed	the road.
Some of the children	were reading	books.

Note that the subject-verb-object pattern illustrates the *active voice*, in which the subject performs the action described by the transitive verb. But when that action is performed by the object, you have a *passive construction* (see Section 18e).

The case was accepted by the lawyer.

The road was destroyed by heavy rains.

The books were being read by some of the children.

Only transitive verbs can be involved in passive constructions, because they require an object that can become a subject. Intransitive verbs don't take objects.

It is important that a transitive verb and its object fit together logically. In the following example, the verb *intimidate* cannot logically convey its action to the object *enthusiasm*. *Enthusiasm* might be *undermined, dampened*, or *eroded*, but we don't usually speak of it as *intimidated*.

FAULTY   The negative attitudes of the senior staff *intimidated* the **enthusiasm** of the volunteers.

REVISED   The negative attitudes of the senior staff *dampened* the **enthusiasm** of the volunteers.

EXERCISE 15.2 Revise any of the following sentences in which the bold-faced verb cannot logically convey its action to its object. First try to explain the problem with the original verb; then change the verb, not the object.

1. At her parents' request, Margery **interrogated** her sister Kyla's low grades at college.

2. Kyla **blasphemed** her instructor's methods of teaching history.

3. Her psychology instructor **jaded** her with long lectures about statistics and methods.

3. Subject + verb (linking) + subject complement. Linking verbs, which are often forms of *to be*, connect a subject to a subject complement, that is, to a word or phrase that extends or completes the meaning of a subject or renames it in some way. Among the common linking verbs are *to seem, to appear, to feel*, and *to become*.

Subject	Linking verb	Subject complement
The lawyer	became	a federal judge.
The storms	seemed	endless.
The children	are	happy.

A complement should be compatible with its subject. When it is not, the sentence is illogical, sometimes subtly so.

FAULTY   **Prejudice** is unacceptable **behavior** in this club.
COMPLEMENT

The problem is that *prejudice* is not behavior; it's an attitude. So the sentence has to be modified to reflect this difference.

REVISED   **Prejudiced behavior** is unacceptable in this club.

For the same reason, it's wrong to use *when* as a complement.

WRONG   **Plagiarism** is **when** a writer doesn't credit her source.

When is an adverb; *plagiarism* is a noun. *Plagiarism* has to be a concept or an idea, so it cannot be *when*.

RIGHT   **Plagiarism** is the **failure** to credit a source.

EXERCISE 15.3 In the following sentences, indicate whether the boldfaced words are objects or complements.

1. Halloween may be the oddest **holiday** of the year.

2. The roots of Halloween are deeply **religious**.

3. But Halloween celebrations today seem quite **secular**.

4. Children and adults wear **costumes** and pull **pranks**.

EXERCISE 15.4 Revise any of the following sentences in which the subject complement cannot work logically with its subject. First explain the problem with the original complement; then change the complement, not the subject. The complement is boldfaced.

1. Photography is an excellent **fun**.

2. Revising every paper in this class four times seems **exorbitant**.

3. Gerald felt **unconscionable** after arriving too late to say farewell.

4. Philosophy is **when** you read Plato and Aristotle.

4. Subject + verb (transitive) + indirect object + direct object.
An **indirect object** explains for whom or what an action is done

or directed. As you can see in this pattern, indirect objects ordinarily precede direct objects.

Subject	Verb (transitive)	Indirect object	Direct object
The lawyer	found	the clerk	a job.
The storms	brought	local farmers	needed rain.
The children	told	their parents	stories.

If you have trouble understanding what an indirect object does in a sentence, turn it into the object of a prepositional phrase.

The lawyer found a job **for the clerk**.

The storms brought needed rain **to local farmers**.

The children told stories **to their parents**.

EXERCISE 15.5 In the following sentences, circle the indirect objects and underline the objects.

1. The IRS agent asked the auditor three tough questions.

2. The placement office finds students jobs after college.

3. Did you send Rosa, Peg, Lester, and Davida the same email message?

4. Give Daisy more cookies.

5. Subject + verb (transitive) + direct object + object complement. Just as a subject complement modifies or explains a subject, an **object complement** does the same for the object of a sentence.

Subject	Verb (transitive)	Direct object	Object complement
The lawyer	called	the verdict	surprising.
The flood	caught	the town	napping.
The children	found	their spinach	vile.

EXERCISE 15.6 In the following sentences, underline the direct objects and circle the object complements.

1. Most men find football entertaining.

2. Thoroughbred horses often turn their wealthy owners poor.

3. Our careful preparation makes us lucky.

4. The mayor called the federal court decision against the city ordinance unfortunate.

2 Understand compound subjects, verbs, and objects. You can develop sentences simply by expanding their subjects, verbs, or objects to include all the ideas you need to express.

Compound subjects. Two subjects attached to the same verb are usually connected by the conjunctions *and* or *or*. No comma is needed between these compound subjects.

> **Lawyers and judges** attended the seminar.
> **Storms or fires** ravage California each year.

When a third subject is added, the items are separated by commas (see Section 31c-3).

> **Storms, fires, and earthquakes** ravage California each year.

Subjects can also be compounded by expressions such as *neither . . . nor* and *either . . . or*, which are called **correlatives**.

> **Neither the judge nor the lawyer** attended the seminar.
> **Either fires or earthquakes** strike California each year.

Compound verbs. Single subjects can perform more than one action. When they do, the verbs attached to them are compound. Like nouns, verbs can be joined by *and, or*, or correlatives such as *either . . . or*. No comma should be used between two verbs that form a compound verb.

> The judge **confused and angered** the prosecutor.
> The earthquake **damaged or destroyed** many homes.
> Children **either like or hate** spinach.

When a third verb is added, the items are separated by commas.

> The judge **confused, angered, and embarrassed** the prosecutor.

Compound verbs can each take separate objects, expanding the sentence structure even more.

> The judge **confused** *the jury* **and angered** *the prosecutor*.
> The earthquake **damaged** *roads* **and destroyed** *homes*.

Compound objects. A verb may also have more than one object. Two objects attached to the same verb are usually connected by the conjunction *and* or *or*. No comma is needed between two objects; commas are required for three or more objects.

> Lawyers attended **the seminar and the dinner**.
> Forest fires ravage **California, Arizona, New Mexico, or Colorado** every year.

Objects can also be connected with correlatives.

Forest fires ravage **either California or New Mexico** every
year.

Many variations of these elements are possible. But don't pile up
more compound expressions than readers can handle easily. Sentences
should always be readable.

15b What do modifiers do?

Modifiers are words, phrases, or clauses that expand what we know
about subjects, verbs, or other sentence elements, including other modifiers and complete sentences. Simple modifiers change the texture of
sentences, while more complex modifiers increase your options for shaping sentences.

1 Use adjectives to modify nouns and pronouns. Adjectives describe
and help to explain nouns and pronouns by specifying *how many, which
size, what color, what condition, which one*, and so on. Single adjectives
are usually placed before the terms they modify.

The **angry** judge scowled at the **nervous** witness.

But adjectives often work in groups. Adjectives in a group are called
coordinate adjectives when each one works on its own, describing different and unrelated aspects of a noun or pronoun.

the **undistinguished, tired-looking** lawyer

our cat, **shedding and overweight**

Placed before a noun or pronoun, coordinate adjectives can be linked
either by conjunctions (usually *and*) or by commas. The order of the
adjectives doesn't affect their meaning.

The **angry, perspiring** judge scowled at the **balding and nervous** witness.
The **perspiring, angry** judge scowled at the **nervous and balding** witness.

Coordinate adjectives may also follow the words they modify, giving
variety to sentence rhythms.

The judge, **angry and perspiring**, scowled at the witness,
balding and nervous.

For a stylish variation, you can also move coordinate adjectives ahead of
an article (*the*) at the beginning of a sentence.

Tired, bored, and underpaid, the jurors listened to an endless interrogation.

Not all clusters of adjectives are coordinate. Often, groups of adjectives must follow a specific sequence to make sense. Changing their sequence produces expressions that are not *idiomatic;* that is, they don't sound right to a native English speaker.

NOT IDIOMATIC	the wooden heavy gavel
IDIOMATIC	the heavy wooden gavel
NOT IDIOMATIC	a woolen green sweater
IDIOMATIC	a green woolen sweater
NOT IDIOMATIC	the American first satellite
IDIOMATIC	the first American satellite

Adjectives in such groupings—which often include numbers—are not separated by commas.

The judge wielded a **heavy wooden** gavel.

The **first American** satellite was Explorer I.

The police rescued **two lucky** kayakers.

Adjectives (along with adverbs and nouns) can also form *compound* or *unit modifiers*, groups of words linked by hyphens that modify a noun (see Section 35b-5). The individual words in compound modifiers need each other; they often wouldn't make sense standing alone in front of a noun.

A **well-known** case would provide a **high-impact** precedent.

The **wine-dark** sea surged in the moonlight.

Finally, adjectives play an important role as subject complements and object complements (see Section 15a-1), modifying words to which they are joined by linking verbs.

The judge's decision seemed **eccentric**.

The children were **sleepy**.

The press called the jury **inept**.

EXERCISE 15.7 Rewrite each of the following sentences so that the adjectives in parentheses modify an appropriate noun or pronoun. Place the adjectives before or after the word they modify, and punctuate them correctly (for example, be sure to add hyphens to unit modifiers and to separate coordinate adjectives with commas or *and* as necessary).

1. The elm trees once common throughout North America have disappeared, victims of disease. (*towering, graceful, Dutch elm*)

2. This infection destroys the vascular system of the elm, causing trees to become husks in a few short weeks. (*fungal, relentless, mature, thriving, leafless*)

3. Few parks in the United States can match the diversity of New York's Central Park, with its zoo, gardens and fields, ponds and lakes, and museum. (*great urban; sizable; pleasant; glistening; world class*)

2 Use adverbs to modify verbs, adjectives, and other adverbs.

Adverbs in sentences explain *how, when, where*, and *to what degree* things happen.

ADVERBS THAT MODIFY VERBS

The prosecutor *spoke* **eloquently** to the jury.

Immediately, the defense attorney *replied*.

The jury *tried* **hard** to follow their summaries.

ADVERBS THAT MODIFY ADJECTIVES

Tornadoes seem **freakishly** *unpredictable*.

Tornado chasing remains **quite** *popular*.

ADVERBS THAT MODIFY OTHER ADVERBS

The reading program has improved **very** *considerably*.

Less *easily* appreciated is a new interest in music at the school.

Adverbs typically can be put in more places than adjectives, enabling you to vary sentence structure and rhythm. All three versions of the following sentence convey the same information, but they do so in subtly different ways.

The news reporter **passionately and repeatedly** defended the integrity of her story.

Passionately and repeatedly, the news reporter defended the integrity of her story.

The news reporter defended the integrity of her story **passionately and repeatedly**.

But this very flexibility causes significant problems. Be sure to review Section 25f on the appropriate placement of adverbs, especially *only*.

EXERCISE 15.8 Rewrite the following sentences so that each adverb in parentheses modifies an appropriate verb, adjective, or adverb. Notice which adverbs work best in one position only and which can be relocated more freely in a sentence.

1. The elm trees once common throughout North America have disappeared, victims of disease. (*sadly, quite, almost, completely*)

2. This lethal infection destroys the vascular system of the elm, causing trees to become husks in a few short weeks. (*nearly, always, completely*)

3. The delicate paintings had not been packed, so they arrived damaged. (*extremely, well, severely*)

3 Understand that nouns can operate as modifiers. In some sentences you may find words that look like nouns but act like adjectives, modifying other words. Don't be confused: nouns often work as modifiers.

> We ordered the **sausage** plate and a **vegetable** sampler.
> The **instrument** cluster glowed red at night.

Proper nouns can serve as modifiers too.

> The choir was preparing for the **Christmas** service.
> We ordered a **New York** strip steak.

EXERCISE 15.9 In the following sentences, underline any nouns that function as modifiers. Discuss disputed cases with colleagues.

1. The Atlanta Braves, Washington Redskins, and Cleveland Indians are sports teams whose names occasionally stir controversy among Native American political interest groups.

2. Car insurance is getting so expensive in urban areas that many college students have to rely on the city bus.

3. Ike signed up for the yoga class because his doctor told him that doing the cobra stretch and the sun salutation would strengthen his injured back muscles.

4 Understand that verbals can operate as modifiers. Especially common as modifiers are participles—words like *dazzling, frightening, broken*. Because participles are based on verbs, they give energy and snap to sentences.

> The waiter brought a **sizzling** steak on a **steaming** bed of rice.
> The officer, **smiling**, wrote us a $100 ticket.
> **Trembling**, I opened the **creaking** door.

For more about participle and infinitive phrases, see Section 15c-2.

EXERCISE 15.10 In the following sentences, underline any participles that function as modifiers. Discuss disputed cases with colleagues.

1. I. M. Pei is one of America's most original and inspiring architects.

2. Born in Guangzhou, China, in 1919, Pei came to the United States in 1935 and became a naturalized citizen in 1954.

3. Pei is responsible for some of the most startling and admired buildings of our era.

4. Pei's work includes the glittering and much debated pyramid that now serves as the main entrance to the Louvre, one of the leading museums in the world.

15c What are phrases?

Technically, a **phrase** is a group of related words without a subject and a finite verb, but this definition is hard to follow. It's probably more helpful to appreciate phrases in action, doing their part to give shape to sentences.

1 Understand prepositional phrases. Among the more mundane of sentence elements, a *prepositional phrase* consists of a preposition and its object, either a noun or a pronoun. The object can be modified.

Preposition	Modifier (optional)	Object(s)
to		Jeff and me
in	your own	words
beyond	the farthest	mountain

Just try writing a paragraph without using a prepositional phrase and you'll appreciate how essential they are. Don't, however, mistake prepositional phrases with *to* (*to Starbucks, to Lila*) for infinitives or infinitive phrases, which include a verb form (*to see, to watch the stars, to be happy*). For more on prepositions and infinitives, see Section 19b.

The power of prepositional phrases resides in their flexibility and simplicity. Moving a prepositional phrase into an unexpected slot gets it noticed. For additional discussion, see Section 16d-7.

EXERCISE 15.11 Study the following passage and discuss the effect of relocating the boldfaced prepositional phrases within the speech. How would the style of the passage be changed—if at all?

With malice toward none, with charity for all, with firmness in the right, let us strive on to finish the work we are in, to bind up the nation's wounds, to care for him who shall have borne the battle and for his widow and his orphan, to do all which may achieve and cherish a just and lasting peace among ourselves and with all nations.

—ABRAHAM LINCOLN

2 Appreciate the versatility of verbals and verbal phrases. Verbals are verb forms that can act as nouns, adjectives, or adverbs (see Chapter 19). Verbals can stand alone, or they can form phrases by taking objects, complements, or modifiers.

	Verbal	Verbal phrase
Infinitive	to serve	to serve the sick
	to prevent	to prevent forest fires
Gerund	serving	serving the sick [is]
	preventing	preventing forest fires [is]
Participle	serving	serving without complaint
	prevented	prevented from helping

Verbals and verb phrases that act as nouns can serve as subjects or direct objects. As modifiers, verbals can function as adverbs or adjectives.

Verbals as subjects. Both infinitives and gerunds can act as subjects in sentences. On their own, they don't look much different from other subjects.

INFINITIVE AS SUBJECT

To serve was the doctor's ambition.

GERUND AS SUBJECT

Serving was the doctor's ambition.

But when they expand into phrases, they can be harder to recognize. Yet they remain subjects and can be either simple or compound.

INFINITIVE PHRASES AS SUBJECTS

To serve the sick was the doctor's ambition.
To serve the sick and to comfort the afflicted were the doctor's ambitions.

GERUND PHRASES AS SUBJECTS

Serving the sick was the doctor's ambition.
Serving the sick and comforting the afflicted were the doctor's ambitions.

Verbals as objects. Both infinitives and gerunds that act like nouns can serve as objects in sentences. On their own, they don't look much different from other objects.

INFINITIVE AS DIRECT OBJECT

The lawyer loved **to object**.

GERUND AS DIRECT OBJECT

The lawyer loved **objecting**.

As phrases, verbals can seem complicated in their role as direct objects. Yet they play that role like any other noun, simple or compound.

INFINITIVE PHRASES AS DIRECT OBJECTS

The lawyer chose **to object to the motion**.
The lawyer chose **to object to the motion and to move for a mistrial**.

GERUND PHRASES AS DIRECT OBJECTS

The lawyer loved **objecting to the prosecutor's motions**.
The lawyer loved **objecting to the prosecutor's motions and winning concessions from the judge**.

Verbals as complements. Both infinitives and gerunds can act as complements in sentences.

INFINITIVE AS SUBJECT COMPLEMENT

To know Rebecca was **to love her**.

GERUND AS OBJECT COMPLEMENT

The IRS caught Elmo **cheating on his taxes**.

Verbals as adjectives. You'll frequently want to use participles and participle phrases to modify nouns and pronouns in your sentences.

PARTICIPLES AS ADJECTIVES

Frowning, the instructor stopped her lecture.
The **suspended** fraternity appealed to the dean.

PARTICIPLE PHRASES AS ADJECTIVES

Frowning at us, the instructor stopped her lecture.
The fraternity, **suspended for underage drinking**, appealed to the dean.
We kept close to the trail, **not knowing the terrain well**.

Notice the freedom you have in placing participle phrases. You do want to be certain, however, that readers can have no doubt what a particular phrase modifies.

Infinitives, too, can function as adjectives, although it can be difficult to perceive the infinitive in this role as a modifier, providing details.

INFINITIVES AS ADJECTIVES

The manager had many items **to purchase**. modifies *items*

Reasons **to stay** were few. modifies *reasons*

INFINITIVE PHRASES AS ADJECTIVES

The manager had many items **to purchase for the grand opening**. modifies *items*

Reasons **to stay calm** were few. modifies *reasons*

Verbals as adverbs. Infinitives and infinitive phrases can act like adverbs, answering such questions as *why, how, to what degree*, and so on.

INFINITIVES AS ADVERBS

Difficult **to please**, Martha rarely enjoyed movies. modifies *difficult*

The sedan seemed built **to last**. modifies *built*

INFINITIVE PHRASES AS ADVERBS

The gardener dug a trench **to stop the spread of oak wilt**. modifies *dug*

The Senate recessed **to give its members a summer vacation**. modifies *recessed*

The pilot found it impossible **to see the runway in the fog**. modifies *impossible*

EXERCISE 15.12 Underline all verbals in the following sentences and then indicate whether they function as subjects, objects, complements, adjectives, or adverbs.

1. Waving at the crowd, the winner of the marathon took a victory lap.

2. The waiter certainly seemed eager to please us.

3. The salesperson enjoyed demonstrating the self-closing door on the minivan.

4. Harriet bought an awning to reduce the light streaming through her bay windows.

5. To cherish the weak and the dying was Mother Teresa's mission in life.

6. Reasons to applaud during the candidate's speech were few.

7. Finding an appealing painting at a reasonable price was impossible.

8. The clerk caught Liza sampling the produce.

9. Surprised by the storm front's ferocity, weather forecasters revised their predictions.

10. We decided we finally had sufficient reason to object.

3 Understand absolute phrases.

Absolutes are phrases that modify whole sentences rather than individual words. They are constructed from participles or infinitives. When absolute phrases are based on participles, they always include a subject and may include modifiers and other elements.

Our representatives will, **time permitting**, read the entire petition to the city council.

The supply craft having docked, the astronauts on the *International Space Station* were ready for their space walk.

Our plane arrived early, **the winds having been favorable**.

When the participle is a form of *to be*, it can often be omitted for a more economical or elegant expression.

The winds [being] favorable, our plane arrived early.

Absolutes based on infinitives don't require a noun or pronoun.

To speak frankly, we are facing the gravest crisis in the history of this company.

Your buzz cut, **to be honest**, would look better on a coconut.

Because absolutes are not attached to particular words, you can place them exactly where they work best in a sentence.

EXERCISE 15.13 Turn the phrases in parentheses into absolutes and incorporate them into the full sentences preceding them.

EXAMPLE   The senator's amendment to the tax bill would fund a worthless pork barrel project. (*to put it bluntly*)

REVISION   The senator's amendment to the tax bill would, to put it bluntly, fund a worthless pork barrel project.

1. Many newspaper reporters don't know beans about their beats. (*to speak candidly*)

2. We should be able to take the launch to the island. (*the weather having cleared*)

3. Johnson became a viable candidate for governor again. (*the tide of public opinion having turned*)

4. Work in the electronic classrooms had to stop for the day. (*the entire network down*)

4 Appreciate appositive phrases. An **appositive** is a noun or noun phrase that restates or expands the meaning of the words it modifies. Appositives are placed immediately after the words they modify and are usually surrounded by commas (see Section 31b-2).

> Napoleon, the **Emperor of France**, crowned himself.
>
> Death Valley, **the largest national park in the continental United States**, blooms with wildflowers in the spring.

Gerund phrases can stand as appositives too.

> Alchemy, **changing base metals into more precious ones**, is discredited medieval lore.

Appositives are also routinely introduced by words or phrases such as *or, as, for example, such as*, and *in other words*.

> Dachshunds, **or wiener dogs**, are growing in popularity.
>
> Katharine Hepburn's best movies, **including *The African Queen* and *The Philadelphia Story***, are classics of American cinema.
>
> The test actually measures college survival skills, **that is, the ability to pass multiple-choice examinations**.

Most appositives are interchangeable with the words they modify: delete those modified terms and the sentence still makes sense.

APPOSITIVES AS MODIFIERS

> Abraham Lincoln, **the first Republican President**, presided over the Civil War.
>
> Halloween, **All Hallows' Eve**, comes two days before All Souls' Day, **also known as the Day of the Dead**.

MODIFIED TERMS REPLACED BY APPOSITIVES

> **The first Republican President** presided over the Civil War.
>
> **All Hallows' Eve** comes two days before **the Day of the Dead**.

Some appositives—often proper nouns—can't be deleted without blurring the meaning of a sentence. These appositives are not surrounded by commas (see Section 31d-5).

> Bob Dylan's masterpiece ***Blonde on Blonde*** is a double album.
>
> Nixon **the diplomat** is more respected by historians than Nixon **the politician**.

EXERCISE 15.14 Turn the phrase(s) in parentheses into appositives and incorporate them into the full sentences preceding them. Be sure to use the right punctuation.

EXAMPLE   Sally Ride served on the presidential commission that investigated the 1986 explosion of the space shuttle. (*America's first woman astronaut*; Challenger)

REVISION   Sally Ride, America's first woman astronaut, served on the presidential commission that investigated the explosion of the space shuttle *Challenger*.

1. Rudolph Giuliani first gained prominence as a federal prosecutor. (*107th mayor of New York City*)

2. In Anasazi architecture, a prominent feature is the kiva. (*a covered circular enclosure sunk in the ground and used for religious ceremonies and community meetings*)

3. The technique called pure fresco produces enduring images such as those on the ceiling of the Sistine Chapel. (*painting with plaster stained with pigment; Michelangelo's masterpiece*)

15d   What do clauses do in sentences?

Clauses are groups of related words that have subjects and verbs. As such, they are the framework for most sentences, the parts to which other modifying words and phrases are attached. The four basic sentence types (*simple, compound, complex*, and *compound-complex*) are based on some combination of independent and dependent clauses (see Section 15e).

1 Understand independent clauses. An **independent clause** can stand alone as a complete sentence. Most independent clauses have an identifiable subject and a predicate (that is, a verb plus its auxiliaries and modifiers). Sometimes a subject is understood and is not stated in the clause.

Subject	Predicate
The house	burned.
The dreams we had	came true today.
The children	caught colds.
[You]	Come here at once.

EXERCISE 15.15 Circle the subject and underline the predicate in the following independent clauses. If the subject is understood, write the word *understood* as the subject in parentheses after the sentence.

1. The wood on the deck warped after only one summer.

2. Jeremy has been trying to reach you all day.

3. Attend the rally this afternoon.

4. Keeping focused on schoolwork is hard on weekends.

2 Understand dependent clauses. A **dependent clause** is one that cannot stand alone as a complete sentence. Many dependent clauses that have identifiable subjects and predicates are introduced by subordinating conjunctions—words such as *although, because, if, until, when, whenever, while*—that place the dependent clause in relationship to another independent clause.

Subordinating conjunction	Subject	Predicate
When	the house	burned . . .
If	the dreams we had	came true today . . .
Because	the children	caught colds . . .

Dependent clauses can have various functions in a sentence, but all dependent clauses must work with independent clauses to create complete sentences.

Adjective clauses. Adjective clauses, also known as *relative clauses*, attach themselves to nouns or pronouns using one of the relative pronouns: *who, whom, whomever, whose, that, which*.

Actress Angelina Jolie, **who was born in Los Angeles**, moved to New York when she was less than a year old.

Venus is the planet **that shines brightest in the sky**.

The new engine, **which is Mercedes-Benz's first V-6**, has a dozen spark plugs and three valves per cylinder.

The adverbs *when* and *where* can introduce adjective clauses when the resulting clauses modify nouns, not verbs.

The immigrants settled in those California cities **where jobs were plentiful**. clause modifies the noun *cities*, not the verb *settled*

We enjoy the winter **when the snow falls**. clause modifies the noun *winter*, not the verb *enjoy*

Adjective clauses are surrounded by commas when they are nonessential—that is, when they can be removed from a sentence without destroying its coherence. When clauses are essential to the meaning of a sentence, they are not surrounded by commas (see Section 31d-5).

EXERCISE 15.16 Add an adjective clause to each of the following sentences at the point indicated. Remember that adjective clauses are usually introduced by *who, whom, whomever, whose, that,* or *which.* An adjective clause may also begin with *where* or *when* if it modifies a noun, not a verb.

1. All the students in class who . . . said they supported the Democratic party's proposals.

2. Companies that . . . are prospering more today than firms that. . . .

3. The original *Star Wars* trilogy, which . . . , has been joined by a new series of films in the saga.

4. Teens prefer to congregate in places where. . . .

5. A person whose . . . is unlikely to find a job quickly.

6. Tom Cruise, whom . . . , remains a top box-office draw.

Adverb clauses. Adverb clauses work just like adverbs, modifying verbs, adjectives, and other adverbs. They are introduced by a subordinating conjunction, such as *after, although, as, before, if, since, though, until, when,* and *while.*

> Liliana left **before the hail fell**. modifies the verb *left*
>
> The bookcase was not as heavy **as we had expected**. modifies the adjective *heavy*
>
> Humberto spoke haltingly **whenever a girl looked him in the eye**. modifies the adverb *haltingly*

Sometimes an adverb or subordinate clause seems to modify an entire sentence or a group of words.

> **Although the stock market plunged**, investors had high hopes for a quick recovery.

For much more about subordination, see Section 15g.

EXERCISE 15.17 Add an adverb clause to each of the following sentences at the point indicated. Remember that adverb clauses are introduced by subordinating conjunctions such as *although, before, since, unless,* and many others.

1. Even though . . . , Americans vote in record low numbers.

2. Many young people put little faith in the Social Security system, since. . . .

3. Because . . . , many students come to college knowing how to operate computers.

4. If . . . , the polar ice caps will melt and the level of the oceans will rise.

5. Although they . . . , surprising numbers of children still smoke.

Noun clauses. Whole clauses that act as nouns are quite common. Such clauses act as subjects or objects, not as modifiers.

> **How a computer works** is beyond my understanding.
> noun clause as subject

> The FAA report did not explain **why the jets collided**.
> noun clause as direct object

> The employment agency found **whoever applied** a job.
> noun clause as indirect object

> You may speak to **whomever you wish**.
> noun clause as an object of a preposition

EXERCISE 15.18 Underline all the noun clauses in the following sentences. Then explain the function of each clause, as either a subject or an object.

1. What politicians say often matters much less than how they say it.

2. Whoever sent a letter of condolence should receive a prompt reply from us.

3. Why so many people care so much about celebrities is beyond my comprehension.

15e   What types of sentences can you write?

While you'll rarely revise sentences just to make a *simple* sentence *compound* or a *compound* sentence *complex*, recognizing these terms will make it easier for you to diagnose problems in your sentences and to talk about them with peer editors. The most familiar sentence types are all built from just two basic components: independent clauses and subordinate clauses (see Section 15d).

	one independent clause
SIMPLE SENTENCE	**Windows rattled**.
	independent clause + independent clause
COMPOUND SENTENCE	**Windows rattled** and **doors shook**.
	dependent clause(s) + one independent clause
COMPLEX SENTENCE	*As the storm blew*, **windows rattled**.
	dependent clause(s) + two or more independent clauses
COMPOUND-COMPLEX SENTENCE	*As the storm blew*, **windows rattled** and **doors shook**.

1 Use simple sentences to express ideas clearly and directly. Simple sentences can attract the attention of readers with the power of their single independent clauses.

> Jesus wept.
>
> I come to bury Caesar, not to praise him.

But don't assume that simple sentences will necessarily be short or without ornament.

> NASA, the federal agency in charge of space exploration, has no current plans for a moon base or for human missions to Mars and Venus, the planets closest to Earth in both size and distance.

Simple sentences can be expanded by compounding or modifying their subjects, verbs, or objects. Despite its increased length, the final sentence still has only one independent clause and no dependent clauses, so it remains a simple sentence.

2 Use compound and complex sentences to express relationships between clauses. These relationships involve *coordination* when independent clauses are joined to other independent clauses.

> The rain fell for days, **but** the city's reservoirs were not filled.
>
> Our fuel pump failed, **so** we were stranded on the expressway.

They involve *subordination* when dependent clauses are joined to independent clauses.

> **Although** the rain fell for days, the city's reservoirs were not filled.
>
> **Because** our fuel pump failed, we were stranded on the expressway.

To write effective sentences, you need to handle both coordination (see Section 15f) and subordination (see Section 15g) confidently.

15f How does coordination build sentences?

Independent clauses can stand on their own grammatically, but they grow richer when they enter into coordinate relationships. These relationships can be established in several ways: with *coordinating conjunctions;* with various *correlative constructions;* with semicolons, colons, and dashes; and with *conjunctive adverbs.*

1 Use coordinating conjunctions to join independent clauses. The **coordinating conjunctions** are *and, or, nor, for, but, yet*, and *so*. They express fundamental relationships between ideas: similarity, addition, or sequence (*and*); exception, difference, or contrast (*or, nor, but, yet*); and process or causality (*for, so*). Commas ordinarily precede coordinating conjunctions (see Section 31c-1).

The solemn service ended, **and** we went home immediately.
sequence

SAT scores in math rose nationally, **but** verbal scores dropped.
contrast

I got a high score on the final examination, **so** I passed geology.
causality

Different coordinating conjunctions give readers different signals, so select them carefully. Many writers habitually choose *and* even when another conjunction might express a relationship more precisely.

Coordinating conjunctions are also useful for linking sentences that are short, choppy, or repetitive.

CHOPPY AND **REPETITIVE**	We liked the features of the computer. It was too expensive for our budgets. We thought it looked complicated.
COMBINED	We liked the features of the computer, **but** it was too expensive for our budgets **and** looked complicated.

But relying too much on coordinating conjunctions (especially *and*) to link ideas can be stylistically dangerous. A string of clauses linked by *ands* quickly grows tedious and should be revised, often by making some clauses subordinate (see Section 15g).

EXERCISE 15.19 Use coordinating conjunctions (*and, or, nor, for, but, yet, so*) to create compound sentences by linking the following pairs of independent clauses. Be sure to punctuate the sentences correctly.

1. The stock market finally rose. Investors remained nervous.

2. Citizens' groups invest time and money on get-out-the-vote campaigns. Many voters still skip general elections.

3. Vitamin C is good for colds. Vitamin E keeps the skin in good condition.

4. Most Americans get their news from television. News anchors are powerful people.

2 Use correlative constructions to join independent clauses. **Correlatives** are conjunctions that work in pairs, expressions such as *if . . . then, either . . . or, just as . . . so,* and *not only . . . but also.* Like coordinating conjunctions, correlatives can be used to form compound sentences that ask readers to examine two ideas side by side.

> **Just as** Napoleon faced defeat in Russia, **so** Hitler saw his dreams of conquest evaporate at the siege of Leningrad.
>
> **Not only** is Captain Janeway a better leader than Kirk, **but** she is **also** a more interesting human being.

EXERCISE 15.20 Create compound sentences by finishing the correlative construction begun for you. Be sure that the sentence you produce is a compound sentence, one with two independent clauses. Punctuate the sentence correctly.

1. If I agree to read *War and Peace* by the end of the summer, then you . . .

2. Not only does the Bill of Rights protect free speech, but it also . . .

3. Just as eating too much fat contributes to poor physical health, so . . .

3 Use semicolons, colons, and dashes to link independent clauses. Semicolons usually join independent clauses roughly balanced in importance and closely associated in meaning.

> We expected chaos; we found catastrophe.
>
> The eyes of the nation were suddenly on the Supreme Court; the nine justices could not ignore the weight of public opinion.

Colons are more directive than semicolons. They imply that the second independent clause explains, exemplifies, or expands on the first.

> There was a lesson in the indictment: even small acts have consequences.

Like colons, dashes can function as conjunctions, connecting clauses with verve and energy. Some writers and editors, however, object to dashes used this way.

> Expect C. Jay Cox's new film to cause controversy—the theme is bold and provocative.
>
> The cathedral of Notre Dame was restored in the nineteenth century—its facade had suffered damage during the French Revolution.

See Chapters 32 and 35 for more on semicolons, colons, and dashes.

EXERCISE 15.21 Use a semicolon, a colon, or a dash to link the following independent clauses. Be prepared to explain why you chose each form of linkage.

1. Don't feel sorry for the spare and thorny plants you see in a desert. They don't want or need more water.

2. Barren stalks, wicked thorns, and waxy spines are their adaptations to a harsh environment. Such features conserve water or protect the plants from desert animals and birds.

3. Spring rains can create an astonishing desert spectacle. Cacti and other plants explode into colorful bloom.

4 Use conjunctive adverbs with semicolons to join independent clauses.
Conjunctive adverbs are words such as *consequently, however, moreover, nevertheless, similarly*, and *therefore*. Like any adverb, they can appear at various places in a sentence. But often the adverb follows a semicolon, illuminating the relationship between clauses and holding our attention.

> Members of the zoning board appreciated the developer's arguments; **however**, they rejected her rezoning request.

> The muffler was leaking dangerous fumes; **moreover**, the brake linings were growing thin.

The comma that typically follows a conjunctive adverb in these constructions also gives weight to the word or phrase.

Note that it is the semicolon, not the adverb, that actually links the independent clauses. That connection becomes more obvious when the conjunctive adverb is moved.

> Members of the zoning board appreciated the developer's arguments; they rejected her rezoning request, **however**.

> The muffler was leaking dangerous fumes; the brake linings, **moreover**, were growing thin.

The punctuation surrounding conjunctive adverbs can be confusing. See Section 32a-3 for more details.

EXERCISE 15.22 Use a semicolon and the conjunctive adverb in parentheses to link the following independent clauses. To gain practice punctuating this tricky construction, use the form illustrated in the example—with the semicolon followed immediately by the conjunctive adverb, followed by a comma.

EXAMPLE   The aircraft lost an engine in flight. It landed safely. (*however*)

REVISED   The aircraft lost an engine in flight; however, it landed safely.

1. Ordinary books are still more convenient than most computerized texts. They employ a technology that doesn't go out of date as quickly—paper. (*moreover*)

2. Most people would save money by using public transportation. They elect to use their private automobiles for daily commuting. (*nevertheless*)

3. American colonists resented England's interference in their political and commercial lives. The 13 colonies decided to fight for independence. (*therefore*)

EXERCISE 15.23 Build coordinate sentences by combining the following independent clauses. You may use coordinating conjunctions, correlatives, conjunctive adverbs, semicolons, or colons. Be sure to get the punctuation right.

EXAMPLE   Pencils were invented in the sixteenth century. Erasers were not added to them until 1858.

COORDINATION   Pencils were invented in the sixteenth century; however, erasers were not added to them until 1858.

1. Today, French Impressionist paintings are favorites among art lovers. The public loudly rejected them at their debut in the nineteenth century.

2. Painters such as Renoir and Monet wanted art to depict life. They painted common scenes and ordinary people.

3. Many critics of the time were disturbed by the Impressionists' banal subjects. They thought the Impressionists' paintings themselves looked crude and unfinished.

15g How does subordination build sentences?

Use subordination to create complex or compound-complex sentences. Subordinating conjunctions provide the link between main ideas (independent clauses) and secondary ones (dependent or subordinate clauses). Subordination can be achieved with the aid of relative pronouns or subordinating conjunctions. The relative pronouns are *that, what, whatever, which, who, whom, whomever,* and *whose.*

chart

(15.1) Subordinating Conjunctions

after	in order that	unless
although	now that	until
as	once	when
as if	provided	whenever
as though	rather than	where
because	since	whereas
before	so that	wherever
even if	than	whether
even though	that	which
if	though	while
if only	till	

A subordinating conjunction or a relative pronoun turns an independent clause into a dependent clause which cannot stand alone as a sentence.

INDEPENDENT	I wrote the paper.
DEPENDENT	**While** I wrote the paper . . .
DEPENDENT	The paper **that** I wrote . . .

1 Use subordination to clarify relationships between clauses. Like most tools for building sentences, subordination provides options for stating and clarifying thoughts. So it's probably misleading to regard the independent clause in a subordinate construction as always more important or more weighty than the dependent clause. In fact, the clauses work together to establish a complex relationship—of time, causality, consequence, contigency, contrast, and so on.

USING SUBORDINATION TO EXPLAIN *WHO OR WHAT*

The *Le Morte d'Arthur*, **which** was the work of Sir Thomas Malory, includes stories about the knights of the Round Table.

USING SUBORDINATION TO EXPLAIN *UNDER WHAT CONDITIONS*

If credit is easy to get, many people go into debt.

USING SUBORDINATION TO CLARIFY *CAUSALITY*

The film enjoyed a brisk summer box office **because** it won an Academy Award last March.

USING SUBORDINATION TO HIGHLIGHT *CONTRAST*

Although members of Congress often campaign for a balanced budget, most of them jealously protect projects in their own districts from cuts in federal spending.

2　Use subordination to shift the emphasis of sentences. Generally, readers will focus on ideas in your independent clauses. Compare the following sentences—both equally good, but with slightly different emphases due to changes in subordination.

> **While** the Supreme Court usually declares efforts to limit the First Amendment unconstitutional, Congress regularly acts to ban forms of speech most citizens find offensive.

> The Supreme Court usually declares efforts to limit the First Amendment unconstitutional, **even though** Congress regularly acts to ban forms of speech most people find offensive.

The first sentence directs readers to consider the efforts of Congress to rein in the First Amendment; the second sentence gives more emphasis to the Supreme Court. The differences are small but significant.

3　Use subordination to expand sentences. You can often use subordination to combine simple clauses into more graceful or powerful sentences.

CHOPPY	Spectators at the air show were watching in horror. An ultralight aircraft struggled down the runway. It was built of kevlar and carbon fiber. It hit a stand of trees and disintegrated in a plume of smoke and fire.
SUBORDINATED	**While** spectators at the air show watched in horror, an ultralight aircraft built of kevlar and carbon fiber struggled down the runway **until** it hit a stand of trees and disintegrated in a plume of smoke and fire.

4　Use subordinate clauses sensibly. If you pile more than two or three subordinate clauses into one sentence, you may confuse readers. Be sure readers can keep up with all the relationships you establish between clauses. If you suspect they can't, simplify those relationships, perhaps by breaking one long complex sentence into several simpler sentences.

TOO MUCH SUBORDINATION	**Although** her book *Harry Potter and the Sorcerer's Stone,* **which** spawned a hugely successful series, **which** has sold millions of copies, was turned down seven times **while** she tried to find a publisher, J. K. Rowling did not quit, **which** suggests the importance of persistence.

REVISED   Persistence counts. J. K. Rowling never gave up,
               even though her *Harry Potter and the Sorcerer's
               Stone*, the first in a string of best-sellers, was
               turned down by seven publishers.

EXERCISE 15.24 Join the following pairs of sentences by making one of the
independent clauses subordinate.

1. The original books of Babylonia and Assyria were collections of
   inscribed clay tablets stored in labeled containers too heavy for one
   person to move. We think of books as portable, bound volumes.

2. Clay tablets had many drawbacks. They remained the most
   convenient medium for recording information until the Egyptians
   developed papyrus around 3000 BC.

3. Egyptian books were lighter than clay tablets but still awkward to
   carry or read. A single papyrus book comprised several large,
   unwieldy scrolls.

4. The Greeks developed papyrus leaflets. They folded and bound the
   leaflets to produce the first modern-looking book.

5. That first book was the Greek Bible. It takes its name from Byblos,
   the Phoenician city that supplied Greece with papyrus.

EXERCISE 15.25   Rewrite the following sentences to reduce any undue
complexity in subordination and in other modification. If necessary,
break longer sentences into shorter ones.

1. Although for many years scientists believed that there might be
   another planet on the fringes of the solar system whose gravitational
   pull influenced the orbit of Uranus, there was no concrete evidence
   that this additional planet existed, even though astronomers spent
   decades speculating about its mass, distance from Earth, and orbital
   mechanics.

2. Because the orbit of Uranus seemed oddly influenced by an unseen
   planetary body, scientists searched for other objects until they
   actually discovered Neptune and, later, Pluto, which, unfortunately,
   did not seem to have the mass necessary to explain the orbital
   disruptions of Uranus that prompted the explorations.

3. If a mysterious Planet X at the fringes of the solar system is an
   appealing notion, few scientists now take the idea seriously because
   Voyager 2 provided data that suggested that the mass of Uranus is
   exactly what it should be if we calculate its orbit accurately.

15h How does parallelism work?

Sentences are easier to read when closely related ideas within them follow similar language patterns. Subjects, objects, verbs, modifiers, phrases, and clauses can be structured to show such a relationship, called **parallelism**.

PARALLEL WORDS	The venerable principal spoke **clearly, eloquently**, and **invariably**.
PARALLEL PHRASES	**Praised by critics, embraced by common readers**, the novel became a best-seller.
PARALLEL CLAUSES	**It was the best of times, it was the worst of times**.

1 Recognize sentence patterns that require parallel construction.

When words or phrases come in pairs or triplets, they usually need to be parallel. That is, each element must have the same form: a noun or noun phrase, an adjective or adjective phrase, an adverb or adverbial phrase.

NOUNS/NOUN PHRASES	**Optimism in outlook** and **egotism in behavior**—those are essential qualities for a leader.
ADJECTIVES	The best physicians are **patient, thorough**, and **compassionate**.
ADVERBS	The lawyers presented their case **passionately** and **persuasively**.

Items in a list should also be parallel.

LIST ITEMS	The school board's objectives are clear: **to hire** the best teachers, **to create** successful classrooms, **to serve** the needs of all families, and **to prepare** students for the twenty-first century.

2 Use parallelism in comparisons and contrasts.

Sometimes parallelism adds a stylistic touch, as in the following example. The first version, though acceptable, is not as stylish as the revised and parallel version.

NOT PARALLEL	Pope was a poet of the mind; Byron wrote for the heart.
PARALLEL	Pope was a poet of the mind, Byron a bard for the heart.

Parallelism is required in comparisons following *as* or *than*.

NOT PARALLEL	The city council is *as* likely **to adopt the measure** *as* **vetoing it**.
PARALLEL	The city council is *as* likely **to adopt the measure** *as* **to veto it**.
NOT PARALLEL	**Smiling** takes fewer muscles *than* **to frown**.
PARALLEL	**Smiling** takes fewer muscles *than* **frowning**.

3 Recognize expressions that signal the need for parallel structure.

These include the following correlative constructions: *not only . . . but also, either . . . or, neither . . . nor, both . . . and, on the one hand . . . on the other hand*.

As Franklin once remarked, *either* **we hang together** *or* **we hang separately**.

A musician's manager sees to it that the performer is *neither* **overworked onstage** *nor* **undervalued in wages**.

We spoke *not only* **to the President** *but also* **to the Speaker of the House**.

4 Use parallelism to show a progression of ideas.
You can set up parallel structures within sentences or entire paragraphs. These structures make ideas easier to follow.

Jane Brody, the *New York Times* health writer, says, "Regular exercise comes closer to being a fountain of youth than anything modern medicine can offer." **Exercise halves** the risk of heart disease and stroke, **lowers** the chance of colon cancer, and reduces the likelihood of osteoporosis. **It lessens** the chances of developing diabetes and **strengthens** the immune system. **Exercise** even **helps** people overcome depression.

5 Use parallelism for emphasis.
Readers really take note when patterns are repeated in longer clauses. By using parallelism of this kind, you will get their attention.

If welfare reform works, **the genuinely needy will** be protected and assisted, **the less conscientious will** be motivated to find work, and **the average taxpayer will** see federal dollars spent more wisely.

You can also use parallelism to express an idea cleverly. Parallelism offers patterns of language perfect for setting up a joke or underscoring sarcasm.

People who serve as their own lawyers in court have *either* **a fool for a client** *or* **a brother for a judge**.

6 Correct faulty parallelism. It is easy for parallel constructions to go off track. When an item doesn't follow the pattern of language already established in a sentence, it lacks parallelism and disrupts the flow of the sentence. To correct faulty parallelism, first identify the items that ought to be parallel; then choose one of the items (usually the first) as the pattern; and finally revise the remaining items to fit that pattern.

NOT PARALLEL   When you open a new computer program, it's easy to **feel overwhelmed by the interface, frustrated by the vague instructions**, and **not know what to do next**.

PARALLEL   When you open a new computer program, it's easy to feel **overwhelmed by the interface, frustrated by the vague instructions**, and **confused about what to do next**.

Sometimes you'll have to decide how much of a parallel structure to repeat. You may want to reproduce a structure in its entirety for emphasis, or you might omit a repeated item for economy.

EMPHASIS   We expect you **to** arrive on time, **to** bring an ID, **to** have three sharpened pencils, and **to** follow instructions.

ECONOMY   We expect you to arrive on time, bring an ID, have three sharpened pencils, and follow instructions.

The difference can be striking. Consider what happens when we remove the artful repetition from a famous speech by Winston Churchill that is a model of parallel structure.

EMPHASIS   **We shall fight** on the beaches, **we shall fight** on the landing grounds, **we shall fight** in the fields and in the streets, **we shall fight** in the hills; we shall never surrender.

ECONOMY   We shall fight on the beaches and landing grounds and in the fields, streets, and hills; we shall never surrender.

EXERCISE 15.26 Read these sentences and decide which ones have faulty parallel structures. Then revise those in which you find inconsistent or faulty patterns.

1. On opening night at the new Tex-Mex restaurant, the manager called the servers together to be sure they understood all the items on the menu, could pronounce *fajitas*, and that they would remember to ask, "Salt or no salt?" when customers ordered margaritas.

2. Two servers had a wager to see whose customers would order the most drinks, devour the most chips, and, of course, leaving the biggest gratuities.

3. Offering the best Southwestern cuisine and to serve the hottest salsa were the restaurant's two goals.

4. But customers soon made it clear that they also expected real barbecue on the menu, so the manager added slow-cooked beef ribs smothered in sauce, hefty racks of pork ribs dripping with fat, and there was smoked sausage on the menu too that was juicy and hot.

15i   How do you craft balanced sentences?

Effective balanced sentences merge the best attributes of coordination and parallelism (see Sections 15f and 15h). In a **balanced sentence**, a coordinating conjunction links two or more independent clauses that are roughly parallel in structure. The result is a sentence so intentional and rhythmic that it draws special attention. For that reason, balanced sentences are often memorable and quotable.

> And so, my fellow Americans, ask not what your country can do for you; ask what you can do for your country.
> —JOHN F. KENNEDY, Inaugural Address

> We live here and they live there. We black and they white. They got things and we ain't. They do things and we can't. It's just like living in jail.
> —RICHARD WRIGHT, *Native Son*

In crafting a balanced sentence, you'll almost always begin with two independent clauses joined to make a compound sentence (see Section 15f). Then you can sharpen the relationship between the clauses by making them reasonably parallel. You may need to revise both clauses quite heavily.

COMPOUND	New programs to end adult illiteracy may be costly, **but** the alternative is continued support of even more expensive welfare programs.
BALANCED	New adult literacy programs may be costly, **but** current welfare programs are costlier still.

EXERCISE 15.27   Complete the following sentences in ways that make them balanced.

1. If Alfred Hitchcock is the master of suspense, then . . .

2. Politics makes strange bedfellows, and . . .

3. If all the world is really a stage, then . . .

4. In theory, college seems the surest pathway to economic security; in practice, . . .

15j   How do you craft cumulative sentences?

The intricate architecture of balanced sentences (see Section 15i) can make them seem formal and even old-fashioned. A structure perhaps better suited to contemporary writing, which tends to be informal, is the **cumulative sentence**, in which an independent clause is followed by a series of modifiers, sometimes simple, sometimes quite complex.

> She [Georgia O'Keeffe] is simply hard, **a straight shooter, a woman clean of received wisdom and open to what she sees**.
>
> —JOAN DIDION, "Georgia O'Keeffe"

In writing a cumulative sentence, you add on to an original thought, expanding and enriching it by attaching modifying words, phrases, and clauses.

> But then they danced down the street like dingledodies, and I shambled after as I've been doing all my life after people who interest me, because the only people for me are the mad ones, **the ones who are mad to live, mad to talk, mad to be saved, desirous of everything at the same time, the ones who never yawn or say a commonplace thing, but burn, burn, burn like fabulous roman candles exploding like spiders across the stars and in the middle you see the centerlight pop and everybody goes "Awww!"**
>
> —JACK KEROUAC, *On the Road*

Almost any of the modifying phrases and clauses described in Sections 15b through 15d can be attached gracefully to the ends of clauses.

1 Attach adjectives and adverbs. Either as individual words or as complete phrases, these modifiers play an important role in shaping cumulative sentences.

> It was a handsome sedan, **black as shimmering oil, deeply chromed, and sleek as a rocket**.
>
> The storm pounded the coast **so relentlessly that residents wondered whether the skies would ever clear again**.

2 Attach prepositional phrases. You can place prepositional phrases (see Section 15c-1) at the ends of sentences to describe or modify nouns or pronouns within the sentence.

> The church was all white plaster and gilt, **like a wedding cake in the public square**.

3 Attach appositives and free modifiers. You can conclude cumulative sentences with modifiers that rename someone or something within the body of a sentence. These *free modifiers* act like appositives (see Section 15c-4), but they may be separated in distance from the noun or pronoun they embellish.

> And more than that, he [Mickey Mantle] was a presence in our lives—a fragile hero to whom we had an emotional attachment so strong and lasting that it defied logic.
>   He got love—love for what he had been; love for what he made us feel; love for the humanity and sweetness that was always there mixed in with the flaws and all the pain that wracked his body and his soul.
>
> —BOB COSTAS

Notice the way these modifiers are introduced by dashes. Notice, too, that the modifying phrase itself can be quite complex and much longer than the original independent clause.

4 Attach clauses. You can experiment with both relative and subordinate clauses (see Section 15d) at the ends of sentences, compounding them and keeping them roughly parallel.

> The astronaut argued that Americans need to return to the moon **because our scientific explorations there have only begun and because we need a training ground for more ambitious planetary expeditions**.

As the lengthy example on page 171 from Jack Kerouac demonstrates, you can combine different kinds of modifiers to extend a sentence considerably.

> The Kennedys had a spark and Jack Kennedy had grown into a handsome man, **a male swan rising out of the Billy the Kid version of an Irish duckling he had been when he was a young senator**.
>
> —STANLEY CROUCH, "Blues for Jackie"

EXERCISE 15.28 Combine the following short sentences into one longer cumulative sentence.

EXAMPLE   Virginia adopted the dog. It was a friendly pup with skinny legs. It had a silly grin.

COMBINED   Virginia adopted the dog, a friendly pup with skinny legs and a silly grin.

1. Caesar was my friend. He had been faithful to me. He had been just to me.

2. Dr. Kalinowski recommended that her patient take up racquetball. It would ease his nerves. It would quicken his reflexes. It would tone his muscles. The muscles had grown flaccid from years of easy living.

3. The members of the jury filed into the courtroom. The members of the jury looked sullen and unhappy. They looked as if they'd eaten cactus for lunch.

4. The reviewer thought the book was a disappointment. It did not summarize the current state of knowledge. It did not advance research in the field.

H◉w Do You Write Stylish Sentences?

16

Just as there's more to cooking than wholesome meals, there's more to writing than competent sentences. As you revise, compose sentences that are varied, rhythmic, rich in detail, even memorable. This chapter focuses on various ways to give your sentences *style*.

16a What are agent/action sentences?

In agent/action sentences, clear subjects (agents) perform strong actions.

agent/action
The **pilot** *ejected*.

agent/action
My **grandmother** *makes* hand-sewn quilts.

Agent/action sentences are highly readable because they answer these important questions.

- What's happening?
- Who's doing it (and to what or to whom)?

1 When possible, make persons or things the subjects of your sentences and clauses. Readers take more interest if people are involved. And they usually are—most issues touch on human lives, one way or another. Start sentences with references to people.

WITHOUT PEOPLE	Although the federally funded student loan program has made education accessible to a low-income population, the increasing default rate among that population has had a significant effect on the program.
WITH PEOPLE	Hundreds of thousands of **young people** have been able to go to college because of federally funded student loans, but **students** who have defaulted on their loans may be jeopardizing the program for **others**.

EXERCISE 16.1 Recast these sentences in agent/action patterns that show more clearly who is doing what to whom. Break the sentences into shorter ones if you like.

1. Raising $3 million to renovate the drama facilities on campus was the goal of Lincoln Brown, the new college president.

2. The experience of playing Horatio in a college production of *Hamlet* had been influential in convincing President Brown of the value of the performing arts.

3. Helping President Brown to convince wealthy donors that restoring and expanding the old theater was a good idea was a small group of actors, all of them alumni of the school.

2 Don't overload the subjects of sentences. Readers will get lost if you bury subjects under abstract words and phrases. When revising, you may have to recover the central idea of a particularly difficult or murky sentence. Ask yourself, "What is its key word or concept?" Make that key word the subject.

OVERLOADED
SUBJECT

The encouragement of total reliance on the federally sponsored student loan program for medical students from low-income families to pay their way through school causes many young doctors to begin their careers deeply in debt.

REVISED

Many young doctors from low-income families begin their careers deeply in debt because they have relied totally on federal student loans to pay their way through medical school.

EXERCISE 16.2   Rewrite the following sentences to simplify their overcrowded openings.

1. Among those who are unhappy about the lack of morality and standards in the television shows coming from Hollywood today and who would like to see pressure on producers for more responsible programming are activists from remarkably different political groups.

2. The elimination of hurtful gender, racial, and ethnic stereotypes, particularly from situation comedies, where they are sometimes a key element of the humor, is a key demand of political groups on the left.

3. TV's almost complete disregard of the role religion plays in the daily lives of most ordinary people, evident in the fact that so few sitcom characters ever go to church or pray, irritates groups on the political right.

3 Make sure verbs convey real actions. Strung-out verb phrases such as *give consideration to* and *make acknowledgement of* slow your writing. Get rid of them. Focus on the action. Ask, "What's happening?" and try to express that action in a single lively verb. Identifying the action will help you spot the real agent in a sentence.

DULL VERB	American society **has** long **had** a fascination with celebrities.
STRONGER VERB	Celebrities **have** long **fascinated** Americans.

EXERCISE 16.3　Rewrite the following sentences to pinpoint their centers of action and to make their verbs stronger.

1. The fears of many prospective students over age 30 are understandable to college counselors.

2. Many such students are apprehensive about seeing textbooks, syllabi, and assignments for the first time in a decade or more.

3. In many schools, counselors have proceeded to establish special groups or programs for older students so that their feelings of dislocation and discomfort will be relieved.

4 Make sure subjects can do what their verbs demand.　Verbs describe actions that subjects perform: *butter melts; scholars read.* In most cases, you know when you've written nonsense: *butter reads; scholars melt.* But as sentences grow longer, you can sometimes lose the logical connection between subjects and predicates, a problem described as **faulty predication**.

FAULTY PREDICATION	The narrative **structure** of Aretha Franklin's song **begins** as a child and continues through her adult life.

Can *narrative structures begin as children?* Unlikely. The writer is probably thinking either of a character in the song or of Aretha Franklin, the singer. The sentence has to be revised.

REVISED	In Aretha Franklin's song, the narrative **structure follows** the life of a character from childhood to adulthood.

Notice how heavily the sentence had to be revised to make it work. Just swapping one verb for another often won't solve the problem.

EXERCISE 16.4　Revise any of the following sentences in which the subject cannot logically perform the action described by the verb. Try to explain what is wrong with the original verb choices, which are boldfaced.

1. Hundreds of miles from any city or large airport, Big Bend National Park in Texas **endeavors** an experience of pristine isolation unlike that of busier parks such as Yellowstone.

2. The park **comprehends** mountain, desert, and riparian environments.

3. While coyotes, road runners, and javelinas are common, a few lucky visitors also **apprehend** mountain lions and bears.

5 Replace *to be* verbs when possible. Though the verbs *is* and *are*, and their variants are often unavoidable, they're not as interesting as verbs that do things.

DULL VERBS	It **is** the tendency of adolescents **to be more concerned** about the opinion of others in their age group than they **are** about the values parents **are** trying to instill in them.
ACTION VERBS	Adolescents **crave** the approval of their peers and often **resist** their parents' values.

EXERCISE 16.5 Replace the *to be* forms in these sentences with active and more lively verbs. The original verbs are boldfaced. (It may help if you make the agent a person or a concrete object.)

1. There **was** an inclination to protest among restaurateurs when the city decided to increase the number of health inspectors.

2. It **had been** the determination of city officials, however, that many restaurants **were** not in a state of compliance with local health ordinances.

3. The occurrence of rodent droppings in pantries and the storage of meat at incorrect temperatures **were** also matters of concern to several TV reporters.

6 Reduce the number of passive verbs. Passive verb constructions (see Section 18e) often make sentences harder to read. It's easy to spot a sentence with a passive verb: the subject doesn't perform the action; the action is *done* to the subject. In effect, the object switches to the subject position, as in the following sentences.

subj.   action
Madison **was selected** by Representative Barton for an appointment to the Air Force Academy.

subj.   action
The candidate **had been nominated** for the academic honor by several teachers.

To identify a passive verb form, look for *both* the past participle and a form of *be*. (See Section 18a for an explanation of past participle.)

> The projects **had been supported** by previous Congresses when they **had been proposed** by other presidents.

When you have identified a passive form, locate the word that actually performs the action in the sentence and make it the subject.

> Previous Congresses had supported the projects when other presidents had proposed them.

But not every passive verb can or should be made active. Sometimes you don't know who or what performs an action.

> Hazardous road conditions **have been predicted**.
> Our flight **has been canceled**.

EXERCISE 16.6 Identify the passive verbs in the following sentences and then rewrite those that might be improved by changing passive verbs to active verbs.

1. The writing of research papers is traditionally dreaded by students everywhere.

2. The negative attitudes can be changed by writers themselves if the assignments are regarded by them as opportunities to explore and improve their communities.

3. When conventional topics are chosen by researchers, apathy is likely to be experienced by them and their readers alike.

16b How can you achieve clarity?

When something is well written, the reader can move along steadily without backtracking to puzzle over the meaning. You can work toward this goal by using a number of strategies.

1 Use specific details. Writing that uses a lot of abstract language is often harder to understand and less pleasurable to read than writing that states ideas more specifically. Abstract terms such as *healthcare provider system, positive learning environment*, and *two-wheeled vehicle* are usually harder to grasp than such concrete terms as *hospital, classroom*, and *Harley*. The more you use specific details, the clearer your sentences will be.

An especially effective way to add texture to sentences is to *downshift*—that is, to state a general idea and then provide more and more details. The resulting sentences will be clear and interesting. Downshifting is the principle behind many cumulative sentences (see Section 15j).

2 State ideas positively. Negative statements can be surprisingly hard to read. When you can, turn negative statements into positive ones.

> DIFFICULT   Do we have the right **not to be victims** of street crime?
>
> CLEARER   Do we have the right **to be safe** from street crime?

EXERCISE 16.7 Revise the following sentences to restate negative ideas more positively or clearly where such a change makes for a better sentence. Not all sentences may need revision.

1. It would not be awful if you never turn in a paper late.

2. The remark wasn't exactly the kind I would not ever repeat to my mother.

3. Would it ever not be inappropriate not to say "Hello" to an ex-spouse?

4. What do I think of your new leopard-skin pillbox hat? Why, it's not unattractive.

3 "Chunk" your writing. Consider breaking lengthy sentences into more manageable pieces or creating a list to present unusually complex information. Most readers like to see information broken into digestible chunks.

TOO LONG

Citing an instance in which a 16-year-old student was working 48 hours a week at Burger King in order to pay for a new car and simultaneously trying to attend high school full time, New York educators have recently proposed legislation that prohibits high school students from working more than 3 hours on a school night, limits the total time they can work in a week to 17 hours when school is in session, and fines employers who violate these regulations as much as $2,000.

REVISED

Educators in New York have recently proposed legislation that prohibits high school students from working more than 3 hours on a school night. In support of the proposal, they cite the example of a 16-year-old student working 48 hours a week at Burger King in order to pay for a new car while simultaneously trying to attend high school full time. The proposed law would limit the total time students can work in a week to 17 hours when school is in session and would fine employers who violate these regulations as much as $2,000.

Another efficient way to cut very specific or technical information to manageable size is to create a list. Lists give readers a sense of order and direction.

EXERCISE 16.8 Make the following sentence more readable by breaking it into manageable chunks.

> Parents are often ambivalent about having their high school–aged children work because almost inevitably it causes a conflict between the demands of schoolwork and extracurricular activities (such as sports, civic clubs, debate teams, band) and the expectations of employers, a balance many high schoolers are simply not mature enough to handle on their own, often choosing the immediate material goods furnished by a job over the less obvious benefits afforded by a good education.

4 Use charts and graphs to present quantitative information. Readers grasp numbers and statistics much more quickly when they see them presented visually. See Chapter 10 for advice on incorporating charts and graphs into your writing.

16c How can you write more economically?

For those who aspire to be good writers, the war against "clutter" never ends. Clutter consists of clichés, strung-out phrases, pointless repetitions, and overstuffed descriptions. Wait, however, until you have a first draft before you start trimming your prose. Many writers overstuff a first draft because they want to get all their ideas down. That's fine: it *is* easier to cut material than to create more.

1 Condense sprawling phrases. Some long-winded expressions slow a reader's way into a sentence, especially at the beginning.

WHY WRITE . . .	WHEN YOU COULD WRITE . . .
in the event that	if
in light of the fact that	since
on the grounds that	because
regardless of the fact that	although
on the occasion of	when
at this point in time	now
it is obvious that	obviously
on an everyday basis	routinely
with regard/respect to	for

We are so accustomed to these familiar but wordy expressions that we don't notice how little they convey.

EXERCISE 16.9 Revise the following sentences to eliminate the sprawling, wordy, or clichéd opening phrase.

1. On the occasion of the newspaper's seventy-fifth anniversary, the governor visited the editorial offices.

2. Regardless of the fact that I have revised the speech three times, I still don't like my conclusion.

3. In the modern American society in which we live today, many people still attend church regularly.

2 Cut nominalizations. **Nominalizations** are nouns made by adding endings to verbs and adjectives. The resulting words tend to be long and abstract.

WORD	NOMINALIZATION
connect	connect**ivity**
customize	customiz**ation**
knowledge	knowledge**ableness**
prioritize	prioritiz**ation**
victimize	victimiz**ation**

Here's a parody of a "bureaucratic" style.

> The **utilization** of appropriate **documentation** will achieve a **maximization** of **accountability**, assuring a **prioritization** and ultimate **finalization** of our budgetary requisitions.

Writing larded with nominalizations gives simple thoughts the appearance of complexity. Avoid such sludge.

EXERCISE 16.10 Revise the following sentences to reduce nominalizations that make the prose wordy.

1. The registrar's note is a clarification of the school's admissions policy.

2. It is a matter of substantial disputation among sociologists whether the gentrification of urban neighborhoods is a beneficial process to inner-city residents.

3. The utilization of creative writing in more and more elementary reading classes is an indication that many teachers are feeling dissatisfaction with more rigid approaches to language instruction.

3 Condense long verb phrases to focus on the action.

To show tense and mood, verb phrases need auxiliaries and helping verbs: I *could have* gone; she *will be* writing. But many verb phrases are strung out by unnecessary clutter. Such expressions sap the energy from sentences.

WHY WRITE . . .	WHEN YOU COULD WRITE . . .
give consideration to	consider
make acknowledgment of	acknowledge
have doubts about	doubt
is reflective of	reflects
has an understanding of	understands
put the emphasis on	emphasize

Similarly, don't clutter active verbs with expressions such as *start to, manage to,* and *proceed to.*

EXERCISE 16.11 Revise the following sentences to condense long verb phrases into more active expressions.

1. Many people are of the opinion that the federal government has grown too large.

2. An almost equal number of people hold the conviction that many citizens have need of services provided by federal programs.

3. This difference in public opinion is indicative of the dilemma faced by many politicians today.

4 Eliminate doublings and redundancies.

Doublings are expressions in which two words say exactly the same thing. One word can usually be cut.

trim ~~and slim~~	~~proper and~~ fitting
ready ~~and able~~	willing ~~and eager~~

Redundancies are expressions in which a concept is repeated unnecessarily. A redundancy compels a reader to encounter the same idea twice.

Our entire society has been corrupted by ~~the evil of~~ commercialism.

Mother's holiday feast on the table was surrounded by our family ~~sitting around it~~.

One might argue, in some cases, that doublings subtly expand the intended meaning. But they usually don't.

Thanksgiving fosters a sense of belonging ~~and togetherness~~.

I am of two worlds, which are forever at odds ~~with each other~~.

Many habitual expressions are in fact redundant.

WHY WRITE . . .	WHEN YOU COULD WRITE . . .
trading activity was heavy	trading was heavy
of a confidential nature	confidential
her area of specialization	her specialty
blue in color	blue

Avoid the repetition of major words in a sentence—unless you have good reasons to emphasize particular terms.

EXERCISE 16.12 Rewrite the following sentences to reduce redundancy and wordiness.

1. I realized that if I were ever to reach law school, I would have to increase my competitiveness in the skill of written prose composition.

2. *Ellen* to me is a daytime talk type of television show.

3. Many traits characterize a truly excellent student adviser, and one of the more important qualities, if not the most important quality of an adviser, is a lively personality.

5 Eliminate surplus intensifiers. An adverb that functions as an **intensifier** should add weight or power to an expression. You waste its energy when you use it carelessly.

WHY WRITE . . .	WHEN YOU COULD WRITE . . .
We're **completely** finished.	We're finished.
It's a **terrible** tragedy.	It's a tragedy.
I'm **totally** exhausted.	I'm exhausted.
That's **absolutely** pointless.	That's pointless.
The work is **basically** done.	The work is done.

EXERCISE 16.13 Review the intensifiers in the following passage and cut any words or phrases you regard as unnecessary.

The Grand Canyon is a quite unique geological treasure in northwestern Arizona, basically formed by the relentless power of the Colorado River cutting a gorge for many, many eons through solid rock. Standing at the edge of the canyon is a totally awesome experience. The canyon walls drop far into the depths, thousands of feet, a seriously deep drop, exposing very different layers of limestone, sandstone, and volcanic rock. These really magnificent canyons recede into the distance like ancient castles, an absolutely remarkable panorama of color and shadow.

6 Cut down on expletive constructions.

Expletives are short expressions such as *it was, there are*, and *this is* that function like starting blocks for pushing into a sentence or clause. For example:

It was a dark and stormy night.

There were five of us huddled in the basement.

There are too many gopher holes on this golf course!

It is a proud day for Bluefield State College.

Although some expletives are unavoidable, using them habitually to open your sentences will make your prose tiresome.

WHY WRITE . . .	WHEN YOU COULD WRITE . . .
There is a desire for	We want
There are reasons for	For several reasons
There was an expectation	They expected
It is clear that	Clearly
It is to be hoped	We hope

EXERCISE 16.14 Revise the following sentences to eliminate unnecessary expletive constructions.

1. There are many different ways to fulfill the science requirement at most colleges.

2. It is usually the case that liberal arts majors benefit from science courses that are geared to the history of the field.

3. Taking a course in the hard sciences is a challenge, and it should be taken seriously.

7 Cut the number of prepositional phrases.

Stylistically, prepositional phrases are capable of dignity and grandeur, thanks to their clarity and simplicity.

In the beginning, God created heaven and earth.

. . . and that government **of the people, by the people, for the people**, shall not perish from the earth.

But that very simplicity can grow tedious if you pack too many prepositional phrases of similar length and tempo into one sentence.

TOO MANY PREPOSITIONS	**In** late summer **on** the road **from** our town **into** the country, we expected to find raspberries **in** the fields **near** the highway **by** the recent construction.
REVISED	We expected to find late summer raspberries **on** the country road, **near** the recent construction.

Avoid strings of prepositional phrases that congeal around abstract nouns, making sentences thick and hard to read. In the example, the abstract nouns are boldfaced and prepositional phrases are underlined.

WORDY   The current **proliferation** of credit cards among college students is the result of extensive **marketing** by banking **institutions** who see college students in terms of their future **affluence**.

Revise a cluttered sentence by looking for the center of action: *who* is doing *what* to *whom*?

REVISED   Banks today are marketing credit cards to college students because they see them as affluent future customers.

For more on prepositional phrases, see Section 15c-1.

EXERCISE 16.15 Revise the following sentences to reduce the number of prepositional phrases where they make the sentences awkward or monotonous. Some sentences may require extensive revision.

1. J.R.R. Tolkein was the author of one of the most popular series of fantasy novels about the battle between good and evil forces in the distant past of the fictional world of Middle Earth.

2. Tolkein's series *The Lord of the Rings* focuses on the adventures of a genial hobbit by the name of Frodo Baggins and his sidekick by the name of Sam who, along with Frodo, becomes involved in the race to destroy a ring of magical but evil power.

3. The novels cover a long period of time, focusing on the colossal struggle for the magical ring and for the future of Middle Earth that goes on between Frodo and his allies and the forces of Sauron, the leader of the forces of evil.

8 Cut relative pronouns (*that, which, who, whom*) when you can do it without changing the meaning of a sentence. Relative pronouns introduce many modifying clauses (see Section 15d-2). You can often cut them for economy.

WORDY   The book **that I had quoted** was missing.

REVISED   The book **I had quoted** was missing.

You may also want to cut them to avoid having to recall the appropriate pronoun: *who* or *whom; which* or *that*?

Millie Liam is a woman (**who? whom?**) everyone likes.

The Cord is an automobile (**which? that?**) collectors cherish.

Cutting the pronoun solves the problem elegantly.

Millie Liam is a woman everyone likes.

The Cord is an automobile collectors cherish.

EXERCISE 16.16 Rewrite these sentences to practice eliminating relative pronouns (*who, whom, that, which*) that might be contributing to wordiness. Retain any such pronouns you regard as necessary for clarity.

1. Some of the people who might be willing to endure a little less environmental consciousness are parents of children whom environmentalists have turned into Green Police.

2. Third graders who used to read Harry Potter novels suddenly can't wait to locate "Tips to Save Our Planet" in the daily newspaper, which carries dozens of slick, unrecyclable inserts.

3. Shrewd are the parents who steer their children's activist impulses in productive directions by asking them to read supermarket labels and find items that are marked "Recyclable."

9 Condense sentences into clauses, and clauses into phrases or words. Often one forceful word can do the work of several. Say more with less.

ORIGINAL   Queen Elizabeth I was a complex and sensuous woman. She seemed to love many men, yet she never came close to marrying any of her suitors.

CONDENSED   Complex and sensuous, Queen Elizabeth I seemed to love men, yet she never came close to marrying.

EXERCISE 16.17 Rewrite the following sentences to reduce clutter by substituting single words for wordy phrases. Rearrange the sentences as necessary.

1. In the event that you are in proximity to Greene County this weekend, you should not miss the opportunity to visit the autumn Concours d'Elegance, an annual exhibit of classic cars.

2. There is the possibility that you may have the chance to touch and feel many quite unusual and different vehicles, from dowdy Edsels with gearshift buttons in the middle of their steering wheels to tiny Corvairs with air-cooled engines under louvered deck lids at the back.

3. However, don't expect to make an inspection of the more unique makes and the basically timeless art of such prestigious automakers as Bugatti, Duesenberg, or Hispano-Suiza.

16d   How can you achieve sentence variety?

Your readers will quickly be bored if all your sentences are of the same type and pattern. Write sentences that move easily and maturely, conveying readers from point to point with appropriate clarity and emphasis. You can't do this without offering variety.

1 Vary sentence types. The familiar sentence types discussed in Section 15e offer you a range of possibilities. Simple sentences attract the attention with economy and punch. Compound sentences put ideas of equal weight side by side. Complex sentences give you a means to state ideas subtly and richly. Varying these sentence types will keep your readers engaged.

2 Vary sentence patterns. The five standard sentence patterns in English (see Section 15a) are reliable but dull when repeated.
     Variations add style. Consider inverting the usual word order.

Gone is the opportunity to win this month's lottery.

Intelligent, cultured, and politically shrewd was Eleanor of Aquitaine, a twelfth-century liberated woman.

Or play with the way a sentence opens.

ORIGINAL	The punk-rock protest songs of the early 1980s were the musicians' way of expressing their criticism of the political establishment.
VARIATION 1	To express their criticism of the political establishment, punk-rock musicians of the early 1980s wrote protest songs.
VARIATION 2	In the early 1980s, punk-rock musicians wrote protest songs as a way of expressing their criticism of the political establishment.

The variations are not necessarily better than the original. They're just different, and they demonstrate the options you have in crafting sentences.
     Still another way to vary the shape of sentences is to put interesting details into modifying clauses or phrases at different points in a sentence.

AT THE BEGINNING	**Convinced that he could not master rhetoric until he knew Greek**, Thomas began studying the language when he was 40.

IN THE MIDDLE	Li Po, **one of the greatest of the Chinese poets**, drowned when he fell out of a boat while trying to kiss the reflection of the moon in the water.
AT THE END	Sixteenth-century Aztec youths played a complex game called *ollamalitzli*, **which some anthropologists believe to have been the forerunner of modern basketball**.

EXERCISE 16.18 The following sentences all begin approximately in the same way. Rewrite them to vary the pattern. Treat the four sentences as a single paragraph; you may not need to change all the sentences.

EXAMPLE	Directors and producers have adapted Shakespeare's plays to contemporary tastes in every age and era.
REVISED	In every age and era, directors and producers have adapted Shakespeare's plays to contemporary tastes.

1. Directors and producers have learned to move Shakespeare from the stage to the screen in the twentieth century.

2. Filmmakers first had to adapt dramas to fit the new medium of film; early Shakespeare movies from the silent era looked much like stage plays presented before a camera.

3. Directors quickly realized that actors on the big screen had to restrain their traditional facial expressions and exaggerated stage gestures.

4. Directors and producers have since produced many Shakespeare films that adapt the dress, music, style, and attitudes of particular decades.

3 Vary sentence length. Readers like a balance between long and short sentences. If you've produced a cluster of short sentences, your writing may seem choppy. If you write only medium-length sentences, your prose may seem monotonous. Give readers a break; vary the rhythm of your prose.

Short sentences catch the attention of readers. They work well to underscore key points. Mixed with longer sentences, they can mark a writer as direct and confident, able to make a bold claim or a clear statement.

EXERCISE 16.19 The sentences in the following paragraph are monotonously brief. Combine some of these short sentences and edit as necessary to produce a more readable passage. Compare your version to others written by classmates.

The National Air and Space Museum is in Washington, D.C. The Air and Space Museum is one of the capital's most popular attractions. It presents the artifacts of aviation history. It presents these artifacts in a creative manner. The museum houses a replica of the Wright brothers' first plane. Lindbergh's plane hangs from the ceiling. The plane carried him across the Atlantic to Paris in 1927. It was a solo flight. Also in the museum are planes from World War II and a full-size lunar landing module. Every manner of flying machine is represented in the museum. There are fighter planes, passenger planes, and space capsules. There are helicopters and balloons. There is even a remarkable movie projected onto a large screen. The screen towers six stories.

Grammar Punctuation and Mechanics

part 5

GRAMMAR

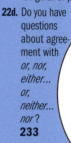

part

5

Grammar

Do You Have Questions bout Subject-Verb Agreement?

17

When subjects and verbs don't agree, careful readers notice. Proofread to be sure you've put singular verb forms with singular subjects and plural verb forms with plural subjects.

17a Agreement: Is the subject singular or plural?

A verb may change its form, depending on whether its subject is singular or plural. The verb is then said to *agree in number* with its subject.

1 Understand how subject-verb agreement works. With verbs in the present tense, agreement in number is simple: most subjects take the base form of the verb. The base form is the word produced when *to* is placed before the verb: to *wait*; to *go*.

First person, singular, present tense:	I predict. I go.
Second person, singular, present tense:	You predict. You go.
First person, plural, present tense:	We predict. We go.
Second person, plural, present tense:	You predict. You go.
Third person, plural, present tense:	They predict. They go.

Subjects and verbs usually agree more readily than politicians.

The notable exception to this pattern occurs with third person singular subjects (for example, *he, she, it, Irene*). A regular verb in the present tense needs an *-s* or *-es* ending.

Third person, singular, present tense: She predicts.
                                          Irene predicts.
                                          He goes.

So to choose a correct verb form in the third person (present tense), you must know whether the subject of a sentence is singular or plural.

sing. subj.
The Weather Channel **predicts** storms today.

plural subj.
Meteorologists **predict** storms today.

sing. subj.
He **goes** to Oklahoma City today.

plural subj.
The teachers **go** to Oklahoma City today.

Agreement is also required with irregular verbs such as *to be* and *to have* in a variety of tenses. (See Section 18d.)

SINGULAR SUBJECTS

The weather forecast **is** clear for today.

The weather forecast **was** clear for today.

The weather forecast **has been** accurate for some time.

PLURAL SUBJECTS

The weather forecasts **are** clear for today.

The weather forecasts **were** clear for today.

The weather forecasts **have been** accurate for some time.

EXERCISE 17.1 Decide which verb in boldface is correct.

1. The most violent of all storms, tornadoes (**occur/occurs**) more often in the United States than in any other country.

2. The rotational winds sometimes (**exceed/exceeds**) 500 miles per hour in the vortex of a tornado.

3. Dust devils (**is/are**) less ferocious vortices of warm air.

4. Rising heat currents (**cause/causes**) dust devils.

2 In most cases, treat subjects joined by *and* as plural. Joining two subjects this way creates a *compound subject* that takes a verb without an *-s* or *-es* ending (in third person, present).

> 1st subj. + 2nd subj.   verb
> *Storm chasers and journalists* alike **want** great videos of destructive storms.

However, a few subjects joined by *and* describe a single thing or idea. Treat such expressions as singular.

> subj.   verb
> *Rock and roll* **is** as noisy as a thunderclap.

Similarly, when a compound subject linked by *and* is modified by *every* or *each*, the verb takes a singular form.

> subj. + subj.   verb
> *Every wall cloud and supercell* **holds** the potential for a tornado.

> subj. + subj.   verb
> *Each spring and each fall* **brings** the threat of more storms.

However, when *each* follows a compound subject, usage varies.

> *The meteorologist and the storm chaser* each **have** their reasons for studying the weather.

> *The meteorologist and the storm chaser* each **has** his or her story to tell.

3 Understand that subjects joined to other nouns by expressions such as *along with, as well as,* or *together with* are not considered compound. So the verb agrees only with the subject, which may be either singular or plural.

> sing. subj.   plural noun
> *The National Weather Service*, as well as many *police officers*,
> verb
> **wishes** amateurs wouldn't chase severe storms in their cars.

> plural subj.   sing. noun   verb
> Many *amateurs*, along with the *press*, **chase** storms in the American heartland.

When subjects linked to the expressions *as well as, along with,* or *together with* sound awkward with a singular verb, join the subjects with *and* instead.

> **SLIGHTLY**   *The National Weather Service*, as well as *local*
> **AWKWARD**   *storm chasers*, **considers** tornadoes unlikely today.

> **BETTER**   *The National Weather Service and local storm chasers*
>   **consider** tornadoes unlikely today.

4 When subjects are joined by *or, neither . . . nor*, or *either . . . or*, be sure the verb (or its auxiliary) agrees with the subject closer to it. In these examples the arrows point to the subjects nearer the verbs.

> plural   sing.
> *Neither police officers nor the National Weather Service* **is** able to prevent people from tracking dangerous storms.

> sing.   plural
> *Either severe lightning or powerful bouts of hail* **mark** the development of a supercell.

> sing.   plural
> **Does** *the danger or the thrills of chasing storms* attract people to the "sport"?

> plural   sing.
> **Do** *the thrills of chasing storms or the danger* attract people to the "sport"?

The rule holds when one or both of the subjects joined by *or, either . . . or*, or *neither . . . nor* are pronouns: the verb agrees with the nearer subject.

> Neither *she* nor *we* admit to fear of thunder.
> Neither *we* nor *she* admits to fear of thunder.

5 When the subject of a sentence is a phrase or a clause, examine the subject closely. Many such constructions will be singular, though they may seem plural.

SINGULAR SUBJECT

That George survived the storms that tore through three Oklahoma counties **is** remarkable.

However, phrases and clauses can form compound subjects, requiring appropriate verb forms.

COMPOUND SUBJECT

That the skies are darkening and that the wind is rising **concern** us.

EXERCISE 17.2 Decide which verb in boldface is correct.

1. Storms of all types (**continue/continues**) to intrigue people.

2. The storm chaser, like other thrill seekers, (**learn/learns**) to minimize the dangers of the hunt.

3. It's unlikely that either the dangers or the boredom of storm chasing (**is/are**) going to discourage the dedicated amateur.

4. The meteorologist and the storm chaser (**know/knows**) that neither ferocious tornadoes nor the less violent waterspout (**is/are**) predictable.

17b Agreement: Is the subject an indefinite pronoun?

Words such as *each, none, everybody, everyone,* and *any* are called **indefinite pronouns** because they do not refer to a particular person, thing, or group. Sometimes it's hard to tell whether an indefinite pronoun is singular or plural.

1 Determine whether an indefinite pronoun is singular, plural, or variable. Consult Chart 17.1 (or a dictionary) to find out. Then select an appropriate verb form.

(17.1) Indefinite Pronouns

SINGULAR	VARIABLE (SINGULAR OR PLURAL)	PLURAL
anybody	all	few
anyone	any	many
anything	either	several
each	more	
everybody	most	
everyone	neither	
everything	none	
nobody	some	
no one		
nothing		
somebody		
someone		
something		

SINGULAR	*Each* **believes** decisive action needs to be taken.
SINGULAR	*Nobody* **knows** what the baseball team will do.
VARIABLE	*None* of the proposals **is** easy to finance.
VARIABLE	*None* but the owners **favor** a big bond issue.
PLURAL	*Many* in sports bars **support** a new stadium.
PLURAL	*Few* **want** to pay higher ticket prices.

2 Be careful when indefinite pronouns are modified. If a pronoun is always singular, it remains singular even if it is modified by a phrase with a plural noun in it.

subj.   verb
Each of the whales **makes** unique sounds.

When the indefinite pronoun varies in number (words such as *all, most, none, some*), the noun in the prepositional phrase determines whether the pronoun (and consequently the verb) is singular or plural.

NOUN IN PREPOSITIONAL PHRASE IS SINGULAR

Some of the research **is** contradictory.

NOUN IN PREPOSITIONAL PHRASE IS PLURAL

Some of the younger whales **are** playful.

EXERCISE 17.3 Decide which verb in boldface would be correct in academic writing.

1. Most of New York's immigrants (**is/are**) now non-European.

2. Everybody (**seem/seems**) to have something to contribute.

3. Nobody in the city (**run/runs**) politics anymore.

4. Everybody (**expect/expects**) a piece of the pie.

5. None of the candidates (**is/are**) qualified.

17c Agreement: Is the subject a collective noun?

Nouns that name a group are called **collective**: *team, choir, band, orchestra, jury, committee, faculty, family*. Some collective nouns may be either singular or plural, depending on how you regard them. Here is a sentence with the subject (the collective noun *family*) treated as singular.

The *Begay family* **expects** that *its* restaurant will benefit from a recent increase in Arizona tourism.

Here's the same sentence with the subject taken as plural.

The *Begay family* **expect** that *their* restaurant will benefit from a recent increase in Arizona tourism.

Both versions are acceptable.

To be sure verbs and collective nouns agree, decide whether a collective noun used as a subject acts as a single unit (the *jury*) or as separate individuals or parts (the twelve members of the *jury*).

SINGULAR   The *jury* **expects** its verdict to be controversial.

PLURAL   The *jury* **agree** not to discuss their verdict with the press.

Usually your writing will be smoother if you treat collective nouns as singular subjects.

Chart 17.2 should help you manage collective subjects.

EXERCISE 17.4 Decide whether the collective subjects in the following sentences are being treated as singular or plural. Then select the appropriate verb form for academic writing.

1. Lieutenant Data (**reports/report**) to Captain Picard that the data on Klingon encroachments of the neutral zone (**is/are**) not subject to interpretation.

2. The crew of the Federation starship (**is/are**) eager to resolve the conflict.

3. Five years (**has/have**) passed since the last intergalactic crisis.

4. A number of weapons still (**needs/need**) to be brought on line, but the chief engineer reports that the actual number of inoperative systems (**is/are**) small.

(17.2) Collective Nouns

chart

SUBJECT	GUIDELINE	EXAMPLES
Measurements	Singular as a unit; plural as individual components.	*Five miles* is quite a long walk. *Five more miles* are ahead of us. *Six months* is the waiting period. *Six months* have passed.
Numbers	Singular in expressions of division and subtraction. Singular or plural in expressions of multiplication and addition.	*Four* divided by *two* is two. *Four* minus *two* leaves two. *Two* times *two* is/are four. *Two* plus *two* is/are four.

SUBJECT	GUIDELINE	EXAMPLES
Words ending in *-ics*	School subjects are usually singular.	*Physics* is a tough major. *Economics* is a useful minor. *Linguistics* is popular.
	Other *-ics* words vary; check a dictionary.	His *tactics* are shrewd. *Athletics* are expensive. *Ethics* is a noble study. Her *ethics* are questionable. *Politics* is fun. Francie's *politics* are radical.
data	Plural in formal writing; often singular in informal writing.	The *data* are reliable. The *data* is reliable.
number	Singular if preceded by *the;* plural if preceded by *a.*	The *number* has grown. A *number* have left.
public	Singular as a unit; plural as individual people.	The *public* is satisfied. The *public* are here in great numbers.

17d Agreement: Is the subject separated from its verb?

A verb agrees with its subject only, not with any nouns in modifying phrases or clauses that come between the subject and verb. Identify the subject; then choose the appropriate verb form.

> sing. subj.   plural noun   verb
> The *power* of Midwestern *tornadoes* often **proves** deadly.

The principle is the same for plural subjects modified by phrases or clauses with singular nouns. The subject remains plural.

> plural subj.   sing. noun verb
> *Storms* that come late in the *spring* **are** sometimes unusually violent.

Be especially careful with lengthy or complicated modifiers.

> subj.   modifying phrase
> The *killer whale*, <u>the most widely distributed of all mammals,</u>
>
> verb
> <u>excepting only humans,</u> **demonstrates** highly complex social
> behavior.

EXERCISE 17.5 Choose the correct verb for academic writing.

1. As the twenty-first century begins, most politicians, regardless of their party or ideology, (**embrace/embraces**) the idea that every child should be able to read by the end of third grade.

2. Almost everyone (**agree/agrees**) with this laudable goal, but trained educators who understand the complex process of learning to read are suspicious of this bandwagon approach.

3. Children's ability to learn how to read (**depend/depends**) on a combination of psychological, physical, and social factors.

4. Moreover, many children from families in low-income neighborhoods, all too common in major cities today, (**need/needs**) intensive tutoring because they are not ready to learn when they arrive in kindergarten.

 Agreement: Is the subject hard to identify?

Occasionally you may simply lose track of a subject because the structure of a sentence is complicated or unusual. Just remember the rule: Keep your eye on the subject.

1 Don't lose track of your subject when a sentence or clause begins with *here* or *there*. In such cases, the verb still agrees with the subject—which usually trails after it.

SINGULAR SUBJECTS

Here **is** a surprising *turn* of events.

There **is** a *reason* for the commotion.

PLURAL SUBJECTS

Here **are** my *tickets*.

There **are** already *calls* for the police chief's resignation.

2 Don't be misled by linking verbs. Common linking verbs are *to be, to seem, to appear, to feel, to taste, to look*, and *to become*. They connect subjects to words that extend or complete their meaning.

A linking verb agrees with its subject even when a singular subject is linked to a plural noun.

> subj.   l.v. plural noun
> Good *evidence* of the power of television **is** its *effects* on political careers.

> subj   l.v.   plural noun
> The *key* to a candidate's success **is** television *appearances*.

3 Don't be misled by inverted sentence order. A sentence is considered inverted when some portion of the verb precedes the subject.

> verb   subj. verb
> **Was** their *motive* **to get** revenge?

A verb agrees with its subject, wherever the subject appears in the sentence.

> verb   subj.
> Also disappointed **is** the *assistant chief*.

4 Don't mistake singular expressions for plural ones. Singular terms such as *series, segment, portion, fragment*, and *part* usually remain singular even when modified by plural words.

A *series* of questions **is** posed by a reporter.

The word *majority*, however, does not follow this guideline; it can be either singular or plural, depending on its use in a sentence.

The *majority* **rules.**

The *majority* of critics **want** Chief Carey's head on a platter.

EXERCISE 17.6 Choose the correct verb.

1. The mayor of the town (**strides/stride**) to the microphone.

2. Among grumbles from the reporters, the crowd (**take/takes**) their seats.

3. (**Does/Do**) the mayor's decision to fire Carey surprise anyone after the last election?

Do You Have Questions bout Verb Tense, Voice, and Mood?

18

18a How do you choose verb tenses?

Perhaps you first discovered the complexity of verb tenses when you tried to learn a foreign language. **Tense** is that quality of a verb that expresses time. Tense is expressed through changes in verb forms and verb endings (*see, saw, seeing; work, worked*) and through the use of auxiliaries—what you may know as *helping verbs* (*had* seen, *will have* seen; *had* worked, *had been* working).

1 Know the tenses and what they do. Tense depends, in part, on *voice*. Verbs that take direct objects—that is, transitive verbs—can be either in **active** or in **passive voice**. They are in active voice when the subject in the sentence actually does what the verb describes.

> subj.   action
> *Professor Gates* **invited** the press to the lecture.

They are in passive voice when the action described by the verb is done *to* the subject.

> subj.   action
> *The press* **was invited** by Professor Gates to the lecture.

Photographer Edward Muybridge (1830–1904) used stop-action photography to study the motion of people and animals: The horse will gallop; the horse gallops; the horse is galloping; the horse has galloped. For more Muybridge images, look for him at <http://www.masters-of-photography.com>.

Chart 18.1 shows English tenses—past, present, and future—in the *active voice*. (See also Section 18e on voice and the more complete Anatomy of a Verb on pp. 212–213.)

chart

(18.1) Verb Tenses in the Active Voice

WHAT IT IS CALLED	WHAT IT LOOKS LIKE	WHAT IT DOES
Past	**I answered** quickly.	Shows what happened at a particular time in the past.
Past progressive	**I was answering** when the alarm went off.	Shows something happening in the past at the same time something else happened in the past.
Present perfect	**I have answered** that question often.	Shows something that has happened one or more times in the past.
Past perfect	**I had answered** the question twice when the alarm went off.	Shows what had already happened before another event, also in a past tense, occurred.
Present	**I answer** when I must.	Shows what happens or can happen now.
Present progressive	**I am answering** now.	Shows what is happening now.
Future	**I will answer** tomorrow.	Shows what may happen in the future.
Future progressive	**I will be answering** the phones all day.	Shows something that will continue to happen in the future.
Future perfect	**I will have answered** all the charges before you see me again.	Shows what will have happened by some particular time in the future.
Future perfect progressive	**I will have been answering** the charges for three hours by the time you arrive at noon.	Shows a continuing future action that precedes some other event also in the future.

Verbs usually look more complicated when they are in the passive voice, as shown in Chart 18.2.

(18.2) **Verb Tenses in the Passive Voice**	
WHAT IT IS CALLED	WHAT IT LOOKS LIKE
Past	I **was invited** to her party last year.
Past progressive	I **was being invited** by Alicia when the phone went dead.
Present perfect	I **have been invited** to many of her parties.
Past perfect	I **had been invited** to this one too.
Present	I **am invited** to everyone's parties.
Present progressive	I **am being invited** now! That's Alicia calling, I'm sure.
Future	I **will be invited** tomorrow.
Future perfect	I **will have been invited** by this time tomorrow.

Many tenses require **auxiliary verbs** such as *will, do, be,* and *have*. These auxiliary or helping verbs combine with other verbs to show relationships of tense, voice, and mood.

Other auxiliary verbs, such as *can, could, may, might, should, ought,* and *must*, help to indicate possibility, necessity, permission, desire, capability, and so on. These verbs are called **modal auxiliaries**.

Rosalind **can** write well.

Audrey **might** write well.

Marco **should** write well.

2 Use the present tense appropriately. The present tense has several special roles. It may be used to introduce the words of authors you are quoting, whether living or dead.

Lincoln **defines** conservatism as "adherence to the old and tried, against the new and untried."

By convention, present tense introduces quotations when you are describing what happens in literary works.

Hester Prynne **wears** a scarlet letter.

The doctor in *Macbeth* **warns** a gentlewoman, "You know what you should not" (5.1.46–47).

Use present tense to make a general statement of fact or to express scientific truths.

Oak trees **lose** their leaves in winter.

Einstein **argues** that the principle of relativity **applies** to all physical phenomena.

Use present tense, too, to describe habitual action.

> We **get up** at five in the morning.
> People today **watch** television more than they **read**.

3 Use perfect tenses appropriately. Perfect tenses enable you to show exactly how one event stands in relationship to another in time. Learn to use these forms; they make a difference.

SIMPLE PAST	She already **quit** her job even before she knew that she **failed** the polygraph.
PAST PERFECT	She **had** already **quit** her job even before she knew that she **had failed** the polygraph.

EXERCISE 18.1 Replace the verb forms in parentheses with appropriate tenses. You may need to use a variety of verb forms (and auxiliaries), including passive and progressive forms. Treat all five sentences as part of a single paragraph. (Consult Chart 18.3 later in the chapter for help with some of the verb forms.)

1. Isambard Brunel (**design**) his ship the *Great Eastern* to be the largest vessel on the seas when it (**launch**) in 1857 in London.

2. Almost 700 feet long, the ship—originally named *Leviathan*—(**weigh**) more than 20,000 tons and (**power**) by a screw, paddle wheels, and sails.

3. Designed originally to be a luxurious passenger ship, the *Great Eastern* (**attain**) its greatest fame only after it (**refit**) to stretch the first transatlantic telegraph cable from England to Newfoundland.

4. In the summer of 1865, the *Great Eastern* (**lay**) cable for many difficult days when the thick line (**snap**) two-thirds of the way to Newfoundland. Nine days (**spend**) trying to recover the cable, but it never (**find**).

How do you choose verb tense in parallel constructions?

Parallelism is an arrangement that gives related words, clauses, and phrases a similar pattern, making it easier for readers to see relationships between the parallel expressions. When verbs that go with the same subject don't share the same verb tense and form, the result is *faulty parallelism*.

LACK OF PARALLELISM

subj.   verb   verb

The *lawyer* **explained** the options to her client and **was recommending** a plea of guilty.

REVISED FOR PARALLELISM

subj.   verb   verb

The *lawyer* **explained** the options to her client and **recommended** a plea of guilty.

Changes in verb tense within a sentence are appropriate when they indicate obvious shifts in time.

Currently, the lawyer **is defending** an accused murderer and soon **will be defending** a bigamist.

For more on parallelism, see Section 15h.

EXERCISE 18.2 Correct any problems with parallelism that the verbs in boldface are causing. Modify the tenses as needed to achieve parallelism.

1. In the middle of the nineteenth century, young French painters **were rejecting** the stilted traditions of academic art, **found** new methods and new subjects, and **would establish** the school of art one critic derided as "Impressionism."

2. The new artists **outraged** all the establishment critics and also **were challenging** all the expectations of Paris gallery owners.

3. Traditionalists thought that painters should **work** indoors, **depict** traditional subjects, and **be using** a balanced style that hid their brushwork.

4. But the youthful Impressionists, including artists like Monet, Degas, and Renoir, soon **were taking** their easels outdoors to the streets of Paris or to public gardens, **laying** on their colors thick and self-consciously, and **had been choosing** scenes from ordinary life to depict.

18c How do you ensure tense consistency in longer passages?

Avoid shifting from tense to tense in longer passages (for instance, from *past* to *present*) unless clarity and good sense require the switch. Choose a time frame and stick with it. The following paragraph shows what can happen when verb forms shift inappropriately.

At the dawn of the nuclear era in the 1950s, many horror movies **featured** monsters **spawned** by atomic explosions or bizarre scientific experiments. For two decades, audiences **flock** to movies with titles like *Godzilla, Them, Tarantula*, and *The Fly*. Theater screens **come** alive with gigantic lobsters, ants, birds, and lizards, which **spent** their time attacking London, Tokyo, and Washington while scientists **look** for ways to kill them.

Making the tenses consistent makes a passage more readable. Here it is in the past tense.

At the dawn of the nuclear era in the 1950s, many horror movies **featured** monsters **spawned** by atomic explosions or bizarre scientific experiments. For two decades, audiences **flocked** to movies with titles like *Godzilla, Them, Tarantula*, and *The Fly*. Theater screens **came** alive with gigantic lobsters, ants, birds, and lizards, which **spent** their time attacking London, Tokyo, and Washington while scientists **looked** for ways to kill them.

18d How do regular and irregular verbs differ?

All verb tenses are built from three basic forms, which are called the *principal parts of a verb*. The three principal parts of the verb are as follows:

- **Infinitive (or present):** This is the base form of a verb, what it looks like when preceded by the word *to: to walk; to go; to choose.*
- **Past:** This is the simplest form of a verb to show action that has already occurred: *walked; went; chose.*
- **Past participle:** This is the form a verb takes when it is accompanied by an auxiliary verb to show a more complicated past tense: *had* **walked**; *will have* **gone**; *would have* **chosen**; *was* **hanged**; *might have* **broken**.

Here are the three principal parts of some regular verbs.

PRESENT	PAST	PAST PARTICIPLE
talk	talked	talked
coincide	coincided	coincided
advertise	advertised	advertised

Regular verbs form their past and past participle forms simply by adding *-d* or *-ed* to the infinitive. **Irregular verbs**, however, change their forms in various ways; a few even have the same form for all three principal parts.

PRESENT	PAST	PAST PARTICIPLE
burst	burst	burst
drink	drank	drunk
arise	arose	arisen
lose	lost	lost

To be sure you're using the correct verb form, consult a dictionary or check Chart 18.3.

(18.3) Irregular Verbs

PRESENT	PAST	PAST PARTICIPLE
arise	arose	arisen
bear (carry)	bore	borne
bear (give birth)	bore	borne, born
become	became	become
begin	began	begun
bite	bit	bitten, bit
blow	blew	blown
break	broke	broken
bring	brought	brought
burst	burst	burst
buy	bought	bought
catch	caught	caught
choose	chose	chosen
cling	clung	clung
come	came	come
creep	crept	crept
dig	dug	dug
dive	dived, dove	dived
do	did	done
draw	drew	drawn
dream	dreamed, dreamt	dreamed, dreamt
drink	drank	drunk
drive	drove	driven
eat	ate	eaten
fall	fell	fallen
find	found	found
fly	flew	flown
forget	forgot	forgotten
forgive	forgave	forgiven
freeze	froze	frozen
get	got	got, gotten
give	gave	given
go	went	gone
grow	grew	grown
hang (an object)	hung	hung
hang (a person)	hanged, hung	hanged, hung
know	knew	known
lay (to place)	laid	laid
lead	led	led

chart

PRESENT	PAST	PAST PARTICIPLE
leave	left	left
lend	lent	lent
lie (to recline)	lay	lain
light	lit, lighted	lit, lighted
lose	lost	lost
pay	paid	paid
plead	pleaded, pled	pleaded, pled
prove	proved	proved, proven
ride	rode	ridden
ring	rang, rung	rung
rise	rose	risen
run	ran	run
say	said	said
see	saw	seen
set	set	set
shake	shook	shaken
shine	shone, shined	shone, shined
show	showed	shown, showed
shrink	shrank, shrunk	shrunk
sing	sang, sung	sung
sink	sank, sunk	sunk
sit	sat	sat
speak	spoke	spoken
spring	sprang, sprung	sprung
stand	stood	stood
steal	stole	stolen
sting	stung	stung
swear	swore	sworn
swim	swam	swum
swing	swung	swung
take	took	taken
tear	tore	torn
throw	threw	thrown
wake	woke, waked	woken, waked
wear	wore	worn
wring	wrung	wrung
write	wrote	written

EXERCISE 18.3 Choose the correct verb form from the choices in parentheses. In some cases, you may want to consult Chart 18.3 or the glossary for assistance.

1. Alicia wondered whether the mayor had (**spoke/spoken**) too soon in welcoming everyone to participate in the town meeting.

2. The residents of Oakhill had not (**shown/shone**) much interest in the environmental issue until this meeting.

3. Now the Oakhill representative pulled a petition out of her purse and (**sat/set**) it before the mayor.

4. She claimed that she had (**got/gotten**) more than enough signatures to stop the proposed freeway extension.

18e Do you understand active and passive voice?

Voice is a characteristic of verbs that is easier to illustrate than to define. Verbs that take objects (called transitive verbs) can be either in **active** or in **passive voice**. They are in active voice when the subject in the sentence actually does what the verb describes.

> subj.   action
> *Keisha* **managed** the account.

They are in passive voice when the action described by the verb is done *to* the subject.

> subj.   action
> The *account* **was managed** by Keisha.

Passive verbs are useful constructions when *who* did an action is either unknown or less important than *to whom it was done*. Passive verbs also work well in scientific writing when you want to focus on the process itself.

The passive is also customary in many expressions where a writer or speaker chooses to be vague about assigning responsibility.

For advice on revising weak passive verbs, see Section 16a-6.

EXERCISE 18.4 Identify all the passive verbs in the following sentences; then revise those passive verbs that might be better stated in the active voice. Some sentences may require no revision.

1. Even opponents of chemical pesticides sometimes use poisons after they have been bitten by fire ants, aggressive and vicious insects spreading throughout the southern United States.

2. These tiny creatures have been given by nature a fierce sting, and they usually attack en masse.

3. Gardeners are hampered in their work by the mounds erected by the ants.

4. By the time a careless gardener discovers a mound, a hand or foot has likely been bitten by numerous ants.

18f What is the subjunctive mood and how do you use it?

As a grammatical term, **mood** indicates how you intend a statement to be taken. Are you making a direct statement? Then the mood is **indicative** ("I enjoy reading science fiction"). Are you giving a command? If so, the mood becomes **imperative** ("Watch out for flying objects!").

When you express a wish or hope, make a suggestion, or describe a possible situation, you may need to indicate the **subjunctive** mood. For example:

> *If* George **were** [not **was**] in charge, we'd be in good hands. The minister wished there **were** [not **was**] more young people in her church.

1 Recognize the subjunctive form of the verb. For all verbs, the present subjunctive is simply the base form of the verb—that is, the present infinitive form without *to*.

VERB	PRESENT SUBJUNCTIVE
to be	be
to give	give
to send	send
to bless	bless

The base form is used even in the third person singular, where you might ordinarily expect a verb to take another form.

> It is essential that *Fernando* **have** [not **has**] his lines memorized by tomorrow.

For all verbs except *be*, the past subjunctive is the same as the simple past tense.

VERB	PAST SUBJUNCTIVE
to give	gave
to send	sent
to bless	blessed

For *be*, the past subjunctive is always *were*. This is true even in the first and third person singular, where you might expect the form to be *was*.

> I wish *I* **were** [not **was**] the director.
> Suppose *you* **were** the director.
> I wish *she* **were** [not **was**] the director.

2 Recognize additional forms of the subjunctive. The subjunctive is employed in *that* clauses following verbs that make demands, requests, recommendations, or motions.

> The presiding officer asked that everyone **be** silent.
>
> I ask only that you **be** courteous to the speaker.

Some common expressions also require the subjunctive.

> **Be** that as it may . . .
>
> As it **were** . . .
>
> **Come** what may . . .
>
> Peace **be** with you.

EXERCISE 18.5 In the following sentences, underline any verbs in the subjunctive mood.

1. It is essential that we be at the airport at 2:00 p.m. today.

2. I wish I were less susceptible to telephone solicitors!

3. Far be it from me to criticize your writing!

4. Come what may, the show must go on.

5. If Avery were to arrive early, what would happen to our plans?

18.4 Anatomy of a Verb: *to pay*

chart

PRINCIPAL PARTS

Infinitive:	pay
Past tense:	paid
Past participle:	paid

TENSE

Present:	I pay
Present progressive:	I am paying
Present perfect:	I have paid
Past:	I paid
Past progressive:	I was paying
Past perfect:	I had paid
Future:	I will pay
Future progressive:	I will have been paying
Future perfect:	I will have paid

PERSON/NUMBER

1st person, singular:	**I** pay
2nd person, singular:	**you** pay

3rd person, singular:	**he** pays
	she pays
	it pays
1st person, plural:	**we** pay
2nd person, plural:	**you** pay
3rd person, plural:	**they** pay

MOOD

Indicative:	I pay.
Imperative:	Pay!
Subjunctive:	I suggested that he pay me.

VOICE

Active:	I pay
	you paid
	he will pay
Passive:	I am paid
	you were paid
	he will be paid

NONFINITE FORMS (VERBALS)

Infinitives:	**to pay** present tense, active voice
	to be paying progressive tense, active voice
	to have paid past tense, active voice
	to have been paying past progressive tense, active voice
	to be paid present tense, passive voice
	to have been paid past tense, passive voice
Participles:	**paying** present tense, active voice
	having paid past tense, active voice
	being paid present tense, passive voice
	paid, having been paid past tense, passive voice
Gerunds:	**paying** present tense, active voice
	having paid past tense, active voice
	being paid present tense, passive voice
	having been paid past tense, passive voice

D🍎 You Have Questions about Verbals?

19

19a What are verbals?

Verbals look like verb forms but act like other parts of speech—nouns, adjectives, and adverbs. Like verbs, verbals can express time (present, past), take objects, and form phrases. Though you may not recognize the three types of verbals by their names—*infinitives, participles*, and *gerunds*—you use them all the time. (See also Section 19a.)

1 Understand infinitives. You can identify an **infinitive** by looking for the word *to* preceding the base form of a verb: *to seek, to find*. Infinitives also take other forms to show time and voice: *to be seeking, to have found, to have been found*. Infinitives sometimes act as nouns, adjectives, and adverbs.

INFINITIVE AS NOUN	**To work** in outer space is not easy. subject of the sentence
INFINITIVE AS ADJECTIVE	Astronauts have many procedures **to learn**. modifies the noun *procedures*
INFINITIVE AS ADVERB	NASA compromised **to fund** the International Space Station. modifies the verb *compromised*

An infinitive can also serve as an *absolute*—that is, a phrase, standing alone, that modifies an entire sentence.

> **To make** a long story short, the current space station is smaller than it might have been.

In some sentence constructions, the characteristic marker of the infinitive, *to*, is deleted.

> Space station crews perform exercises to help them **[to] deal** with the consequences of weightlessness.

2 Understand participles. A **participle** is a verb form that acts as a modifier. The present participle ends with *-ing*. For regular verbs, the past participle ends with *-ed*; for irregular verbs, the form of the past participle varies. Participles take various forms, depending on whether the verb they are derived from is regular or irregular. Chart 19.1 shows the participle forms of two verbs.

(19.1) Forms of the Participle

perform (a regular verb)	PARTICIPLES
Present, active:	performing
Present, passive:	being performed
Past, active:	performed
Past, passive:	having been performed

write (an irregular verb)	PARTICIPLES
Present, active:	writing
Present, passive:	being written
Past, active:	written
Past, passive:	having been written

(For the forms of some irregular past participles, check the list of irregular verbs on pp. 208–209.)

As modifiers, participles may be single words.

> **Waving**, the astronaut turned a cartwheel in the space station for the television audience.

Participles often take objects, complements, and modifiers to form verbal phrases.

> The designers of the station, **knowing** they had to work within budget constraints, used their ingenuity to solve many problems.

Like an infinitive, a participle can also serve as an *absolute*—that is, a phrase, standing alone, that modifies an entire sentence.

> All things **considered**, the International Space Station is a remarkable machine.

3 Understand gerunds. A **gerund** is a verb form that acts as a noun. Because most gerunds end in *-ing*, they look exactly like the present participle. The important difference is that gerunds function as nouns, while participles act as modifiers. Gerunds usually appear in the present tense, but they can take other forms.

GERUND AS SUBJECT	**Keeping** within current budget restraints poses a problem for NASA.
GERUND AS OBJECT	Some NASA engineers prefer **flying** space missions without crews.

GERUND AS APPOSITIVE	Others argue that NASA needs to cultivate its great talent, **executing** daring missions.

GERUNDS AS SUBJECT AND COMPLEMENT	subj. comp. **Exploring** the heavens is **fulfilling** the dreams of humankind.

EXERCISE 19.1 Identify the boldfaced words or phrases as infinitives, participles, or gerunds.

1. **Regretting** compromises in the original design, engineers refined the space shuttle after the *Challenger* explosion.

2. At the time, the press questioned both NASA's **engineering** and its **handling** of the shuttle program.

3. **To be** fair, NASA's safety record in the **challenging** task of space exploration has been remarkable.

4. **Costing** even more than the space shuttle, the International Space Station is sure **to stimulate** new controversies over the years.

19b How do verbals cause sentence fragments?

A verbal phrase that stands alone can create a sentence fragment—that is, a clause without a complete subject or verb.

Verbals are called **nonfinite** (unfinished) verbs. A complete sentence requires a **finite** verb, which is a verb that changes form to indicate person, number, and tense.

NONFINITE VERB—INFINITIVE	**To have found** success . . .
FINITE VERB	**I have found** success.
NONFINITE VERB—PARTICIPLE	The comedian **performing** the bit . . .
FINITE VERB	The comedian **performs** the bit.
NONFINITE VERB—GERUND	**Directing** a play . . .
FINITE VERB	She **directed** the play.

Although verbal phrases often stand alone in informal writing such as advertising copy, in academic writing, sentence fragments should be revised. For help on recasting such fragments, see Section 30a.

19c What is a split infinitive?

An infinitive interrupted by an adverb is considered split.

to **boldly** go   to **really** try   to **actually** see

Some writers believe that constructions such as these are incorrect, a point disputed by grammarians. Split infinitives are such common expressions in English that most writers use them without apology. In academic and business writing, however, it's probably best to revise a split infinitive to keep *to* and the verb together.

SPLIT INFINITIVE	Words fail **to** adequately **describe** the cluelessness of some public figures.
REVISED	Words fail **to describe** adequately the cluelessness of some public figures.

EXERCISE 19.2 Find the split infinitives in the following sentences and revise them. Decide which revisions are necessary, which optional. Be prepared to defend your decisions.

1. In his comic monologue, Harold decided to candidly describe his own inept campaign for city council.

2. Harold usually didn't allow his personal life to too much color his comedy routines.

3. But to really appreciate how absurd politics could be, a person had to basically run for office himself.

4. Harold quickly discovered that it wasn't easy to persuade contributors to only support the best candidate.

Do You Have Questions about Plurls, Possessives, and Articles?

20a How do you form the plurals of nouns?

Most plurals in English are formed by adding *-s* or *-es* to the singular forms of nouns.

> demonstration → demonstrations
>
> picture → pictures
>
> dish → dishes

However, substantial numbers of words are simply irregular.

> **IRREGULAR**
>
> man → m**e**n
>
> ox → ox**en**
>
> mouse → m**ic**e
>
> goose → g**ee**se
>
> child → child**ren**
>
> fungus → fung**i** (or funguses)

Plurals may vary, too, according to how a word is used. You might find maple *leaves* on your driveway but several Toronto Maple *Leafs* on the cover of *Sports Illustrated*.

1 Check the dictionary for the plural form of a noun. Most up-to-date college dictionaries provide the plurals of all troublesome words. If your dictionary does not give a plural for a particular noun, assume that it forms its plural with *-s* or *-es*.

2 Use *-es* when the plural adds a syllable to the pronunciation of the noun. If the noun already ends in *-e*, you add only *-s*.

> dish → dish**es**
>
> glass → glass**es**
>
> bus → bus**es** or buss**es**
>
> buzz → buzz**es**
>
> choice → choic**es**

3 Add -*s* to form a plural when a noun ends in -*o* and a vowel precedes the -*o*; add -*es* when a noun ends in -*o* and a consonant precedes the -*o*.

VOWEL BEFORE -*O* (ADD -*S*)	CONSONANT BEFORE -*O* (ADD -*ES*)
video → video**s**	hero → hero**es**
rodeo → rodeo**s**	tomato → tomato**es**
studio → studio**s**	veto → veto**es**

4 Add -*s* to form a plural when a noun ends in -*y* and a vowel precedes the *y*. When a consonant precedes the *y*, change the *y* to an *i* and add -*es*.

VOWEL PRECEDES -*Y* (ADD -*S*)	CONSONANT PRECEDES -*Y* (CHANGE -*Y* TO -*IES*)
attorney → attorney**s**	foundry → foundr**ies**
Monday → Monday**s**	candy → cand**ies**
boy → boy**s**	sentry → sentr**ies**

An exception to this rule occurs with proper nouns. They usually retain the -*y* and simply add -*s*.

PROPER NAMES ENDING IN -*Y*	EXCEPTIONS TO THE EXCEPTION (ADD -*S*)
Gary → Gary**s**	Rocky Mountains → Rock**ies**
Nestrosky → Nestrosky**s**	Smoky Mountains → Smok**ies**
Germany → Germany**s**	

5 Check the plural of nouns ending in -*f* or -*fe*. Some form plurals by adding -*s*, some change -*f* to -*ves*, and some have two acceptable plural forms.

ADD -*S* TO FORM PLURAL	CHANGE -*F* TO -*VES* IN PLURAL
chief → chie**fs**	leaf → lea**ves**
belief → belie**fs**	knife → kni**ves**

TWO ACCEPTABLE FORMS

elf → el**fs**/el**ves**
scarf → scar**fs**/scar**ves**

6 Check the plural of certain nouns that derive from other languages.

analysis → analys**es**	medium → medi**a**
criterion → criter**ia**	syllabus → syllab**i**

7 Check the plural of compound words. In most compounds, pluralize the last word.

dishcloth → dishcloth**s**

housewife → housewi**ves**

But pluralize the first word in a compound when it is the important term. This is often the case in hyphenated expressions.

attorney general → attorney**s** general

father-in-law → father**s**-in-law

passerby → passer**s**by

Words that end with *-ful* add *-s* to the end of the whole word, not to the syllable before *-ful*.

handful**s** [not hand*s*ful]

tablespoonful**s** [not tablespoon*s*ful]

8 Check the plural of letters, abbreviations, acronyms, and numbers. These constructions usually form their plurals by adding *-s*.

the SAT**s**   all CEO**s**   the 1800**s**   four Ph.D.**s**

Use *-'s* only where adding *-s* without the apostrophe might cause a misreading.

three *e*'**s** and two *y*'**s**

For more on apostrophes see Sections 20b and 23c.

9 Use plurals consistently within a passage. For example, if the subject of a clause is plural, be sure that words related to it are appropriately plural.

INCONSISTENT	**Leaders** able to make up their **mind** usually hold on to their **job**.
CORRECTED	**Leaders** able to make up their **minds** usually hold on to their **jobs**.

EXERCISE 20.1 Form the plurals of the following words. Use the guidelines above or a dictionary as necessary.

basis	gas	soliloquy
duo	loaf	zero
tooth	alkali	mongoose
alumnus	datum	heir apparent
moose	Oreo	court-martial

Do you have questions about possessives?

A noun or pronoun takes a possessive form to show ownership or some similar relationship: *Rita's, the students', the governor's approval, the day's labor, the city's destruction, hers, his, theirs.* Possession can also be signaled by the pronoun *of*: *the pride of Brooklyn, the flagship of the company, the signature of the author.*

1 Add an apostrophe + -s to most singular nouns and to plural nouns that do not end in -s.

SINGULAR NOUNS	PLURALS NOT ENDING IN *-S*
dog**'s** life	geese**'s** behavior
that man**'s** opinion	women**'s** attitude
the NCAA**'s** ruling	children**'s** imaginations

Singular nouns that end in *-s* or *-z* may take either an apostrophe + *-s* or the apostrophe alone. Use one form or the other consistently throughout a paper.

Ross**'s** handball or Ross**'** handball

Goetz**'s** play or Goetz**'** play

The apostrophe alone is used with singular words ending in *-s* when the possessive does not add a syllable to the pronunciation of the word.

Texa**s'** first settlement

Jesus**'** words

2 Add an apostrophe (but not an s) to plural nouns that end in -s.

hostesse**s'** job	senators**'** chambers
student**s'** opinion	Smiths**'** home

3 Show possession only at the end of compound or hyphenated words.

president-elect**'s** decision

fathers-in-law**'s** Cadillacs

the United States Post Office**'s** efficiency

4 Show possession only once when two nouns share ownership.

Marge and Homer**'s** family

Smith-Fallows and Luu**'s** project

But when ownership is separate, each noun shows possession.

Marge's and Homer's educations
Smith-Fallows' and Luu's offices

5 Use an apostrophe + -s to form the possessive of living things and titled works; use *of* with nonliving things.

TAKE APOSTROPHE + -*S*	TAKE *OF*
the dog's bone	the size **of** the bone
Professor Granchi's taxes	the bite **of** taxes
Time's cover	the timeliness **of** the cover

Use *of* when an apostrophe + -*s* seems awkward or ridiculous.

RIDICULOUS   The **student** sitting next to Peg's opinion was radical.

REVISED   The opinion **of the student** sitting next to Peg was radical.

In a few situations, English allows a double possessive, consisting of both -'s and *of*.

That idea **of** Mariah's didn't win support, although an earlier one did.

6 Do not use an apostrophe with personal pronouns. Personal pronouns don't take an apostrophe to show ownership: *my, your, her, his, our, their, its*. The forms *it's* and *who's* are contractions for *it is* and *who is* (see Section 23c). . . . it's an idea that has **its** opponents alarmed.

Indefinite pronouns—such as *anybody, each one, everybody*—do form their possessives regularly: *anybody's, each one's, everybody's*. For more about possessive pronouns, see Section 23b.

EXERCISE 20.2 Decide whether the forms boldfaced in these sentences are correct. Revise any that you believe are faulty.

1. That claim **of her's** may be right.

2. **Moufida's** belief was that the main concern **of most citizens'** was a thriving economy.

3. **Society's** problems today are not as great as they were in the **1900s'**; each generation benefits from its **parent's** sacrifices while tackling **it's** own problems.

4. **Its** a shame that people forget how much they have benefited from **someone elses** labor.

20c   Are possessives needed before gerunds?

Gerunds (see Section 19a-3) are verb forms that function like nouns: *eating, biking, walking.* Usually you use the possessive form when the word preceding the gerund is a noun or a pronoun.

Dejuan**'s** snoring kept everyone awake that night.

Use the common form of the noun when the subject of the gerund is modified by other words.

The complainers admitted they had forgotten about the *Irish* **being** discriminated against in nineteenth-century Boston.

EXERCISE 20.3 Select the appropriate form for the nouns or pronouns used before gerunds in the sentences below. Gerunds are boldfaced.

1. The same discussions had been going on at the (*art commission/art commission's*) **gatherings** for the past several years.

2. The question was always this: should the commission sponsor local (*artists/artists'*) **painting** or should it seek work from nationally famous figures?

3. Unfortunately, whatever the members of the commission decided, they could count on (*someone/someone's*) **being** unhappy.

4. Mayor Casterbridge and City Councilwoman Meredith decided the (*local artists/local artists'*) **contributing** was the most important concern.

20d   Is it *a* or *an*?

Use *a* when the word following it begins with a consonant *sound*; use *an* when the word following it begins with a vowel *sound*. In most cases, it works out that *a* comes before words beginning with consonants, *an* before words with vowels.

INITIAL CONSONANTS	INITIAL VOWELS
a **b**oat	an **a**ardvark
a **c**lass	an **E**gyptian monument
a **d**uck	an **i**gloo
a **f**inal opinion	an **o**dd event
a **h**ouse	an **O**edipus complex
a **X**erox product	an **u**tter disaster

But *an* is used before words beginning with a consonant when the consonant is silent, as is sometimes the case with *h*. It is also used when a consonant itself is pronounced with an initial vowel sound (*f* → *ef; n* → *en; s* → *es*), as often happens in acronyms.

SILENT CONSONANT	CONSONANT WITH A VOWEL SOUND
an **h**eir	an **S**AT score
an **h**onest man	an **H**MO
an **h**ors d'oeuvre	an **X**-ray star
an **h**our	an **F** in this course

Similarly, *a* is used before words beginning with a vowel when the vowel is pronounced like a consonant. Certain vowels, for example, sound like the consonant *y*, and in a few cases, an initial *o* sounds like the consonant *w*.

VOWEL WITH A CONSONANT SOUND

a European vacation (**eu** sounds like **y**)

a unique painting (**u** sounds like **y**)

a one-sided argument (**o** sounds like **w**)

a U-joint (**u** sounds like **y**)

EXERCISE 20.4 Decide whether *a* or *an* should be used before each of the following words or phrases.

1. L-shaped room

2. hyperthyroid condition

3. zygote

4. *X*-rated movie

5. Euclidean principle

6. evasive answer

Do You Have Questions about Prnoun Reference? **21**

21a Do pronouns lack antecedents?

Pronouns stand in for and act like nouns, but they don't name a specific person, place, or thing—*I, you, he, she, it, they, whom, this, that, one*, and so on. The person, place, or thing a pronoun stands in for is called the **antecedent**. This connection between a pronoun and antecedent is called *pronoun reference.*

Jill demanded that the clerk speak directly to **her**.

ANTECEDENT	PRONOUN
JILL	HER
Number: singular	*Number:* singular
Gender: feminine	*Gender:* feminine

Workers denied that **they** intended to strike.

ANTECEDENT	PRONOUN
WORKERS	THEY
Number: plural	*Number:* plural
Gender: neuter	*Gender:* neuter

A pronoun must agree with its antecedent in *number* (singular or plural), in *case* (subjective, objective, or possessive), and sometimes in *gender* (masculine or feminine). You must revise a pronoun reference if readers can't find a specific word in your sentence that could logically serve as an antecedent, the word the pronoun replaces.

When you aren't sure that the pronoun has an antecedent, ask yourself whether another word in the sentence or passage could substitute for the pronoun. If none can, replace the vague pronoun with a word or phrase that explains precisely what it is.

> **VAGUE** The pollsters chose their participants scientifically, but **it** did not prevent a faulty prediction of the mayoral election.
>
> **REVISED** The pollsters chose their participants scientifically, but **their random sampling** did not prevent a faulty prediction of the mayoral election.

EXERCISE 21.1 Revise or rewrite the following sentences to eliminate vague pronouns. Treat the sentences as a continuous passage.

1. Leah read avidly about gardening, although she had never planted one herself.

2. Her fondness for the convenience of apartment living left Leah without a place for one.

3. Leah found herself buying garden tools, seeds, and catalogs, but it did not make much sense.

4. Leah's friends suggested building planters on her deck or installing a window garden, but Leah doubted that the landlord would permit it.

5. As for her parents' idea that she invest in a condominium, they overestimated her bank account.

 ## Are pronoun references unclear?

You have a problem with pronoun reference when a pronoun could refer to more than one antecedent.

> AMBIGUOUS   When Ms. Walker talked to Mrs. Mendoza that noon, **she** did not realize that **she** might be resigning before the end of the day.

Eliminate confusion by replacing the ambiguous pronouns with more specific words or by recasting the sentence. Sometimes you have to do both.

> REVISED   When **they** talked to each other at noon, **Ms. Walker** did not realize that **Mrs. Mendoza** might be resigning before the end of the day.

EXERCISE 21.2 Revise the following sentences to eliminate ambiguous pronoun references. Treat the sentences as a continuous passage. Several versions of each sentence may be possible.

1. Amanda could hardly believe that the representatives from Habitat for Humanity would visit wintry Madison, Wisconsin, when it was so bad.

2. When she met them at their hotel, the winds were howling, the visitors were hungry, and it was predicted that they would get worse.

3. But the two women were bundled up and ready to brave the elements, so she figured this wasn't a problem.

4. Later Amanda learned that one of the visitors, Sarah Severson, had been born in Wisconsin, and she told her she knew a great deal about northern winters.

5. The three of them took off through the blizzard in Amanda's lumbering SUV, but it didn't slow them down a bit.

 # Do you have questions about *this*, *that*, *which*, and *it*?

Readers may be confused if you use the pronouns *this, that, which,* or *it* to refer to ideas you haven't named specifically in your writing. Vague pronouns reflect vague thinking.

1 Revise a sentence or passage to make clear what *this*, *that*, *which*, or *it* means.

CONFUSING | The minutes of the committee are usually filled with data, charts, and vivid accounts of the debate. I especially like **this**.

REVISED | I especially like **this detailed reporting of information**.

VAGUE | While atomic waste products are hard to dispose of safely, **it** remains a reasonable alternative to burning fossil fuels to produce electricity.

REVISED | While atomic waste products are hard to dispose of safely, **nuclear power** remains a reasonable alternative to burning fossil fuels to produce electricity.

2 Avoid using *they* or *it* without antecedents to describe people or things in general.

VAGUE | In Houston, **they** drive worse than in Dallas.

REVISED | In Houston, **people** drive worse than in Dallas.

3 Avoid sentences in which a pronoun merely repeats the obvious subject. Such constructions are unacceptable in writing.

INCORRECT | The **mayor**, a Democrat, **he** won the election.

REVISED | The **mayor**, a Democrat, won the election.

4 Don't let a nonpossessive pronoun refer to a word that is possessive.

VAGUE | As for the television **pundits'** coverage, they either mock third-party candidates or ignore them.

REVISED | As for the television **pundits, they** either mock third-party candidates or ignore them.

EXERCISE 21.3 Decide whether a reader might find the pronouns in boldface unclear. Revise the sentences as necessary.

1. Even tourists just visiting the building soon noticed the aging state capitol's sagging floors, unreliable plumbing, and exposed electrical conduits. **This** was embarrassing.

2. When an electrical fire in the office of the Speaker of the House was soon followed by another in the Senate chamber, it was clear **it** was a problem.

3. Old paintings and sculptures were grimy and cracked, **which** had been donated by citizens over the decades.

Do You Have
Questions abut
Pronoun Agreement?

22

22a Do antecedents and pronouns agree in number?

Pronouns and nouns are either singular or plural. Singular pronouns (such as *she, it, this, that, her, him, my, his, her, its*) refer to something singular; plural pronouns (such as *they, these, them, their*) refer to plural nouns. This connection is called **agreement in number**.

The soccer **players** gathered **their** equipment.

ANTECEDENT	PRONOUN
players	*their*
Number: plural	*Number:* plural

The **coach** searched for **her** car.

ANTECEDENT	PRONOUN
coach	*her*
Number: singular	*Number:* singular

1 Be sure that singular pronouns refer to singular antecedents and plural pronouns to plural antecedents.

sing.
AGREEMENT ERROR   An **American** always takes it for granted that
plural
government agencies will help **them** when trouble strikes.

plural
REVISED   **Americans** always take it for granted that
plural
government agencies will help **them** when trouble strikes.

sing.
REVISED   An **American** always takes it for granted that
sing.
government agencies will help **him or her** when trouble strikes.

229

2 Keep pronouns consistent in number throughout a passage. Don't switch back and forth from singular to plural forms of pronouns and antecedents.

> One reason some **teenagers [pl.]** quit school is to work to support **their [pl.]** families. If **he or she [sing.]** is the eldest child, the **teen [sing.]** may feel an obligation to provide for the family. So **they [pl.]** look for a minimum wage job.

To correct such a tendency, be consistent throughout the passage.

> One reason some **teenagers [pl.]** quit school is to work to support **their [pl.]** families. If **they [pl.]** are the eldest children, such **teens [pl.]** may feel an obligation to provide for **their [pl.]** families. So **they [pl.]** look for minimum wage jobs.

EXERCISE 22.1 Revise the following sentences wherever pronouns and antecedents do not agree in number. You may change either the pronouns or the antecedents.

1. Many a college class is conducted using the Socratic method, but they aren't always successful.

2. In the Socratic method, a teacher leads a student through a series of questions to conclusions that they believe they've reached without the instructor's prompting.

3. Yet when instructors ask leading questions, the cleverer students sometimes answer it in unexpected ways.

4. However, no instructor, except perhaps for Socrates himself, can foresee all the questions and answers eager students might have for them.

 ## **22b** Do you have questions about agreement with indefinite pronouns?

Common indefinite pronouns include *everyone, anybody, anyone, somebody, all, some, none, each, few,* and *most.* It is not always easy to tell whether one of these indefinite words is singular or plural.

> Everyone should keep (**his? their?**) temper.
> No one has a right to more than (**his or her? their?**) share.

1 Use Chart 22.1 or a dictionary to determine whether an indefinite pronoun or noun in your sentence is singular, variable, or plural.

chart

22.1 Indefinite Pronouns

SINGULAR	VARIABLE (SINGULAR OR PLURAL)	PLURAL
anybody	all	few
anyone	any	many
anything	either	several
each	more	
everybody	most	
everyone	neither	
everything	none	
nobody	some	
no one		
nothing		
somebody		
someone		
something		

2 If the indefinite word is regarded as singular, make any pronouns that refer to it singular.

sing.   sing.
No one has a right to more than **his or her** share.

In a few situations, however, the singular indefinite pronoun does take a plural referent.

sing.   plural
Because **each** of the players arrived late, the coach gave **them** a stern lecture on punctuality.

sing.   plural
Nobody was late, were **they?**

sing.   plural
Everybody has plenty of money, and **they** are willing to spend it.

3 If the indefinite word is usually plural, make any pronouns that refer to it plural.

plural   plural
Several of the jet fighters had to have **their** wings stiffened.

plural   plural
Few, however, had given **their** pilots trouble.

4 If the indefinite word is variable, use your judgment to determine which pronoun suits the sentence better.

var.   plural   var.
All of the portraits had yellowed in **their** frames. **Some** will be
           plural
restored to **their** original condition.

var.   sing.   var.
All of the wine is still in **its** casks. **Some** of the vintage is certain
       sing.
to have **its** quality evaluated.

EXERCISE 22.2 Select the word or phrase in parentheses that would be correct in formal and college writing.

1. Anybody can learn to drive an automobile with a manual transmission if (**they are/he or she is**) coordinated.

2. But not everyone will risk (**his or her/their**) (**life/lives**) trying.

3. Few today seem eager to take (**his or her/their**) driver's tests in a five-speed.

4. Everyone learning to drive a manual car expects (**his or her/their**) car to stall at the most inopportune moment.

Do you treat collective nouns as singular or plural?

Questions about agreement occur when pronouns refer to collective nouns, that is, to nouns that describe groups of things: *class, team, band, government, jury*. Collective nouns can be either singular or plural, depending on how they are used in a sentence.

The **chorus** sang **its** heart out.
The **chorus** arrived and took **their** seats.

The **team** looks sharp today.
The **team** lost **their** luggage.

In most cases, your sentences will sound more natural if you treat collective nouns as single objects.

AWKWARD   The **band** are unhappy with **their** latest recordings.
BETTER   The **band** is unhappy with **its** latest recordings.

EXERCISE 22.3 In the following sentences, select the appropriate words in parentheses. Be prepared to defend your answers.

1. The **class** entered the lecture hall and took (**its/their**) seats, eager to hear from the architect after (**its/their**) field trip to several of his buildings.

2. He belonged to a revitalized **school** of design that had enjoyed (**its/their**) best days four decades ago.

3. The aging architect was accompanied by several **members of his firm**, carrying (**its/their**) designs in huge portfolios.

22d Do you have questions about agreement with *or, nor, either . . . or, neither . . . nor*?

The choice of a pronoun can be puzzling.

1 When two nouns joined by *or, nor, either . . . or*, or *neither . . . nor* are singular, be sure any pronoun referring to them is singular.

sing.
Neither Brazil nor Mexico will raise **its** oil prices today.

2 When two nouns joined by *and* or *or* are plural, be sure any pronoun referring to them is plural.

plural
Players or managers may file **their** grievances with the commissioner.

3 When a singular noun is joined to a plural noun by *or, nor, either . . . or*, or *neither . . . nor*, any pronoun should agree in number with the noun nearer to it.

sing.   plural
Either poor **diet** or long, stress-filled **hours** in the office will take
plural
their toll on an executive's health.

plural   sing.
Either long, stress-filled **hours** in the office or poor **diet** will take
sing.
its toll on an executive's health.

EXERCISE 22.4 In the sentences below, select the appropriate words in parentheses.

1. Neither the tour guide nor any of his customers had bothered to confirm (**his/their**) flight from Chicago's O'Hare Airport back to Toledo.

2. Either the ticket agents or a flight attendant working the check-in desk had misread (**their/her**) computer terminal and accidentally canceled the group's reservations.

3. Either the tourists or their guide had to make up (**their/his**) (**minds/mind**) quickly about arranging transportation back to Toledo.

4. Neither the guide nor his wife relished the thought of spending (**his/her/their**) hard-earned money on yet another expensive ticket.

D You Have Questions about Pronoun Case?

23

Some personal pronouns (and *who*) change their form according to how they are used in a sentence. These different forms are called **case**. **Subjective** (or **nominative**) **case** is the form a pronoun takes when it is the subject of a sentence or a clause: *I, you, she, he, it, we, they, who*. A pronoun is also in the subjective case when it follows a linking verb as a **predicate nominative**, a word that renames the subject.

> It is **I**.
>
> It was **they** who cast the deciding votes.

Objective case is the form a pronoun takes when something is done to it: Elena broke *them*; Will loved *her*. This is also the form a pronoun takes after a preposition: (to) *me, her, him, us, them, whom*. The subjective and objective forms of the pronouns *you* and *it* are identical.

The **possessive case** is the form a pronoun takes when it shows ownership: *my, mine, your, yours, her, hers, his, its, our, ours, their, theirs, whose*.

23a How do you use pronouns in subjective and objective case?

Choose subjective forms when pronouns act as subjects, and objective forms when pronouns act as objects (especially in prepositional phrases).

(23.1) Pronoun Case

chart

SUBJECTIVE FORMS	OBJECTIVE FORMS
I	me
we	us
you	you
he	him
she	her
it	it
they	them
who	whom

235

1 Check pronoun case when pronouns are paired. The second pronoun in a pair is often troublesome. To choose the right pronoun, figure out what the pronoun does in the sentence: Is it a subject or a predicate nominative? Is it an object?

WHICH CASE?	You and (**I/me**) don't have the latest designs yet.
	These pronouns are subjects, so the subjective form *I* is correct.
CORRECT	You and **I** don't have the latest designs yet.
WHICH CASE?	The winners are (**he/him**) and (**I/me**).
	The pronouns are predicate nominatives and should be in the subjective case.
CORRECT	The winners are **he** and **I**.
WHICH CASE?	Forward the email to (**he/him**) and (**I/me**).
	Pronouns are objects of the preposition *to*; they take the objective case.
CORRECT	Forward the email to **him** and **me**.

Alternatively, conduct a simple test by taking out the first pronoun and recasting the sentence with only the troublesome pronoun. You can often tell immediately which choice to make.

EXERCISE 23.1 Select the correct pronoun from the choices offered in parentheses.

1. In the reporter's opinion, neither (**she/her**) nor (**he/him**) had done a good job in covering the city's financial crisis.

2. It was likely that both political parties would now accuse (**she/her**) and (**he/him**) of media bias.

3. Knowing her colleagues at the competing TV stations, the reporter was convinced that both she and (**they/them**) had rushed their stories.

4. "You and (**I/me**) will just have to accept the criticism," the reporter told a professional colleague.

2 Check pronoun case when first person plural pronouns are followed by nouns. The pronoun and noun must share the same case, either subjective or objective.

	subjects
SUBJECTIVE	**We** *lucky sailors* missed the storm.

	objects
OBJECTIVE	The storm missed **us** *lucky sailors*.

	obj. of preposition
OBJECTIVE	For **us** *engineers*, the job market looks promising.

You can test for the correct form by leaving out the noun and recasting the sentence using only the pronoun.

WHICH CASE?	Us *lucky sailors* missed the storm.
WRONG	**Us** missed the storm.
CORRECT	**We** *lucky sailors* missed the storm.

3 Check pronoun case with *who* and *whom*. Select the subjective form (*who*) when pronouns act as subjects and the objective form (*whom*) when pronouns act as objects.

SUBJECTIVE	**Who** wrote this letter?
OBJECTIVE	You addressed **whom**?
OBJECTIVE	To **whom** did you write?

When *who* or *whom* (or *whoever/whomever*) is part of a dependent clause, *who* or *whom* takes the form it would have in the dependent clause, not in the sentence as a whole. Constructions of this kind are quite common. The words in italics in the following examples are clauses within full sentences.

noun clause

The system rewards ***whoever*** *works hard.*
Whoever is the subject of the noun clause in which it appears. It has its own verb, *works*.

noun clause

Whomever *the party nominates* is likely to be elected.
The pronoun is the object of *nominates*.

adverbial clause

The deficit will increase *no matter **whom** we elect president.*
The main verb of the subordinate clause is *elect* and its subject is *we*. So the pronoun *whom* is the object of *we elect* and *president* modifies *whom*. The chart on page 235 tells you that *whom*, not *who*, is correct.

EXERCISE 23.2 Decide which of the pronoun forms in parentheses is correct in each of the following sentences.

1. Jon Stewart looks like a man (**whom/who**) wouldn't trust a nun with a prayer.

2. To (**who/whom**) would you go for sound financial advice?

3. Are these the young children (**who/whom**) you took by bus to Charleston?

4. Officials couldn't determine (**who/whom**) rigged the state elections.

4 Check pronoun case in comparisons. To determine pronoun case after *than* or *as*, it helps to complete the comparison.

WHICH CASE?	I am taller *than* (**him/he**).
CORRECT	I am taller *than* **he** (is).
WHICH CASE?	We don't invest as much *as* (**she/her**).
CORRECT	We don't invest as much *as* **she** (does).

Some comparisons can be expanded two ways.

WHICH CASE?	Politics does not interest me as much *as* (**she/her**).
POSSIBLE EXPANSIONS	Politics does not interest me as much *as* **she** (does).
	Politics does not interest me as much *as* (it interests) **her**.

In such cases, the pronoun you select will determine what the sentence means. In these situations it's probably better to write out the full comparison.

EXERCISE 23.3 Select the correct pronoun from the choices offered in parentheses.

1. Although the Cowardly Lion needed the Wizard's help as much as Dorothy did, the King of the Jungle was less determined than (**she/her**) to hike to Oz.

2. Dorothy probably felt more confident than (**he/him**) that she could deal with the wonderful Wizard.

3. Perhaps Dorothy could relate more easily to (**he/him**) than a lion could.

4. Although more cautious in his appraisal of the Wizard than Dorothy, the Scarecrow was no less eager for guidance than (**she/her**).

5 Check pronoun case in appositives. *Appositives* are nouns or phrases that add information to a previous noun.

appositive

The teacher gave special help to two of the *students*, **Cheryl and me**.

When an appositive contains a pronoun, the pronoun should be in the same case as the noun it modifies.

The teacher called *two students*, **Cheryl and (I/me)**, to the front of the classroom.

Two students, the noun phrase being modified, is the object of *called*. So the pronoun should also be in the objective case.

The teacher called *two students*, **Cheryl and me**, to the front of the classroom.

6 Check pronoun case after linking verbs. Linking verbs, such as *to be, to seem, to appear, to feel, to become*, connect a subject to a word or phrase that extends or completes its meaning—the predicate nominative. In most cases, use the subjective case of a pronoun when it is the complement of a linking verb.

      subj.   l. v.   subj. comp.
The *culprits are* obviously **they**.

Such constructions are fairly common. Yet many writers have a tough time deciding which of the following pairs of sentences are correct.

In academic and professional writing, the left-hand column is considered correct.

It is **I**.	*It* is **me**.
The next president will be **she**.	*The next president* will be **her**.
You are **who**?	*You* are **whom**?

To work around the problem, rather than write "The director was he," reverse the order and try "He was the director."

EXERCISE 23.4 Select the correct pronoun from the choices in parentheses below.

1. That is (**he/him**) in the office there.

2. The guilty party certainly was not (**she/her**).

3. Spying three men in uniform, we assumed that the pilots were (**they/them**).

4. They are (**who/whom**)?

23b Do you have questions about possessive pronouns?

The most common way of showing ownership in English is to add an apostrophe + *-s* to a noun: *Akilah's book*, the *dog's owner*. The familiar *-'s* is not, however, used with **personal pronouns** (or *who*): do not add an apostrophe + *-s* with personal pronouns used to show ownership (possession). This is true whether the possessive pronoun comes before or after a noun.

INCORRECT	The coat is **her's**.
CORRECT	The coat is **hers**.
INCORRECT	The TV station made **it's** editorial opinion known.
CORRECT	The TV station made **its** editorial opinion known.

The following examples show the various forms of possessive pronouns. Notice that they don't add apostrophes.

BEFORE THE NOUN	AFTER THE NOUN
That is **my** book.	The book is **mine**.
That is **your** book.	The book is **yours**.
That is **her** book.	The book is **hers**.
That is **his** book.	The book is **his**.
That is **our** book.	The book is **ours**.
That is **their** book.	The book is **theirs**.
Whose book is this?	This book is **whose**?

Understand, too, that while indefinite pronouns such as *everybody* or *someone* form the possessive by adding *-'s*, others, like *all, any, each, most, none, some*, and *few*, do not.

INCORRECT	**Some's** opinion
CORRECT	The opinion of **some**

23c Are you confused by *its/it's* and *whose/who's*?

Don't mistake the possessive pronoun *its* for the contraction *it's* (which means *it is* or *it has*). This error is both very common and easy to fix. Remember that *its* is a possessive form; *it's* is a contraction of *it is*.

POSSESSIVE FORM	The iron left **its** grim outline on the silk shirt.
CONTRACTION	**It's** a silly proposal.

Of course, the apostrophe makes the contracted form—*it's*—look suspiciously like a possessive. And the possessive form—*its*—sounds like a contraction. But don't be fooled. The possessive forms of personal pronouns never take an apostrophe, while contractions always require one.

WRONG	The school lost **it's** charter because of low test scores.
RIGHT	The school lost **its** charter because of low test scores.

WRONG	**Its** unlikely that the aircraft will lose **it's** way in the dark. **Its** equipped with radar.
RIGHT	**It's** unlikely that the aircraft will lose **its** way in the dark. **It's** equipped with radar.

If you consistently misuse *its/it's*, circle these words whenever they appear in your work and then check them. It may help if you always read *it's* as *it is*. Eventually you will eliminate this error.

A related error is mistaking *whose*, a possessive pronoun, for *who's*, which is the contraction for *who is* or *who has*.

POSSESSIVE FORM	**Whose** teammate is on first base?
CONTRACTION	**Who's** on first?

EXERCISE 23.5 Circle all occurrences of *its/it's* in the following passage and correct any errors.

1. Its been decades since Americans have felt as comfortable traveling in Eastern Europe as they do now.

2. Its likely that tourism will remain a major industry in Hungary, Poland, and the Czech Republic.

3. Each of these countries has much to attract tourists to its cities.

4. Yet its the small towns of Eastern Europe that many Americans may find most appealing.

Do You Have Questions about Prnoun Choices?

24

24a When should you use *I*, *we*, *you*, or *one*?

Pronouns change the distance between writers and readers. Choosing *I* or *you* puts you closer to readers; using *one* creates distance.

1 Use *I* when you or your opinions belong in what you're writing. In general, avoid the first person *I* in scientific reports and expository essays.

> AWKWARD   **I learned** through a survey **I did** that students who drive a car on campus are more likely to have jobs than those who do not.

> REVISED   **A survey showed** that students who drive a car on campus are likely to have jobs.

However, when you find that avoiding *I* makes you resort to an awkward passive verb, use *I* instead.

> AWKWARD   **It is believed** that procedures for voting in campus elections are too complex.

> REVISED   **I believe** that procedures for voting in campus elections are too complex.

You can often eliminate an awkward passive without using *I*.

> REVISED WITHOUT *I*   Procedures for voting in campus elections are too complex.

2 Use *we* whenever two or more writers are involved in a project or when you are writing to express the opinion of a group.

> When **we** compared our surveys, **we** discovered the conflicting evidence.

> **We** believe that the city council has an obligation to reconsider its zoning action.

Or use the first person *we* to indicate a general condition when it is appropriate to comment editorially.

> **We** need better control of our medical care systems in the United States.

Avoid *we* or *us* as a chummy way of addressing your reader. In most college writing, *we* used this way sounds pompous.

3 Use *you* to address readers personally or to give orders or directions. Because *you* is both vague and potentially personal, it is a pronoun to avoid in most academic writing.

INAPPROPRIATE	A recent student government survey suggested that **you** will cheat in two courses during **your** college career.
REVISED	A recent student government survey suggested that **most students** will cheat in two courses during **their** college careers.

You may be more appropriate in persuasive writing, however, where your goal is to move people to act.

4 Use *one* to express a general thought. *One* may sometimes be useful for conveying moral sentiments or sweeping claims.

Consider the anxiety of not knowing where **one's** next meal is coming from.

One learns a great deal about pre-revolutionary Russia from reading Dostoevsky.

But notice that *one* makes the sentence more formal than it would be if *one* were replaced by *I* or *you*.

5 Whatever pronouns you choose, be consistent. Don't switch pronoun forms in the middle of a sentence or paragraph.

NONSTANDARD	**One** cannot know what **their** future holds.

Here the pronoun shifts incorrectly from *one* to the plural form *their*. Several revisions are possible.

CORRECT	**One** cannot know what **his or her** future holds.
CORRECT	**People** cannot know what **their** future holds.

EXERCISE 24.1 Revise the sentence below to create a passage appropriate for a college report. Pay particular attention to the words and phrases in boldface.

1. **I was amazed to learn that** the Chinese speak a variety of dialects of a language **they** describe as Han.

2. Although there are only eight major varieties of Han, **you would find them** as different from each other as one Romance language is from another.

3. **One finds,** moreover, that each of the eight versions of Han occurs in a great many dialects, adding to **your** linguistic confusion.

4. **You will be glad to know**, however, that the Chinese use only one system of writing—a set of common ideographs—for expressing all **their** dialects.

24b Do your pronouns treat both sexes fairly?

Today, members of either sex may belong to almost every profession or group—students, athletes, coal miners, truckers, secretaries, nurses. Let your pronoun usage reflect that diversity. In situations where you cannot assume that members of a group will all be male or female, be sure your language accommodates both sexes. You can do that in a variety of ways.

1 Use the expressions *he or she, him or her*, or *his or her* instead of the pronoun of either sex alone.

SEXIST	Every secretary may invite **her husband**.
REVISED	Every secretary may invite **his or her partner**.

2 Make singular pronoun references plural. Because plural pronouns do not have a specific gender in English, you can often avoid the choice between *he* and *she* simply by turning singular references into plural ones.

SEXIST	**Every** secretary may invite **her husband**.
REVISED	**All** secretaries may invite **their partners**.
TIRESOME	Before **he or she** leaves, **each** band member should be sure **he or she** has **his or her** music.
REVISED	Before leaving, **all** band members should be sure **they** have **their** music.

Notice that these revisions eliminate *he or she* entirely.

3 Cut troublesome pronouns.

ORIGINAL	*Each student* may bring **his or her** favorite CD.
REVISED	*Each student* may bring **a** favorite CD.

ORIGINAL   *Nobody* should leave until **he or she** has signed the guest book.

REVISED   *Nobody* should leave without **signing** the guest book.

These options are useful, but they are not always available.

4 Switch between *he* and *she*. In most cases, you can vary the pronouns sensibly and naturally within chunks of prose—between paragraphs, for example, or between the examples in a series. Handled skillfully, the shift between masculine and feminine references need not attract a reader's attention.

The dean of students knew that any student could purchase term papers through mail-order term paper services. If **he** could afford the scam, a student might construct **his** entire college career around papers **he** had purchased.

Yet the dean also acknowledged that the typical plagiarist was rarely so grossly dishonest and calculating. **She** tended to resort to such highly unethical behavior only when **she** believed an assignment was beyond **her** capabilities or **her** workload was excessive.

Avoid varying pronoun gender within individual sentences.

EXERCISE 24.2 Revise the following sentences to make them read better and to eliminate exclusionary pronouns. Treat the sentences as part of one paragraph.

1. Earlier this century, a laborer might fear that heavy equipment would mangle his limbs or that pollutants might damage his lungs.

2. Today, a worker has to be concerned with new threats to her health.

3. Anybody who faces a computer terminal eight hours a day must worry about his exposure to radiation and wonder whether his muscles and joints are being damaged by the repetitive limb motions required by his job.

4. Frankly, the typical worker is often so concerned with her job performance that she may not consider that her workplace poses risks.

24c Do you have questions about *that, which,* and *who*?

1 Use *that* to introduce essential (restrictive) clauses. A clause introduced by *that* will almost always be essential. No commas are used around such clauses.

The concept **that** intrigued the shareholders most involved profit sharing.

Only the report **that I** wrote recommended that concept.

2 Use *which* to introduce nonessential (nonrestrictive) clauses. Such clauses are ordinarily surrounded by commas.

NONESSENTIAL CLAUSE	The Web site, **which** is not on the university's server, contains controversial advice about plagiarism.
NONESSENTIAL CLAUSE	The agency, **which** was created in 1978, helps businesses use energy more efficiently.

But understand that many writers use *which* to introduce essential clauses as well. In these clauses, context and punctuation may determine whether a *which* clause is essential or not. If the clause is essential, no commas separate it from the rest of the sentence; if nonessential, commas enclose the clause.

ESSENTIAL CLAUSE	The business plan **which** intrigued the shareholders was the simplest one.
NONESSENTIAL CLAUSE	The business plan, **which** intrigued the shareholders, was quite simple.

Some readers still prefer to distinguish between *that* and *which* even though the distinction is disappearing in general usage. For more about this issue, see Section 21c.

3 Use *who* rather than *that* or *which* when modifying a person.

INAPPROPRIATE	The woman **that** was promoted is my boss.
BETTER	The woman **who** was promoted is my boss.
INAPPROPRIATE	The delegates, **which** represented all regions of the country, met in Philadelphia for their convention.
BETTER	The delegates, **who** represented all regions of the country, met in Philadelphia for their convention.

EXERCISE 24.3 Decide among *that / which / who* in the following sentences. Add commas where needed.

1. Charlie Chaplin's tramp (**that/which/who**) wore a derby, baggy trousers, and a mustache may still be the most recognized character on film.

2. The popularity (**that/which/who**) Chaplin had in the early days of film may never be equaled, either.

3. His graceful gestures and matchless acrobatics (**that/which/who**) some critics likened to ballet were perfectly suited to the silent screen.

4. A flaw (**that/which/who**) weakens many of Chaplin's films is sentimentality.

 # Do you have questions about reflexive and intensive pronouns?

Reflexive and **intensive pronouns** are created when *-self* is added to singular personal pronouns and *-selves* to plural personal pronouns: *myself, yourself, herself, himself, itself, oneself, ourselves, yourselves, themselves.* These words are *reflexive* in sentences like the following, where both the subject and the object of an action are the same person or thing.

subj.   obj.
They took **themselves** too seriously.

These words are *intensive* when they modify a noun or another pronoun to add emphasis.

noun   pron.
Warren **himself** admitted he was responsible.

noun   pron.
I never vote, **myself**.

1 Don't use reflexive pronouns to make sentences sound more formal.

NONSTANDARD   The memo is for Ms. Matthews and **yourself**.

REVISED   The memo is for Ms. Matthews and **you**.

Use the pronoun reflexively only when the subject and object in a sentence refer to the same person or thing.

subj.   obj.
Maggie rediscovered herself in her paintings.

subj.   obj.
Jones had only **himself** to blame.

Similarly, don't use *myself* in place of a more suitable *I* or *me*.

NONSTANDARD   *Jose and myself* wrote the **lab report**.

REVISED   *Jose and I* wrote the **lab report**.

Compare the sentence above to a similar one using *myself* correctly as an intensive pronoun.

I wrote the lab report **myself**.

2 Use intensive pronouns for emphasis.

The gift is for *you* **yourself**.

The *residents* did all the plumbing and wiring **themselves**.

3 Never use *hisself* or *theirselves*. Although you may hear these expressions in speech, the correct forms in writing are always *himself* and *themselves*.

WRONG   They saw **theirselves** on television.

CORRECT   They saw **themselves** on television.

EXERCISE 24.4   Correct any problems with reflexive or intensive pronouns in the sentences below.

1. "God helps them who help themselves" is an adage credited to Benjamin Franklin.

2. The delegates to the Constitutional Convention in 1787 were not sure they could agree among theirselves on a new form of government.

3. Aaron and myself wrote a paper on Madison's contribution to the Constitution.

4. You might want to read about the topic yourself.

Do You Hve Questions about Modifiers?

25

Much of the work in sentences is handled by modifiers—especially adjectives and adverbs (see Section 15b). These modifying words and phrases expand what we know about subjects, verbs, and other sentence elements.

25a What's the problem with misplaced or dangling modifiers?

Adjectives and adverbs can cause confusion if they become detached from the words they are supposed to modify in a sentence. Two forms of this common problem are **misplaced modifying phrases** and **dangling modifiers**. A modifier is considered misplaced when it hooks up with the wrong word or phrase, sometimes with comic effect. A modifier dangles when it doesn't have a word or phrase to connect with in a sentence. As a result, it doesn't make a logical connection.

DANGLING MODIFIER	**Angered by the crowd's booing**, the concert was canceled.
CORRECTED	**Angered by the crowd's booing**, the band canceled the concert.

1 Be sure that an introductory modifying phrase is followed by the word it modifies.

MISPLACED MODIFIER	**Insulting and predictable**, fewer and fewer television viewers are attracted to the comedian's monologues.
REVISION	**Insulting and predictable**, the comedian's monologues attracted fewer and fewer television viewers.

2 Supply a word for a dangling modifier to modify.

DANGLING MODIFIER	**On returning to the office**, the furniture had been rearranged.
ONE POSSIBLE REVISION	**On returning to the office**, the staff found that the furniture had been rearranged.

3 Distinguish between absolute phrases and dangling modifiers.

Some modifying phrases may look like dangling modifiers but are actually **absolute phrases;** that is, they are complete in themselves.

> absolute
>
> **Given the fiasco at dinner**, the guests weren't surprised when Martha pushed her husband into the pool.

For more on absolute phrases, see Section 15c-3.

EXERCISE 25.1 Rewrite or rearrange these sentences, placing modifiers in appropriate positions. You may need to add a noun for the modifier to modify. Not all of the sentences need to be revised.

1. Although they are among the most famous of reptiles, biologists have only recently begun to study rattlesnakes.

2. The deadly snakes, which take their name from the two characteristic pits on their snouts, belong to the family of pit vipers.

3. After studying the habits of pit vipers, the pits, which serve as infrared sensors and enable the snakes to seek heat, evolved to detect danger rather than to hunt prey.

4. Given their lethal capabilities, it is not surprising that pit vipers are universally loathed.

25b Where should adjectives go?

Adjectives are words that modify nouns or pronouns. They explain how many, which color, which one, and so on.

> A **simple** tax return is **rare** these days.
>
> The **darkest** nights are **moonless**.
>
> The truck, **tall** and **ungainly**, rolled down the hill.
>
> **Pale** and **redheaded**, she looked **Irish**.

Place adjectives carefully to avoid ambiguity and pileups. An adjective becomes ambiguous when readers can't tell which word it modifies.

1 Relocate adjectives that are potentially confusing or ambiguous.

| AMBIGUOUS | Ana had her **enthusiastic parents' support**. |
| CLARIFIED | Ana had her p**arents' enthusiastic support**. |

2 Consider placing adjectives after the words or phrases they modify.

TEDIOUS   A **new, powerful, quick**, and **easy-to-use** database
           program was installed today.

REVISED   A new database program, **powerful, quick**, and **easy to
           use**, was installed today.

EXERCISE 25.2 Rearrange the adjectives to make each of these sentences
clearer or more effective. Several options are possible.

1. Lisa and Julia wanted to find a politically sophisticated women's
   group that could help them plan their lobbying strategy.

2. Professional children's care in the workplace of employed parents was
   one of their goals.

3. They viewed the negative board members' attitudes as a challenge to
   their persuasive abilities.

4. Before explaining their plan, Lisa asked for the undivided employees'
   attention.

25c How do you handle predicate adjectives?

An adjective that follows a linking verb is called a **predicate adjective**.

I *feel* **bad**.
You *seem* **uneasy**.
The lawyer *became* **angry**.
The perfume *smells* **vile**.
Iris *appears* **calm**.

1 Remember that only adjectives, not adverbs, can modify a noun.

INCORRECT   Lillian appears **pessimistically** about her chances for
             getting into the graduate program.

CORRECT   Lillian appears **pessimistic** about her chances for
             getting into the graduate program.

2 Learn to manage *good/well* and *bad/badly*. *Good* and *bad* are
always adjectives and *well* is usually an adverb; but *well* can also be an
adjective that describes someone's physical condition.

He feels **good** about being a father too.

Most college students feel **well** in spite of their eating habits.

NO   The students don't eat **good**.

YES   The students don't eat **well**.

EXERCISE 25.3 In these sentences, replace the boldfaced modifier with a better one.

1. In developed countries, most people feel **confidently** that their drinking water is safe.

2. In many parts of the world, however, even water that looks **well** can be full of bacteria and pollution.

3. Some relief organizations feel **optimistically** that they can bring clean water to the rural areas of Africa and India.

4. They teach villagers what must be done to keep a sanitation system running **good**.

Do you have questions about absolute adjectives?

Some words called *absolute adjectives* cannot be compared or qualified—at least not logically. For example, since *equal* means "exactly the same," you shouldn't write that something is *more equal* any more than you'd say it is *more empty*.

Avoid using qualifiers (such as *less, more, most, least, very*) with the following absolute words: *unique, perfect, singular, empty, equal, full, definite, complete, absolute*, and, of course, *pregnant*.

Consider these examples.

ILLOGICAL   We doubted that the new operating system was **absolutely perfect**.

REVISED   We doubted that the new operating system was **perfected yet**.

ILLOGICAL   Jack's story is **more unique** than Jane's.

REVISED   Jack's story is **unique;** Jane's is not.

EXERCISE 25.4 Working with other students in a group, read over these sentences and decide which ones have faulty modifiers. Confer to decide how any problems with modifiers might be solved.

1. The technician assured me that the service work on my computer was almost complete.

2. The machine had frozen because my hard drive was totally full of illegal downloads.

3. The repair had required a very complete erasure of my files.

4. Now my drive was mostly empty of music and video files.

25e Do you have questions about adverb form?

Adverbs are words that modify verbs, adjectives, or other adverbs, explaining where, when, and how. Many adverbs end in *-ly*.

> The Secretary of State spoke **angrily** to the press.
> The water was **extremely** cold.
> The candidate spoke **evasively**.

Some adverbs have both short and long forms.

slow/slowly	fair/fairly	rough/roughly
quick/quickly	tight/tightly	deep/deeply

You'll do better to use the *-ly* form.

COLLOQUIAL	The computer booted **quick**.
STANDARD	The computer booted **quickly**.
COLLOQUIAL	The employees expected to be treated **fair**.
STANDARD	The employees expected to be treated **fairly**.

25f Where should adverbs go?

Adverbs can take various positions in a sentence. For example:

> George daydreamed **endlessly** about his vacation, **thoroughly** reviewing each travel brochure.
> George daydreamed about his vacation **endlessly**, reviewing **thoroughly** each travel brochure.
> **Endlessly** George daydreamed about his vacation, reviewing each travel brochure **thoroughly**.

But it's also easy to drop them in inappropriate spots, particularly when a sentence has two verbs and the adverb might modify either one of them.

ADVERB MISPLACED	Analyzing an argument **effectively** improves it.

1 Place adverbs so it is clear which words they modify.

ADVERB MISPLACED   Before the Battle of Agincourt, King Henry V urged his troops to fight **eloquently**.

ADVERB REPOSITIONED   Before the Battle of Agincourt, King Henry V **eloquently** urged his troops to fight.

2 Place the adverbs *almost* and *even* next to the words they modify.

ADVERB MISPLACED   Much to his dismay, Hugo realized he had **almost** dated every woman at the party.

ADVERB BETTER PLACED   Much to his dismay, Hugo realized he had dated **almost** every woman at the party.

3 Place the adverb *only* directly ahead of the word you want it to modify. The word *only* means "this one and no other."

CONFUSING   Javier **only** plays the piano.

CLEARER   Javier plays **only** the piano.
Only Javier plays the piano.

EXERCISE 25.5 Rewrite the sentences to clarify them.

1. People who attend the theater regularly complain that the manners of the average audience member are in severe decline.

2. Far from listening in respectful if not attentive silence, he broadcasts a running commentary frequently modeled, no doubt, on his behavior in front of the television at home.

3. Sitting next to a woman who spends most of the evening unwrapping Tootsie Rolls slowly can provoke even the most saintly theatergoer to violence.

4. Cellular phones, beepers, and wristwatch alarms even go off intermittently causing an evening in the theater to resemble a trip to an electronics store.

25g What's wrong with double negatives?

Sentences that say *no* in two different ways are emphatic and usually very colloquial.

Ain't no way I'm revising this paper again!

They make their point, but you need to avoid them in academic and professional writing.

1 Check that you don't have two *no* words (a *double negative*) in the same sentence or independent clause. In addition to *no*, look for such words as *not, nothing, nobody*, and *never*.

DOUBLE NEGATIVE	The child does **not** want **no** help tying his shoes.
CORRECTED	The child does **not** want help tying his shoes.

2 Don't mix the adverbs *hardly, scarcely,* or *barely* with another negative word or phrase. Such pairings create double negatives, which should be edited.

DOUBLE NEGATIVE	The morning was so cool and clear that the hikers **couldn't hardly** wait to get started.
CORRECTED	The morning was so cool and clear that the hikers **could hardly** wait to get started.

Double negatives shouldn't be confused with negative statements that express ideas indirectly—and perhaps with ironic twists. Consider the difference in tone between these simple sentences, framed negatively and positively.

NEGATIVE TONE	The proposal was not unintelligent.
POSITIVE TONE	The proposal was intelligent.

EXERCISE 25.6 Rewrite sentences that contain double negatives to eliminate the problem.

1. Some critics claim that in our multimedia age, young people don't hardly read anymore.

2. Yet many cities haven't never had so many bookstores.

3. Many bookstores aren't no longer just places to buy books.

4. They serve as community centers where people can buy coffee, go to poetry readings, and get on the Internet without never buying any books.

25h How do comparatives and superlatives differ?

The comparative and superlative forms of most adjectives and a few adverbs can be expressed two ways.

ugly (an adjective)

Comparative	uglier	more ugly
Superlative	ugliest	most ugly

slowly (an adverb)

Comparative	slower	more slowly
Superlative	slowest	most slowly

As a general rule, use *-er* and *-est* endings with one-syllable adjectives and adverbs but use the terms *more* and *most* (or *less* and *least*) before words of two or more syllables.

Curtis likes **brighter** colors than Kyle.

Kyle wears **more conservative** clothes than Curtis.

1 Be sure to use the comparative, not the superlative, when comparing two items.

FAULTY COMPARISON Marta was the **smartest** of the two children.
Smartest is the superlative, not the comparative, form.

REVISED Marta was the **smarter** of the two children.

2 Use the superlative form when comparing more than two objects or qualities.

Of all the children in her kindergarten class, Marta was the **liveliest**.

3 Avoid doubling the comparative or superlative forms.

CONFUSING Jasper was **more stricter** as a parent than Janice was.

CLEAR Jasper was **stricter** as a parent than Janice was.

CONFUSING Of all the members of the archery team, Diana was the **most angriest** about the stolen targets.

CLEAR Of all the members of the archery team, Diana was the **angriest** about the stolen targets.

EXERCISE 25.7 Write sentences in which you use the appropriate forms of comparison for the situation given.

1. Today community librarians are constantly trying to decide what is (**more/most**) important: expanding computer facilities or buying more books.

2. These librarians consider who among their clients has the (**greater/greatest**) need—schoolchildren, working adults, or retired people.

3. In general, librarians enjoy the reputation of being among the (**most helpful/helpfullest**) of city employees.

4. In good libraries, librarians are also likely to be among the (**most bright/brightest**) city employees.

25i Do you have questions about nonessential and essential modifiers?

In order to know how to introduce and punctuate modifying clauses, you first have to recognize whether they are essential or nonessential.

1 Understand nonessential modifiers. A modifier is **nonessential** when it adds information to a sentence but can be cut without a loss of sense. It is typically surrounded by commas.

WITH NONESSENTIAL MODIFIER	The police officers, **who were wearing their dress uniforms**, marched in front of the mayor's car.
MODIFIER REMOVED	The police officers marched in front of the mayor's car.

2 Understand essential modifiers. When you can't remove a modifying expression from a sentence without affecting its meaning, you have an *essential modifier*.

ESSENTIAL MODIFIER	Diamonds **that are synthetically produced** are more perfect than natural diamonds.
ESSENTIAL MODIFIER REMOVED	Diamonds are more perfect than natural diamonds. The sentence now makes little sense.

Context will determine whether a modifier is essential. Remember this sentence?

NONESSENTIAL	The police officers, **who were wearing their dress uniforms**, marched in front of the mayor's car.

We can make its nonessential modifier essential just by pairing the sentence with another that affects its overall meaning.

ESSENTIAL	The police officers **who were wearing their dress uniforms** marched in front of the mayor's car. The officers **who were in plain clothes** mingled with the crowd as part of a security detail.

Notice that the punctuation changes too, with the modifiers no longer surrounded by commas.

Any clause introduced by *that* will be essential (restrictive) and should not be surrounded by commas. (See Section 24c.)

WRONG	The committee, that I chair, meets every Monday.
RIGHT	The committee that I chair meets every Monday.

EXERCISE 25.8 Following the model provided, first write a sentence with a nonessential modifier. Then add a second sentence that would make the modifier in the first sentence essential. Be sure your version shows the same changes in punctuation that occur in the model.

NONESSENTIAL   The students, who had stood for hours in line, applauded when the ticket window opened.

ESSENTIAL   The students **who had stood for hours in line** applauded when the ticket window opened. Those **who had only just arrived** despaired at ever getting seats for the game.

Is English a Second Language for Yu (ESL)?

26

With Jocelyn Steer and Carol Rhoades

ESL (English as a Second Language) is still the most familiar term to designate language instruction for people whose native tongue may not be English. But the expression fails to capture the circumstances of many people in college writing classes today. For many, English may indeed be a second language—or a third or fourth. For others, English and another language may play equal, if different, roles, one the language of home and community, the other of school and workplace. For people living in border regions, two national languages may merge, so much so that so-called ESL "problems" may reflect attempts to negotiate hybrid grammars and vocabularies. We continue to use ESL as a familiar term, but we appreciate the huge range of writers for whom more technical instruction in edited American English may be helpful. There is no single type of ESL writer.

That said, it is obvious that you will face challenges while working to express ideas in a new language. Writing in a familiar language is not always simple, and writing in a second can be even harder. But because you have experienced the grammatical systems and vocabularies of at least two languages, you have already acquired a lot of linguistic knowledge and skill that should help you become a proficient writer in English.

The next three chapters of this book are designed to help you to build on your language skills and further develop your abilities to manage English.

- This chapter, **Chapter 26**, reviews common problem areas for ESL (English as a Second Language) writers. We list common proofreading errors and identify resources to which you can turn for more help.

- **Chapter 27** gives detailed guidelines for choosing the proper verb forms in your writing.

- **Chapter 28** offers detailed advice for using gerunds, articles, count and noncount nouns, and other grammatical elements that ESL writers often question.

26a What are some common problem areas for ESL writers?

All writers should proofread papers for grammar and punctuation errors before handing in the final copy. (See Section 5c.) Reading your work aloud is the best way to help you find errors. Mistakes you notice when you are proofreading are usually mistakes you know how to correct. Many errors that instructors mark on final drafts could probably have been corrected by more thorough proofreading.

If you know what your most common errors are, check for them first. Also, make sure that you haven't typed some words or word endings in your own language rather than English.

In this section you'll find a list of the most common problems for ESL writers—and their solutions.

1 Be sure each clause has a subject. Every clause in English must have a subject, except for imperative sentences ("Sit down").

INCORRECT	˄Is difficult to write in English.
CORRECT	**It** is difficult to write in English.
	You must have *it* before the verb *is*.

2 Be sure a main or an auxiliary verb isn't missing.

INCORRECT	The teacher˄extremely helpful. *verb missing*
CORRECT	The teacher **is** extremely helpful.
INCORRECT	Hurry! The plane˄leaving right now. *verb missing*
CORRECT	Hurry! The plane **is** leaving right now.

3 Don't forget the -s on verbs used with third person singular nouns and pronouns (*he, she, it*). Check all present tense verbs to make sure you haven't forgotten an -s.

INCORRECT	The library close at 5:00 today. *3rd person sing. -s*
CORRECT	The library closes at 5:00 today.

When you have the auxiliary *do* or *does* in a sentence, add -s to the auxiliary, not to the main verb.

INCORRECT	He **don't** know the answer to the question. *3rd person sing. -s*
CORRECT	He **doesn't** know the answer to the question.

4 Don't forget -*ed* endings on past participles. Use the past participle (-*ed* ending) for verbs in the following cases. (See Section 18d for a list of the three parts of a verb.)

In passive voice (see Section 18e).

INCORRECT	The documents were **alter** by the thief.
CORRECT	The documents were **altered** by the thief.

In the past perfect tense (see Section 27a-3).

INCORRECT Juan had **finish** the race before Fred came.

CORRECT Juan had **finished** the race before Fred came.

In participle adjectives (see Section 15c-2).

INCORRECT She was **frighten** by the dark.

CORRECT She was **frightened** by the dark.

Be sure that you *don't* add endings to infinitives.

INCORRECT George started to **prepared** dinner.

CORRECT George started to **prepare** dinner.

5 Don't confuse adjective pairs such as *bored* and *boring*. The following sentences are different in meaning, although they look similar.

John is bored. This means that John is bored by *something*—maybe his class or his homework; it is a feeling he has as a result of something.

John is boring. This means that John has a personality that is not interesting; he is a boring person.

Adjectives ending in *-ed* have a passive meaning. Adjectives ending in *-ing* have an active meaning. (See Section 18e for an explanation of passive voice.)

The English spelling system often confuses Jorge.

-ED ENDING Jorge is **confused** by the English spelling system. passive

       The **confused** student looked up words in his spelling dictionary. passive

-ING ENDING English spelling is **confusing**. active

       It is a **confusing** system. active

Joan's work satisfies her.

-ED ENDING She is **satisfied** by her work. passive

       She is a **satisfied** employee. passive

-ING ENDING Her work is **satisfying**. active

       Joan does **satisfying** work. active

Chart 26.1 shows some common pairs of adjectives that confuse students, along with the preposition that is used after the *-ed* adjectives.

26.1 Adjective Pairs

	amusing	amused by	exciting	excited by/about
	annoying	annoyed by	frightening	frightened by
	boring	bored by	interesting	interested in
	confusing	confused by	irritating	irritated by
	embarrassing	embarrassed by	satisfying	satisfied with

6 Avoid repeating sentence elements.

In adjective clauses.

The store that I told you about ~~it~~ closed down.
It is not necessary because *that* replaces *it*.

The man whom I met ~~him~~ yesterday was kind.
Whom replaces *him*.

The school where I go ~~there~~ is very expensive.
Where replaces *there*.

In the subject of the sentence.

My brother ~~he~~ is the director of the hospital.
Because *my brother* and *he* refer to the same person, the *he* is unnecessary repetition.

Multiple connectors.

Although the employee was diligent, ~~but~~ she was fired.
Although and *but* both express contrast. You don't need two connectors in one sentence with the same meaning. You must remove one of them.

Because she fell asleep after eating a big lunch, ~~so~~ she missed her class.
So and *because* both express cause. Cut one of them.

7 Place adverbs correctly in the sentence. There are a few positions where adverbs *can't* be placed. (For more help with adverb placement, see Section 25f.)

Don't put an adverb between the verb and its object.

	verb	adverb	obj.
INCORRECT	She answered (slowly) the question.		

	verb	obj.	adverb
CORRECT	She answered the question **slowly**.		

Don't place adverbs of frequency before the verb *be*.

INCORRECT   Louise (regularly) is late for class.

CORRECT   Louise is **regularly** late for class.

Don't place adverbs of frequency after other verbs.

INCORRECT	Juan arrives often late to class.
CORRECT	Juan **often** arrives late to class.

EXERCISE 26.1 Review Section 26a. Then read the following paragraph and proofread it for the mistakes described in that section. In some cases you will need to add something and in others you will delete an element. (There are seven errors. For answers, see p. 265)

> There are long lines at the cashier's office because students signing up for financial aid. Is extremely frustrating to spend the entire day in line. Because some students they have other jobs and classes, so they can't wait very long. Then you very tired when you finally arrive at the desk where you can talk to the clerk there. The clerk usually give you a form to fill out, and then you have to wait in another line!

26b How do you find other ESL resources?

1 Consult relevant material in other chapters of this book. Chart 26.2 lists possible questions, each with the chapter or section in this handbook that covers that problem.

26.2 Where to Find More Help with ESL Grammar Questions

chart

IF YOU HAVE A QUESTION ABOUT	EXAMPLES	GO TO THIS CHAPTER/ SECTION
Abbreviations	Dr., APA, Ms.	37a
Adjective clauses	clauses beginning with *who, which, that*	15d, 24c
Capitalization	English, Japanese	36b–36c
Comparatives/ superlatives	more interesting/the most interesting	25h
Dangling modifiers	Reading the paper, the phone rang.	25a

continued on next page

26.2 Where to Find More Help with ESL Grammar Questions continued

IF YOU HAVE A QUESTION ABOUT	EXAMPLES	GO TO THIS CHAPTER/ SECTION
Irregular verbs	*sit, sat, sat*	18d
Parallelism	I like swimming and fishing.	15h
Passive voice	I was hit by a car.	18e
Plural nouns	child: children	20a
Possessives	the teacher's book	20b–20c
Pronouns	his gain; their loss	21–24
Punctuation	commas, periods	29–35
SENTENCE PROBLEMS		
Run-ons	I am a student I come from Mexico.	30d
Fragments	Because it is my house.	30a–30b
Subject-verb agreement		17

2 Consult reference books especially designed for ESL writers. See the following list of ESL reference books.

hi◉hlight | *References for ESL Students*

We suggest the following reference books and Web sites for ESL students who have questions about grammar and usage.

- Betty S. Azar. *Basic English Grammar: English as a Second Language*. 3rd ed. New York: Pearson ESL, 1996.
- Betty S. Azar. *Understanding and Using English Grammar*. 3rd ed. New York: Pearson ESL, 1998.
- *Dave's ESL Café* <http://www.eslcafe.com/>.
- ESL Resources at OWL—the Online Writing Lab at Purdue University <www.owl.english.edu>.

We also recommend the following dictionary written for the ESL student.

- *Longman Dictionary of American English*. 3rd ed. New York: Longman, 2004.

3 Look for opportunities to listen to, speak, read, and write English in your everyday activities. The best way to increase your proficiency in English is to practice, practice, practice. Look for opportunities to use English every day: email friends and classmates in English; write letters; join a Web chat; read English novels and newspapers; and watch the news in English. When you converse with friends or colleagues who are native speakers of English, ask them to explain expressions that are unfamiliar to you. Enriching your knowledge of English in these ways will enable you to write and speak more easily and fluently.

ANSWER KEY

EXERCISE 26.1

There are long lines at the cashier's office because students **are** signing up for financial aid. **It** is extremely frustrating to spend the entire day in line. Because some students ~~they~~ have other jobs and classes, ~~so~~ they can't wait very long. Then you **are** very tired when you finally arrive at the desk where you can talk to the clerk ~~there~~. The clerk usually **gives** you a form to fill out, and then you have to wait in another line!

Do You Have ESL Questions bout Verbs? **27**

With Jocelyn Steer and Carol Rhoades

English verbs are complicated. If you are a nonnative speaker, you will probably still have questions about them, even after many years of studying English. For additional help with verbs, see Chapter 18.

27a Which verb tense should you use?

A verb's tense expresses time. Chart 27.1 shows the 12 most commonly used verb tenses, along with a list of common adverbs and expressions that accompany them. Each diagram illustrates the timeline for a tense; in the diagram, an *X* indicates an action, and a curved line indicates an action in progress.

27.1 Verb Tenses

chart

WHAT IT IS CALLED	WHAT IT LOOKS LIKE	WHAT IT DESCRIBES	TIME WORDS USED WITH IT
Simple present	• I *sleep* eight hours every day.	Habits, regular activities	• every day • often • regularly • always
	• Water *freezes* at 0°C.	Facts, general truths	• usually • habitually
Simple past	• I *slept* only four hours yesterday. • He *went* to sleep three hours ago.	A finished action in the past	• yesterday • last year • ago
Simple future	• I *am going to sleep* early tonight. • I *will* try to sleep more.	A single action in the future A planned action in the future (use *be going to*)	• tomorrow • in *x* days • next year

WHAT IT IS CALLED	WHAT IT LOOKS LIKE	WHAT IT DESCRIBES	TIME WORDS USED WITH IT
Present perfect 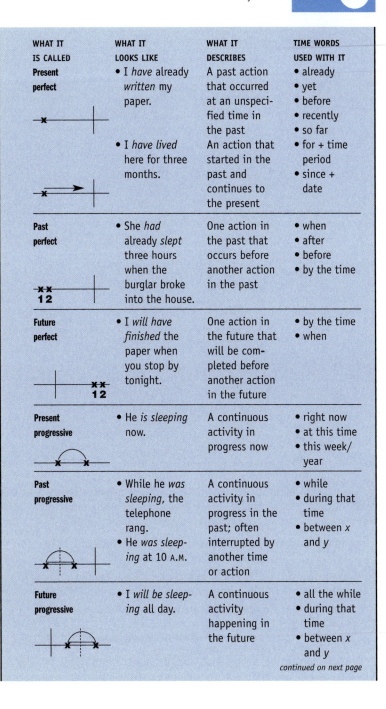	• I *have* already *written* my paper. • I *have lived* here for three months.	A past action that occurred at an unspecified time in the past An action that started in the past and continues to the present	• already • yet • before • recently • so far • for + time period • since + date
Past perfect	• She *had* already *slept* three hours when the burglar broke into the house.	One action in the past that occurs before another action in the past	• when • after • before • by the time
Future perfect	• I *will have finished* the paper when you stop by tonight.	One action in the future that will be completed before another action in the future	• by the time • when
Present progressive	• He *is sleeping* now.	A continuous activity in progress now	• right now • at this time • this week/year
Past progressive	• While he *was sleeping*, the telephone rang. • He *was sleeping* at 10 A.M.	A continuous activity in progress in the past; often interrupted by another time or action	• while • during that time • between *x* and *y*
Future progressive	• I *will be sleeping* all day.	A continuous activity happening in the future	• all the while • during that time • between *x* and *y*

continued on next page

27.1 Verb Tenses *continued*

chart

WHAT IT IS CALLED	WHAT IT LOOKS LIKE	WHAT IT DESCRIBES	TIME WORDS USED WITH IT
Present perfect progressive	• The woman *has been waiting* for many hours. • He *has been sleeping* since eight o'clock.	A continuous activity that began in the past and continues to the present; emphasis is on the duration	• for + time period • since + exact date
Past perfect progressive	• She *had been waiting* for three hours before he arrived. • He *had been sleeping* for an hour when the train crashed.	A continuous activity in the past that is finished before another action in the past	• for • since
Future perfect progressive	• I *will have been sleeping* for twelve hours by the time you arrive.	A continuing future activity which started before another future event	• by • when

1 Review the difference between the simple present tense and the present progressive tense.
Use the simple present tense when you want to talk about *regular, repeated* activity.

SIMPLE PRESENT	The mail carrier usually **arrives** at 10 A.M. This is an activity that is repeated daily.
PRESENT PROGRESSIVE	Look! She **is putting** the mail in the box now. This is an activity occurring at the moment of speaking—now.
PRESENT PROGRESSIVE	She **is delivering** mail for John this month. This is an activity that is in progress over a period of time. Use the progressive tense with the expression *this + time period*.

2 Review nonaction verbs and the present tense.
Some verbs in English can't be used in a progressive form because they express a state and not an activity. Nonaction verbs include verbs of existence, of

thought, of emotions, and of sense perceptions. Chart 27.2 lists some of these verbs. To use one of these nonaction verbs, you must use a simple form of the verb even though the time intended is *now*.

INCORRECT	I can't study because I **am hearing** my roommate's singing.
CORRECT	I can't study because I **hear** my roommate's singing.
INCORRECT	Maria **is preferring** Carlos's apartment to her own.
CORRECT	Maria **prefers** Carlos's apartment to her own.

27.2 Nonaction Verbs*

chart

appear	forget	owe	seem
be	hate	own	smell
belong	have	possess	sound
consist	hear	prefer	surprise
contain	know	recognize	taste
deserve	like	remember	think
desire	love	require	understand
dislike	mean	resemble	want
feel	need	see	wish

*There are exceptions to the nonaction rule ("I **am thinking** about getting a job"; "He **is seeing** a doctor about his insomnia"). These exceptions can usually be paraphrased using other verbs ("He **is seeing** a doctor about his insomnia" means "He **is consulting** a doctor about his insomnia").

---

3 Review the difference between the simple past tense and the present perfect tense. If an action happened in the past and is finished, you can always use the simple past tense to describe it. (See Chapter 18 on how to form the past tense and for a list of irregular verbs.) Often you will also use a time word such as *ago* or *yesterday* to specify the time of the past action.

SIMPLE PAST	My brother **saw** that movie three days ago.
	We know exactly when the brother saw the movie—three days ago. You *must* use the simple past in this sentence.

Use the **past tense** to show that something is completed, and use the **present perfect tense** to indicate that the action may continue or that it still has the possibility of occurring in the future.

SIMPLE PAST	My grandmother never **used** a computer.
	This implies that the grandmother may no longer be alive.
PRESENT PERFECT	My mother **has** never **used** a computer.
	This sentence indicates that the mother is still alive and may use a computer in the future.

When you don't know or you don't want to state the exact time or date of a past action, use the present perfect tense.

PRESENT PERFECT · Sarah **has seen** that movie before.
We don't know when Sarah saw the movie; she saw it at an unspecified time in the past.

You must use the present perfect for an action that began in the past and continues up to the present moment, especially when you use the time words *for* and *since*.

PRESENT PERFECT · This theater **has shown** the same film for three months! I hope they change it soon.
The action started in the past—three months ago—and continues to the present. The film is still playing.

4 Review the difference between the present perfect tense and the present perfect progressive tense. You can use a **present perfect progressive** tense to show that an action is still in progress.

PRESENT PERFECT
PROGRESSIVE · Catherine **has been writing** that letter
since this morning. She hasn't finished; she's still writing.

In general, when the statement emphasizes *duration* (length of time), you need to use a present perfect progressive tense.

PRESENT PERFECT
PROGRESSIVE · My best friend **has been writing** her novel
for five years.
This tells us how long the friend has been writing; the emphasis is on duration, or length of time.

However, when the statement emphasizes *quantity* (how much), you will use a **present perfect tense**.

PRESENT PERFECT · Toni Morrison **has written** several well-received novels.
This tells us how many books; it talks about quantity.

EXERCISE 27.1 Review Sections 27a-1 and 27a-2. Choose the correct tense—simple present or present progressive. (For answers, see p. 279.)

1. Many people have bizarre dreams, but I usually (**dream/am dreaming**) about something that (**happens/is happening**) during the day.

2. I often (**remember/am remembering**) my dreams right after I (**wake/am waking**) up.

3. Sometimes when I (**hear/am hearing**) a noise while I (**dream/am dreaming**), I will incorporate that into my dream.

4. I (**know/am knowing**) a lot about dreams because I (**write/am writing**) a paper about them this semester.

EXERCISE 27.2 Review Section 27a-3. Choose the best verb tense—simple past or present perfect. Use the present perfect when possible. (For answers, see p. 279.)

1. This month the newspapers (**had/have had**) many articles about a phenomenon called the glass ceiling.

2. This refers to an unofficial limitation on promotion for women who (**worked/have worked**) in a corporation for several years and who cannot advance beyond middle management.

3. Last year my mother (**applied/has applied**) for the position of vice president of the company she works for, but they (**did not promote/ have not promoted**) her.

4. She (**had/has had**) the most experience of all the candidates for the job, but a man was chosen instead.

EXERCISE 27.3 Review Section 27a. Fill in the blanks with the most precise and appropriate tense of the verb *talk*. Pay special attention to time words. Incorporate the adverbs in parentheses into your answers. (For answers, see p. 280.)

1. They _____ about the issue since yesterday.

2. Some employees _____ about it when we arrived at work.

3. They _____ (**probably**) about the issue when they leave work.

4. We _____ about it many times in the past.

5. I never _____ about this topic last week.

27b How do you use transitive and intransitive verbs?

A **transitive verb** is a verb that has a direct object. This means that the verb has an effect on, or does something to, that object. A transitive verb without a direct object is incomplete; it does not make sense.

INCORRECT	She raised.
	This thought is incomplete; we need to know *what* she raised.
CORRECT	She raised **her children** on a farm.

There are two types of transitive verbs. (See Chart 27.3 for a list of them.) One type—verb + direct object—*must* be followed directly by a noun or pronoun.

VERB + DIRECT OBJECT (TRANS. V. = TRANSITIVE VERB)

subj.   trans. v.   noun
This university **needs** more parking lots.

subj.   trans. v.   pronoun
The trustees **discussed** it at the last meeting.

The second type—verb + (indirect object) + direct object—*can* be followed by an indirect object (a person receiving the action) before the direct object. When you use *to* or *for* in front of the indirect object, the position changes, as you can see in these examples.

VERB + (INDIRECT OBJECT) + DIRECT OBJECT

dir. obj.
Ron bought **a rose**.

indir. obj. dir. obj.
Ron bought *his wife* **a rose**.

or

dir. obj. + *for/to* + indir. obj.
Ron bought **a rose** *for his wife*.

An **intransitive verb** is complete without a direct object. In fact, you cannot put a direct object after an intransitive verb.

| INCORRECT | She grew up **her children**. *Her children cannot come after the verb grew up because her children is an object; objects cannot come after intransitive verbs.* |

However, other words can come after intransitive verbs.

| CORRECT | She grew up **quickly**. *Quickly is an adverb. You can put an adverb after this verb. This sentence means that she matured at a very fast rate.* |
| CORRECT | She grew up **on a farm**. *On a farm is a prepositional phrase, not a direct object.* |

There are two kinds of intransitive verbs—linking verbs and action verbs. (See Chart 27.3 for a list of these verbs.)

subj. l.v.   comp.
LINKING VERBS   This book **seems** very old. l.v. = linking verb

subj. l.v. comp.
Your professor **is** an expert in law.

subj.   a.v.

ACTION VERBS   Jacqueline **complained**. a.v. = action verb

subj.   a.v.   prep. phrase

Jacqueline **complained** to me before breakfast.

(For more information on transitive and intransitive verbs, see Section 18e.)

 Transitive and Intransitive Verbs

TRANSITIVE VERBS*

- **Verb + direct object:** *attend, bring up, choose, do, have, hit, hold, keep, lay, need, raise, say, spend, use, want, watch, wear*
- **Verb + (indirect object) + direct object:** *bring, buy, get, give, make, pay, send, take, tell*

INTRANSITIVE VERBS*

- **Linking verbs:** *appear, be, become, seem, look*
- **Action verbs:** *arrive, come, get dressed, go, grow up, laugh, lie, listen, live, rise, run, sit, sleep, walk, work*

*These lists are not complete. You can always consult your dictionary to find out whether a verb is transitive or intransitive.

27c How do you use two-word and three-word verbs?

Some verbs in English consist of two or three words, usually a main verb and a preposition. These verbs are idioms because you can't understand the meaning of the verb simply by knowing the separate meaning of each of the two or three words. There are many two- and three-word verbs in English. It's best for you to learn them as you hear them and to keep a list of them for reference. Chart 27.4 lists common two- and three-word verbs. Two-word verbs that are transitive—which means they can have a direct object—are divided into two groups: **separable** and **inseparable**. (See Section 27b for an explanation of transitive verbs.)

27.4 **Common Two-word and Three-word Verbs**

chart

This list is not complete; there are many more such verbs. An asterisk (*) indicates an *inseparable* verb: the verb and the preposition cannot be separated by an object. A cross (+) indicates verbs that have additional meanings not given here.

VERB	DEFINITION
break down*	stop functioning
bring on	cause something to happen
call off	cancel
catch up with*+	attain the same position, place
check into*	explore, investigate
come across*	encounter unintentionally
cut down on*	reduce the amount of
do over	repeat
figure out	solve a problem, dilemma
find out	discover
get along with*	have harmonious relations
get in*+	enter a car
get off*+	exit from (a bus, a train, a plane)
get on*	enter (a bus, a train, a plane)
get over*	recover from (a sickness, a relationship)
give up	stop trying
go over*	review
grow up*	mature, become an adult
keep up with*	maintain the same level
look after*	take care of
look into*	explore, investigate
make up+	invent
pass away*	die
pick out	make a selection
put off	postpone
put up with*	tolerate
run into*+	meet by chance
show up*	appear, arrive
stand up for*	defend, support
sum up	summarize, conclude
take after*	resemble, look alike
touch on*	discuss briefly

1 Separable verbs. You can place the object *before* or *after* the preposition.

CORRECT   Lee checked **the book** *out* from the library.
The object (*the book*) is placed *before* the preposition (*out*).

CORRECT	Lee checked *out* **the book** from the library.
	The object comes *after* the preposition.

However, when the object is a *pronoun* (such as *it* in the following example), the pronoun *must* come *before* the preposition.

INCORRECT	Gary checked out **it** from the library.
CORRECT	Gary checked **it** out from the library.

2 Inseparable verbs. You cannot separate the verb and the preposition.

INCORRECT	My sister **majored** history **in**.
CORRECT	My sister **majored in** history.

INCORRECT	The frantic student **stayed** all night **up** to study.
CORRECT	The frantic student **stayed up** all night to study.

EXERCISE 27.4 Review Sections 27a through 27c. Each of the following sentences contains errors related to verb tense, transitive/intransitive verbs, and two-word verbs. Identify the errors and correct them. (For answers, see p. 280.)

1. Before I study psychology, I thought it was an easy subject.

2. Now I am knowing that it isn't easy.

3. It has had a lot of statistics.

4. I am studying psychology since April, and I only begin to learn some of the concepts.

5. I have been tried to learn more of the concepts every day.

6. Last night I have studied from 9:00 to midnight.

27d Which modal should you use?

You already know that a verb's tense expresses time. A *modal*, which is an auxiliary or helping verb, expresses necessity, obligation, regret, and formality. Modals can be used to express ideas about the past, present, or future.

PAST	I **could** speak Japanese as a child.
PRESENT	My brother **can** speak Japanese now.
FUTURE	I **might** learn another language next semester.

The common modals are *could, should, must*, and *have to*. You may have questions about others, such as *had better, have to*, and *ought to*.

1 Choose the modal that best expresses your idea. Chart 27.5 summarizes the functions of modals. It also lists the past form of the modals. Modals in the present are followed by the base form of the verb—for example, "Kim **may** win the prize" (subject + modal + base form of the verb). The form of modals in the past varies. (See Section 27d-3 for more details.)

(27.5) Modals

WHAT IT MEANS	PRESENT OR FUTURE FORM	PAST FORM
Permission *(Informal → Formal)*		
can	**Can** I be excused?	He **could have**
could	**Could** I be excused?	**been** excused, but
may	**May** I be excused?	he didn't ask.
would you mind*	**Would you mind if** I *brought* my dog?	**Would you have minded if** I *had brought* my dog?
Ability		
can	Joe **can** drive a car.	He **couldn't** drive a car last year.
be able to	Carl **is able to** study and listen to music at the same time.	Celia **was never able to** play the Mozart concertos.
Advice		
should	You **should** quit.	He **should have**
ought to	You **ought to** quit.	quit last year.
had better	You **had better** quit.	He didn't quit; this sentence shows regret.
Necessity		
have to	He **has to** pay a fine.	He **had to** pay a fine last week.
must	She **must** pay her taxes.	No past form; use *had to.*
Lack of necessity		
not have to	You **don't have to** attend school in summer.	He **didn't have to** take the final exam last year.
not need to	You **don't need to** pay in advance.	You **didn't need to** pay in advance.

Would you mind is followed by *if* + the past tense of the verb.

WHAT IT MEANS	PRESENT OR FUTURE FORM	PAST FORM
Possibility (More sure → Less sure)		
can	It **can** get cold in May.	No past form.
may	It **may** get cold in June this year.	I'm not sure, but it **may have** just happened.
could	It **could** get cold in July this year.	It **could have** just happened.
might	It **might** get cold in July this year.	It **might have** just happened.
Conclusion		
must	Your eyes are all red; you **must have** allergies. I'm almost certain that this is true.	You got an *A* on your test. You **must have studied** hard! I'm certain that you did this in the past.
Expectation		
should/ ought to	Your keys **should be** on the desk where I left them. I expect them to be there.	John **should have been** elected. He didn't get elected, but I expected him to.
Polite requests (Informal → Formal)		
can	**Can** you give me a hand?	No past forms.
will	**Will** you give me a hand?	
could	**Could** you give me a hand?	
would you mind + present participle	**Would you mind** giving me a hand?	

2 Use the correct form of the modal auxiliary and the main verb that follows it. Modals that express present and future time have this form.

SUBJECT + MODAL + BASE FORM OF VERB

Clarissa **had better** register for classes soon.

- Don't use *to* or a present participle (*-ing* form of a verb) after the modal.

INCORRECT	Jacquie **can** ~~to~~ play the guitar very well.
CORRECT	Jacquie **can** play the guitar very well.
INCORRECT	**Must** I ~~to~~ hand in this paper tomorrow?
CORRECT	**Must** I hand in this paper tomorrow?
EXCEPT	We **have to** write a 10-page paper.
INCORRECT	They **should reading** before class.
CORRECT	They **should read** before class.

- There is no *-s* on the third person singular of a modal.

INCORRECT	Kwang **might~~s~~** go to graduate school.
CORRECT	Kwang **might** go to graduate school.

- Never use two modals together.

INCORRECT	They **might co~~u~~ld** drive all night.
CORRECT	They **might** drive all night.

- *Do, does,* and *did* are not used in questions with modals, except for the modal *have to.*

INCORRECT	**Do** I **must** answer all the questions?
CORRECT	**Must** I answer all the questions?
EXCEPT	**Do** I **have to** answer all the questions?

- *Do, does,* and *did* are not used in negative statements with modals; use *not* instead, placed after the modal.

INCORRECT	They **do not can** enter the test room.
CORRECT	They **cannot** enter the test room.
INCORRECT	Jorge **did not could** have worked any harder.
CORRECT	Jorge **could not have** worked any harder.

3 Use the perfect form to express past time The past of modals that give advice or express possibility, expectation, and conclusion have a *perfect* verb form (modal + *have* + past participle), as you can see in the following examples.

ADVICE	Gail **should have taken** that marketing job last year.
	Gail didn't take the job.

POSSIBILITY	Although he chose not to, Bob **could have gone** to Mexico over spring break. Bob didn't go to Mexico.
EXPECTATION	Where is Sue? She **should have been** here by now. Sue hasn't arrived yet.
CONCLUSION	Ted finished; he **must have worked** all night.

EXERCISE 27.5 Review Section 27d-1. Fill in the blanks with a modal from the list below. More than one answer is possible for each blank. Try to use each modal only once. (For answers, see p. 280.)

would	must	have to	ought to	should have
should	can	might	had better	must have

1. Can you believe the line waiting to see the movie *Superman Returns*? That _____ be a good movie!

2. Where is my purse, Mom? It _____ be on the table where you put it last night.

3. I'm sorry, Professor Lopez, but I _____ not take the test tomorrow because I _____ go to Immigration about my visa.

4. Jason, you _____ eat your vegetables or you won't get any dessert.

EXERCISE 27.6 Review Section 27d. Each of the following sentences contains errors related to modal auxiliaries. Identify the errors and correct them. (For answers, see p. 280.)

1. Megan's boss told her, "You had better to improve your attitude, or we will have to take disciplinary action."

2. Megan was very distressed by this news; she did not could understand the basis for her boss's complaints.

3. She tried to think of things that she had done wrong. She knew that she should had been more enthusiastic at the last meeting, but she felt she couldn't be hypocritical. She simply didn't agree with her boss.

ANSWER KEY

EXERCISE 27.1
1. dream; happens
2. remember; wake
3. hear; am dreaming
4. know; am writing

EXERCISE 27.2
1. have had
2. have worked
3. applied; did not promote
4. had

EXERCISE 27.3
1. have been talking
2. were talking
3. will probably be talking
4. have talked
5. talked

EXERCISE 27.4
1. Before I **studied** psychology, I (**had**) **thought** it was an easy subject.
2. Now I **know** that it isn't easy.
3. It **has** a lot of statistics.
4. I **have been studying** psychology since April, and I **have only begun** to learn some of the concepts.
5. I **have been trying** to learn more of the concepts every day.
6. Last night I **was studying** from 9:00 to midnight.
   or
   Last night I **studied** from 9:00 to midnight.

EXERCISE 27.5
1. must; should
2. should; ought to; must; had better
3. cannot/might have to; might/should
4. had better; must; should; ought to

EXERCISE 27.6
1. Megan's boss told her, "You had better ꭓ improve your attitude, or we will have to take disciplinary action."
2. Megan was very distressed by this news; she **could not** (*or* **did not**) understand the basis for her boss's complaints.
3. She tried to think of things that she had done wrong. She knew that she **should have been** more enthusiastic at the last meeting, but she felt she couldn't be hypocritical. She simply didn't agree with her boss.

Do You Have ESL Questions About Gerunds, Infinitives, Articles, r Numbers? 28

With Jocelyn Steer and Carol Rhoades

This chapter offers guidelines for handling grammatical concepts that many ESL writers find confusing: gerunds, infinitives, articles, and number agreement.

28a How do you use gerunds and infinitives?

In English, gerunds and infinitives have several functions. (See Section 19a for definitions of *gerund* and *infinitive*.)

Gerunds can function as subject, object, complement, and object of a preposition. (See Sections 15a-1 and 15c for explanations of *complement* and *object of a preposition*.)

An **infinitive** can be the subject of a sentence, and it can be the object of a verb.

ESL writers often have difficulty with gerunds and infinitives that act as objects in a sentence.

1 Review which form—gerund or infinitive—to use. Some verbs in English are followed by gerunds and other verbs are followed by infinitives.

GERUND (BASE FORM OF VERB + -*ING*)

He enjoys **jogging** in the park.

INFINITIVE (*TO* + BASE FORM OF VERB)

I want **to go** with you.

Other verbs, however, can have *either* a gerund or an infinitive after them without a difference in meaning.

GERUND OR INFINITIVE (NO CHANGE IN MEANING)

gerund
The dog began **barking** at midnight.

infinitive
The dog began **to bark** at midnight.
These two sentences have exactly the same meaning.

Finally, some verbs in English (including *forget, regret, remember, stop, try*) can be followed by *either* a gerund or an infinitive, but with a change in meaning.

GERUND OR INFINITIVE (CHANGE IN MEANING)

Paul stopped **working** in the cafeteria.
Paul *no longer* works in the cafeteria.

Paul stopped his tennis game early **to work** on his homework.
Paul stopped his game *in order to* work on his homework.

Paul forgot **to visit** his cousin while he was in Mexico.
He did *not* visit his cousin.

Paul will never forget **visiting** Mexico.
Paul visited Mexico and he will always remember the trip.

Native speakers know intuitively whether to use a gerund or an infinitive after a verb, but this is not usually true for ESL students.

Chart 28.1 can help you; be sure to keep this chart handy when you write.

28.1 Verbs Followed by Gerunds or Infinitives

VERB + INFINITIVE
These verbs are followed by **infinitives**, but not gerunds.

afford	consent	intend	pretend
agree	decide	learn	promise
appear	deserve	manage	refuse
arrange	expect	mean	seem
ask	fail	need	threaten
beg	hesitate	offer	wait
claim	hope	plan	wish

VERB + GERUND
These verbs are followed by **gerunds**, but not infinitives.

admit	deny	mention	recommend
anticipate	discuss	miss	resent
appreciate	dislike	postpone	resist
avoid	enjoy	practice	risk
complete	finish	quit	suggest
consider	can't help	recall	tolerate
delay	keep	recollect	understand

VERB + GERUND OR INFINITIVE
These verbs can be followed by either a **gerund** or an **infinitive**, with no change in meaning.

begin	can't stand	hate	prefer
can't bear	continue	like	start

> **VERB + GERUND OR INFINITIVE WITH A CHANGE IN MEANING**
> These verbs can be followed by either a **gerund** or an **infinitive**, but the meaning of the sentence will change depending on which one you use.
>
> | VERB | MEANING |
> | --- | --- |
> | try (to be) | make an attempt to be |
> | try (being) | do an experiment |
> | regret (to be) | feel sorry about |
> | regret (being) | feel sorry about *past* action |
> | remember (to be) | not forget |
> | remember (being) | recall, bring to mind |
> | forget (to be) | not remember |
> | (never) forget (being) | always remember |
> | stop (to be) | stop in order to be |
> | stop (being) | interrupt an action |

2 Review when a verb must be followed by a noun or a pronoun. With some verbs, a noun or pronoun must come between the verb and the infinitive that follows it. The noun or pronoun usually names the person who is affected by the verb.

INCORRECT   I told∧to write me a letter.
   The object is missing; the sentence is incomplete.

CORRECT   I told **my son** to write me a letter.
   My son is the indirect object; this sentence is complete.

Chart 28.2 lists the verbs that follow this pattern.

> **(28.2) Verbs Followed by Nouns, Pronouns, or Infinitives**
>
> **chart**
>
> **VERB + (NOUN OR PRONOUN) + INFINITIVE**
> These verbs must be followed by a **noun** or a **pronoun** + an **infinitive**.
>
> | | | |
> | --- | --- | --- |
> | advise | forbid | persuade |
> | allow | force | remind |
> | cause | hire | require |
> | challenge | instruct | tell |
> | convince | invite | urge |
> | encourage | order | warn |

3 Instead of being followed by an infinitive, the verbs *have*, *make*, and *let* are followed by a noun or pronoun and the base form of the verb. This means that you omit *to* before the verb.

HAVE   I **had** my mother *cut* my hair.
   Here *had* means to cause someone to do something.

MAKE The teacher **made** him *leave* the class.
Here *made* means to force someone to do something; it is stronger than *had*.

LET Professor Betts **let** the class *leave* early.
Here *let* means to allow someone to do something.

4 Use a gerund after a preposition. Always use a gerund, not an infinitive, after prepositions.

      verb   adj.   prep.   gerund

Carla has been very worried **about passing** her statistics class.

      verb   prep.   gerund

Mrs. Short apologized **for interrupting** our conversation.

Chart 28.3 lists common preposition combinations with verbs and adjectives.

(28.3) **Common Verb (+ Adjective) + Preposition Constructions**

Chart

be accustomed to	be faithful to	pray for
be afraid of	be familiar with	prevent from
approve of	be fond of	prohibit from
be aware of	be good at	protect from
believe in	be grateful to	be proud of
be capable of	be guilty of	rely on
be committed to	hope for	be responsible for
complain about	insist on	be satisfied with
be composed of	be interested in	be scared of
consist of	be jealous of	stop from
depend on	look forward to	succeed in
be disappointed in	be made of	take advantage of
be divorced from	be married to	take care of
dream of/about	object to	be tired of
be envious of	be opposed to	be worried about
be excited about	be patient with	

EXERCISE 28.1 Fill in the blanks with the infinitive, gerund, or base form of the verbs in parentheses. (For answers, see p. 280.)

1. Women who have not wanted (**work**) _____ because of health threats can now relax.

2. A recent study completed in California shows that women who work outside the home seem (**have**) _____ fewer health problems than those who work inside the home.

3. Another federal study reports that women employed outside the home do not risk (**have**) _____ more "stress-induced" heart attacks than women working inside the home.

4. In fact, this study appears (**support**) _____ the benefits of working outside the home for women.

5. In general, working women are found (**be**) _____ physically and mentally healthier than women who stay at home.

28b Do you have questions about articles and number agreement?

This section gives you general guidelines about articles and expressions of quantity. For the finer points about articles not covered here, please consult one of the ESL grammar references listed on page 264.

1 Decide whether the noun is count or noncount. In order to know which article to use, you first need to determine whether the noun in question is *count* or *noncount*. A **count noun** refers to something that you can count or that you can divide easily.

A **noncount noun** generally refers to something that cannot usually be counted or divided. Noncount nouns include **mass nouns** such as materials (*wood, plastic, wool*), food items (*cheese, rice, meat*) and liquids (*water, milk*), and **abstract nouns** (*beauty, knowledge, glory*).

Some nouns that are noncount may seem like things that you can count, such as *money*. Many other noncount nouns can confuse ESL students: *furniture, hair, traffic, information, advice*.

Unlike count nouns, which can be singular or plural, noncount nouns have only the singular form. In addition, since you can't count these nouns, you can't use numbers or words that express number (*several, many*) to describe them. You will use other types of expressions to indicate quantity for noncount nouns; these expressions, called *quantifiers*, are discussed in Section 28b-5.

Most nouns are either count or noncount. However, some noncount nouns can change to have a count meaning. Instances in which a noncount noun changes to a count noun include when you mean *an instance of, a serving of*, or *a type of* the noncount noun.

count noun
His grandmother started a **business**. one instance of business

count noun
I'd like two **coffees** to go, please. two servings of coffee

count noun
There are three new **wines** on the menu. three kinds of wine

2 Decide whether the count noun requires a definite article (*the*) or an indefinite article (*a/an*).

When the count noun is singular, you'll need an article, either *a/an* or *the*, in front of it. Generally, when you introduce the noun, without having referred to it before, then you will use the *indefinite* article, *a* or *an*. (See Section 20d for the difference between *a* and *an*.)

INDEFINITE MEANING

Bob: I just signed up for a literature class.

Ted: Oh, really? I didn't know you were interested in that.
This is the first time Bob has mentioned the class to Ted.

After that, when both of them know what is being discussed, Bob will use the *definite* article, *the*.

DEFINITE MEANING

Bob: Can you believe **the** class meets on Friday evenings?
Both Bob and Ted now share the same information.

Certain other situations also require the definite article, *the*.

- When there is only one of the noun.

  The earth is round. There is only one earth.

- When the noun is superlative.

  This is **the best** brand you can buy.
  There can only be one brand that is the best.

- When the noun is limited. You will usually use *the* before a noun that has been limited in some way to show that you are referring to a *specific* example of the noun.

  The book **that I read** is informative.
  That I read limits the book to a specific one.

If you are making a *generalization*, however, *the* is not always used.

  A book **on plants** can make a nice gift.
  On plants limits the noun, but the sentence does not refer to a specific book on plants—it refers to *any or all books on plants*. The definite article, *the*, would not be correct here.

3 Choose articles before general nouns carefully.

When you want to make generalizations, choosing the correct article can be tricky. As a rule, use *a/an* or *the* with most *singular count nouns* to make generalizations.

  A dog can be good company for **a** lonely person.
  Use *a/an* to mean any dog, one of many dogs.

  The computer has changed the banking industry dramatically.
  Use *the* to mean *the computer in general*.

  The spotted owl is an endangered species.

The capitalist believes in free enterprise.
Use *the* to make general statements about specific species of animals (*spotted owl*) or groups of people (*capitalists*).

He was ill and went to **the** hospital.
American English uses the definite article with *hospital* even when we do not refer to a specific hospital; British English does not use the article with *hospital*.

Use a *plural count noun* to make general statements, without *the*.

Capitalists believe in free enterprise.

Computers have changed the banking industry dramatically.

Finally, *noncount nouns* in general statements do not have an article in front of them.

Sugar is a major cause of tooth decay.

Many educators question whether **intelligence** can be measured.

Consumed in moderate amounts, **red wine** is thought by some researchers to reduce chances of heart disease.

4 Be aware of two possible article problems with noncount nouns.
Don't use *a* / *an* with noncount nouns.

INCORRECT	I need a work.
CORRECT	I need work.

Second, a noncount noun can never be plural.

INCORRECT	Joe needs some informations about the class.
CORRECT	Joe needs some information about the class.

5 Pay careful attention to quantifiers.
The words that come before nouns and tell you *how much* or *how many* are called **quantifiers**. Quantifiers are not always the same for both count and noncount nouns. Chart 28.4 provides a list of quantifiers.

(28.4) Quantifiers — chart

USE THESE WITH COUNT AND NON-COUNT NOUNS	USE THESE WITH COUNT NOUNS ONLY	USE THESE WITH NONCOUNT NOUNS ONLY
some books/money	**several** books	**a good deal of** money
a lot of books/money	**many** books	**a great deal of** money
plenty of books/money	**a couple of** books	**(not) much** money*
a lack of books/money	**a few** books	**a little** money
most of the books/money	**few** books	**little** money

Much is ordinarily used only in questions and in negative statements: "Do you have *much* milk left?" "No, there isn't *much* milk."

A few/a little and ***few/little*** It may not seem like a big difference, but the article *a* in front of the quantifiers *few* and *little* changes the meaning. *A few* or *a little* means "not a lot, but enough of the item."

There are **a few books** in the library on capital punishment.
Use *a few* with count nouns.

There is **a little information** in the library on capital punishment.
Use *a little* with noncount nouns.

Few or *little* (without *a*) means that there is *not enough* of something. These quantifiers have a negative meaning.

There are **few** female leaders in the world.
not enough of them

My mother has **little** hope that this will change.
not much hope

Most and ***most of*** Using *most of* can be tricky. You can use *most of* before either a count or a noncount noun, but if you do, don't forget to put *the* before the noun.

MOST OF + THE + SPECIFIC PLURAL NOUN

Most of the *women* in the class were married. Not: *most of women*

MOST OF + THE + SPECIFIC NONCOUNT NOUN

Most of the *jewelry* in the house was stolen. Not: *most of jewelry*

MOST + GENERAL PLURAL NOUN

Most *cars* have seat belts. Not: *most of cars*

EXERCISE 28.2 In the list of nouns below, write *C* after the count nouns and *NC* after the noncount nouns. If you are not sure, consult an ESL dictionary. Then make a note of the nouns you had to check. (For answers, see p. 289.)

1. furniture
2. work
3. dollar
4. job
5. advice
6. people
7. equipment
8. money
9. newspaper
10. traffic

EXERCISE 28.3 Review Section 28b. Each of the following sentences has at least one error in the use of articles or quantifiers. Circle the error and correct it. (For answers, see p. 289.)

1. Much people have visited the new restaurant downtown called Rock-and-Roll Hamburger Haven.

2. Most of customers are young people because music in restaurant is very loud.

3. The restaurant serves the usual food—hamburgers, pizza, and pasta. It is not expensive; in fact, most expensive item on the menu is only $8.

4. Food is not very good, but the atmosphere is very appealing to these young men and women.

EXERCISE 28.4 Write a descriptive paragraph about ordering and eating a meal at your favorite restaurant. Refer to Chart 28.4 on page 287, which lists quantifiers used with count and noncount nouns, and use at least four words from this list in your paragraph. Underline all the nouns in your paragraph and write *C* (for count nouns) and *NC* (for noncount nouns) above them. Then check your use of articles. (For help, refer to Sections 28b-2 through 28b-4.) Make sure your subject-verb agreement is correct.

ANSWER KEY

EXERCISE 28.1
1. to work
2. to have
3. having
4. to support
5. to be

EXERCISE 28.2
1. NC
2. NC
3. C
4. C
5. NC
6. C
7. NC
8. NC
9. C
10. NC

EXERCISE 28.3
1. **Many** people have visited the new restaurant downtown called Rock-and-Roll Hamburger Haven.
2. Most of **the** customers are young people because **the** music in **the** restaurant is very loud.
3. The restaurant serves the usual food—hamburgers, pizza, and pasta. It is not expensive; in fact, **the** most expensive item on the menu is only $8.
4. **The** food is not very good, but the atmosphere is very appealing to these young men and women.

EXERCISE 28.4
Answers will vary.

part

6

Punctuation and Mechanics

How Do Yu Punctuate Sentence Endings?

29

29a When do you use periods?

Sentences and some abbreviations end with periods. Periods say, "That's all there is."

1 Use periods at the end of statements.

Hannibal, a Carthaginian general, was a brilliant military strategist.

2 Use periods at the end of indirect questions and mild commands.

Military theorists wonder whether any battle plan has been more tactically perfect than Hannibal's at Cannae (216 B.C.).

On the map, locate the Roman and Carthaginian positions.

3 Use periods to punctuate some abbreviations.

Cong.	natl.
sing., pl.	pp.

When a statement ends with an abbreviation, the period at the end of the sentence is not doubled.

We visited the Folger Library in Washington, D.C.

When the sentence is a question or an exclamation, the period at the end of the abbreviation is retained.

Have you ever been to Washington, D.C.**?**
Our flight departs at 6:00 A.M.**!**

When an abbreviation occurs in the middle of a sentence, it retains its period. The period may even be followed by another punctuation mark.

Though he signed his name Quentin P. Randolph, Esq., we called him Bubba.

Abbreviations for institutions, corporations, networks, or government agencies usually don't require periods; neither do words shortened by common use.

NCAA	GM	HBO	FEMA
lab	auto	dorm	co-op

Similarly, acronyms—first-letter abbreviations pronounced as words—don't take periods.

CARE   NATO   NOW

When do you use question marks?

Question marks terminate questions; they can also be used to suggest doubt or uncertainty.

1 Use question marks to end direct questions.

Have you ever heard of the Battle of Cannae**?**
Who fought in the battle**?**

2 Use question marks to indicate that a name, date, or fact cannot be established with certainty. Such a question mark should not be used to indicate that a writer is unsure of facts that might be available with more research.

Hannibal (247**?**–183 B.C.) was a Carthaginian general and military tactician.

3 Do not use question marks to terminate indirect questions. Indirect questions are statements that seem to have questions within them.

INDIRECT QUESTION	The reporter asked how the new agency would be funded.
DIRECT QUESTION	How will the new agency be funded**?**

4 Punctuate as questions any compound sentences that begin with statements but end with questions.

The strategy seemed reasonable, but would it work on the battlefield**?**

5 Place question marks after direct questions that appear in the middle of sentences.

Skeptical of their tour guide's claim—"Would Hannibal really position his cavalry here**?**"—the scholars in the group consulted a map.

6 Place question marks outside quotation marks except when they are part of the quoted material itself.

Was it Terence who wrote "Fortune helps the brave"**?**

The teacher asked, "Have you read any Cicero**?**"

For a more detailed explanation of quotation marks, see Section 33a.

7 Do not allow question marks to bump against other punctuation marks.

WRONG   "Where did the battle begin**?,**" the tourist asked.

RIGHT   "Where did the battle begin**?**" the tourist asked.

Don't multiply question marks to add emphasis. One mark is sufficient.

WRONG   Are you serious**???**

RIGHT   Are you serious**?**

29c When do you use exclamation marks?

Exclamations give emphasis to statements.

1 Use exclamation marks to express strong reactions or commands.

Our time has come at last**!**

Save exclamations for those occasions—rare in business and academic writing—when your words really deserve emphasis. Too many exclamations can make a passage seem juvenile.

OVERDONE   The Roman forces at the Battle of Cannae outnumbered
            Hannibal's forces roughly two to one! Yet Roman
            casualties would be ten times higher than those suffered
            by Hannibal's army!

BETTER   The Roman forces at the Battle of Cannae outnumbered
            Hannibal's forces roughly two to one. Yet Roman
            casualties would be ten times higher than those suffered
            by Hannibal's army.

2 Do not allow exclamation marks to bump against other punctuation marks.

WRONG   "Please check your records again**!,**" the caller demanded.

RIGHT   "Please check your records again**!**" the caller demanded.

Don't multiply exclamation marks to add emphasis. One mark is sufficient.

WRONG   Don't shout**!!**

RIGHT   Don't shout**!**

EXERCISE 29.1 Edit the following passage, adding, replacing, and deleting periods, question marks, exclamation points, and any other marks of punctuation that need to be changed.

1. Hannibal simply outfoxed the Roman general Varro at Cannae!!!

2. Hannibal placed his numerically smaller army where the Aufidius River would protect his flank—could the hotheaded Varro appreciate such a move—and arrayed his forces to make the Roman numbers work against themselves!

3. It must have seemed obvious to Hannibal where Varro would concentrate his forces?

4. "Advance!," Hannibal ordered!

5. Is it likely that Varro and the Romans noticed how thin the Carthaginian forces were at the center of the battle line?

6. Predictably, the Romans pressed their attack on the weakened Carthaginian center. But in the meantime, Hannibal's cavalry had destroyed its Roman counterpart!

Do You Have Questions About Sentence Boundaries: Fragments, Comma Splices, and Run-ons?

30

Three of the most troublesome and common punctuation problems are the fragment, the comma splice, and the run-on. All three problems arise from confusion about sentence boundaries—that is, where sentences begin and end.

30a How do you repair sentence fragments?

Sentence fragments are phrases or clauses that look like complete sentences, but either they lack subjects or verbs (see Section 15a-1) or they are subordinate constructions (see Section 15g).

NO SUBJECT	Fits perfectly!
NO VERB	The gold ring.
SUBORDINATE	That I found on the subway.
COMPLETE SENTENCE	The gold ring that I found on the subway fits perfectly.

1 Check that all sentences have complete subjects and verbs, either stated or implied.
To avoid a fragment, you need a subject and verb that can stand alone. Sometimes subjects may be understood rather than stated—for example, in commands.

The sun rose. subject is *sun;* verb is *rose*

It was a beautiful morning. subject is *it;* verb is *was*

Keep quiet. subject *you* is understood; verb is *keep*

2 Check that you have not allowed a dependent or subordinate clause to stand alone as a sentence.
Subordinate clauses—that is, clauses that begin with words such as *although, because, if, since, unless, when, while*—won't work as sentences by themselves even though they have a subject and a verb (see Section 15d-2).

FRAGMENT   It will be a miracle. **If the mail comes on time.**

Usually, such fragments can be repaired by attaching them to surrounding sentences.

COMPLETE SENTENCE   If the mail comes on time, it will be a miracle.

3 Check that you have not allowed a relative clause or appositive to stand alone as a sentence.

Words like *who, which, that*, and *where* typically signal the beginning of a relative clause that must be connected to a sentence to make a complete thought (see Section 15d-2). If the clause is left unattached, a fragment results.

FRAGMENT   The Capitol is on Congress Avenue. **Which is the widest street in the city.**

CORRECTED   The Capitol is on Congress Avenue, which is the widest street in the city.

The appositive, a group of words that gives more information about a noun, is another construction that produces fragments when allowed to stand alone (see Section 15c-4).

FRAGMENT   Dr. Anderson resigned her professorship. **The Herstein Chair of Psychology.**

CORRECTED   Dr. Anderson resigned her professorship, **the Herstein Chair of Psychology**.

4 Check that you have not substituted a verbal for the verb in a sentence.

Verbals (see Sections 19a and 19b) are tricky constructions because they look like verbs, but they act as nouns, adjectives, or adverbs. To eliminate fragments caused by verbals, it helps to remember the following:

- An *-ing* word by itself can never act as the verb of a sentence. To qualify as a verb, the *-ing* word must have an auxiliary such as *have been, is*, or *were*.

- An infinitive, such as *to run* or *to go*, can never act as the verb of a sentence.

Here are examples of verbals causing sentence fragments. The fragments are boldfaced.

FRAGMENT   The reporter from Reuters asked the senator probing questions. **Suspecting a coverup.**

CORRECTED   Suspecting a coverup, the reporter from Reuters asked the senator probing questions.

FRAGMENT   **To break the story.** That was the reporter's goal.

CORRECTED   To break the story was the reporter's goal.

5 Check that you have not treated a disconnected phrase as a sentence. Turning a disconnected phrase into a full sentence usually means adding a subject or a verb (sometimes both), depending on what has been left out of the phrase.

> FRAGMENTS   David cleaned his glasses. **Absentmindedly. With the hem of his lamb's-wool sweater.**
>
> CORRECTED   Absentmindedly, David cleaned his glasses with the hem of his lamb's-wool sweater.

6 Check that you have not treated a list as an independent sentence. Sometimes a list gets detached from the sentence that introduced or explained it.

Lists are often introduced by words or phrases such as *especially, for example, for instance, such as*, and *namely*. If a fragment follows such an expression, be sure to correct it—usually by attaching the fragment to the preceding sentence.

> FRAGMENT   People suffer from many peculiar phobias. **For example, ailurophobia (fear of cats), aviophobia (fear of flying), ombrophobia (fear of rain), and vestiphobia (fear of clothes).**
>
> CORRECTED   People suffer from many peculiar phobias—for example, ailurophobia (fear of cats), aviophobia (fear of flying), ombrophobia (fear of rain), and vestiphobia (fear of clothes).

EXERCISE 30.1 Rewrite the following passage to eliminate any sentence fragments.

> The news agenda in the United States used to be set by just a few institutions. Mainly, the major three television networks (CBS, NBC, and ABC). Along with three or four major papers. These news outlets were located mainly on the East and West Coasts. Giving these regions extra clout in political affairs. Especially influential was the *New York Times*. Considered the paper of record of the United States. However, in recent years, 24-hour news channels, radio talk shows, and Internet news outlets have challenged the power of the traditional media. Widening the range of news topics. Creating outlets for regional opinions. Providing spaces to critique mainstream news sources. The *New York Times* has become a favorite target of many critics. Especially bloggers, who have had a field day finding what they purport to be errors and omissions in its coverage.

30b   When are fragments okay?

You might wonder why incomplete sentences occur so often in public media when you've been told to avoid fragments in your own work. Are sentence fragments considered wrong at some times but not at others? The answer is yes, depending on your purpose and audience. In advertising copy, email messages, instant messaging, and much fiction—phrases without subjects or verbs are routinely punctuated as sentences.

> The classic sports chronometer. Rugged but elegant. Engineered to aviation standards. A cut above.

> A Starbucks in Muleshoe? Bad idea. Won't get financing. Not from any local bank.

Such fragments are not actually puzzling or confusing when audiences expect them—as they might in informal, popular, or creative writing. But for that reason, fragments are generally considered out of place in serious academic, professional, or technical writing. As a rule, avoid intentional fragments in academic assignments, job applications, or any piece of serious writing going to an audience you do not know well.

However, don't be confused by commands—words or phrases in the imperative mood. They may look like sentence fragments because they do not state a subject, but the subject is assumed—the silent or "understood" *you*. "Don't give an inch in the negotiations!" is a sentence. So is "Vote for Pedro."

EXERCISE 30.2 Bring to class some advertisements, such as the ones above, that use sentence fragments—or locate a Web site or listserv that routinely uses fragments. Working with other students in a small group, identify the fragments and then rewrite them to eliminate the incomplete sentences. Discuss the differences between the original material and your revised versions. Why do you think the writers may have used fragments?

30c How do you avoid comma splices?

A comma splice occurs when you try to join two independent clauses with a comma only.

COMMA SPLICE

Local shopkeepers were concerned about a recent outbreak of graffiti, they feared that it indicated the arrival of troublesome gangs in the neighborhood.

The groups of words on each side of the comma could stand alone as complete sentences. The error is common and considered serious in academic and professional writing—but it is easy to identify and fix.

1 Remember that commas can't link complete sentences. They require a linkage stronger than a comma alone to show their relationship.

COMMA SPLICE	The report is highly critical of the media, it has received little press coverage.
CORRECTED	The report is highly critical of the media, **so** it has received little press coverage.
COMMA SPLICE	Shawna is an outstanding orator, she has no formal training in speech.
CORRECTED	Shawna is an outstanding orator, **although** she has no formal training in speech.

Although the independent clauses are obviously connected, the comma splices do not explain how. Inserting conjunctions relieves the confusion.

COMMA SPLICE	Maria was supposed to be on stage in five minutes, however, she was still donning her costume.
CORRECTED	Maria was supposed to be on stage in five minutes; however, she was still donning her costume.

Very short sentences, usually in threes, may be joined by commas. These constructions are rare.

I came, I saw, I conquered.
He ate, I paid, we left.

2 Eliminate a comma splice by replacing the faulty comma with a semicolon. Use this option when the relationship between the sentences is so close that you don't need any connecting word.

COMMA SPLICE	When David detailed his Mustang, every brush, sponge, and swab was arranged in one neat row, he laid out each towel, chamois, and duster in another.
CORRECTED	When David detailed his Mustang, every brush, sponge, and swab was arranged in one neat row; he laid out each towel, chamois, and duster in another.

3 Eliminate a comma splice by replacing the faulty comma with a period.

Use a period when you want a clear separation between two ideas or a dramatic pause.

COMMA SPLICE	David polished a square inch of his car at a time, by the end of the day he had finished the hood and one fender.
CORRECTED	David polished a square inch of his car at a time. By the end of the day, he had finished the hood and one fender.

4 Eliminate a comma splice by inserting a coordinating conjunction after the comma.

Add a conjunction when you need a word that explains the relationship between the two ideas. The coordinating conjunctions are *and, or, nor, for, but, yet*, and *so*.

COMMA SPLICE	His progress was slow because he did every step by hand, it was satisfying work.
CORRECTED	His progress was slow because he did every step by hand, but it was satisfying work.

5 Eliminate a comma splice by subordinating one of the independent clauses.

You can do that by introducing one of the independent clauses with a subordinating word such as *although, because, since*, or *when*. For more on subordination, see Section 15g.

COMMA SPLICE	Detailing a vehicle requires skill, learning to do it can pay off in a profitable career.
CORRECTED	Although detailing a vehicle requires skill, learning to do it can pay off in a profitable career.

EXERCISE 30.3 Identify the sentences that have comma splices and correct them.

1. At one time the walls in many Philadelphia neighborhoods were covered with graffiti, however they are covered with murals today.

2. Since 1984 a city-sponsored program has been teaming young graffiti writers with professional artists, the result is the creation of over a thousand works of public art.

3. The murals are large, they are colorful, they are 99 percent graffiti-free.

4. A forty-foot-tall mural of Julius ("Dr. J") Erving has become a local landmark, even Dr. J himself brings friends by to see it.

30d How can you fix run-on sentences?

A *run-on* occurs when no punctuation separates two independent clauses (see Section 15d-1). The reader is left to figure out where one sentence ends and a second begins. You need to provide a boundary strong enough to separate the independent clauses clearly. You usually have several options for repairing a run-on.

RUN-ON	We were surprised by the package quickly we tore it open.
CORRECTED	We were surprised by the package. Quickly we tore it open.

1 Correct a run-on by separating independent clauses with a period.

RUN-ON	Politicians fear reforming the Social Security system someday they will scramble to prevent its bankruptcy.
CORRECTED	Politicians fear reforming the Social Security system. Someday they will scramble to prevent its bankruptcy.

2 Correct a run-on by inserting a semicolon between independent clauses. A semicolon suggests that the ideas in the two sentences are closely related.

RUN-ON	Emily's entire life revolves around ecological problems she can speak of little else.
CORRECTED	Emily's entire life revolves around ecological problems; she can speak of little else.

For more on semicolons, see Section 32a.

3 Correct a run-on by joining independent clauses with a comma and a coordinating conjunction. The coordinating conjunctions are *and, or, nor, for, but, yet*, and *so*.

RUN-ON	Poisonous giant toads were introduced to Australia in the 1930s to control beetles they have since become an ecological menace.
CORRECTED	Poisonous giant toads were introduced to Australia in the 1930s to control beetles, **but** they have since become an ecological menace.
RUN-ON	The manager suggested a cut in our hourly wages then I walked out of the negotiations.
CORRECTED	The manager suggested a cut in our hourly wages, **so** then I walked out of the negotiations.

4 Correct a run-on by subordinating one of the independent clauses to the other.

RUN-ON	Albert had to finish the financial report by himself his irresponsible co-author had lost interest in the cause.
CORRECTED	Albert had to finish the financial report by himself **because** his irresponsible co-author had lost interest in the cause.

How Do Y◉u Use Commas? **31**

Commas are interrupters or signals to pause. Commas make a reader slow down and pay attention to the words and ideas they set off. For this reason, it's just as important to omit commas where they aren't needed as it is to include them where they are.

31a When are commas needed to separate items in a sentence?

Some commas keep words, phrases, and clauses from colliding. Use too many commas, and your writing will seem plodding and fussy; use too few, and your readers may be confused.

1 Use commas after introductory phrases of more than three or four words. Phrases—which come in several varieties (see Section 15c)—are groups of words without subjects or verbs.

> Well before the end of the day, we were in Amarillo.
>
> Having driven non-stop most of the afternoon, we decided to spend the night in Raton.

A comma isn't needed when an introductory phrase is only a few words long and the sentence is clear without it. You may use a comma in these situations, however, when you believe it makes a sentence easier to

In some situations, commas have the message of a yield sign—slow down, but don't quite stop.

read. Commas would be optional, though acceptable, in the following sentences.

> On Tuesday, we were in Mesa Verde National Park.
> Very carefully, we climbed the ladder at Balcony House.

2 Use a comma after an introductory dependent clause. Dependent clauses are signaled by words such as *after, although, as, because, before, if, since, unless, when, while*.

> **Although** the vote was close, we passed the motion.
> **While** the military band played taps, the flag was lowered.

When there is no comma after such an introductory clause, the reader may not understand where the main clause of the sentence begins.

COMMA MISSING	While the crack in the roadway had opened months before the bridge inspector who found it seemed surprised.
	Does *before* go with the dependent clause or the main clause?
COMMA ADDED	While the crack in the roadway had opened months before, the bridge inspector who found it seemed surprised.

3 Use a comma to set off contrasts. Often the contrast will occur in a phrase following the main clause.

> Marietta makes mediocre pottery, **though her prices are steep**.
> In most cities, owning a car is a necessity, **not a luxury**.

Do not use a comma, however, when the additional clause or phrase is closely related to the main idea of the sentence.

> The NASDAQ market plunged **despite new rules to control computer trading**.

4 Use commas after conjunctive adverbs at the beginning of sentences or clauses. Commas are needed because words of this kind—*consequently, nevertheless, however, therefore*—are interrupters that mark a shift or contrast in a sentence.

INCORRECT	The poll was poorly designed. Nevertheless those who commissioned it had faith in the answers.
CORRECT	The poll was poorly designed. Nevertheless, those who commissioned it had faith in the answers.

In a compound sentence (one made up of two or more independent clauses), those clauses may be joined by a semicolon. In that case, put the comma after the conjunctive adverb in the second clause.

The budget cuts are final; **therefore,** you'll have to reduce staff.

But when a conjunctive adverb occurs in the middle of the clause modified, put a comma before and after it.

It seemed to us **, however,** that the flames were spreading.

See Section 32a for more on using and punctuating conjunctive adverbs.

5 Use commas to set off absolute phrases. Absolutes are phrases made up of nouns and participles. You are most likely to recognize them through examples.

The question settled, the strikers returned to their jobs.
All things considered, the fund drive was a success.

6 Use commas to introduce quotations or to follow them. Commas set off quotations introduced or followed by phrases such as *he said, she repeated, he argued, she insisted*.

The lawyer kept repeating, "My client can't be held responsible for that."
"Don't tell me he can't be held responsible, " retorted the judge.

A phrase that interrupts a single independent clause is set off by commas.

"I am sure, " she said, "you will remember our earlier conversation."

No commas are needed when a quotation fits neatly into a sentence without a separate introductory phrase.

Oscar Wilde defines experience as "the name we give to our mistakes."

See Section 33a for more on punctuating quotations.

7 Learn other uses of commas that separate.

- Commas separate words where repetitive phrases have been left out.

   Brad Pitt once worked as a giant chicken; Rod Stewart, as a gravedigger; Whoopi Goldberg, as a makeup artist for corpses.

- Commas separate parts of sentences that might cause confusion.

  The motto of some critics seems to be**,** whatever is**,** is wrong.

- Commas separate conversational expressions from the main body of the sentence.

  No, I'm sure the inspector wasn't there.

- Commas set off direct address.

  "**Jane,** bring in the newspaper when you come," I said.

- Commas separate mild interjections—short exclamations or expressions of emotion—from the main body of the sentence.

  Oh, I'm sure it will be all right.

- Commas set off tag questions.

  You did remember the salsa**, didn't you**?

EXERCISE 31.1 Insert commas in these sentences where needed.

1. When Mount St. Helens erupted in 1980 the north slope collapsed sending torrents of mud and rock down into the Toutle River valley.

2. Stripped of all vegetation for fifteen miles the valley was left virtually lifeless; whatever trees there were were dead.

3. In an effort to prevent erosion and speed the valley's recovery ecologists planted grasses and ground covers.

4. However the species they planted were not native but alien or exotic.

31b When should commas enclose words and phrases?

Enclosing some words and phrases with commas makes sentences more readable; the commas chunk information into manageable units.

1 Use commas to set off nonessential (nonrestrictive) modifiers.
When you can remove a modifier from a sentence without affecting the primary meaning of the sentence, the modifier is *nonessential*. Such modifiers are surrounded by commas.

NONESSENTIAL **MODIFIER**	The police officers, **who had been carefully** **screened,** marched in front.
MODIFIER REMOVED	The police officers marched in front.

When you can't remove the modifier without affecting meaning, the modifier is *essential* (restrictive). Essential modifiers do not take commas.

> The car **that we had received** was not the car **that we had custom-ordered**.

A good rule of thumb: Do not use commas to set off clauses beginning with *that*.

INCORRECT	The bill, that was passed by the city council, will raise property taxes again.
CORRECT	The bill that was passed by the city council will raise property taxes again.

For more on essential and nonessential clauses, see Section 25i.

2 Use commas to enclose appositives that are nonessential. An *appositive* is a noun or noun phrase that describes another noun or pronoun more fully. Usually it is nonessential.

> Franklin Delano Roosevelt, **the only President to serve more than two terms,** died in office.

There are, however, essential appositives that follow a noun and give information necessary to the sentence. The following sentence needs the essential appositive to clarify *which* of Hemingway's many novels is being discussed.

> The Hemingway novel ***The Sun Also Rises*** is set in Pamplona, Spain.

But when it's clear from the rest of the sentence which novel is meant, the appositive becomes nonessential.

> Hemingway's first successful novel, ***The Sun Also Rises,*** is set in Pamplona, Spain.

3 Use commas to enclose various interrupting words, phrases, and clauses. It is important to use commas in pairs when the interruptions come in the middle of sentences.

> The president intends, **predictably,** to veto the bill in its current form.

The first landmark we recognized, **well before the plane landed,** was the Washington Monument.

She could not, **in good conscience,** ignore the clamor for passage of the measure.

Some contemporary editors, however, are moving toward using fewer commas around words such as *however* and *therefore*. In many newspapers and magazines—even the linguistically conservative *New York Times*—you will often find no commas around *of course* when it appears in the middle of a sentence. If you are unsure of whether to use a comma in such situations, consult your instructor or a style manual.

EXERCISE 31.2 Discuss the following sentences to decide which modifiers are essential and which are not; then fix the sentences that need to be changed.

1. Carter a salesclerk with a passion for Native American art urged Iona his manager at a gallery in Alpine to increase her stock of Navajo rugs.

2. On a sales trip, Carter had met with several art dealers who specialized in Native American crafts; the dealer Carter met in Gallup had offered rugs produced by several well-known artists.

3. The rugs that he showed Carter included examples of all the classic Navajo designs produced from wool which the weavers had shorn, carded, and dyed themselves.

4. Iona who had managed the store for ten years was uncertain that her regular customers would buy the premium rugs which cost as much as $6,000.

When are commas needed to connect parts of a sentence?

Although commas often mark separations, they can also tell readers that certain ideas belong together.

1 Use commas before the coordinating conjunctions *and, or, nor, for, but, yet,* and *so* when those words link independent clauses to form compound sentences.

Texas is larger in land area than California, **and** its history is different too.

West Texas can seem empty at times, **yet** the vastness of its deserts and high plains is part of its appeal.

A comma is especially important when the two clauses separated by the conjunction are long.

> Experts have tried to explain why dogs wag their tails, **but** they have not come up with a satisfactory reason for this attention-grabbing behavior.

Be careful—commas don't *follow* coordinating conjunctions between two independent clauses.

> **WRONG**   My friends shared my opinion but, they were afraid to say so.
>
> **RIGHT**   My friends shared my opinion, but they were afraid to say so.

Remember not to join two independent clauses by a comma. If you do, you'll create a comma splice. (See Section 30c.)

2 Use commas to link items in a series of three or more.

> The mapmaker had omitted the capital cities of Idaho, New York, and Delaware!

Newspaper and magazine articles follow the conventions of journalism and typically omit the final comma.

> The mapmaker had omitted the capital cities of Idaho, New York and Delaware!

No comma is needed between just two items in a series.

> The mapmaker had omitted the capital cities of Idaho and Delaware!

3 Use commas to link coordinate adjectives in a series. Coordinate adjectives modify the noun they precede, not each other (see Section 13b-1).

> The job calls for a **creative, experienced, intelligent** manager.

When adjectives are coordinate, they can be switched around without affecting the sense of a phrase.

> The job calls for an **intelligent, experienced, creative** manager.

Do not use commas to mark off noncoordinate adjectives in a series. *Noncoordinate adjectives* work together to modify a term. They cannot be switched around or have *and* inserted between them.

> He drives a **sharp blue Mustang** convertible.
>
> Tom Cruise has already been nominated for the **best supporting actor** Oscar.

EXERCISE 31.3 Rewrite the following sentences, adding commas where they are needed to link ideas, moving commas that are misplaced, and correcting comma splices. Some sentences may be correct.

1. Many people freeze when they enter an electronics store cluttered with merchandise shoppers and grinning hyperactive sales staffs.

2. Shrewd, and careful shoppers know exactly what they intend to buy when they walk in but, they routinely discover that those gizmos have been discontinued modified or reordered.

3. Fifteen-year-old, sales clerks direct them to ten, megapixel digital, cameras that cost an arm, and a leg.

4. When a customer explains that she just wants a clock radio, the pimply, faced sales representative will steer her toward a 52-inch plasma-screen TV that has a clock function.

31d Where are commas unnecessary or incorrect?

Every comma in a sentence should be placed for a reason: to mark a pause, to set off a unit, to keep words from running together. Cut those that don't serve any such purpose.

1 Eliminate commas that interrupt the flow of a sentence. Sometimes a comma disrupts what would otherwise be a clear statement.

| UNNECESSARY COMMA | Five years into graduate school, Frida found herself**,** without a degree or prospects for a job. |
| COMMA CUT | Five years into graduate school, Frida found herself without a degree or prospects for a job. |

At other times, unneeded commas seem to follow a guideline, but they really don't. In the following example, the writer may recall that commas often follow introductory words, phrases, and clauses.

| UNNECESSARY COMMA | However**,** cold it gets, the train arrives on time. |
| COMMA CUT | However cold it gets, the train arrives on time. |

2 Don't let a comma separate a subject from a verb. Such problems usually occur when the subject of a sentence is more complex than usual—perhaps a noun clause or a verb phrase.

UNNECESSARY COMMA	What happened to the team since last season, isn't clear.
COMMA CUT	What happened to the team since last season isn't clear.

Only in rare cases may a comma be required between subject and verb to assure clarity.

Those who hope, thrive; those who despair, fail.

3 Don't let a comma separate a verb from its object.

UNNECESSARY COMMA	During the Cold War, the Pentagon developed and deployed, nuclear submarines, cruise missiles, and MIRV warheads.
COMMA CUT	During the Cold War, the Pentagon developed and deployed nuclear submarines, cruise missiles, and MIRV warheads.

4 Don't use commas to separate compound subjects, predicates, or objects.

WRONG	The Mississippi, and the Missouri are two of the United States' great rivers.
RIGHT	The Mississippi and the Missouri are two of the United States' great rivers.
WRONG	We toured the museum, and then explored the monument.
RIGHT	We toured the museum and then explored the monument.
WRONG	Alexander broke his promise to his agent, and his contract with his publisher.
RIGHT	Alexander broke his promise to his agent and his contract with his publisher.

Of course, commas are used to separate full independent clauses joined by conjunctions. Compare the following sentences, both punctuated correctly.

RIGHT	We toured the museum and then explored the monument.
RIGHT	We toured the museum, and then we explored the monument.

5 Don't use commas to introduce lists.

WRONG	States with impressive national parks include, California, Utah, Arizona, and New Mexico.

RIGHT States with impressive national parks include California, Utah, Arizona, and New Mexico.

Note, though, how commas work in the following sentences to set off lists introduced by "including" and "such as."

RIGHT Many states have impressive national parks, **including** California, Utah, Arizona, and New Mexico.

RIGHT Many states, **such as** California, Utah, Arizona, and New Mexico, have impressive national parks.

Commas may be used to enclose lists that function as nonessential modifiers.

RIGHT Universities with major football programs, Notre Dame, Michigan, and LSU **among them,** benefit from generous alumni contributions.

In such cases, however, all the commas can be confusing. The modifier might be better enclosed by dashes (see Section 35a).

RIGHT Universities with major football programs—Notre Dame, Michigan, and LSU among them—benefit from generous alumni contributions.

EXERCISE 31.4 Working in a group, analyze these sentences to see if all the commas are needed. Then work together to rewrite sentences to get rid of commas that cause awkward interruptions. Notice that some of the commas are necessary.

1. Psychologists, who have studied moods, say that such emotional states are contagious, and compare them to social viruses.

2. Moreover, some people are emotionally expressive, and likely to transmit moods; others, seem to be more inclined to "catch" moods.

3. Trying to pinpoint the exact means by which moods are transmitted, is difficult, since the process happens almost instantaneously.

4. One transmission mechanism is imitation: by unconsciously imitating facial expressions, people produce, in themselves a mood that goes with the expression.

31e What special uses do commas have?

Aside from the important role commas play within sentences both in linking and separating ideas, commas have many conventional uses you simply have to know to get right.

1 Use commas correctly to separate units of three within numbers.
Commas are optional in four-digit numbers.

4,110 or 4110

99,890

1,235,470

Do not use commas in decimals, Social Security numbers, street addresses, or zip codes.

2 Use commas correctly in dates.
In American usage, commas separate the day from the year. Note that a year is enclosed by commas when it appears in the middle of a sentence.

World War II began on September 1, 1939.

Germany expanded the war on June 22, 1941, when its armies invaded Russia.

Commas aren't required when only the month and year are given.

World War II began in September 1939.

Commas are not used when dates are given in British form, with the day preceding the month.

World War II began on 1 September 1939.

3 Use commas correctly in addresses.
Commas ordinarily separate street addresses, cities, states, and countries. When these items occur in the middle of a sentence, they are enclosed by commas.

Miami University is in Oxford, Ohio.

Though born in London, England, Denise Levertov is considered an American writer.

The prime minister lives at No. 10 Downing Street, Westminster, London, England.

Commas aren't used between states and zip codes.

Austin, Texas 78712

4 Use commas correctly to separate proper names from titles and degrees that follow.

Tonya Galvin, Ph.D., has been chosen to replace Howard Brill, M.D.

5 Use commas to follow the salutation in personal letters.

Dear Aunt Sue,

EXERCISE 31.5 Review the following sentences and add commas where necessary.

1. In the autumn of 1863, Abraham Lincoln President of the United States traveled to Gettysburg Pennsylvania to speak at the dedication of a cemetery there.

2. The cemetery was for the soldiers who had fallen at the Battle of Gettysburg, and Lincoln's speech—now known as the Gettysburg Address—opened with the famous words "Fourscore and seven years ago."

3. The Battle of Gettysburg had started on July 1 1863 and had raged for three days.

4. The Civil War would not end until April 1865.

How Do You Use
Semicolons nd Colons?   32

32a When do you use semicolons?

A semicolon marks a stronger pause than a comma, but a weaker pause
than a period.

1 Use semicolons to separate items of equal grammatical weight.
Semicolons can be used to separate one independent clause from
another, one phrase from another, one item in a list from another.

> independent clause; independent clause
> Director John Ford released *Stagecoach* in 1939; a year later, he
> made *The Grapes of Wrath*.

> phrase; phrase
> My course in cinema taught the basics of movie production,
> including how to write treatments, outlines, and scripts; how to
> audition and cast actors; and how to edit 16-mm film.

> item in a list; item in a list; item in a list
> We rented DVDs of *Resident Evil: Apocalypse*; *Napoleon Dynamite*;
> and *Blade Runner—The Director's Cut*.

Because semicolons work only between comparable items, it would be
wrong to place a semicolon between an independent clause and a prepositional phrase. Also incorrect would be a semicolon separating a dependent clause and an independent clause.

	independent clause, prepositional phrase
WRONG	Many young filmmakers regularly exceed their budgets; in the tradition of the finest Hollywood directors.
RIGHT	Many young filmmakers regularly exceed their budgets, in the tradition of the finest Hollywood directors.

	dependent clause, independent clause
WRONG	Although director Alfred Hitchcock once said that actors should be treated like cattle; he won fine performances from many of them.
RIGHT	Although director Alfred Hitchcock once said that actors should be treated like cattle, he won fine performances from many of them.

2 Use semicolons to join independent clauses closely related in thought. Coordinating conjunctions (such as *and, or, nor, for, but, yet, so*) aren't needed when clauses are linked by semicolons.

> Italian cinema blossomed after World War II; directors like Fellini and Antonioni won critical acclaim.

Omitting the semicolons in the examples above would create run-on sentences (see Section 30d). Using a comma would produce a comma splice (see Section 30c). Both run-ons and comma splices are major sentence errors. Sometimes, however, placing semicolons between very short independent clauses, while correct, can seem like punctuation overkill.

> WITH SEMICOLONS For best director, Todd picked Alfred Hitchcock; Ryan nominated François Truffaut; and Aimee chose Agnes Varda.

When such clauses are short and closely related, they can be separated by commas.

> WITH COMMAS For best director, Todd picked Alfred Hitchcock, Ryan nominated François Truffaut, and Aimee chose Agnes Varda.

3 Use semicolons between independent clauses joined by words such as *however, therefore, nevertheless, nonetheless, moreover*, and *consequently*. These words by themselves cannot link sentences.

> The original *Rocky* was an Oscar-winning movie; **however**, its many sequels exhausted the original idea.
>
> Films about British spy 007 have been in decline for years; **nevertheless**, new James Bond films continue to appear.

But here's an important point: when a word such as *however* or *therefore* occurs in the middle of an independent clause, it *is* preceded and followed by commas. In the following pair of sentences, note where the boldfaced words appear and how the shifts in their location change the punctuation required.

> *Casablanca* is now admired as a film classic; **however**, its producers and stars regarded it as an average spy thriller.
>
> *Casablanca* is now admired as a film classic; its producers and stars, **however**, regarded it as an average spy thriller.

32.1 Frequently Used Conjunctive Adverbs

consequently	meanwhile	rather
furthermore	moreover	then
hence	nonetheless	therefore
however	otherwise	thus

4 Use semicolons to join independent clauses connected by words or phrases such as *indeed, in fact, at any rate, for example,* and *on the other hand*. These expressions, like conjunctive adverbs, ordinarily require a semicolon before them and a comma after.

> Box office receipts for *Spider-Man*'s opening week were spectacular**; in fact**, the film unexpectedly broke records for a summer release.

A period could be used instead of the semicolon in these situations.

> Naturally, *Spider-Man* will spawn many sequels. **In fact**, *Spider-Man 2* was a better film than the original.

5 Use semicolons to separate clauses, phrases, or items in a series that might be confusing if commas alone were used to mark boundaries. Use semicolons when phrases or items in a list already contain commas or other punctuation.

> Matt Damon's filmography includes *School Ties*, which is set in an upper-class prep school; *Saving Private Ryan*, a Steven Spielberg movie in which Damon plays the title character; and *Good Will Hunting*, a drama that earned him an Oscar for best screenplay.

6 Do not use semicolons to introduce quotations.

> **WRONG**   Wasn't it Mae West who said**;** "When I'm good I'm very good, but when I'm bad, I'm better"?

> **RIGHT**   Wasn't it Mae West who said**,** "When I'm good I'm very good, but when I'm bad, I'm better"?

7 Do not use semicolons to introduce lists.

> **WRONG**   Paul Robeson performed in several classic films**;** *Show Boat, Song of Freedom, King Solomon's Mines.*

> **RIGHT**   Paul Robeson performed in several classic films**:** *Show Boat, Song of Freedom, King Solomon's Mines.*

8 Use semicolons correctly with quotation marks. Semicolons ordinarily fall outside quotation marks (see Section 33a-6).

> The first Edgar Allan Poe work filmed was "The Raven"; movies based on the poem appeared in 1912, 1915, and 1935.

EXERCISE 32.1 Revise the following sentences, adding or deleting semicolons as needed. Not all semicolons below are incorrect. You may have to substitute other punctuation marks for some semicolons.

1. For many years, biblical spectacles were a staple of the Hollywood film industry, however, in recent years, few such films have been produced.

2. Cecil B. DeMille made the grandest epics; he is quoted as saying; "Give me any couple of pages of the Bible and I'll give you a picture."

3. He made *The Ten Commandments* twice, the 1956 version starred Charlton Heston as Moses.

4. The most famous scene in *The Ten Commandments* is the parting of the Red Sea; the waters opening to enable the Israelites to escape the pursuing army of Pharaoh.

32b When do you use colons?

Colons point attention precisely to what you wish to highlight: an idea, a list, a quotation, or even another independent clause. Their functions are limited and quite specific.

1 Use colons to direct readers to examples, explanations, or significant words and phrases.

> Orson Welles's greatest problem may also have been his greatest achievement: the brilliance of his first film, *Citizen Kane*.

A colon that highlights an item in this way ordinarily follows a complete sentence. Do not place colons after linking verbs.

WRONG	America's most bankable film star is: Julia Roberts.
RIGHT	America's most bankable film star is Julia Roberts.

2 Use colons to direct readers to lists. Colons that introduce lists ordinarily follow complete sentences. Here is a pair of sentences—both correct—demonstrating your options.

VERSION 1— WITH A COLON	The filmmakers the professor admired most were a diverse group: Ang Lee, François Truffaut, Spike Lee, and Penny Marshall.
VERSION 2— WITHOUT A COLON	The filmmakers the professor admired most were Ang Lee, François Truffaut, Spike Lee, and Penny Marshall—a diverse group.

Colons are omitted after expressions such as *like, for example, such as*, and *that is*. In fact, colons are intended to replace these terms.

WRONG	Shoestring budgets have produced many artistically successful films, such as: *March of the Penguins, Napoleon Dynamite*, and *Hustle and Flow*.
RIGHT	Shoestring budgets have produced many artistically successful films, such as *March of the Penguins, Napoleon Dynamite*, and *Hustle and Flow*.

Never introduce a list with a colon that separates a preposition from its object(s).

WRONG	Katharine Hepburn starred in: *Little Women, The Philadelphia Story*, and *The African Queen*.
RIGHT	Katharine Hepburn starred in *Little Women, The Philadelphia Story*, and *The African Queen*.

Colons are used, however, after phrases that specifically announce a list, expressions such as *including these, as follows*, and *such as the following*. Compare the following sentences to understand the difference.

VERSION 1— WITH A COLON	The producer trimmed her budget by cutting out some **frills:** special lighting, rental costumes for the cast, and crew lunches.
VERSION 2— WITHOUT A COLON	The producer trimmed her budget by cutting out **frills, such as** special lighting, rental costumes for the cast, and crew lunches.
VERSION 3— WITH A COLON	The producer trimmed her budget by cutting out **frills such as these:** special lighting, rental costumes for the cast, and crew lunches.

3 Use colons to direct readers to quotations or dialogue.

Orson Welles commented poignantly on his own career: "I started at the top and worked down."

Don't introduce short quotations with colons. A comma or no punctuation mark at all will suffice. Compare the following sentences.

Dirty Harry said, "Make my day!"

As Dirty Harry said, "Make my day!"

We recalled Dirty Harry's memorable phrase: "Make my day!"

In the last example, the colon *is* appropriate because it directs attention to a particular comment.

4 Use colons to join two complete sentences when the second sentence illustrates or explains the first.

Making a film is like writing a paper: it absorbs all the time you'll give it.

Don't use more than one colon in a sentence. A dash can usually replace one of the colons.

PROBLEM   Most critics agree on this point: Orson Welles made one of the greatest of films: *Citizen Kane*.

SOLUTION   Most critics agree on this point: Orson Welles made one of the greatest of films—*Citizen Kane*.

Colons and semicolons are not interchangeable, but you can use both marks in the same sentence. A colon, for example, might introduce a list of items separated by semicolons.

The 1950s produced an odd array of science fiction films: *It! The Terror from Beyond Space; Earth vs. the Flying Saucers; Forbidden Planet*.

5 Use colons to separate titles from subtitles.

A Nightmare on Elm Street 3: Dream Warriors

6 Use colons in conventional situations. Colons separate numbers when indicating time or citing Bible passages—though MLA style uses a period in biblical citations.

12:35 p.m.   Matthew 3:1 (or Matthew 3.1 in MLA style)

Colons traditionally follow salutations in business letters.

Dear Ms. Dowd: Dear Mr. Ebert:

Colons separate place of publication from publisher and separate date from page numbers in various MLA bibliography entries.

Glenview: Scott, 1961   14 August 1991: 154–63

Colons appear in Web addresses, with no space left after the mark.

<http://google.com>

EXERCISE 32.2 Revise the following sentences by adding colons or making sure colons are used correctly. Don't assume that every sentence contains an error.

1. No one ever forgets the conclusion of Hitchcock's *Psycho*; the discovery of Norman's mother in the rocking chair.

2. Hitchcock liked to use memorable settings in his films, including: Mt. Rushmore in *North by Northwest*, Radio City Music Hall in *Saboteur*, and the British Museum in *Blackmail*.

3. One actor appears in almost every Hitchcock film Hitchcock himself.

4. Hitchcock probably summed up his own technique best; "There is no terror in a bang, only in the anticipation of it."

How Do You Use Quotation Marks nd Ellipses?

33

33a When do you use quotation marks?

Quotation marks, which always occur in pairs, highlight whatever appears between them. Use double marks (" ") around most quoted material and around titles. Use single quotation marks (' ') to mark quotations (or titles) that fall within quotations.

1 Use quotation marks around material you are borrowing word for word from sources.

> Emerson reminds us that "nothing great was ever achieved without enthusiasm."

> "Next to the originator of a good sentence is the first quoter of it," writes Emerson.

2 Use quotation marks to set off dialogue.
When writing a passage with several speakers, start a new paragraph each time the speaker changes.

> Mrs. Bennet deigned not to make any reply; but unable to contain herself, she began scolding one of her daughters.
> "Don't keep coughing so, Kitty, for heaven's sake! Have a little compassion on my nerves. You tear them to pieces."
> "Kitty has no discretion in her coughs," said her father; "she times them ill."
> "I do not cough for my own amusement," replied Kitty fretfully.
> —JANE AUSTEN, *Pride and Prejudice*

When dialogue is provided not for its own sake but to make some other point, the words of several speakers may appear within a single paragraph.

> Professor Norman was confident that his colleagues would eventually see his point. "They'll come around," he predicted. "They always do." And Professor Brown, for one, was beginning to soften. "I've supported many proposals not half so intelligent."

3 Use quotation marks to cite the titles of short works. These include titles of songs, essays, magazine and newspaper articles, TV episodes, unpublished speeches, chapters of books, and short poems. Titles of longer works appear in *italics* (see Section 36a-1).

> "Love Is Just a Four-Letter Word" song
> "Love Is a Fallacy" title of an essay

4 Use quotation marks to draw attention to specific words. Italics can also be used in these situations (see Section 36a-3).

> Politicians clearly mean different things when they write about "democracy."

You might also use quotation marks to signal that you are using a word ironically, sarcastically, or derisively.

> The clerk at the desk directed the tourists to their "suites"—bare rooms crowded with cots. A bathroom down the hall would serve as the "spa."

But don't overdo it. Highlighting a tired phrase or cliché just makes it seem more fatigued.

> Working around electrical fixtures makes me more nervous than "a cat on a hot tin roof."

5 Surround quotation marks with appropriate punctuation. A quotation introduced or followed by *said, remarked, observed*, or a similar expression takes a comma.

> Benjamin Disraeli *observed*, "It is much easier to be critical than to be correct."

Commas are used, too, when a single sentence quotation is broken up by an interrupting expression such as *he asked* or *she noted*.

> "If the world were a logical place," Rita Mae Brown *notes*, "men would ride sidesaddle."

When such an expression comes between two successive sentences quoted from a single source, a comma and a period are required.

> "There is no such thing as a moral or an immoral book," *says* Oscar Wilde. "Books are well written, or badly written. That is all."

No additional punctuation is required when a quotation runs smoothly into a sentence you have written.

> Abraham Lincoln observed that "in giving freedom to the slave we assure freedom to the free."

See Section 42a for guidelines on introducing and framing quotations.

6 Use quotation marks correctly with other pieces of punctuation.
Commas and periods ordinarily go *inside* closing quotation marks.

"This must be what the sixties were like," I thought.

Down a dormitory corridor lined with antiwar posters, I heard someone humming "Blowin' in the Wind."

However, when a sentence ends with a citation in parentheses, the period follows the parenthesis.

Mike Rose argues that we hurt education if we think of it "in limited or limiting ways" (3).

In American usage, colons and semicolons go *outside* closing quotation marks.

Riley claimed to be "a human calculator": he did quadratic equations in his head.

The young Cassius Clay bragged about being "the greatest"; his opponents in the ring soon learned he wasn't boasting.

Question marks, exclamation points, and dashes can fall either inside or outside quotation marks. They fall *inside* when they apply only to the quotation.

When Mrs. Rattle saw her hotel room, she muttered, "Good grief!" She turned to her husband and said, "Do you really expect me to stay here?"

They fall *outside* the closing quotation mark when they apply to the complete sentence.

Who was it who said, "Truth is always the strongest argument"?

EXERCISE 33.1 Rework the following passage by adding or deleting quotation marks, moving punctuation as necessary, and indenting paragraphs where you think appropriate.

Much to the tourists' surprise, their "uproar" over conditions at their so-called "luxury resort" attracted the attention of a local television station. (In fact, Mrs. Rattle had read "the riot act" to a consumer advocate who worked for the station.) A reporter interviewed Mrs. Rattle, who claimed that she had been promised luxury accommodations. This place smells like old fish she fumed. Even the roaches look unwell. Didn't you check out the accommodations before paying? the reporter asked, turning to Mr. Rattle. He replied that unfortunately they had prepaid the entire vacation. But Mrs. Rattle interrupted. I knew we should have gone to Paris. You never said that! Mr. Rattle objected. As I was trying to say, Mrs. Rattle continued, I'd even rather be in Philadelphia.

33b When do you use ellipses?

In a sentence an ellipsis mark (. . .) indicates that words or even whole sentences have been cut from a passage you are quoting.

1 Place ellipses where material has been omitted from a direct quotation. This material may be a word, a phrase, a complete sentence, or more.

COMPLETE PASSAGE

Abraham Lincoln closed his First Inaugural Address (March 4, 1861) with these words: "We are not enemies, but friends. We must not be enemies. Though passion may have strained it must not break our bonds of affection. The mystic chords of memory, stretching from every battlefield and patriot grave to every living heart and hearthstone all over this broad land, will yet swell the chorus of the Union, when again touched, as surely they will be, by the better angels of our nature."

PASSAGE WITH ELLIPSES

Abraham Lincoln closed his First Inaugural Address (March 4, 1861) with these words: "We are not enemies, but friends. . . . The mystic chords of memory . . . will yet swell the chorus of the Union, when again touched, as surely they will be, by the better angels of our nature."

2 Use ellipses to indicate pauses of any kind or to suggest that an action is incomplete or continuing.

We were certain we would finish the report on time . . . until the computer crashed and wouldn't reboot.

The rocket rumbled on its launch pad as the countdown ended, "four, three, two, one. . . . "

3 Use the correct spacing and punctuation before and after ellipsis marks. An ellipsis is typed as three spaced periods (. . . not ...). When an ellipsis mark appears in the middle of a quoted sentence, leave a space before the first and after the last period.

> mystic chords of memory **. . .** will yet swell

If punctuation occurs before the ellipsis, include the mark when it makes your sentence easier to read. The punctuation mark is followed by a space, then the ellipsis mark.

> The mystic chords of memory, **. . .** all over this broad land, will yet swell the chorus of the Union.

When an ellipsis occurs at the end of a complete sentence from a quoted passage or when you cut a full sentence or more, place a period at the end of the sentence, followed by a space and then the ellipsis.

> We must not be enemies. **. . .** The mystic chords

When a parenthetical citation follows a sentence that ends with an ellipsis, leave a space between the last word in the sentence and the ellipsis. Then provide the parenthetical reference, followed by the closing punctuation mark.

> passion may have strained it **. . .** " (2001).

4 Keep ellipses to a minimum at the beginning and end of sentences.

If your quoted material begins with a capital letter, readers will know you are quoting a complete sentence.

> According to Richard Bernstein, "The plain and inescapable fact is that the derived Western European culture of American life [has] produced the highest degree of prosperity in the conditions of the greatest freedom ever known on planet Earth" (11).

If the quoted material begins with a small letter, readers can assume introductory words have been cut, so no ellipses are needed.

> According to Richard Bernstein, the United States has "produced the highest degree of prosperity in the conditions of the greatest freedom ever known on planet Earth" (11).

Similarly, if your quoted material begins with a capital letter in brackets, readers should understand that you've added that capital because the quoted material is not from the beginning of a sentence. No ellipses are required.

"[T]he derived Western European culture of American life,"
according to Richard Bernstein, has "produced the highest degree
of prosperity" (11).

You need ellipses at the beginning of a quotation only when a capital
letter in a proper noun (or the pronoun *I*) might lead readers
to believe that you're quoting a complete sentence when, in fact, you
are not.

According to Richard Bernstein, ". . . American life [has]
produced the highest degree of prosperity in the conditions of the
greatest freedom ever known on planet Earth" (11).

When you use an ellipsis, be sure your shortened quotation accurately
reflects the meaning of the uncut passage.

5　Use a full line of spaced dots when you delete more than a line of verse.

For Mercy has a human heart,
Pity a human face,

. . . .
And Peace, the human dress.
　　　　　　　　—**William Blake**, "The Divine Image" (1789)

EXERCISE 33.2 Abridge the following passage, using at least three
ellipses. Be sure the passage is still readable after you have made your
cuts.

Within a week, the neglected Victorian-style house being repaired
by volunteers began to look livable again, its gables repaired, its
gutters rehung, its roof reshingled. Even the grand staircase,
rickety and worm-eaten, had been rebuilt. The amateur artisans
made numerous mistakes during the project, including painting
several windows shut, papering over a heating register, and
hanging a door upside down, but no one doubted their
commitment to restoring the historic structure. Some spent hours
sanding away layers of varnish accumulated over almost six
decades to reveal beautiful hardwood floors. Others contributed
their organizational talents—many were managers or paper-
pushers in their day jobs—to keep other workers supplied with
raw materials, equipment, and inspiration. The volunteers
worked from seven in the morning to seven at night, occasionally

pausing to talk with neighbors from the area who stopped by with snacks and lunches, but laboring like mules until there was too little light to continue. They all felt the effort was worth it every time they saw the great house standing on the corner in all its former glory.

H⬤w Do You Use Parentheses and Brackets? 34

Parentheses are enclosures for comments, asides, or extra information added to sentences; the marks also enclose in-text notes for MLA and APA documentation (see Chapters 44–45). Parentheses are much more common than brackets, which are used in a few specific situations (see Section 34b).

1 Use parentheses to separate material from the main body of a sentence or paragraph. This material may be a word, a phrase, a list, even a complete sentence.

> The airplane flight to Colorado was quick **(only about ninety minutes)** and uneventful.

> The emergency kit contained all the expected items **(jumper cables, tire inflator, roadside flares).**

> The buses arrived early, and by noon the stagehands were working at the stadium. **(One of the vans carried a portable stage.)**

Don't use parentheses to explain what will be obvious to most readers.

2 Use parentheses to insert examples, directions, or other details into a sentence.

If the children get lost, have them call the school **(346-1317)** or the church office **(471-6109)**.

3 Use parentheses to highlight numbers or letters used in listing items.

The labor negotiators realized they could **(1)** concede on all issues immediately, **(2)** stonewall until the public demanded a settlement, or **(3)** hammer out a compromise.

4 Use the correct punctuation with or around parentheses. When a complete sentence standing alone is surrounded by parentheses, place its end punctuation inside the parentheses.

The neighborhood was run-down and littered. **(Some houses looked as if they hadn't been painted in decades.)**

However, when a sentence concludes with a parenthesis, the end punctuation for the complete sentence falls outside the final parenthesis mark.

On the corner was a small church **(actually a converted store)**.

When parentheses enclose a very short sentence within another sentence, the enclosed sentence ordinarily begins without capitalization and ends without punctuation.

The editor pointed out a misplaced modifier **(the writer glared at her)**, crossed out three paragraphs **(the writer grumbled)**, and then demanded a complete rewrite.

Punctuation may be used, however, when an enclosed sentence is a question or exclamation.

The snowstorm ended **(who would have guessed it?)** almost as quickly as it began.

5 Don't use punctuation before a parenthesis in the middle of sentences. A comma before a parenthesis is incorrect; if necessary, a parenthesis may be followed by a comma.

WRONG   Although the Crusades failed in their announced objective, **(Jerusalem still remained in Muslim hands afterward)** the expeditions changed the West dramatically.

RIGHT   Although the Crusades failed in their announced objective **(Jerusalem still remained in Muslim hands afterward)**, the expeditions changed the West dramatically.

EXERCISE 34.1 Add parentheses as needed to the following sentences.

1. Native Americans inhabited almost every region of North America, from the peoples farthest north the Inuit to those in the Southwest the Hopi, the Zuni.

2. In parts of what are now New Mexico and Colorado, during the thirteenth century, some ancient tribes moved off the mesas no one knows exactly why to live in cliff dwellings.

3. One cliff dwelling at Mesa Verde covers an area of 66 meters 217 feet by 27 meters 89 feet.

4. Spectacular as they are, the cliff dwellings served the tribes known as the Anasazi for only a short time.

34b   When do you use brackets?

Like parentheses, brackets are enclosures. But brackets have fewer and more specialized uses. Brackets and parentheses are usually *not* interchangeable.

1 Use brackets to insert comments or explanations into direct quotations. Although you cannot change the words of a direct quotation, you can add information between brackets.

> "He [**George Lucas**] reminded me a little of Walt Disney's version of a mad scientist."
>
> —STEVEN SPIELBERG

In other cases, you can insert bracketed material to make the grammar of a quotation fit smoothly into your own syntax. But use this strategy sparingly, taking care not to change the meaning of the original.

Any change you make in an original text, even if only from an uppercase to a lowercase letter or vice versa, should be signaled with brackets.

> In *The Dinosaur Heresies*, Robert T. Bakker rejects "[**o**]rthodox theory."
>
> Dinosaurs, he argues, are not just big reptiles with a "metabolism [**that is**] pitifully low compared to mammals'."

The brackets around the letter *o* indicate that you have changed Bakker's original capital letter to lowercase.

2 Use brackets to avoid one set of parentheses falling within another.
Turn the inner pair of parentheses into brackets.

> The Web site included a full text of the resolution (expressing the sense of Congress on the calculation of the consumer price index **[H.RES.99]**).

3 Use brackets to acknowledge or highlight errors that originate in quoted materials. In such cases the Latin word *sic* ("thus") is enclosed in brackets immediately after the error. See Section 42c-1 for details.

> The sign over the cash register read "We don't except **[sic]** personal checks for payment."

H⬤w Do You Use Dashes, Hyphens, and Slashes?

35

35a When do you use dashes?

Dashes can either link or separate ideas in sentences. They are bold marks of punctuation to be used with care and a little flair.

1 Use dashes to add illustrations, examples, or summaries to the ends of sentences. A dash gives emphasis to any addition.

> Beethoven's Ninth Symphony was a great accomplishment for an artist in bad health—and completely deaf.

2 Use pairs of dashes to insert information into the middle of a sentence. Information between dashes gets noticed.

> Many regard Verdi's *Otello*—based on Shakespeare's story of a marriage ruined by jealousy—as the greatest of Italian tragic operas.

3 Use dashes to highlight interruptions, especially in dialogue. The interruption can even be punctuated.

> Candice sputtered, "The opera lasted—I can hardly believe it—five hours!"

> "When—perhaps I should say if?—I ever sit through Wagner's *Ring*, I expect to be paid for it," Joshua remarked.

4 Use dashes to set off items, phrases, or credit lines.

> Charles Ives, William Grant Still, Aaron Copland, George Gershwin—these composers sought to create an American musical idiom.

> Members of the audience are asked
> —to withhold applause between movements
> —to stifle all coughing and sneezing
> —to refrain from popping gum.

> "Music is the universal language."—Henry Wadsworth Longfellow

5 Don't use a hyphen when a dash is required.

WRONG Beethoven's music-unlike Mozart's-uses emphatic rhythms.

RIGHT Beethoven's music—unlike Mozart's—uses emphatic rhythms.

6 Don't use too many dashes. One pair per sentence is the limit.

WRONG Mozart—recognized as a genius while still a child—produced more than six hundred compositions during his life—including symphonies, operas, and concertos.

RIGHT Mozart, recognized as a genius while still a child, produced more than six hundred compositions during his life—including symphonies, operas, and concertos.

EXERCISE 35.1 Add and delete dashes as necessary to improve the sentences below.

1. Legend has it that Beethoven's Third Symphony was dedicated to Napoleon Bonaparte the champion of French revolutionary ideals until he declared himself emperor.

2. Scholars believe—though they can't be sure—that the symphony was initially called *Bonaparte*—testimony to just how much the idealistic Beethoven admired the French leader.

3. The Third Symphony a revolutionary work itself is now known by the title *Eroica*.

4. The Third, the Fifth, the Sixth, the Seventh, the Ninth Symphonies, they all contain musical passages that most people recognize immediately.

35b When do you use hyphens?

Hyphens either join words or divide them between syllables. They should not be confused with dashes.

1 Learn common hyphenation patterns. Hyphenate words beginning with the prefixes *all-*, *self-*, and *ex-* or ending with the suffix *-elect*.

all-encompassing	**ex**-hockey player
self-contained	mayor-**elect**

Hyphenate most words beginning with *well-*, *ill-*, and *heavy-*.

well-dressed	**ill**-suited	**heavy**-handed

Most common nouns beginning with *un-*, *non-*, *anti-*, *pro-*, *co-*, and *pre-* are not hyphenated.

uncertain	**anti**slavery	**co**ordinate
nonviolent	**pro**democracy	**pre**recorded

2 Follow the conventional uses of hyphens.
Use hyphens to write out numbers from twenty-one to ninety-nine. Fractions also take hyphens, but use only one hyphen per fraction.

twenty-nine	one forty-seventh of a mile
one-quarter inch	two hundred forty-six

Use hyphens to indicate double titles, elements, functions, or attributes.

the secretary-treasurer of our club

members of the AFL-CIO

a city-state such as Sparta

in the space-time continuum

Use hyphens in some technical expressions:

uranium-235	A-bomb

Use hyphens to link prefixes to proper nouns and their corresponding adjectives.

pre-Columbian	**anti**-American
mid-Victorian	**neo**-Darwinism

Use hyphens to prevent words from being misread.

a recreation area	the re-creation of an event
a chicken coop	a student co-op

3 Use hyphens to link some compound nouns and verbs.
The conventions for hyphenating words are complicated and inconsistent. Here are some expressions that do take hyphens.

brother-in-law	great-grandmother
two-step	walkie-talkie
water-skier	hit-and-run
hocus-pocus	president-elect
cold-shoulder	double-talk
strong-arm	off-Broadway

Here are some compounds that aren't hyphenated. Some can be written as either single words or separate words.

cabdriver	best man	sea dog
cab owner	blockhouse	

When in doubt whether to hyphenate, check a dictionary or a style manual.

4 Use hyphens to create compound phrases and expressions.

Some classmates resented her **holier-than-thou** attitude.

Product innovation suffered because of a **not-invented-here** bias.

5 Use hyphens to link compound modifiers before a noun. The hyphen makes the modification easier to read and understand.

an **up-or-down** vote

an **English-speaking** country

a **sharp-looking** suit

a **stop-motion** sequence

a **seventeenth-century** vase

Do not use hyphens with adverbs that end in -*ly*. Nor should you use hyphens with *very*.

a **sharply honed** knife	a **quickly written** note
a **bitterly cold** morning	a **very hot** day

When compound modifiers follow a noun, omit the hyphen.

The artist was **well known**.

The scream was **bone chilling**.

6 Handle suspended modifiers correctly. Sometimes a word or phrase may have more than a single hyphenated modifier. These **suspended modifiers** should look like the following.

Anne planned her vacation wardrobe to accommodate **cold-**, **cool-**, and **wet-**weather days.

Whether the math class should be a **first-** or **second-**semester course was the one thing we couldn't determine.

7 Do not hyphenate words at the end of lines. Most style manuals advise against such divisions when typing. On a computer, word wrap automatically eliminates end-of-line divisions.

If you must divide a word, break it only at a syllable. Check a dictionary for accurate syllable breaks. Don't guess.

Never hyphenate contractions, numbers, abbreviations, acronyms, or one-syllable words at the end of lines. The following divisions would be inappropriate.

would- n't	250,- 000,000
NA- TO	U.S.- M.C.
Ph.- D.	ES- PN

EXERCISE 35.2 In the following sentences, indicate which form of the words in parentheses is preferable. Use a dictionary if you are not familiar with the terms.

1. Local citizens have a (**once in a lifetime/once-in-a-lifetime**) opportunity to preserve an (**old-growth/oldgrowth**) forest.

2. A large, wooded parcel of land is about to be turned into a shopping mall by (**real-estate/realestate**) speculators and (**pinstripe suited/pinstripe-suited**) investors.

3. The forest provides a haven for (**wild-life/wildlife**) of all varieties, from (**great horned owls/great-horned owls**) to (**ruby throated/ruby-throated**) hummingbirds.

4. Does any community need (**video stores/video-stores**), (**T shirt/T-shirt**) shops, and (**over priced/overpriced**) boutiques more than acres of natural habitat?

35c When do you use slashes?

Slashes are used to indicate divisions. They are rare pieces of punctuation with a few specific functions. About the only problem slashes pose concerns the spacing before and after the mark. That spacing depends on how the slash is being used.

1 Use slashes to separate expressions that indicate a choice. In these cases, no space is left before or after the slash.

either/or	he/she	yes/no	pass/fail
win/lose	up/down	on/off	right/wrong

2 Use slashes to indicate fractions.

2/3   2 2/3   5 3/8

3 Use slashes in typing World Wide Web addresses.

<http://www.nps.gov/parks.html>

Note that no spaces precede or follow slashes in World Wide Web addresses.

4 Use slashes to divide lines of poetry quoted within sentences.
When used in this way, a space is left on either side of the slash.

```
Only then does Lear understand that he has been a failure

as a king: "O, I have taken / Too little care of this!"
```

If you cite more than three lines of verse, set the passage as a block quotation and break the lines as they occur in the poem itself. No slashes are required.

```
Poor naked wretches, wheresoever you are,

That bide the pelting of this pitiless storm,

How shall your houseless heads and unfed sides,

Your looped and windowed raggedness, defend you

From seasons such as these?
```

Do You Have Questions Abut Italics and Capitalization? **36**

36a When do you use italics?

Italics, like quotation marks, draw attention to a title, word, or phrase. In a printed text, italics are *slanted letters*. In typed or handwritten papers, italics are signaled by underlining the appropriate words. If you are using a computer that can print italicized words, ask your instructor or editor whether you should print actual italics in a paper. He or she may still prefer that you use an underscore.

1 Use italics to set off some titles. Some titles and names are italicized; others appear between quotation marks. Chart 36.1 provides guidance.

Neither italics nor quotation marks are used for the names of *types* of trains, ships, aircraft, or spacecraft.

DC-10   Trident submarine

Neither italics nor quotation marks are used with titles of major religious texts, books of the Bible, or classic legal documents.

the Bible   the Qur'an
the Constitution   the Declaration of Independence

2 Use italics to set off foreign words or phrases. Italics emphasize scientific names and foreign terms that haven't become accepted into the English vocabulary.

Pierre often described his co-workers as *les bêtes humaines*.

36.1 Titles *Italicized* or "In Quotes"

Chart

TITLES *ITALICIZED*
books   *Blink* or Blink
magazines   *Time* or Time
journals   *JAMA* or JAMA
newspapers   *USA Today* or USA Today
films   *Casablanca* or Casablanca

TV shows	*Punked* or Punked
radio programs	*All Things Considered* or All Things Considered
plays	*Macbeth* or Macbeth
long poems	*Beowulf* or Beowulf
long musical pieces	*The Mikado* or The Mikado
albums	Green Day's *American Idiot* or American Idiot
paintings	Schnabel's *Adieu* or Adieu
sculptures	Christo's *Running Fence* or Running Fence
dances	Antonio's *Goya* or Goya
ships	*Titanic* or Titanic
	U.S.S. *Saratoga* or U.S.S. Saratoga
trains	the *Orient Express* or the Orient Express
aircraft	*Enola Gay* or Enola Gay
spacecraft	*Apollo 11* or Apollo 11
software programs	*Microsoft Word* or Microsoft Word

TITLES "IN QUOTES"

chapters of books	"Lessons from the Pros"
articles in magazines	"Is the Stock Market Too High?"
articles in journals	"Vai Script and Literacy"
articles in newspapers	"Inflation Heats Up"
sections in newspapers	"Living in Style"
TV episodes	"The Soup Nazi"
radio episodes	"McGee Goes Crackers"
short stories	"Araby"
short poems	"The Red Wheelbarrow"
songs	"God Bless America"

Foreign words absorbed by English over the centuries should not be italicized. To be certain, look them up in a recent dictionary.

crèche   gumbo   gestalt   arroyo

Common abbreviations from Latin appear without italics or underscoring.

etc.   et al.   i.e.   viz.

3 Use italics (or quotation marks) to emphasize or clarify a letter, a word, or a phrase.

Does that word begin with an *f* or a *ph*?

When some people talk about *school spirit*, they really mean "Let's party."

EXERCISE 36.1 Indicate whether the following titles or names in boldface should be italicized, in quotation marks, or unmarked. If you don't recognize a name below, consult an encyclopedia or another reference work.

1. launching a **Titan III** at Cape Kennedy

2. **The Phantom of the Opera** playing at the **Paramount Theater**

3. watching **I Love Lucy**

4. sunk on the passenger ship **Andrea Doria**

5. returning **A Farewell to Arms** to the public library

6. watching **Casablanca** again on a **Sony** DVD player

7. discussing the colors of Picasso's **The Old Guitarist**

8. reading Jackson's **The Lottery** one more time

36b When do you capitalize?

Capital letters can cause problems simply because you have to remember the conventions guiding their use. Fortunately, you can observe the guidelines for capital letters in almost every sentence you read.

1 Capitalize the first word in a sentence.

Naomi picked up the tourists at their hotel.
What a remarkable city Washington is!

2 Capitalize the first word in a direct quotation that is a full sentence.

Ira asked, "**W**here's the National Air and Space Museum?"
"**G**ood idea!" Naomi agreed. "**L**et's go there."

Use lowercase for quotations that continue after an interruption.

"It's on the Mall," Naomi explained, "**n**ear the Hirschhorn gallery."

3 Don't capitalize the first word of a phrase or clause that follows a colon unless you want to emphasize the word. You may also capitalize the first word after a colon if it is part of a title.

NO CAPS AFTER COLON	They ignored one item while parking the car: **a** no-parking sign.
CAPS FOR EMPHASIS	The phrase haunted her: **Y**our car has been towed!
CAPS FOR TITLE	*Marilyn: **T**he Untold Story*

4 Don't capitalize the first word of a phrase or sentence enclosed by dashes.

Audrey's first screenplay—a thriller about industrial espionage—had been picked up by an agent.

5 Capitalize the titles of papers, books, articles, poems, and so on. In MLA style, capitalize the first and last word of the title. Capitalize all other words *except* articles (*a, an, the*), prepositions, the *to* in infinitives, and coordinating conjunctions—unless they are the first or last words.

Book: *Freakonomics*

Magazine article: "Confessions of a Sports Car Bolshevik"

Title of a term paper: "Can Quality Survive the Standardized Test?"

Articles and prepositions are capitalized when they follow a colon, usually as part of a subtitle.

A Dream Deferred: The Second Betrayal of Black Freedom in America

Note, however, that the the American Psychological Association (APA) does not follow these guidelines for capitalizing titles (see Chapter 45).

6 Capitalize the first word in lines of quoted poetry unless the poet has used lowercase letters.

Sumer is ycomen in,	**I**da,
Loude sing cuckoo!	**h**o, and Oh,
Groweth reed and bloweth meed,	**I**o!
And springth the wode now.	**s**paces
Sing cuckoo!	**w**ith places
—"The Cuckoo Song"	**t**ween 'em
	—T. Beckwith, "Travels"

EXERCISE 36.2 Correct the problems in capitalization in the following sentences.

1. The passenger next to me asked, "do you remember when air travel used to be a pleasure?"

2. I couldn't reply immediately: My tray table had just flopped open and hit me on the knees.

3. The plane we were on—A jumbo jet that seated nine or ten across—had been circling Dulles International for hours.

4. "We'll be landing momentarily," the flight attendant mumbled, "If we are lucky."

36c When do you capitalize persons, places, and things?

When you are unsure whether a particular word needs to be capitalized, check a dictionary. Don't guess, especially when you are dealing with proper nouns (nouns that name a particular person, place, or thing—*Geoffrey Chaucer*, *Ohio*, *Lincoln Memorial*) or proper adjectives (adjectives formed from proper nouns—*Chaucerian*).

1 Capitalize the names and initials of people and characters.

W. C. Fields	**A**nzia **Y**ezierska
Cher	**M**innie **M**ouse
I. M. Pei	**J. H**ector **St. J**ean **C**rèvecoeur

A few people prefer that their names not be capitalized. Respect that choice.

e. e. cummings   bell hooks

2 Capitalize titles that precede names.

Senator Hillary Clinton
Vice President Cheney
Judge Joe Brown
Aunt Josephine

3 Capitalize titles after names when the title describes a specific person.

But don't capitalize such a title when the title is more general. Compare:

Robert King, the **D**ean of Liberal Arts
Robert King, a **d**ean at the university

Don't capitalize the titles of relatives that follow names. Compare:

Anthony Pancioli, Cathy's **u**ncle
Cathy's **U**ncle Anthony

Exception. Capitalize academic titles that follow a name.

Iris Miller, **P**h.**D**.
Enrique Lopez, **M**aster of **A**rts

4 Don't capitalize minor titles when they stand alone without names.

a **l**ieutenant in the Air Force
the first **p**resident of our club

Exceptions. Prestigious titles are regularly capitalized even when they stand alone. Lesser titles may be capitalized when they clearly refer to a particular individual or when they describe a position formally.

> **P**resident of the **U**nited **S**tates
> the **P**resident
> **S**ecretary of **S**tate
> the **C**hair of the **C**lassics **D**epartment argued . . .

5 Capitalize the names of national, political, and ethnic groups.

> **C**hinese   **R**epublicans   **C**hicanos

Exception. The names of racial groups, economic groups, and social classes are usually not capitalized.

> blacks   whites
> the proletariat   the knowledge class

6 Capitalize the names of businesses, corporations, organizations, unions, clubs, schools, and trademarked items.

> **T**ime, **I**nc.
> **O**klahoma **S**tate **U**niversity
> **A**mnesty **I**nternational
> **C**hemical **W**orkers **U**nion
> **K**leenex
> **X**erox copy

Note that some companies and institutions capitalize more than just an initial letter in their names or logos.

> **D**aimler**C**hrysler
> **F**ed**E**x
> **AOL**

7 Capitalize the names of religious figures, religious groups, and sacred books.

> **G**od   the **S**avior   **B**uddha
> **B**uddhism   **C**atholics   **J**udaism
> the **B**ible   the **Q**ur'an   **T**almudic tradition

Exceptions. The terms *god* and *goddess* are not capitalized when used generally. When *God* is capitalized, pronouns referring to God are also capitalized.

The Greeks had a pantheon of **g**ods and **g**oddesses.

The **G**oddess of **L**iberty appears on our currency.

The cardinal praised **G**od and all **H**is works.

8 Do not routinely capitalize academic ranks. Such ranks include the terms *freshman, first-year, sophomore, junior, senior, graduate, postgrad.*

The college had many fifth-year **s**eniors.

The **f**reshman dormitory was a dump.

The teacher was a **g**raduate student.

Exception. Capitalize academic ranks when these groups are referred to as organized bodies or institutions.

a representative of the **S**enior **C**lass

the **F**reshman **C**otillion

9 Capitalize academic degrees when they are abbreviated. Abbreviated degrees include *Ph.D., LL.D., M.A., M.S., B.A., B.S.* Do not capitalize those degrees when they are spelled out. (Note that MLA style omits the periods in these abbreviations.)

Maria earned her **Ph.D.** the same day Mark received his **LL.D.**

Leon Railsback, **M.A.**

Leon has a **m**aster of **a**rts degree.

Exception. Academic degrees spelled out in full are capitalized when they follow a name.

Leon Railsback, **M**aster of **A**rts

Maria Ramos, **D**octor of **P**hilosophy

10 Capitalize the names of places. Also capitalize words based on place names and the names of specific geographic features such as lakes, rivers, and oceans.

Asia	**O**ld **F**aithful
Asian	the **A**mazon
the **B**ronx	the **G**ulf of **M**exico
Lake **E**rie	**D**eaf **S**mith **C**ounty

Exception. Don't capitalize compass directions unless they name a specific place or are part of a place name.

north	North America
south	the South
eastern Ohio	the Middle East

Capitalize words that identify nationalities or countries—words such as *English, French*, or *Mexican*.

WRONG	Kyle has three english courses.
RIGHT	Kyle has three English courses.
WRONG	Janet drives only american cars.
RIGHT	Janet drives only American cars.

11 Capitalize abstractions when you want to give them special emphasis.

Terms such as *love, truth, mercy*, and *patriotism* (which ordinarily appear in small letters) may be capitalized when you discuss them as concepts or when you wish to give them special emphasis, perhaps as the subject of a paper.

What is this thing called Love?

The conflict was between Truth and Falsehood.

There is no need to capitalize abstractions used without special emphasis.

Byron had fallen in love again.

Either tell the truth or abandon hope of rescue.

12 Capitalize the names of buildings, structures, or monuments.

Yankee Stadium	Hoover Dam
the Alamo	the Golden Gate Bridge

13 Capitalize the names of particular objects.

SS *Titanic*	Boeing 777
Ford Fusion	Eskimo Pie
Super Bowl XXX	the Constitution
Rolling Stones	Fifth Amendment

14 Capitalize most periods of time.

Periods of time include days, months, holidays, historical epochs, and historical events.

Monday	the Reformation
May	World War II
Middle Ages	Bastille Day
Fourth of July	Pax Romana

Exception. Seasons of the year are usually not capitalized.

winter   spring   summer   fall

15 Capitalize terms ending in -ism when they name specific literary, artistic, religious, or cultural movements. When in doubt, check a dictionary.

Impressionism	Vorticism
Judaism	Catholicism
Buddhism	Romanticism

Exception. Many terms ending in -*ism* are not capitalized.

socialism   capitalism   monetarism

16 Capitalize school subjects and classes only when the subjects themselves are proper nouns.

biology	chemistry
English	Russian history
French	physics

Exception. Titles of specific courses (such as you might find in a college catalog) are capitalized.

Biology 101   Chemistry Lab 200   English 346K

17 Capitalize all the letters in acronyms and initialisms. (See Section 37a for more detail.)

NATO	OPEC	NASCAR
DNA	GMC	MCAT

Exception. Don't capitalize familiar acronyms that seem like ordinary words. When in doubt, check a dictionary.

radar   sonar   laser

EXERCISE 36.3 Capitalize in the following sentences as necessary.

1. The east asian students visiting the district of columbia were mostly juniors pursuing b.a.'s while the african-american students were predominantly graduate students seeking master's degrees.

2. The constitution and the declaration of independence are on view at the national archives.

3. I heard the doorkeeper at the hilton speaking spanish to the general secretary of the united nations.

4. At the white house, the president will host a conference on democracy and free enterprise in the spring, probably in april.

Do You Have Questions About Abbreviations nd Numbers?

37

37a How do you handle abbreviations?

Using abbreviations, acronyms (*NATO, radar*), and initialisms (*HBO, IRS*) can make some writing simpler. Many conventional abbreviations are acceptable in all kinds of papers.

a.m.	p.m.
Mrs.	Mr.
B.C.	A.D.
Ph.D.	M.D.

Other abbreviations are appropriate on forms, reports, and statistics sheets, but not in more formal writing.

Jan.—January	no.—number
ft.—foot	mo.—month

1 Be consistent in punctuating abbreviations and acronyms. Abbreviations of single words usually take periods.

vols.	Jan.	Mr.

Initialisms are usually written without periods. You may still use periods with these terms, but be consistent.

HBO	IRS	AFL-CIO	URL

Acronyms ordinarily do not require periods.

CARE	NATO	NOW

Consistently use three periods or none at all in terms such as the following. Current usage generally omits the periods.

m.p.g. *or* mpg	r.p.m. *or* rpm	m.p.h. *or* mph

2 Be consistent in capitalizing abbreviations, acronyms, and initialisms. Capitalize the abbreviations of words that are capitalized when written out in full.

General Motors—GM   University of Toledo—UT
U.S. Navy—USN   98° Fahrenheit—98° F.

Don't capitalize the abbreviations of words not capitalized when written out in full.

pound—lb.   minutes—min.

Capitalize most initialisms.

IRS   CRT   UCLA   NBC

Always capitalize *B.C.E.* and *C.E.* or *B.C.* and *A.D.* Printers may set these items in small caps: B.C.E. and A.D.
You may capitalize *A.M.* and *P.M.*, but they often appear in small letters: *a.m.* and *p.m.* Printers may set them as small caps: A.M. and P.M.

3 Use the appropriate abbreviations for titles, degrees, and names.

Some titles are almost always abbreviated (*Mr., Ms., Mrs., Jr.*). Other titles are normally written out in full, though they may be abbreviated when they precede a first name or initial.

President   President Bush   Pres. George W. Bush
Senator   Senator Clinton   Sen. Hillary Clinton
Reverend   Reverend Call   Rev. Ann Call
                 the Reverend Dr. Call   Rev. Dr. Call

Give credit for academic degrees either before a name or after—not both. Don't, for example, use both *Dr.* and *Ph.D.* in the same name.

WRONG   **Dr.** Katherine Martinich, **Ph.D.**

RIGHT   **Dr.** Katherine Martinich
         Katherine Martinich, **Ph.D.**

Abbreviations for academic titles often stand by themselves, without names attached.

Professor Kim received her **Ph.D.** from Penn State and her **B.S.** from St. Vincent College.

4 Use the appropriate technical abbreviations.

Abbreviations are often used in professional, governmental, scientific, military, and technical writing.

DNA   UHF   EKG   START

When writing for nontechnical audiences, spell out technical terms in full the first time you use them. Then in parentheses give the specialized abbreviation you will use in the rest of the paper.

> The two congressional candidates debated the effects a tax increase might have on the gross national product (GNP).

5 Use the appropriate abbreviations for agencies and organizations.
In some cases, the abbreviation or acronym regularly replaces the full name of a company, agency, or organization.

FBI   IBM   MC   AT&T

6 Use the appropriate abbreviations for dates.
Dates are not abbreviated in most writing. Write out in full the days of the week and months of the year.

7 Use the appropriate abbreviations for time and temperatures.
Abbreviations that accompany time and temperatures are acceptable in all kinds of writing.

43 B.C.	A.D. 144	1:00 a.m.	98° F
143 B.C.E.	1066 C.E.	4:36 p.m.	13° C

Notice that the abbreviation *B.C.* appears after a date, *A.D.* usually before one. Both expressions are always capitalized. You may also see *B.C.E.* (*Before the Common Era*) used in place of *B.C.* and *C.E.* (*Common Era*) substituted for *A.D.* Both follow the date. MLA style deletes the periods in these items: BC, BCE, AD, CE.

8 Use the appropriate abbreviations for weights, measures, and times.
Technical terms or measurements are commonly abbreviated when used with numbers, but they are written out in full when they stand alone in sentences. Even when accompanied by numbers, the terms usually look better in sentences when spelled out completely.

28 mpg   1 tsp.   40 km.   450 lbs.

> Ella didn't really care how many **miles per gallon** her Escalade got in the city.

The abbreviation for number—*No.* or *no.*—is appropriate in technical writing, but only when immediately followed by a number.

NOT   The **no.** on the contaminated dish was **073**.

BUT   The contaminated dish was **no. 073**.

No. also appears in footnotes, endnotes, and citations.

9 Use the appropriate abbreviations for places. In most writing, place names are not abbreviated except in addresses and in reference tools and lists. However, certain abbreviations are accepted in academic and business writing.

USA　　　　USSR　　　　UK　　　　Washington, D.C.

In addresses (but not in written text), use the standard postal abbreviations, without periods, for the states. All the various terms for *street* are written out in full, except in addresses.

boulevard　　　　road　　　　avenue　　　　parkway

But *Mt.* (for *mount*) and *St.* (for *saint*) are acceptable abbreviations in place names when they precede a proper name.

Mt. Vesuvius　　　　**St.** Charles Street

10 Use the correct abbreviations for certain expressions preserved from Latin.

i.e. (*id est*—that is)
e.g. (*exempli gratia*—for example)
et al. (*et alii*—and others)
etc. (*et cetera*—and so on)

In most writing, it is better to use English versions of these and other Latin abbreviations. Avoid using the abbreviation *etc.* in formal or academic writing. Never write *and etc.*

11 Use the appropriate abbreviations for divisions of books. The many abbreviations for books and manuscripts (*p., pp., vols., ch., chpts., bk., sect.*) are fine in footnotes or parenthetical citations, but don't use them alone in sentences.

WRONG　　Richard stuck the **bk.** in his pocket after reading **ch.** 5.

RIGHT　　Richard stuck the **book** in his pocket after reading **chapter** 5.

12 Use symbols as abbreviations carefully. Symbols such as %, +, =, ≠, <, > make sense in technical and scientific writing, but in other academic papers, spell out the full words. Most likely to cause a problem is % for *percent*.

ACCEPTABLE	Mariah was shocked to learn that **80%** of the cars towed belong to tourists.
PREFERRED	Mariah was shocked to learn that **80 percent** of the cars towed belong to tourists.

You can use a dollar sign—$—in any writing as long as it is followed by an amount. Don't use both the dollar sign and the word *dollar*.

WRONG	The fine for parking in a towing zone is $125 dollars.
RIGHT	The fine for parking in a towing zone is **$125**.
RIGHT	The fine for parking in a towing zone is **one hundred twenty-five dollars**.

The ampersand (&) is an abbreviation for *and*. Do not use it in formal writing except when it appears in a title or name: *Road & Track*.

EXERCISE 37.1 Correct the sentences below, abbreviating where appropriate or expanding abbreviations that would be incorrect in college or professional writing. Check the punctuation for accuracy and consistency. If you insist on periods with acronyms and initialisms, use them throughout the passage.

1. There's a better than 70% chance of rain today.

2. Irene sent angry ltrs. to a dozen networks, including NBC, A.B.C., ESPN, and CNN.

3. The Emperor Claudius was born in 10 b.c. and died in 54 A.D.

4. Dr. Kovatch, M.D., works for the Federal Department of Agriculture (FDA).

37b How do you handle numbers?

You can express numbers in writing either through numerals or through words.

1	one
25	twenty-five
100	one hundred
1/4	one-fourth
0.05%	five hundredths of a percent *or*
	five one-hundredths of a percent

You'll likely use numerals in technical, scientific, and business writing. In other kinds of documents, you may combine words and numerals.

(For guidelines on using hyphens with numbers that are spelled out, see Section 35b-2.)

1 Write out numbers from one to nine; use numerals for numbers larger than nine.

10	15	39
101	115	220
1001	1021	59,000
101,000	10,000,101	50,306,673,432

In most cases, spell out ordinal numbers (that is, numbers that express a sequence): *first, second, third, fourth*, and so on. Spell out numbers that identify centuries.

in the fifteenth century

twentieth-century philosophers

2 Combine words and figures when you need to express large round numbers.

100 billion	$32 million	103 trillion

Avoid shifting between words and figures. When you need numerals to express some numbers in a sentence, use numbers throughout.

There were over **125,000** people at the protest and **950** police officers, but only **9** arrests.

When one number follows another, alternate words and figures for clarity.

33 fifth graders	12 first-term representatives
2 four-wheel-drive vehicles	five 5-gallon buckets

3 Use numerals when comparing numbers or suggesting a range. Numerals are easier to spot and compare than words.

A blackboard at the traffic office listed a **$50** fine for jaywalking, **$100** for speeding, and **$125** for parking in a towing zone.

4 Don't begin sentences with numerals.

WRONG 32 people were standing in line at the parking violation center.

RIGHT Thirty-two people were standing in line at the parking violation center.

5 Use numerals for dates, street numbers, page numbers, sums of money, and various ID and call numbers.

July 4, 1776   1860–1864
6708 Beauford Dr.   1900 East Blvd.
p. 352   pp. 23–24
$2,749.00   43£
Channel 8   103.5 FM
PR 105.5 R8   SSN 111-00-1111

Don't use an ordinal form in dates.

WRONG   May 2nd, 1991

RIGHT   May 2, 1991 *or* 2 May 1991

6 Use numerals for measurements, percentages, statistics, and scores.

35 mph   13° C   Austin, TX 78750
75 percent   0.2 liters   5.5 pupils per teacher
2 1/2 miles   15%   Browns 42—Steelers 7

Use numerals for time with *a.m.* and *p.m.*; use words with *o'clock*.

2:15 p.m.   **6:00** a.m.   **six** o'clock

7 Form the plural of numbers by adding -s or -'s.

five **6s** in a row   five **98's**

See Section 17a for more on plurals.

EXERCISE 37.2 Decide whether numbers used in the following sentences are handled appropriately. Where necessary, change numerals to words and words to numerals. Some expressions may not need revision.

1. 4 people will be honored at the ceremony beginning at nine p.m.

2. The culture contained more than 500,000,000,000 cells.

3. We forgot who won the Nobel Peace Prize in nineteen ninety-one.

4. The examination will include a question about the 1st, the 4th, or the Tenth Amendment.

Research and Writing

MLA, APA, and CMS Documentation

Research and Writing
MLA, APA, CMS Documentation

part

7

Research
and Writing

How Do You Design Research Project?

Research papers are important exercises in handling information responsibly.

Today, students in college courses can find many tools, media, and audiences to support serious academic writing and research. Students and instructors can explore and create online resources that couldn't be imagined just a decade ago.

Where just a few years ago, a research paper was typically a 10-page effort with a dozen sources—six books and six articles—a research project today can be that very same paper, or that paper moved to a Web site, or a Web site itself, or a multimedia presentation, a service-learning project, a CD-ROM, or any combination of these forms. College researchers, often working collaboratively, now reach beyond the walls of their classrooms to "publish" their work themselves for ever widening audiences.

Of course, the electronic tools that make this possible do not supplant the need for clear, powerful, and responsible writing. You still need to know how to find a topic for a project, how to use research tools, and how to evaluate, organize, and document information. You need reliable methods for managing research, whether you are preparing a traditional paper, an electronic project, or

For more about research opportunities, see the Council on Undergraduate Research at <http://www.cur.org>.

The Library of Congress in Washington, D.C., is one of the world's greatest storehouses of knowledge. Visit its Web site at <http://lcweb.loc.gov> to tour its online collections. You'll have to visit in person to study the main reading room, depicted here.

something in between. So be creative: the point of research is to expand your horizons.

38a How do you claim a topic?

Research is an active process of creating knowledge. Projects you begin now can last a lifetime; you may find yourself changing and redirecting your life as a result of work you began in a paper or a service project. That's normal and wonderful.

1 Size up an assignment carefully. When you are assigned a major college research project, go over your instructions carefully. Consider issues such as the following.

- **Scope and medium.** Conventional paper, oral report, Web project, community service project—be sure you understand what you must do and at what length. Look for word, page, or time limits.

- **Due dates.** There may be separate due dates for different stages of the project: topic proposal, annotated bibliography, outline, first draft or prototype, final version.

- **Presentation.** Note exactly what you must eventually turn in, such as a cover sheet, abstract, appendixes, bibliographies, illustrations, charts, and so on.

- **Format and documentation.** Note any specific requirements for margins, placement of page numbers, line spacing, titles, headings, illustrations and graphics. If an instructor doesn't specify a format, use one of the documentation styles explained in this book: MLA—for papers in English; APA—for psychology and the social sciences; CMS—for humanities. In the sciences, consult guides to CSE style.

- **Collaboration.** Instructors may encourage or require collaboration on research projects. Read ground rules carefully to see how work may be divided and what reports and self-assessments may be required from project participants.

- **Key words.** Take notice of key words in the assignment: *analyze, classify, define, discuss, evaluate, review, explain,* *compare, contrast, prove, disprove, persuade, survey.* Each of these words means something different.

2 Browse your topic area. When you can pick your own topic, look for a subject about which you can say, "I'd love to learn much more about it." Avoid stale controversies that have been written about for decades.

Get closer to your subject by spending a few hours browsing, first in your library and then on the Web. While browsing your topic, try to identify issues that help narrow the scope of your project. Will enough resources exist to support your project in the time available? One way to begin exploring an academic topic is to read a specialized encyclopedia, one that deals specifically with your subject. Library reference rooms have dozens of specialized encyclopedias covering many fields. Checklist 38.1 lists some of these.

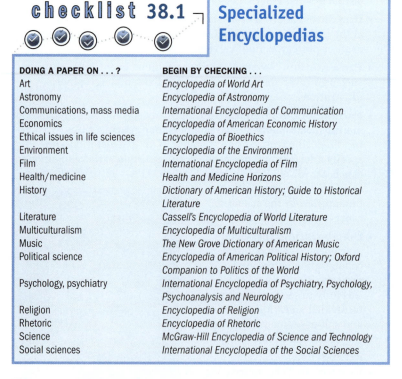

checklist 38.1 ⌐ Specialized Encyclopedias

DOING A PAPER ON . . . ?	BEGIN BY CHECKING . . .
Art	*Encyclopedia of World Art*
Astronomy	*Encyclopedia of Astronomy*
Communications, mass media	*International Encyclopedia of Communication*
Economics	*Encyclopedia of American Economic History*
Ethical issues in life sciences	*Encyclopedia of Bioethics*
Environment	*Encyclopedia of the Environment*
Film	*International Encyclopedia of Film*
Health/medicine	*Health and Medicine Horizons*
History	*Dictionary of American History; Guide to Historical Literature*
Literature	*Cassell's Encyclopedia of World Literature*
Multiculturalism	*Encyclopedia of Multiculturalism*
Music	*The New Grove Dictionary of American Music*
Political science	*Encyclopedia of American Political History; Oxford Companion to Politics of the World*
Psychology, psychiatry	*International Encyclopedia of Psychiatry, Psychology, Psychoanalysis and Neurology*
Religion	*Encyclopedia of Religion*
Rhetoric	*Encyclopedia of Rhetoric*
Science	*McGraw-Hill Encyclopedia of Science and Technology*
Social sciences	*International Encyclopedia of the Social Sciences*

Then examine books and journals in the field. Find two or three books on the subject you are researching and compare their bibliographies. Books that appear in more than one bibliography are likely to be key sources on the subject.

Check out your subject on the Internet, too. Most university and college libraries now offer extensive online databases and subscription services where you can easily access academic sources. Also browse the Web, consulting both newsgroups and Web sites. Not all sources are equally helpful, but remember that at this point you're simply selecting a topic; you aren't seeking research material.

You can usually access newsgroups from your Web browser and explore them with a search engine. To search Usenet groups, try <http:// groups.google.com>.

38b How do you plan a project?

Be organized from the start. Plan to deal with the complexities of a research project that may draw on many different kinds of sources and technologies.

1 Write a research proposal. You may be asked to prepare a proposal that outlines your project. Such proposals vary in scope: a proposal for a short project might fit on a single page; one for a senior thesis might require many pages. Any proposal will include some of the following elements.

- **Identification of a topic or topic area.** Explain your topic area and your reason for selecting this subject. (See Chapter 2.)

- **A hypothesis, research question, or thesis.** State your hypothesis or question and explain its significance, relevance, or appropriateness. Explain any assumptions on which you base your claim(s). See Chapter 3 for help in formulating a thesis.

- **Background information or review of literature.** Identify the books, articles, and other materials you expect to use. For major projects, do a thorough review of the literature in your research area.

- **A review of research resources.** Identify materials you'll need and determine their availability: books, articles, newspapers, documents, manuscripts, recordings, videos, artworks, databases, online sources, and so on. See Chapter 39 for much more about research resources.

- **A description of your research methodology.** Outline the procedures you will follow and justify your choice of methodology.
- **An assessment of the ethics of your project if it involves experiments on people or animals.** Most universities have review boards that govern research ethics, especially in psychology and the social sciences.
- **A schedule or timeline.**

2 Decide how you will handle your research materials. Most writers now use word processors or database research programs (such as *TakeNote!* or *ProCite*) to organize their work. Many projects today also require materials created on software or downloaded from electronic sources. Store this data both on the hard disk in your computer and a backup such as a USB drive or Web server.

Consider other resources you may need including software or electronic equipment such as voice or video recorders, digital cameras, and printers. Keep the materials you accumulate in a rugged portfolio with ample pockets and safe storage for printouts, notebooks, and disks. To prevent loss, label your portfolio and all your important materials with your contact information.

3 Prepare a working bibliography. Whether you are using print or electronic sources, you need to know where your information came from. Develop a bibliography of all the sources you use (see p. 368). Eventually you will need the bibliographical data to generate the Works Cited or References pages required of every standard academic paper. Each bibliographical record should contain all the information necessary to find a source again later.

The exact information you need will vary considerably for books, articles, newspapers, and electronic sources: check the MLA, APA, and CMS Models in Chapters 44–46. When using a Web page, always record the URL and the date you viewed the site.

4 Make photocopies and note cards for printed sources. Photocopy or print out passages that you expect to quote. Be sure your copies are complete and legible (especially any page numbers). When copying from a book or magazine, duplicate the title page and publication/editorial staff information page that follows. You'll need that information later.

Also write bibliographical information directly on photocopies and printouts, making sure each document is keyed to a full bibliographic record. Use highlighter pens to mark passages in photocopies and printouts that you expect to refer to later, and keep all these materials in a folder. Never mark in library books.

checklist 38.2 ┐ | **Information for Note Cards**

Some writers still prefer to keep notes on index cards. Here's what such cards might contain:

- Author's last name and a shortened version of the source's title (for accurate reference to the corresponding bibliography card)
- A heading to identify the nature of the information on the card
- The actual data or information, correctly summarized, paraphrased, or quoted
- Page numbers or correct Web address for locating the source

5 Print or download electronic sources. How you record data from an electronic source will depend on how you expect to use it. If you're simply looking for facts, you may want to treat it like a printed source, recording the data on note cards or printing out the source itself. Printouts may be the easiest way to preserve information on Web resources whose content changes from day to day. Some of this material may be archived electronically, but it is always safer to print out material you will later cite. Be sure to record when you made the printout, since most documentation for electronic material requires a date of access.

It is possible to copy most electronic sources directly to disk. The finder on your computer may already have folders where you can store text files, movies, pictures, music files, and Web sites. Label any folders you create carefully so that you or a co-worker on the project can find information easily. Do back up all such materials. Know where *all* downloaded images come from and who owns their copyrights; you will have to document and credit all copyrighted pictures, photographs, and images borrowed from the Web. To use copyrighted material in your own electronic publications, you must get permission from the holder of the copyright.

6 Consider collaborative research. You may work as part of a team for some projects. Careful management is an important part of any collaborative effort. In a group you may want to discuss questions such as the following.

- What research and writing skills will your project require?
- What qualities and skills should you look for in your colleagues?
- How will you organize your team?

- How will decisions be made?
- Who—if anyone—will be in charge?
- How will you communicate and coordinate your efforts?
- How will you schedule the work, and how will you deal with deviations from the schedule?
- How will you assess your work and share the credit?

How Do You Find Inf⬤rmation?

39

As you begin a research paper or project, your goal is to find sources and to prepare a *working bibliography*, that is, a preliminary list of materials related to your topic (see pp. 47 for an example). Today, you can tap into more information than ever before.

39a How do you use a library?

A first priority for any college student is to learn the physical arrangement of campus libraries and research facilities. Tour these buildings, study the collections, and, above all, get to know the research librarians.

1 Explore your library. Be sure you can locate the following places, features, and services.

- **Online catalog.** Learn how to use these terminals, which are the pathway into your library's books, journals, and other materials. Many libraries also have comprehensive online catalogs and Web sites with links to available indexes, databases, and online reference tools.

- **Card catalog.** Most libraries now have extensive electronic catalogs. But online terminals sometimes may not cover older library materials or special collections.

- **Reference room.** Study this useful collection. Notice how its materials are arranged and where heavily used items (encyclopedias, almanacs, phone books, databases) are located. Find out, too, where the reference librarian is stationed.

- **Databases and bibliographies.** Research databases will usually be arrayed around computer

terminals, with information either online or accessed via CD-ROM disks. Older print bibliographies in various fields will often be large multivolume collections. Ask librarians for help.

- **Microforms collections.** Some older documents, newspapers, and periodicals have been preserved on rolls of film called *microfilm* or rectangular sheets of film called *microfiche*. Know where these collections are and learn how to use them.

- **Periodical collections.** Know where to find both current journals and periodicals and older bound or microfilmed copies.

- **Newspapers.** Current newspapers are usually available in a reading room. A limited selection of older newspapers will often be available on microfilm or in online archives.

- **Special collections.** Note the location of any important collections in your library: pictures and photographs, maps, government documents, and so on.

- **Audio/video collections.** Know where to locate audio/video materials as well as facilities for listening to or viewing CDs, DVDs, tapes, and video disks.

- **Circulation desk/library services.** Learn about circulation desk services. You can usually recall materials already on loan. Most libraries also offer interlibrary loan programs that enable you to borrow materials your library may not own. (These orders take time; don't wait until the last minute.)

- **Directories.** Look for directories or pamphlets to help you locate materials.

- **Photocopiers/computers/study areas.** Look for quiet places to study, photocopiers, and computer terminals, ports and plugs for laptops, and wireless areas.

2 Use traditional and online library catalogs efficiently. Almost all libraries now provide access to their resources via computer terminals or the World Wide Web. If your library has an electronic catalog, study its screens and learn its basic search techniques and commands. Most basic screens support a variety of author-title-subject keyword search combinations, and more advanced searches enable you to pick the date, location, format, and language of the research material. Librarians find that most people use online catalogs by using keyword searches. For more about keyword searches, see Section 39d.

For a list of online library catalogs, examine the LIBCAT Web site at <http://www. metronet.lib.mn.us/lc/lca.cfm>.

An online catalog offers detailed information about most library holdings. On screen, you'll often be given a list of brief entries on your subject—typically the author, title, publishing information, date, and call number—with an option to select a fuller listing. The full listing describes additional features of the item.

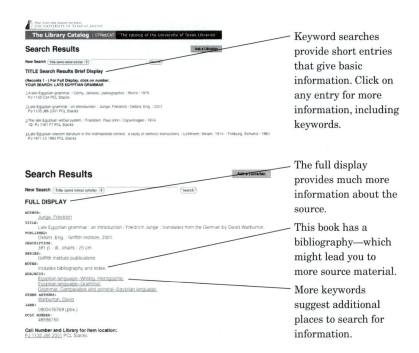

Keyword searches provide short entries that give basic information. Click on any entry for more information, including keywords.

The full display provides much more information about the source.

This book has a bibliography—which might lead you to more source material.

More keywords suggest additional places to search for information.

Most card and online catalogs use subject headings determined by the Library of Congress and compiled in the multivolume *Library of Congress Subject Headings* (*LCSH*). Consult this volume (or its electronic equivalent) in the reference room of your library at the start of your research: It will tell you how your topic is described and treated in the library catalog. On any given subject card or screen, pay attention, too, to any additional subject headings offered because these may be keywords to use for additional searches.

39b　How do you find research materials?

Today, resources on almost any topic are plentiful. It helps to know what kinds of materials provide what types of information.

1 Locate suitable bibliographies. Bibliographies are lists of books, articles, and other documentary materials that deal with particular subjects. Ask a reference room librarian whether a bibliography on your specific subject has been compiled. If not, consult a more general bibliography.

39.1 **Types of Printed Bibliographies**

chart

- **Selective bibliographies** usually list the best-known or most respected books and articles in a subject area.

- **Annotated bibliographies** briefly describe the works they list and may evaluate them.

- **Annual bibliographies** catalog the works produced within a field or discipline in a given year.

Printed bibliographies are losing ground to electronic databases, but they are still available on many subjects. Also look for bibliographies at the back of scholarly books, articles, and dissertations you examine. Such bibliographies offer a focused look at a specific topic.

Only a few of the hundreds of bibliographic resources in specific disciplines are listed below.

checklist 39.1   **Bibliographies**

DOING A PAPER ON . . . ?	CHECK THIS BIBLIOGRAPHY . . .
American history	*Bibliographies in American History*
Anthropology	*Anthropological Bibliographies: A Selected Guide*
Art	*Guide to the Literature of Art History*
Astronomy	*A Guide to the Literature of Astronomy; Astronomy and Astrophysics: A Bibliographic Guide*
Classics	*Greek and Roman Authors: A Checklist of Criticism*
Communications	*Communication: A Guide to Information Sources*
Engineering	*Science and Engineering Literature*
Literature	*MLA International Bibliography*
Mathematics	*Using the Mathematical Literature*
Music	*Music Reference and Research Materials*
Philosophy	*A Bibliography of Philosophical Bibliographies*
Physics	*Use of Physics Literature*
Psychology	*Harvard List of Books in Psychology*
Social work	*Social Work Education: A Bibliography*

Electronic subject guides offer lists of print and electronic resources on a vast number of subjects and disciplines, from art and architecture to women's studies. You may find the following Web sites especially helpful.

- New York Public Library: search for Research Guides and Subject Guides at <http://www.nypl.orgl>
- Columbia University Library Web "Selected Subject Guides and Resources" at <http://www.columbia.edu/cu/lweb/eguides>
- The University of California at Berkeley Libraries: search for Subject Guides at <http://www.lib.berkeley.edu>
- The University of Chicago "Libraries, Collections, and Subjects" at <http://www.lib.uchicago.edu/e/lcs.html>
- The University of Texas at Austin Subject Guides at <http://www.lib.utexas.edu/subject/>
- The University of Virginia Subject Guides at <http://www.lib.virginia.edu/resguide.html>

2 Locate suitable indexes to search the periodical literature. Indexes list important items that cannot be recorded in a library catalog: journal articles, magazine pieces, and stories from newspapers, for instance. Such material is called *periodical literature*. You shouldn't undertake any college-level research paper without surveying the periodical literature in the subject area.

In the past, periodical indexes were printed works, and you may still have to use these to find older sources. More recent materials, however, are indexed electronically.

You may want to begin periodical searches with general and multidisciplinary indexes such as the following.

Expand Academic ASAP (electronic)

EBSCOhost (electronic)

LEXIS-NEXIS Academic Universe (electronic)

Readers' Guide to Periodical Literature (print)

A new and developing resource is *Google Scholar* at *Scholar.google.com*. You can search for authors, articles, and more—but begin by checking Scholar Help.

All major academic fields and majors now have several indexes for their periodical literatures, most of them computerized—a few of these are listed in Checklist 39.2. And because new indexes may be added at any time, check with your reference librarian or your library's Web site to find the index best suited to your work.

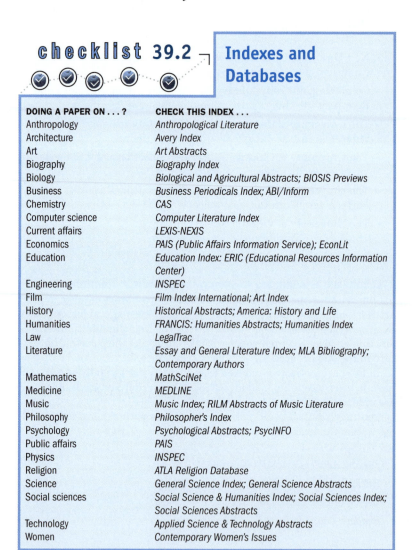

checklist 39.2 — Indexes and Databases

DOING A PAPER ON . . . ?	CHECK THIS INDEX . . .
Anthropology	*Anthropological Literature*
Architecture	*Avery Index*
Art	*Art Abstracts*
Biography	*Biography Index*
Biology	*Biological and Agricultural Abstracts; BIOSIS Previews*
Business	*Business Periodicals Index; ABI/Inform*
Chemistry	*CAS*
Computer science	*Computer Literature Index*
Current affairs	*LEXIS-NEXIS*
Economics	*PAIS (Public Affairs Information Service); EconLit*
Education	*Education Index: ERIC (Educational Resources Information Center)*
Engineering	*INSPEC*
Film	*Film Index International; Art Index*
History	*Historical Abstracts; America: History and Life*
Humanities	*FRANCIS: Humanities Abstracts; Humanities Index*
Law	*LegalTrac*
Literature	*Essay and General Literature Index; MLA Bibliography; Contemporary Authors*
Mathematics	*MathSciNet*
Medicine	*MEDLINE*
Music	*Music Index; RILM Abstracts of Music Literature*
Philosophy	*Philosopher's Index*
Psychology	*Psychological Abstracts; PsycINFO*
Public affairs	*PAIS*
Physics	*INSPEC*
Religion	*ATLA Religion Database*
Science	*General Science Index; General Science Abstracts*
Social sciences	*Social Science & Humanities Index; Social Sciences Index; Social Sciences Abstracts*
Technology	*Applied Science & Technology Abstracts*
Women	*Contemporary Women's Issues*

Ordinarily, you can access indexes on your library's Web site or in the reference room. Most indexes, printed or electronic, are easy to use—if you read the instructions that come with them. Checklist 39.3 provides some useful tips.

checklist 39.3 — **Searching an Electronic Index or Database**

- Be sure you are logged on to the right index. A library terminal may provide access to several different databases or indexes. Find the one appropriate for your subject.

- Read the description of the index to find out how to use its information. Not all databases and indexes work the same way.

- When searching by keyword, check whether a list of subject headings is available. To save time, match your search terms to those on the list before you begin.

- Try synonyms if an initial keyword search turns up too few items.

3 Consult biographical resources. If you need information about famous people, living and dead, good places to start are the *Biography Index, BioBase, LEXIS-NEXIS, Current Biography*, and *The McGraw-Hill Encyclopedia of World Biography*.

There are also *Who's Who* volumes for living British, American, and world notables, as well as volumes for African Americans and women. Deceased figures may appear in *Who Was Who*. Probably the two most famous dictionaries of biography are the *Dictionary of National Biography* (British) and the *Dictionary of American Biography*.

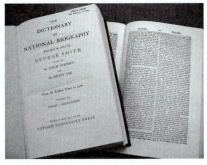

On the World Wide Web, you might look at the database maintained by the Arts and Entertainment Network program *Biography* at <http://www.biography.com>. For information about writers and authors, check the Internet Public Library's "Authors" page at <http://www.ipl.org/ref/RR/static/hum60.10.00.html>. For the wisdom of famous people, check out the Web version of the 1919 version of *Bartlett's Familiar Quotations* at <http://www.bartleby.com/100> or, for more recent remarks, *The Quotation Page* at <http://www.quotationspage.com>. To search for private individuals, you can use features such as *Yahoo!*'s "people search" on the World Wide Web.

checklist 39.4 ┐ **Biographical Information**

YOUR SUBJECT IS IN...?	CHECK THIS SOURCE...
Art	*Index to Artistic Biography*
Music	*The New Grove Dictionary of Music and Musicians*
Politics	*Politics in America; Almanac of American Politics*
Religion	*Dictionary of American Religious Biography*
Science	*Dictionary of Scientific Biography*

YOUR SUBJECT IS...?	CHECK THIS SOURCE...
African American	*Dictionary of American Negro Biography*
Asian	*Encyclopedia of Asian History*
Australian	*Australian Dictionary of Biography*
Canadian	*Dictionary of Canadian Biography*
Female	*Index to Women; Notable American Women*
Mexican American	*Mexican American Biographies*

4 Locate statistics. Statistics are available in library reference rooms and online. Be sure to find up-to-date and reliable figures.

checklist 39.5 ┐ **Statistics**

TO FIND...	CHECK THIS SOURCE...
General statistics	*World Almanac; Current Index to Statistics* (electronic)
Statistics about the United States	*Historical Statistics of the United States; Statistical Abstract of the United States; STAT-USA* (electronic); *GPO Access* (electronic)
World information	*The Statesman's Yearbook; National Intelligence Factbook; UN Demographic Yearbook; UNESCO Statistical Yearbook*
Business facts	*Handbook of Basic Economic Statistics; Survey of Current Business; Dow Jones–Irwin Business Almanac*
Public opinion polls	*Gallup Poll*
Population data	*Population Index* (electronic)

5 Check news sources. For information published earlier than the mid-1990s, you'll have to rely on printed papers or microfilm copies. More recent editions will be indexed online. If you know the date of a particular event, you can usually locate the information you want. Only a few printed papers are fully indexed. Most common is the *New York*

Times, usually available on microfilm. The *New York Times Index* provides chronological summaries of articles on a given subject. A reference librarian can guide you to other news indexes—products such as *Newsbank* or *InfoTrac.*

For current events, you can search hundreds of online newspapers and news services. They offer immediate information from around the globe and with many points of view. When reporting information you find on the Web, make sure that the source is reputable (see Section 40a). The following online news resources are worth consulting.

@tips

Also consult resources such as *The Internet Public Library* at <http://ipl.sils.umich.edu/div/subject>, <iTools.com> and *Wikipedia: The Free Encyclopedia* at <http://en.wikipedia.org/wiki/Main_Page>. For statistics from more than 70 agencies of the federal government, explore FedStats, at <http://www.fedstats.gov>.

NEWS RESOURCE	ADDRESS
CNN Interactive	<http://www.cnn.com>
C-SPAN Online	<http://c-span.org>
Google News	<http://news.google.com>
London Times	<http://www.thetimes.co.uk>

news resources continued on page 374

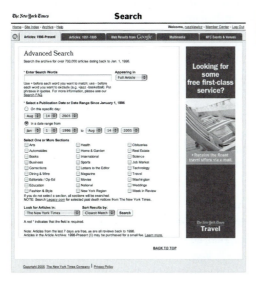

Advanced search screen from the *New York Times on the Web.*

news resources continued from page 373

MSNBC	<http://msnbc.com/news>
New York Times	<http://www.nytimes.com>
Reuters	<http://reuters.com>
USA Today News	<http://usatoday.com>

Yahoo! at <http://www.yahoo.com> can point you to hundreds of online newspapers. Check under its "News & Media" category. You may have to register to use some online newspapers and pay to download archived materials.

6 Check book and film reviews. To locate reviews of books, see *Book Review Digest* (1905), *Book Review Index* (1965), or *Current Book Review Citations* (1976). *Book Review Digest* lists fewer reviews but summarizes those it does include. Many electronic periodical indexes also catalog book reviews. Enter "book reviews" on a search engine or directory, and you will turn up many sites, such as the *New York Times Sunday Book Review* at <http://www.nytimes.com/books/yr/mo/day/home/contents.html> and *The New York Review of Books* at <http://www.nybooks.com>.

For film reviews and criticism, see the printed volumes *Film Review Index* (1986) and *Film Criticism: An Index to Critics' Anthologies* (1975) as well as the electronic index *Film Index International*. Numerous Web sites—of wildly varying quality—are devoted to films and film reviews.

7 Write or email professional organizations. Almost every subject, cause, concept, or idea is represented by a professional organization, society, bureau, office, or lobby. For mailing addresses of organizations, consult the *Encyclopedia of Associations*, published by Gale Research. Use a search engine to find Web sites.

The U.S. government publishes information on just about every subject of public interest. Check the *Index to U.S. Government Periodicals* or the *Monthly Catalog of United States Government Publications* for listings. Or use a Web site such as *Fedworld Information Network* at <http://www.fedworld.gov>.

8 Consult collections of images. Online resources make it possible to locate images. Among the numerous collections of images and clip art on the Web are the following.

IMAGE SITE	ADDRESS
About.com	<http://webclipart.about.com>

Surveys clip art and graphic sites on the Web.

Google Maps	<http://maps.google.com>

Provides both maps and satellite images of all locations.

GraphicMaps.com   <http://www.graphicmaps.com>
Provides information about maps on the Web.

Time & Life Pictures   <http://www.timelifepictures.com>
Presents images from the Time, Inc. collection.

Note that you may have to pay to acquire or use some images. You'll also need to document any borrowed images you include in your finished project, just as you cite and document other research sources.

39c   How do you choose electronic resources?

Many electronic sources were not designed with researchers and scholars in mind. For instance, the Web presents a jumble of information, leaving users to screen nuggets of gold from mountains of slag. It's essential that your searches be efficient and critical.

1 Check the World Wide Web. The Web is not, like a library, designed, catalogued, and selected to support research. So while finding information is easy, finding *reliable* source material can be more of a challenge. You probably do most of your Web searching using Google or Yahoo!. But you should be careful not to let these resources become your only tool for research. Try several search engines for any major project.

SEARCH TOOLS	ADDRESS
About.com	<http://about.com>
AltaVista	<http://altavista.com>
Ask Jeeves	<http://ask.com>
Dogpile	<http://www.dogpile.com>
Excite	<http://excite.com>
Lycos	<http://www.lycos.com>

Libraries, universities, and government agencies have also created hundreds of reference tools with more scholarly goals. Here are just a few places to look. (Be warned that Web addresses change frequently.)

REFERENCE SITE	ADDRESS
Books on the Internet	<http://www.lib.utexas.edu/Libs/PCL/Etext.html>
Infomine	<http://infomine.ucr.edu>
The Internet Public Library	<http://www.ipl.org>
Librarians' Index to the Internet	<http://lii.org>
Library of Congress Research Centers	<http://lcweb.loc.gov/rr/research-centers.html>

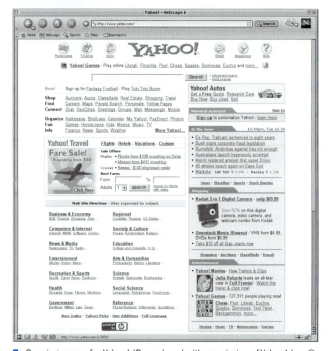

Opening screen for *Yahoo!* (Reproduced with permission of Yahoo! Inc. © 2007 by Yahoo! Inc. *Yahoo!* and the *Yahoo!* logo are trademarks of Yahoo! Inc.)

The basic tool of many search engines and databases is the keyword search. For keyword search strategies, see Section 39d.

2 Investigate Usenet groups and blogs. Usenet groups make it possible for you to read or participate in discussions on a huge variety of topics—arts, sciences, religion, popular culture, and so on. You can access these groups easily by selecting "Groups" at either Yahoo.com or Google.com. These tools can furnish you with up-to-the-second information on a topic offered from many points of view. But be cautious with any information you take from such an open environment: Confirm any statistic, fact, or claim from such a source with information from a second and different type of authority.

Similarly, many blogs offer commentary on the news and critiques of mainstream media sources. The best of these often highly personal and frequently updated sites can be useful when you want to gauge opinion on almost any subject. Political blogs often critique mainstream news sources, so they provide an important perspective on public discussions.

39d How do you search by keywords?

Writers now routinely find information online by typing names, phrases, or other key terms into Google to see what pops up. That habit has largely replaced more refined keyword searches. Yet you still will need keyword search techniques to explore many electronic resources, including the online library catalogs and electronic indexes and databases. A *keyword search* is simply a scan of an electronic text or database to find each occurrence of a given word or phrase.

Our best advice is to read the instructions for any tool you are using, whether it is an electronic catalog, a search engine, or a directory. Your ability to get results depends on knowing how to direct that search. The rules and "filters" controlling any given catalog or database may differ.

1 Understand how a simple keyword search works. A keyword search finds the titles in a catalog or database that contain the keyword(s) you have typed into a box or line on the screen. The *Library of Congress Subject Headings (LCSH)* in the reference room of your library may be a good source for keyword ideas. Or ask a librarian for help.

To find new, powerful keywords, look for cross-listings for your particular subject—that is, other terms under which your subject is entered—and then probe the catalog using each of these new terms as keywords.

The keywords you choose—whether names, places, titles, concepts, or people—will shape your search. You have to be ingenious and dogged. If you begin with overly general keywords, you might never find the particular information you need. Try searching combinations of terms to narrow your search.

An online library catalog may ask you to indicate whether a word you are searching is a title (t), author (a), subject (s), or some other term the system recognizes.

2 Understand the principles of Boolean searching. A Boolean search combines keywords in specific ways to give you more control over narrowing your search. Most search engines in online catalogs, databases, or Web sites use some form of Boolean search.

You initiate a Boolean search in different ways. By linking keywords with the term AND, you can identify only those items in which all the individual keywords appear.

Schnauzer AND Training

Washington AND Jefferson AND Constitution

Another way to initiate a Boolean search is to select an appropriate command from a search engine menu, such as an "all the words" option.

Other Boolean operators allow you to direct database searches in different ways.

OR   Using OR between keywords directs the search engine to find any examples of either keyword. Using OR might widen a search, but it would also allow you to locate all documents that cover related concepts.

     Congress OR Senate

NOT   Using NOT between terms permits you to search for sites that include one term but not another. This may be useful when you want to exclude certain meanings of a term irrelevant to your search.

     Indians NOT Cleveland
     democratic NOT party

( )   Putting items in parentheses allows for additional fine tuning of a search. In the first example below, you could locate documents that mention either Senator Clinton or Senator Hutchison but not Senator Kennedy or Senator Hatch.

     Senator AND (Clinton OR Hutchison)
     pickup NOT (Ford OR Dodge)

3 Search by exact phrase. To narrow a search even more, you can search for a specific and distinctive phrase either by placing it between quotation marks or selecting the "exact phrase" option on a search screen.

You can use exact-phrase searches when you can't recall who is responsible for a particular expression—for example, "defining deviancy down." On a Web search, you may find the expression attributed to former Senator Daniel Patrick Moynihan.

You can also combine exact-phrase searches with various Boolean commands.

"Ten Commandments" AND ("Charlton Heston" OR "Yul Brynner")

"pickup truck" NOT (Ford OR Dodge)

4 Focus your search. Search tools give you flexibility in how to search information and how to report it.

Where to search. Many search engines allow you to limit a keyword search to a specific type of information. For example, the search engine *Google* allows you to make any of the following choices under its "Advanced Search" option.

- Language (any language—Arabic, Bulgarian, etc.)
- File Format (for example, Adobe Acrobat @ rft)
- Occurrences (anywhere in the page, in the title, in the text)

Your search may return suggestions for additional searches. You may see links marked "More like this."

When to search. Many keyword searches can be limited to specific periods of time, making your search narrower and more efficient.

Searches limited by time also can show who was thinking what, when. How often were the terms *multiculturalism* and *partial birth abortion* being used 10 years ago? How often are they being used today? You could find out on a database such as *LEXIS-NEXIS*.

How to report information. With online library catalogs and electronic indexes, you can usually print out the information you see on screen. Sometimes you have to select individual items to get full bibliographic data.

On the Web, you can usually see how many "hits" a search has found, and you can decide how many of them to view. It often makes sense to look at the abstracts for the sites first; then you can get full listings for sites that interest you.

To learn more about using Web search engines, see Ellen Chamberlain's "Bare Bones 101," a site that includes detailed descriptions of important search engines, at <http://sc.edu/beaufort/library/bones.html>.

How DYou Evaluate Sources?

40

Throughout the research process you'll find yourself gathering additional information. At the same time, you'll be assessing the sources you've gathered, first *positioning* them to understand their purpose and limitations and then *evaluating* their quality. How can your sources best support the claims you wish to make?

40a How do you position research sources?

Before you annotate (see Section 41a), summarize, or paraphrase a source (see Section 41b), be sure you understand its context—what we call *positioning a source.* You position a source by identifying its point of view, biases, strengths, and limitations. Of course, you will use different sources in different ways. Sometimes you'll want sources that offer the most balanced or authoritative treatment of a subject. At other times you'll choose sources that exemplify specific points of view—a leftist view or a right-wing perspective. Positioning a source assures that you'll make such decisions with your eyes open and not misconstrue information when you report it.

Utne Reader at <http://utne.com> appeals to a predominantly left-of-center readership concerned with issues of culture, earth, body, spirit, and politics.

The titles of articles in *The Weekly Standard* at <http://www.weeklystandard.com> might suggest its right-of-center politics. Or you might recognize the names of some of its authors.

The perspectives of a magazine like *Rolling Stone*, which focuses on popular culture, may not be as self-evident or consistent as those of a political journal. But the magazine will still reflect the interests and biases of its writers and publishers. To position such a source, you might examine the titles of its articles, the tone of its editorials (if any), the character of its illustrations and graphics, and even the types of ads it attracts. View its Web site at <www.rollingstone.com>.

checklist 40.1    **Positioning a Source**

- What are the background and interests of the author(s)?
- What are the interests and biases of the publisher?
- How much authority does the source claim?
- Are the assertions of authority justified?
- Does the source purport to be objective and/or scientific?
- Does the source present itself as subjective and/or personal?
- Whose interests does the source represent?
- Whose interests does the source seem to ignore?
- To what audience(s) is the source directed?
- What do readers need to know about the source?
- Where do links in the source lead? Who advertises in the source?
- What role should the source play in my project: Authority? Opinion? Illustration?

40b How do you evaluate research sources?

It falls to you to judge the authority, quality, and credibility of the sources you use. You can make sound judgments if you remember a few basic principles. (For detailed advice on reading critically, see Chapter 7.)

1 Consider the purpose of a source. Sources aren't simply *good* or *bad*. Their value depends, in part, on how you use them. You can devise information from almost any source. Sources that lack the authority and perspective of scholarly works may still provide a valid snapshot of current political attitudes.

Even if sources can't be described as simply good or bad without considering their purposes, they do have strengths and weaknesses to weigh. We've summarized some of those qualities in the table on pages 384–385, but our guidelines should be taken with caution. Any single source might differ from our characterizations.

In researching a subject, the best sources for you are likely to be those just a step or two above your current level of knowledge. Push yourself to learn more without exceeding your depth.

2 Consider the authority and reputation of a source. Certain books, articles, and reference tools are cited more often than others. These are likely to be essential materials that people in the field assume most other researchers know. If you haven't already consulted these materials, go and review them. Ask librarians or instructors about the authority of sources that you use. They can direct you to reliable materials.

Do the same with electronic sources: track down the best items so far as you can determine. Inevitably, the most valuable sites will appear on many "favorites" lists. Checking the domain in the address will give you some sense of who is sponsoring the site.

.edu—an educational institution

.org—a nonprofit organization

.gov—a government-sponsored site

.com—a commercial site

.net—a network site

3 Consider the credentials of authors and sponsoring agencies. You'll quickly pick up the names of people mentioned frequently as experts or authorities. Look for these familiar authors. But be wary when the names of famous people are attached to subjects about which they may have no special expertise.

You can be more confident about electronic information when the sponsoring agency of the source is one you would trust in a print environment. Acquiring information online from *Reuters News Service* or the *New York Times* is equivalent to seeing the same information in print. But don't hesitate even in these cases to raise questions about fairness, bias, and completeness.

With Web sites, Usenet groups, blogs, and other online sources, you may find yourself clueless about the credentials of your "authors." When you report factual information from such sources, confirm it when possible through second, more familiar sources. (Reporting opinion is a different matter.)

4 Consider the timeliness and stability of a source. Timeliness is relative. In general, you want to support your projects with the most current and reputable information in a field. But your instructors and librarians may refer you to classic writings, many of which may have shaped thinking in your topic area.

Timeliness is a different matter in newer electronic environments. In general, electronic sources are not yet as stable, comprehensive, and dependable over the long run as printed books and articles—though the situation is improving rapidly and some materials (such as scholarly e-journals) may be available only online. Writers online have become better about furnishing bibliographical information—especially dates. In general, avoid sites that do not date either their original postings or

Assessing Sources

Source	Purpose	Authors	Audience/Language
Scholarly books	Advance or report new knowledge	Experts	Academic/Technical
Scholarly articles	Advance or report new knowledge	Experts	Academic/Technical
Serious books & articles	Report or summarize information	Experts or professional writers	Educated public/Formal
Popular magazines	Report or summarize information	Professional writers or journalists	General public/Informal
Newspapers, news services	Report current information	Journalists	Popular/Informal
Sponsored Web sites	Varies from report information to advertise	Varies, usually Web expert	Varies/Usually informal
Individual Web sites/ Web logs	Varies	Expert to novice	Varies/Casual to slang
Interviews	Consult with experts	Experts	Varies/Technical to colloquial
Listservs	Discuss specific subjects	Experts to interested amateurs	Varies/Technical to colloquial
Usenet newsgroups	Discuss specific subjects	Open to everyone	Varies/Technical to colloquial

updates. The turnover of some online material (blogs, newsgroups) is very rapid, changing from day to day. Obviously, you need to print out or download relevant postings from such sources. Check also whether a site archives its materials. If it doesn't, it may not be useful for research.

5 Consider special interest intrusions into a source. Sponsored Web sites—especially search engines—can be difficult to use when they bring up specific advertising messages to direct you to a sponsor's material. Sponsored sites may also reflect the commercial connections of their owners, especially when they are owned by larger companies with other commercial interests. Be wary of attempts to influence your judgment, and make it a point to visit many different sites when exploring a subject.

@ etips

For additional advice on evaluating Web sites, see <http://www.library.cornell.edu/ okuref/research/webeval.html> and <http://www.library.ucla. edu/libraries/college/help/ critical/index.htm>. For an exercise on evaluating a Web site, see <http://www.lib.vt. edu/research/evaluate/ evaluating.html>.

Publisher or Medium	Reviewed/Documented?	Current/Stable?	Dialogic/Interactive?
University Press	Yes/Yes	No/Yes	No/No
Scholarly or professional journal	Yes/Yes	Usually no/Yes	No/No (unless online)
Commercial publishers	Yes/No	Depends on subject/Yes	No/No (unless online)
Commercial publishers	Yes/No	Yes/Yes	No/No (unless online)
Commercial press or online	Yes/No	Yes/Yes	No/No (unless online)
Online WWW	Sometimes/Links to other sites	Regularly updated/Sometimes	Sometimes/Often
Online WWW	Usually no/Links to other sites	Varies/Varies	Sometimes/Sometimes
Notes, recordings, email	No/No	Yes/No	Yes/Yes
Online email	No/No	Yes/Sometimes	Yes/Yes
Online email	No/No	Yes/No	Yes/Yes

checklist 40.2

Evaluating a World Wide Web Site

- Is the site sponsored by a reputable group you can identify?
- Do the authors of the site give evidence of their credentials?
- Is the site conveniently searchable?
- Is information in the site logically arranged?
- Is the site easy to navigate?
- Does the site provide an email address where you might send questions?
- Is the site updated regularly or properly maintained?
- Does the site archive older information?
- Is the content of the site affected by commercial sponsorship?

How Do You Use Sources Responsibly?

41

Once you have sources for your project, you must make use of the information in them. How you handle these materials will vary, but certain techniques make sense for getting the most out of them: annotating, and summarizing and paraphrasing.

41a How do you annotate research materials?

Once you have positioned and evaluated a source (see Chapter 40), you can begin mining it for information. One way to do this is to annotate the material—that is, to attach comments, questions, and reactions to it directly. The point of annotation is to identify ideas and information worth returning to and, more important, to engage in a dialogue with the authors and sources you are encountering.

When you are reading library books and material, you'll have to record your reactions in notes, summaries, and paraphrases (see Section 41b).

With photocopied materials, highlighting important passages is part of effective annotation. Each highlight should also be accompanied by a marginal comment that explains the importance of the passage or states your reaction to it. Be sure to highlight any passages worthy of direct quotation.

Use the annotation features of word-processing programs to record your reactions to downloads. These annotations can later be incorporated into the paper or project itself if they are thoughtful and entirely in your own words.

Also, you should take conventional notes on all your important sources, online or off. (See Section 7a–4 for advice about preparing *content*, *context*, and *response* notes.)

Here is an example of a source that has been annotated in its margins. This same article is both summarized and paraphrased in Section 41b.

@tips

For a detailed online guide to *Microsoft Word's* commenting features, see <http://www.cwrl.utexas.edu/teachers/word_commenting.shtml>. The tutorial explains how to either edit or comment on any document you can download in *Word*.

An Annotated Essay

"Educational Insensitivity"

Diane Ravitch

An enterprising parent of a high school senior recently discovered that the literary texts on the New York Regents examinations had been expurgated. Excerpts from the writings of many prominent authors were doctored, without their knowledge or permission, to delete references to religion, profanity, sex, alcohol or other potentially troublesome topics.

The story was a huge embarrassment to the New York State Education Department, which prepares the examinations, and yesterday Richard P. Mills, the state education commissioner, ordered the practice stopped. From now on, all literary passages used on state tests will be unchanged except for length.

Mr. Mills is to be commended for this new policy. But the dimensions of this absurd practice reach far beyond the borders of New York, and there are many culprits. Censorship of tests and textbooks is not merely widespread: across the nation, it has become institutionalized.

For decades, American publishers have quietly trimmed sexual and religious allusions from their textbooks and tests. When publishers assemble reading books, they keep a wary eye on states like California, Texas and Florida, where textbooks are adopted for the entire state and any hint of controversy can prevent a book's placement on the state's list. In Texas, Florida and other southern states, the religious right objects to any stories that introduce fantasy, witchcraft, the occult, sex or religious practices different from its own. In California, no textbook can win adoption unless it meets the state's strict demands for gender balance and multicultural representation and avoids mention of unhealthy foods, drugs or alcohol.

Over the past several decades, the nation's testing industry has embraced censorship. In almost every state, tests are closely scrutinized in an official process known as a bias and sensitivity review. This procedure was created in the late 1960's and early 1970's to scrutinize questions for any hint of racial or gender bias. Over the years, every test development company in the nation has established a bias and sensitivity review process to ensure that test questions do not contain anything that might upset students and prevent them from showing their true abilities on a test. Now these reviews routinely expurgate references to social problems, politics, disobedient children or any other potentially controversial topic.

Original audience was readers of the New York Times, America's paper of record. Find out more about NY Regents exams.

What's the issue now if the policy has been changed?

Ravitch's claim.

Can both right and left be responsible for censorship?

Looks like good intentions gone haywire. Shouldn't good literature challenge students?

This is the rationale now used within the testing industry to delete references to any topic that someone might find objectionable. As a top official in one of the major testing companies told me: "If anyone objects to a test question, we delete it. Period."

This self-censorship is hardly a secret. Every major publisher of educational materials uses "bias guidelines," which list hundreds of words and images that are banned or avoided. Words like "brotherhood" and "mankind" have been banished. A story about mountain climbing may be excluded because it favors test-takers who live near mountains over those who don't. Older people may not be portrayed walking with canes or sitting in rocking chairs.

Is Ravitch being sarcastic in this ¶ or are her examples real?

I serve on the board of a federal testing agency, the National Assessment Governing Board, which is directly responsible for reviewing all test questions on the National Assessment of Educational Progress. We have learned that bias and sensitivity rules are subject to expansive interpretations. Once reviewers proposed to eliminate a reading passage about Mount Rushmore because the monument offends Lakota Indians, who consider the Black Hills of South Dakota a sacred site.

This censorship is now standard practice in the testing industry and in educational publishing. One way to end it is to expose the practice to public scrutiny, forcing officials like Mr. Mills to abandon it. Another way, adopted by the National Assessment Governing Board, is to review every deletion proposed by those applying bias and sensitivity standards to determine whether it passes the test of common sense. I would also recommend that whenever material is deleted from a literary passage in a test, the omission should be indicated with ellipses.

Proposals to solve censorship in schools and textbooks.

The bias and sensitivity review process, as it has recently evolved, is an embarrassment to the educational publishing industry. It may satisfy the demands of the religious right (in censoring topics) and of the politically correct left (in censoring language). But it robs our children of their cultural heritage and their right to read—free of censorship.

Ravitch's actual claim—and a possible quotation.

Diane Ravitch, a historian of education at New York University, is writing a book about censorship in the educational publishing industry.

What else has she written? What are her politics?

41b How do you summarize, paraphrase, and synthesize research materials?

1 Understand the difference between summary and paraphrase.

Summarizing and paraphrasing represent different ways of responding to materials you read.

A *summary* captures what is relevant and boils it down to a few words or sentences.

To prepare a summary, assemble the key claim and supporting elements into a concise restatement of the overall argument. The summary should make sense on its own, forming a complete statement you might use later in the project itself. The summary should also be entirely in your own words.

A *paraphrase* usually reviews a source in greater detail than does a summary. When paraphrasing a work, you restate it point by point *in your own words*. You will typically want to paraphrase any materials that provide detailed facts or ideas your readers will need.

An effective paraphrase will meet the following conditions.

- The paraphrase reflects the structure of the original piece.
- The paraphrase reflects the ideas of the original author, not your reflections on them.
- Each important fact or direct quotation is accompanied by a specific page number from the source when possible.
- The material you record is relevant to your project.
- The material is entirely in your own words—except for clearly marked quotations.

2 Compose accurate, effective summaries and paraphrases.
Now let's look at a source first summarized and then paraphrased. We will use the article "Educational Insensitivity" by Diane Ravitch annotated in Section 41a (see pp. 387–388). This op-ed piece originally appeared in the *New York Times* on June 5, 2002, shortly after the New York State Department of Education admitted that, to avoid offending students, it had been censoring works of literature included in a standard examination.

EFFECTIVE SUMMARY	Diane Ravitch, a professor at New York University, argues in the *New York Times* (5 June 2002) that attempts by educators and textbook publishers to avoid objectionable topics or language are depriving students of their right to read uncensored literature.

Don't make the summary too succinct and leave out crucial details. Such a summary might be useless when, days later, you try to make sense of it.

> **INEFFECTIVE**   She argues that it's wrong to censor
> **SUMMARY**   literature. Both the left and right want it.

Don't miss the central point.

> **INACCURATE**   Diane Ravitch, a professor at New York
> **SUMMARY**   University, knows about censorship in
>   education because she serves on the National
>   Assessment Governing Board, which reviews
>   questions on tests.

Don't use the actual words of the original author without both quotation marks and documentation. This is plagiarism (see Section 41d). In the example following, language taken directly and inappropriately from Ravitch's op-ed piece is underlined.

> **PLAGIARIZED**   Diane Ravitch, a professor at New York
> **SUMMARY**   University, argues in the *New York Times*
>   (5 June 2002) that the expurgation of literary
>   works by educators and textbook publishers
>   <u>robs our children of their cultural heritage</u>
>   <u>and their right to read—free of censorship</u>.

To avoid plagiarism, the safest practice is *always* to use your own words in summaries.

A paraphrase of "Educational Insensitivity" would be appreciably longer than a summary. Here's one possible paraphrase of Ravitch's op-ed article.

> **EFFECTIVE**   Responding to criticism that it had edited
> **PARAPHRASE**   sensitive and controversial passages from
>   literary works on its Regents examinations,
>   the New York State Education Department
>   announced that it would abandon the practice.
>   But Diane Ravitch argues in a *New York Times*
>   op-ed piece (5 June 2002) that the practice
>   of trimming controversial materials from

educational materials is so common that it is
institutionalized. Those on the political
right demand that morally offensive topics
and ideas be cut from exams and textbooks;
those on the political left demand gender and
ethnic balance. Standardized tests are now
routinely subject to reviews for bias and
insensitivity, as are other educational
materials. Ravitch argues that this practice
should be ended by letting the public know
what is happening and by carefully reviewing
any standards applied to educational
materials. Censorship robs students of their
cultural right to read literature as it was
written.

Notice that this paraphrase covers all the major points in the editorial in the same order as the original. It also borrows none of the author's language. With proper documentation, any part of the paraphrase could become part of a final research project without a need for quotation marks.

Don't insert your personal notes or annotations in a paraphrase.

INACCURATE Responding to criticism that it had edited
PARAPHRASE sensitive and controversial passages from
literary works on its Regents examinations,
the New York State Education Department
announced that it would abandon the practice.
But Diane Ravitch argues in a *New York Times*
op-ed piece (5 June 2002) that trimming
controversial materials from educational
materials is so common that it is
institutionalized. Those on the political
right, who probably don't want their children
exposed to any challenging ideas, demand that
morally offensive topics be cut from exams
and textbooks; those on the political left

demand gender and ethnic balance, <u>which
Ravitch should admit is often lacking in so-
called classical works of literature</u>.
Standardized tests are now routinely subject
to reviews for bias and insensitivity, as are
other educational materials. Ravitch argues
that this embarrassing practice should be
ended by letting the public know what is
happening and by carefully reviewing any
standards applied to educational materials.
Censorship robs students of their cultural
right to read literature as it was written.

These reactions don't represent an accurate paraphrase of the original article.

Don't reorganize or improve on the structure or argument of the original piece. For example, the following paraphrase doesn't actually add material to Ravitch's editorial, but it rearranges its information radically.

INACCURATE   Children in school should not be robbed of
PARAPHRASE   their cultural heritage by educators and
publishers worried that reading what literary
authors actually wrote might harm their
tender sensitivities. But that's what is
happening all across the country according to
Diane Ravitch, a member of the National
Assessment Governing Board, a group that
reviews questions posed on the National
Assessment of Educational Progress. Maybe if
Ms. Ravitch served in the New York State
Education Department, it would not have
gotten into the business of censoring the
literary works that appeared on its Regents
examinations—sparking a controversy about how
much censorship is occurring in education

```
today as a result of pressure from both the
right and the left to advance their political
agendas in our nation's schools.
```

The most dangerous and dishonest paraphrase borrows the ideas, structure, and details of a source wholesale, changing a few words here and there in order to claim originality. This sort of paraphrase is plagiarism even if the material is documented in the research project; writers can't just change a few words in their sources and claim the resulting material as their own work. (See Section 41d-1.)

PLAGIARIZED
PARAPHRASE

```
An inquisitive parent of a high school
student figured out recently that the works
of literature used on the New York Regents
examinations had been cut and edited.
Passages from the novels and poems of many
famous writers were changed, without their
permission or knowledge, to remove all
mention of religion, drugs, sexuality, and
other such offensive subjects.
    The story embarrassed the New York State
Education Department, which creates the
tests, and so the state education
commissioner ordered a stop to the practice.
Henceforth, all literary passages used on New
York tests will be unchanged except for
length. . . .
```

3 Connect and synthesize your research materials. Once you have taken notes from a variety of sources, consider what you have learned. Think of your project as a conversation among authors. Let the sources *talk* with each other in your mind.

Examine the sources you have selected, reading them as both believer and doubter (see Section 7b–1) and posing these practical questions.

- What information represents "fact" and what "opinion"?
- What have I actually learned from my sources?
- What do I still have to discover?

- What conflicts in the evidence do I need to address?
- What position(s) will I take?

When you actually begin to write, build your project from a variety of materials, drawing on different voices to create a coherent whole. Don't depend on just one or two sources. If you do, you may begin to sound like a parrot quoting others with a few squawks of your own. Try to take a discussion further than it has progressed so far. To do that, combine what you learn from many sources into a coherent argument of your own.

41c How do you document a research project?

Acknowledge your sources in academic or professional projects conscientiously, honestly, and gracefully, using an appropriate system of documentation. *Documentation* refers to the forms devised to keep track of sources used in a project—typically some type of notes (endnotes, footnotes, parenthetical notes) and a full bibliography. In college, most student writers learn the documentation procedures established by the Modern Language Association (MLA). But different rules about documentation and style have evolved in other fields. Use the documentation style appropriate to your field or recommended by your instructor.

This section examines the general principles for acknowledging and using sources.

1 Provide a source for every direct quotation. A *direct quotation* is any material repeated word for word from a source. Direct quotations in college papers typically require some form of parenthetical documentation—that is, a citation of author and page number (MLA) or author, date, and page number (APA).

> **MLA**   It is possible to define literature as simply "that text which the community insists on having repeated from time to time intact" (**Joos 51-52**).

> **APA**   **Hashimoto (1986)** questions the value of attention-getting essay openings that "presuppose passive, uninterested (probably uninteresting) readers" (**p. 126**).

Similarly identify the sources for any diagrams, statistics, charts, or pictures in your paper. You need not document famous sayings, proverbs, or biblical citations.

In less formal writing, you should still identify the author, speaker, or work from which you borrow any passage and indicate why the words you are quoting are significant. Many phrases of introduction or attribution are available (see Section 42a). Here are just a few.

One noted astronomer **reported** that . . .

Condoleezza Rice **asserts** that . . .

According to the GAO, the figures . . .

2 Document all ideas, opinions, facts, and information that cannot be considered common knowledge. *Common knowledge* includes the facts, dates, events, information, and concepts that an educated person can be assumed to know. You don't have to document common knowledge.

What experts assume collectively constitutes the common knowledge within a field; what they claim individually—their opinions, studies, theories, research projects, hypotheses—is the material you *must* document in a paper.

3 Document materials that readers might question or wish to explore further. If your subject is controversial, you may want to document even those facts or ideas considered common knowledge. When in doubt, document.

4 Furnish dates, credentials, and other information to assist readers. Provide dates for important events, major figures, and works of literature and art. Identify any person readers might not recognize.

After the great fire of London (**1666**), the city was . . .

Henry Highland Garnet (**1815–82**), American abolitionist and radical, . . .

When quoting from literary works, help readers locate the passages you are citing. For novels, identify page numbers; for plays, give act/scene/line information; for long poems, provide line numbers and, when appropriate, division numbers (book, canto, or other divisions).

5 Use computer programs to document your project. Be sure to read the instructions for such software carefully and to proofread the output to be sure you have entered your data accurately.

41d Do you understand academic responsibility?

Taking notes carelessly or documenting sources inadequately may raise doubts about the integrity of a paper. Representing as your own the words or ideas you found in a source constitutes *plagiarism*, a serious

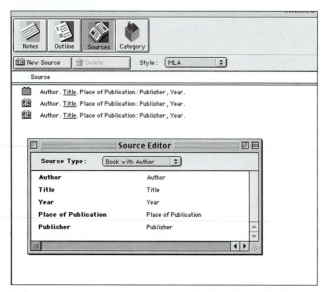

Here is a source screen from the program *TakeNote!* designed to help writers organize notes and information. After providing author, title, year, and publication information, you will get a properly formatted entry for a Works Cited or References page.

breach of academic ethics. Plagiarism is easily avoided if you take good notes (see Section 41b) and follow these guidelines.

1 For conventional sources, acknowledge all direct uses of anyone else's work. Use quotation marks (or indention) to indicate that you are borrowing a writer's exact words. Identify the author, work, publisher, date, and location of the passage through documentation. Use *both* quotation marks and the parenthetical note when you quote directly. Quotation marks alone would not tell what your source was. A note alone would not explain which specific words were not entirely your own.

2 Summarize and paraphrase carefully. When you summarize or paraphrase a source (see Section 41b), be certain that your notes are entirely in your own words. Some writers mistakenly believe that they can avoid a charge of plagiarism just by rearranging the elements or changing a few words in a source they are using. They are flat wrong. Review Section 41b for detailed advice on how to write effective summaries and paraphrases and how to avoid plagiarizing in the process.

3 Appreciate the unique features of electronic discourse. The basic
rules of scholastic honesty apply in electronic environments. You may
not copy and paste information from a Web site, listserv, newsgroup, or
other electronic source to your own project without documenting that
material. Nor may you call it your own just because you have altered it
in some minor way. For ways to cite electronic sources, consult the chapters on MLA, APA, and CMS documentation.

4 Understand the special nature of collaborative projects. Although it
can be tough to remember who
wrote what, joint authorship ought
not to be a problem. But legitimate
questions do arise.

- Must we write the whole
  project together?
- Can we break the project into
  separately authored sections?
- Can one person research a
  section, another write it, a
  third edit and proofread?
- Which author gets listed first?
- What do we do if someone is
  not pulling his or her weight?
- Do we all get the same grade?

Ask these questions at the beginning of a collaborative effort.

> The Web offers a great deal of
> information on plagiarism,
> collusion, and cheating. Use
> keywords in a search engine and
> you will discover many
> academic sites (they end in
> *.edu*) that discuss the definition
> and terms of scholastic
> dishonesty. Or you might use
> the search engine at the Center
> for Academic Integrity at
> <http://academicintegrity.org>
> to explore more than 7,000 Web
> pages dealing with these issues.

How Do You Intrduce and Quote from Sources?

42

No stylistic touch makes a research project work quite so well as quotations deftly handled. But using quotations skillfully is not simply a matter of style. Every quotation should contribute something your own words cannot. Use quotations for various reasons.

- To focus on a particularly well-stated key idea in a source
- To show what others think about a subject—either experts, people involved with the issue, or the general public
- To give credence to important facts or concepts
- To add color, power, or character to your argument or report
- To show a range of opinion
- To clarify a difficult or contested point
- To demonstrate the complexity of an issue
- To emphasize a point

Never use quotations to avoid putting ideas in your own words or to pad your work.

42a How do you introduce all direct and indirect borrowings in some way

Short introductions, attributions, or commentaries are needed to frame materials you've gathered from sources. Such frames can be relatively simple, and they can *precede, follow*, or *interrupt* the borrowed words or ideas. Here are examples of ways that material can be introduced.

- *Frame precedes borrowed material:*

  In 1896, Woodrow Wilson, who would become Princeton's president in 1902, declared, "It is not learning but the spirit of service that will give a college a place in the public annals of the nation."

  —ERNEST L. BOYER

- *Frame follows borrowed material:*

  "One reason you may have more colds if you hold back tears is that, when you're under stress, your body puts out steroids which affect your immune system and reduce your resistance to disease," **Dr. Broomfield comments**.

—BARBARA LANG STERN

- *Frame interrupts borrowed material:*

"Whatever happens," **he [Karl Marx] wrote grimly to Engels,** "I hope the bourgeoisie as long as they exist will have cause to remember my carbuncles."

—PAUL JOHNSON

- *Surrounding sentences frame borrowed material:*

In the meantime, [Luis] Jimenez was experimenting with three-dimensional form. "Perhaps because of the experience of working in the sign shop, I realized early on that I wanted to do it all—paint, draw, work with wood, metal, clay." **His images were those of 1960s pop culture, chosen for their familiarity and shock value.**

—CHIORI SANTIAGO

- *Borrowed material integrated with passage:*

The study concludes that a faulty work ethic is not responsible for the decline in our productivity; quite the contrary, the study identifies "a widespread commitment among U.S. workers to improve productivity" **and suggests that** "there are large reservoirs of potential upon which management can draw to improve performance and increase productivity."

—DANIEL YANKELOVICH

You should also introduce ideas that you borrow when you summarize or paraphrase a source, even if you do not directly quote from it. (See Section 41a).

Attributions either name (directly or indirectly) the author, the speaker, or the work the passage is from, or explain why the quote is significant. Note that the verb of attribution can shape the way readers perceive the quotation. Compare your reactions to the following.

Benson **reports** that "high school test scores have dropped again."

Benson **laments** that "high school test scores have dropped again."

Benson **complains** that "high school test scores have dropped again."

chart	**42.1** Verbs of Attribution				
	accept	allege	confirm	emphasize	propose
	add	argue	contend	insist	say
	admit	believe	deny	mention	state
	affirm	claim	disagree	posit	verify

42b Modify quotations carefully to fit your needs

You must always quote accurately and fairly. You cannot leave out a word or phrase to make a source seem to agree with you or support your thesis. But you can use a variety of techniques to make quotations flow naturally. These techniques preserve the integrity of quotations while giving you flexibility.

1 Tailor your language so that direct quotations fit into the grammar of your sentences.

CLUMSY The chemical capsaicin that makes chili hot: "it is so hot it is used to make antidog and antimugger sprays" (Bork 184).

REVISED Capsaicin, the chemical that makes chili hot, is so strong "it is used to make antidog and antimugger sprays" (Bork 184).

CLUMSY Computers have not succeeded as translators of language because, says Douglas Hofstadter, "nor is the difficulty caused by a lack of knowledge of idiomatic phrases. The fact is that translation involves having a mental model of the world being discussed, and manipulating symbols in the model" (603)

REVISED "A lack of knowledge of idiomatic phrases" is not the reason computers have failed as translators of languages. "The fact is," says Douglas Hofstadter, "that translation involves having a mental model of the world being

```
discussed, and manipulating symbols in the
model" (603).
```

2 Use ellipses (three *spaced* periods . . .) to indicate where you have cut material from direct quotations. An ellipsis tells readers where words, phrases, and even whole sentences have been cut.

ORIGINAL PASSAGE

The text of the Old Testament is in places the stuff of scholarly nightmares. Whereas the entire New Testament was written within fifty to a hundred years, the books of the Old Testament were composed and edited over a period of about a thousand. The youngest book is Daniel, from the second century B.C. The oldest portions of the Old Testament (if we limit ourselves to the present form of the literature and exclude from consideration the streams of oral tradition that fed it) are probably a group of poems that appear, on the basis of linguistic features and historical allusions contained in them, to date from roughly the twelfth and eleventh centuries B.C. . . .

—**BARRY HOBERMAN**, "Translating the Bible"

PASSAGE AS CUT FOR USE IN AN ESSAY

```
    Although working with any part of an original
scripture text is difficult, Hoberman describes the text
of the Old Testament as "the stuff of scholarly
nightmares." He explains in "Translating the Bible" that
while "the entire New Testament was written within fifty
to a hundred years, the books of the Old Testament were
composed and edited over a period of about a thousand. . . .
The oldest portions of the Old Testament . . . are probably
a group of poems that appear . . . to date from roughly the
twelfth and eleventh centuries B.C."
```

See Section 33b for much more about ellipses.

3 Use square brackets [ ] to add necessary information to a quotation. You may want to explain who or what a pronoun refers to, or you may have to insert a short explanation, furnish a date, and explain or translate a puzzling word.

```
        Some critics clearly prefer Wagner's Tannhäuser to
Lohengrin: "The well-written choruses [of Tannhäuser] are
```

```
combined with solo singing and orchestral background into

long, unified musical scenes" (Grout 629).
```

But don't overdo it. Readers will resent the explanation of obvious details.

42c Observe the conventions of quotation

Following are some specific conventions that apply to direct quotations. Review Section 33a to appreciate all their uses.

1 Use [sic] to indicate an obvious error copied faithfully from a source. Quotations must be copied accurately, word by word, from your source—errors and all. To show that you have copied a passage faithfully, place the expression *sic* (the Latin word for "thus" or "so") in brackets one space after any mistake.

```
    Mr. Vincent's letter went on: "I would have preferred

a younger bride, but I decided to marry the old window

[sic] anyway."
```

If *sic* is placed outside the quotation itself, it appears between parentheses, not brackets.

```
    Molly's paper was titled "King Leer" (sic).
```

2 Place prose quotations shorter than four typed lines (MLA) or 40 words (APA) between quotation marks.

```
    In Utilitarianism (1863), John Stuart Mill declares,

"It is better to be Socrates dissatisfied than a pig

satisfied."
```

3 Indent more than three lines of poetry (MLA). Up to three lines of poetry may be handled just like a prose passage, with slashes marking the separate lines. Quotation marks are used.

```
    As death approaches, Cleopatra grows in grandeur and

dignity: "Husband, I come! / Now to that name my courage

prove my title! / I am fire and air" (5.2.287-89).
```

More than three lines of poetry are indented 10 spaces and quotation marks are not used. (If the lines of poetry are unusually long, you may indent fewer than 10 spaces.) Be sure to copy the poetry accurately, right down to the punctuation.

> Among the most famous lines in English literature are
> those that open William Blake's "The Tyger":
>> Tyger tyger, burning bright,
>>
>> In the forests of the night;
>>
>> What immortal hand or eye,
>>
>> Could frame thy fearful symmetry? (1-4)

4 Indent any prose quotation longer than four typed lines (MLA) or 40 words (APA). MLA form recommends an indention of one inch, or 10 spaces if you are using a typewriter; APA form requires five spaces. Quotation marks are *not* used around the indented material. If the quotation extends beyond a single paragraph, the first lines of subsequent paragraphs are indented an additional quarter inch, or three typed spaces (MLA) or five spaces (APA). In typed papers, the indented material—like the rest of the essay—is double spaced.

You may indent passages of fewer than four lines when you want them to have special emphasis. But don't do this with every short quotation or your paper will look choppy.

5 Refer to events in works of fiction, poems, plays, movies, and television shows in the present tense. When quoting passages from novels or describing scenes from a movie or events in a play, think about the actions as performances that occur over and over again.

> In his last speech, Othello **orders** those around him to
> "Speak of me as I am. Nothing extenuate, / Nor set down
> aught in malice" (V. ii. 338-39). Then he **stabs** himself
> and **dies**, falling on the bed of the innocent wife he has
> murdered only moments before.

How Do You Produce a Final Draft?

43

You must meet exacting standards as you bring academic research projects to completion. Requirements vary, but the principles examined in this section apply to most papers and projects. (See also Chapter 5.)

43a Is the organization solid?

Create a framework that will make your project an effective response to the original assignment. Be deliberate and strategic. In a research project, you can't rely on chance to bring the parts together.

1 Test your organization. For organizing a long paper, check the structure using a method such as the following.

- **Underline the topic idea, claim, or thesis, in your draft.** It should be clearly stated somewhere in the first few paragraphs.

- **Underline just the first sentence in each subsequent paragraph.** If the first sentence is very short or closely tied to the second, underline the first two sentences.

- **Read the underlined sentences straight through as if they formed an essay in themselves.** Ask whether each sentence advances the thesis statement. If the sentences—taken together—read coherently, chances are good that the paper is well organized.

- **If the underlined sentences don't make sense, reexamine those paragraphs not clearly related to the topic idea.** If the ideas really are not related, delete the whole paragraph. If the ideas are related, consider how to revise the paragraph to make the connection clearer.

- **Test your conclusion against your introduction.** Sometimes the conclusions of essays contradict their openings. When you've completed a draft, set it aside for a time and then reread the entire piece. Does it hang together? If not, revise it.

Test the structure of other projects similarly. For a brochure, make sure the headings and sections are in correct sequence and contain all pertinent information. In a Web site, will users find what they are seeking? Check that links work in both directions, that there are no dead ends, and that every page provides a link to your home page or another helpful location in the site.

43b Is the format correct?

Here we focus chiefly on research papers, but you can find advice about crafting other types of projects in Part 3, Document Design.

1 Pay attention to the format of work you submit. Be sure a paper is submitted on good-quality white paper. Print on only one side of the pages, double-spacing the body of your essay and the notes. Keep fonts simple and use boldface rarely, perhaps to highlight important headings.

If required, follow specifications for MLA and APA papers (Sections 44d and 45d, respectively). These guidelines, which explain where page numbers go, the width of margins, and the placement of headings, can be applied even to papers that don't need to follow a specific professional style.

2 Insert tables and figures as needed. Use graphics to help readers understand your ideas. Be careful not to clutter your work with "chartjunk." Develop an eye for clean and attractive presentations on paper or on screen.

MLA form requires that you label tables (columns of data) and figures (pictures or illustrations), number them, and briefly identify what they illustrate.

Spell out the word *Table*, and position the heading above the table, aligned with the left margin.

Table 43.1

First-Year Student Applications by Region

	Fall 1995	Fall 1994	Difference	Percent Change
Texas	12,022	11,590	432	+4
Out of state	2,121	2,058	63	+3
Foreign	756	673	83	+11

Figure, which is usually abbreviated in the caption as *Fig.*, appears below the illustration, flush left.

Fig. 1 Mountain bike.

When preparing an APA paper, check the detailed coverage of figures and tables in the *Publication Manual of the American Psychological Association*. For APA-style student papers, figures (including graphs, illustrations, and photos) and tables may appear in the body of the essay itself, placed on separate pages, immediately following their mention in the text.

> Chromosomes consist of four different nucleotides or
>
> bases—adenine, guanine, thymine, and cytosine—which,
>
> working together, provide the code for different genes
>
> (see Figure 1).

Short tables may even appear on the same page as text material.

Figures and tables are numbered consecutively. Captions for figures appear below the item. If the illustration is borrowed from a source, you must get permission to reproduce it and acknowledge the borrowing as shown.

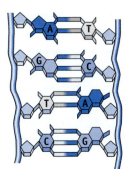

Fig. 2. The four bases of the genetic code: adenine (A), guanine (G), thymine (T), and cytosine (C). From *Your Genes, Your Choice*, by C. Baker, 1997. Copyright 1997 by the American Association for the Advancement of Science. Reprinted with permission.

Titles for tables appear above the item.

Table 2

Errors by Levels of Difficulty

3 Be consistent with headings. A short research paper (five to six pages) ordinarily needs only a title. Longer papers, however, need headings that explain the content of major sections. Heads should be brief, parallel in phrasing, and consistent in format like the items in a formal outline (see Section 3d-3). For academic papers, you probably won't use more than one level of heading after the title.

MLA style (described in detail in Chapter 44) provides fairly loose standards for headings. Titles of MLA papers are ordinarily centered on the first page of an essay. Headings appear in the text, flush with the left-hand margin. If you descend to a second level, distinguish second-level heads by numbering or lettering them or by setting them off typographically (usually by variations in capitalization or underlining). MLA style leaves you to decide how you will handle such choices, but keep the headings clean and unobtrusive.

APA style (described in detail in Chapter 45) defines five levels of headings for professional articles—more than you'll probably use in a college paper. Here's how to handle two levels of headings.

- First-level heads are centered, using both uppercase and lowercase letters as shown below.
- Second-level heads are capitalized like titles, but also underlined or italicized and placed flush with the left-hand margin.

Here's how those APA guidelines look in operation.

Differences in Reading Habits of	
College Sophomores	Title
Abstract	1st level
Method	1st level
Participants	2nd level
Materials	2nd level
Design and Procedure	2nd level
Results	1st level
Discussion	1st level

Web pages also need accurate, well-focused headings and titles. Succinct and descriptive titles are easier for Web search engines and directories to locate. Create titles that make sense when they get shortened as bookmarks or favorites: the first few words of the title should include the keywords. A heading such as "The Beauty and Mystery of Anasazi Cliff Dwellings" might be clipped back to the not very helpful "The Beauty and Mystery." Instead, title the Web page "Anasazi Cliff Dwellings: Beauty and Mystery" to highlight pertinent information.

Are the details correct?

Give the final version of your project a final review. Don't skip this step.

1 Include all the components your project requires. Before you submit a project, reread the guidelines you are following. Must you, for instance, include an abstract or an outline? Check to see what leeway (if any) you have in arranging the title page, notes, bibliography, and other features. A research paper typically follows a specific order.

- Title page (not recommended in MLA; required in APA)
- Outline (optional; begins on its own page; requires separate title page)

- Abstract (optional, but common in APA; usually on its own page)
- Body of the essay (in MLA, Arabic pagination begins with the body of the essay in MLA; in APA, with the title page)
- Content or bibliographic notes
- Works Cited/References (begins on its own page separate from the body of the essay and any content or bibliographic notes)

The sample research essay in Section 44d illustrates MLA style, and the essay in Section 44d illustrates APA style. For a more complex paper such as a master's thesis or a doctoral dissertation, follow the order recommended in a volume such as *The MLA Style Manual* (MLA) or the *Publication Manual of the American Psychological Association* (APA). Many schools publish their own guidelines for submitting graduate-level theses.

2 Follow the rules for documentation right down to the punctuation and spacing.
Accurate documentation is a part of professional research. Perhaps the two most common errors in handling the MLA format, for example, are forgetting to put a period at the end of entries in the Works Cited list and placing a comma where none is needed in parenthetical documentation.

WRONG   Pluto, Terry. *The Curse of Rocky Colavito*. New
York: Simon, 1994. Print.

RIGHT   Pluto, Terry. *The Curse of Rocky Colavito*. New
York: Simon, 1994. Print.

WRONG   (Pluto, 132–36)

RIGHT   (Pluto 132–36)

You will survive both errors, but they are easy to avoid.

3 Submit your project professionally.
Whether you've written a paper, designed a brochure, or created a Web site, be sure the work meets appropriate standards. Examine what you've produced to see that everything looks "detailed." Ensure the writing is sharp and correct, the images are crisp and labeled, the pagination is right, the links are operative, the documentation is solid.

Don't overdo it, but be sure to follow all instructions. See the Web site for this handbook at <www.prenhall.com/SFCompact>.

checklist 43.1 ⌐ Research Project Requirements

- Have you placed your name, your instructor's name, the date, and the course name on the first or title page?
- Is the title centered? Are only the major words capitalized? (Your title should not be underlined or appear between quotation marks.)
- Did you number the pages? Are they in the right order?
- Have you used quotation marks and parentheses correctly and in pairs? (The closing quotation mark and parenthesis are often forgotten.)
- Have you placed quotation marks around all direct quotations that are shorter than four lines?
- Have you indented all direct quotations of more than four typed lines (MLA) or of 40 words or more (APA)?
- Have you remembered that indented quotations are not placed between quotation marks?
- Did you introduce all direct quotations with some identification of their author, source, or significance?
- Did you use the correct form for parenthetical notes?
- Have you handled titles correctly, italicizing books and putting the titles of articles between quotation marks?
- Did you include a Works Cited or References list? Is your list of works cited alphabetized? Did you indent the entries correctly?

part

8

Documentation

How Do You Use MLA Documentati🍏n?

44

MLA (Modern Language Association) documentation usually involves two steps: creating a note at the point where you use a source in a paper or project (Section 44a) and then creating an entry on a Works Cited page for that source (Section 44b).

Some instructors still prefer footnotes at the bottom of a page or endnotes gathered in a single list at the end of the paper to the in-text notes we demonstrate here. We provide examples of these footnote forms in Checklist 44.5 on page 467. If you run into documentation problems not discussed here, refer to the *MLA Handbook for Writers of Research Papers*, seventh edition (2009). Style updates are also available at the MLA Web site at <http://www.mla.org/style>.

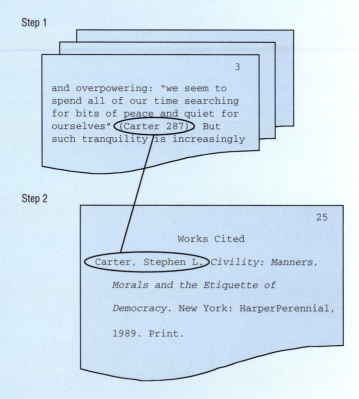

Step 1

```
                                          3
and overpowering: "we seem to
spend all of our time searching
for bits of peace and quiet for
ourselves" (Carter 287). But
such tranquility is increasingly
```

Step 2

```
                                         25

              Works Cited

    Carter, Stephen L. Civility: Manners,

       Morals and the Etiquette of

       Democracy. New York: HarperPerennial,

       1989. Print.
```

Step 1: In the body of your paper, place a note for each source you use.

44a

Each time you quote, paraphrase, or use ideas from outside sources, you must acknowledge that you've done so with some form of note. You can create in-text notes several ways. One is to use *parenthetical citations*, which put information about a source between parenthesis, usually at the end of a sentence: (Prosek 246–47). Or you may use *signal phrases*, which identify sources within the normal flow of the sentence: According to Eric Foner in *The Story of American Freedom.* . . . Or you may combine these basic forms, using both a signal phrase and a page number in parentheses: Anderson claims that the TV show *South Park* "spares no sensitivity" (76).

1 Identify outside sources clearly each time you use them. Whether you introduce sources with parenthetical notes or signal phrases, readers need to know precisely which source on the works-cited list you're using (see Section 44b for more on creating a works-cited list). Establish that connection by making certain that the in-text note clearly refers to the word by which a source is alphabetized in the works-cited list (for example, the last name of the author). Here are some guidelines to help you.

- **Citing a source listed under a single person's name.** This is a common type of note.

      As one historian says, "The scientist, like the
      artist, is one of us" (**Jardine** 5).

In signal phrases, you may use full first names to make your passage more readable.

      "Today's secular disruption between the creative
      aspect of art and that of science," anthropologist
      Loren Eiseley contends, "is a barbarism that would have
      brought lifted eyebrows in a Cro-Magnon cave" (271).

When your works-cited listing contains sources by different people having the same last name, use initials or full first names to refer to their works without confusion.

- **Citing a source listed under a group of people's names.** Provide the *last names of all individuals* in the same order they will appear at the beginning of the works-cited entry. When a source is listed under four or more persons' names, you have the option of using the Latin abbreviation *et al.* (*et alia,* "and others") after the first person's name.

> **Varela, Thompson, and Rosch** ask, "What challenges
>
> does human experience face as a result of the
>
> scientific study of the mind?" (xvii).

> The Royal Society was chartered in 1662 to
>
> further scientific enquiry and advance the study of
>
> natural philosophy (**Abrams et al.** 1: 1571).

- **Citing a source listed under a corporate or group author.** In this case, a signal phrase is often more readable than a parenthetical note. When you do use a parenthetical note to identify the source, abbreviate the name of the author.

> "The Shuttle will return to flight only after we
>
> have met all the safety requirements and milestone
>
> goals—and not before" (**NASA**).

- **Citing a source listed by title.** Put the *title* in your in-text citation when a work doesn't have an author or creator. Shorten that title as much as possible: the shortened title should, however, always include its first word (excluding *A, An,* and *The*), so readers can easily find the entry on the alphabetized Works Cited page.

> Scientific creativity tends to be limited more by
>
> money than ideas (**"Art"**).

- **Citing a source that is one of many listed under the same person's name.** Mention *both* the *last name* of the author and the *title* of the particular source. When using parenthetical citation, follow the person's last name with a comma and a shortened version of the title (see the preceding section).

> Even the most cultivated "habit of thought" can be
>
> questioned when we acknowledge that "conviction of the
>
> 'truth' . . . is founded exclusively on rather incomplete
>
> experience" (**Einstein,** *Relativity* 3-4).

A readable way of handling such a citation is to mention the person's name in a signal phrase and then to use a parenthetical citation to clarify which work you are referring to in the particular passage.

> **Spielberg**'s recent films have explored how science and technology shape our views of morality (***Minority***), as well as how they challenge our ideas of humanity (***A.I.***).

- **Citing material from sacred texts, classical literary works, and legal documents.** These works are often identified by standard abbreviations. For classical literary works, look for a standard abbreviation in the textual notes of the edition you're using, or find a list compiled by scholars—if none is available, follow the guidelines presented in "Citing a source listed by title" above.

> **Shakespeare**'s Caliban values his education in the language arts only because it helped him "know how to curse" (***Tmp.*** I.ii.364).

For sacred texts, standard abbreviations are often used to identify the work in both signal phrases and parenthetical notes. When you use the generic name of a sacred work—including terms such as the Bible, Torah, Qur'an, as well as sections and chapters within them—do *not* italicize the title in your in-text notes.

> The spiritual value of pursuing the truth is articulated in the **King James Version** of the **Bible**: "He that hath knowledge spareth his words: and a man of understanding is of an excellent spirit" (**Prov.** 17.27).

Do, however, italicize the title of any particular published editions of such works.

> It is not clear how the works that comprise the Torah came to be seen as one book (***New Oxford Annotated Bible***, HB 6).

Similar rules apply to historic legal documents (for example, the Declaration of Independence), and also to specific government acts and laws (for example, the Selective Service Act). You would, ordinarily, not italicize such titles.

- **Citing multiple sources in a single parenthetical note.** Separate each citation by a semicolon, following the other guidelines listed above. Do this sparingly, however, since such notes can become long and distracting.

> Newer editions of literary anthologies include scientific texts of historical significance (**Abrams, et al.** xxiii; **Henderson and Sharpe** vii, xii).

- **Citing material repeatedly from the same source.** Omit the source identifier in notes referring repeatedly to the same work when no other is mentioned.

> Dr. Frankenstein, whose "sole occupation" is "natural philosophy" (**M. Shelley** 49; vol. 1, ch. 4), studies the human animal through biological experiments. His creation, a so-called "monster" (60; vol. 1, ch. 5), learns to be human by reading poetry and history (124-127; vol. 2, ch. 7).

2 Locate referenced material as precisely as possible. Besides identifying a source, in-text notes tell readers exactly where to find that material you are citing. The guidelines below present your options.

SINGLE PAGE
(You can omit the page reference when the source is only one page long)

(Jones **142**)
According to Jones . . . (**142**)
("Blame" **21**)

RANGE OF PAGES
Separate the first and last pages in the range with a hyphen

(Dyson, *Disturbing* **11-13**)
(Savlov **E4-E5**)

NON-CONSECUTIVE PAGES
Separate by a comma and space each page where idea is referenced

(**151, 156, 198**)
(Gilbert and Gubar **xxix, xxxiv**)

PAGES IN MULTI-VOLUME SOURCES
Insert the volume number, a colon, and a space before page references

```
(2: 132)
(Churchill 4: 3461-62)
```

SOURCES WITH NO PAGINATION
After the source identifier (if given in the note), insert a comma, an abbreviation for the numbering scheme, and a reference number

```
(Neruda, lines 2-9)
(USPTO, "Intellectual," par. 4)
(screen 3)
```

LITERARY WORKS WITH PAGINATION
Follow the page reference with a semicolon and reference to the chapter, section, etc.

```
(Eliot, Middlemarch 273; ch. 28)
(75-76; ch. 4, sec. 1.5)
(Stoppard 58-59; act 2)
```

WORKS WITH TRADITIONAL NUMBERING
Classic works that are divided into precise hierarchical sections need no page references. Instead, list each section from largest to smallest with periods in between—even between chapter and verse in biblical citations. Use hyphens to indicate a range.

```
(Aristotle, Prior 68b. 9-15)
(Ham. 3.6.4-5)
(Interpreter's Bible, Mark 10.25)
```

When you quote or paraphrase a statement that your source itself quotes. Start a note with "qtd. in" to indicate that the author of the work did not make these statements, but rather someone named within the source:

> According to Albert Einstein, "Imagination is more important than knowledge" (**qtd. in** Thomas 1).

3 Place and punctuate parenthetical citations correctly. Place parenthetical citations after closing quotation marks but before ending or connecting punctuation marks.

AFTER BORROWED IDEA OR QUOTE, BEFORE END PERIOD

> As Carter notes, "we seem to spend all of our time searching for bits of peace and quiet" (287).

TWO PARENTHETICAL NOTES	The seclusion of the Lake
IN ONE SENTENCE	District would often result in
	"the deepest melancholy" (D.
	Wordsworth 19), but the lakes
	themselves could be "soft . . . and
	beautiful" (36).
AFTER FINAL PUNCTUATION	Fixed ideas of permanence
FOR BLOCK QUOTATIONS	And transience,
(SEE CHECKLIST 44.3)	Finitude and infinity,
	Have no place when all is well.
	(Nagarjuna, lines 28–31)

44b Step 2: On a separate page at the end of your project, list alphabetically every source you have cited.

This list of sources is titled "works cited." It should include only sources you actually mention in the body of the project itself. A typical MLA Works Cited entry includes the following basic information with many variations.

- **Author(s)**, last name first, followed by a period.
- **Title of the work**, followed by a period. Book titles and the titles of Web sites are italicized, while titles of articles or individual Web pages are placed between quotation marks.
- **Publication information.** For books, provide place of publication (followed by a colon), the name of publisher (followed by a comma), and year of publication (followed by a period). For articles, give the title of the journal (italicized), the volume and issue numbers, the date of publication in parentheses followed by a colon, and the page numbers followed by a period. For Web sites, the publication information includes a date of publication and the date you looked at the information.
- **Medium of publication.** All works cited entries must include the medium of publication. Include as the last element of the works cited entry the designation *Print* for sources such as books, journal articles, and newspapers. Include the designation *Web* for sources accessed online, including Web sites, articles accessed via an online database, and online newspapers. The medium of publication for *Web* sources is placed after the date of publication and before the date of access. Other types of sources may require more specific medium of publication designations, such as *DVD*, *CD*, *Television*, or *Performance*, included as the last element of the works cited entry.

Appropriate forms for dozens of Works Cited items appear in the list of MLA models in Section 44c. See Chart 44.1 for a list of abbreviations used in MLA Works Cited entries.

The Works Cited page is placed after the body of the essay (and the endnotes, if there are any). For a sample Works Cited list, see pages 463–465. A checklist for setting up your own Works Cited list appears on page 466. The first entries on a Works Cited page might look like this.

Subsequent lines indented one-half   "Works Cited"   All items
inch or five spaces   centered   double spaced

```
                        Works Cited

Arni, Sherry. "I Can Live With It." English

      Journal 79.7 (1990): 76. Print.

Corbett, H. Dickson, and Bruce L. Wilson. Testing,

      Reform, and Rebellion. Norwood: Ablex, 1991.

      Print.

Dinan, John. "Standardized Tests: Multiple Choices

      of the Wrong Kind." English Journal 67.7

      (1978): 54-56. Print.
```

44.1   Useful MLA Abbreviations

chart

Secondary Acknowledgements

Adapted by	adapt.	Introduction by	introd.
Compiler	comp.	Narrator	narr.
Conductor	cond.	Performer	perf.
Director	dir.	Preface by	pref.
Editor	ed.	Producer	prod.
Foreword by	fwd.	Translator	trans.
Illustrator	illus.	Written by	writ.

Publication Information

Book	bk.	Press	P
Chapter	ch.	Scene	sc.
Edition	ed.	Section	sec or sect.
Line	line or l.	Series	ser.
Lines	lines or ll.	University	U
Page	p.	University Press	UP
Pages	pp.	Volume	vol.
Paragraph	par.	Volumes	vols.

44c MLA models

(See the inside back cover of this book for an alphabetical index of MLA model entries.)

1 MLA: Books checklist

BASIC INFORMATION	EXAMPLE (SEE MODEL 1)
Name of author(s) or editors(s)	*Prosek, James.*
Title of the book (italicized)	*The Complete Angler . . .*
Publisher's location	*New York:*
Publisher (brief name)	*Harper,*
Year of publication	*1999.*
Medium of publication	*Print.*

OTHER INFORMATION	
Edition number	
Volume number	
Translator's name	
Series name	

1. Book, Generic—MLA Provide author, title, place of publication, publisher, year of publication, and medium of publication. For an online book, see model 42.

> IN-TEXT NOTE: (Prosek 246–47)
>
> ### Works Cited
>
> Prosek, James. *The Complete Angler: A Connecticut Yankee Follows in the Footsteps of Walton.* New York: Harper, 1999. Print.

2. Book, Two or Three Authors or Editors—MLA

> IN-TEXT NOTE: (Collier and Horowitz 24)
>
> ### Works Cited
>
> Collier, Peter, and David Horowitz. *Destructive Generation: Second Thoughts About the '60s.* New York: Summit, 1989. Print.

Note that the names of second and third authors are given in their normal order, first names first.

3. Book, Four or More Authors or Editors—MLA You have two options. You can name all the authors in both the note and the Works Cited entry.

IN-TEXT NOTE: (Guth, Rico, Ruszkiewicz, and Bridges 95)

Works Cited

Guth, Hans P., Gabriele L. Rico, John Ruszkiewicz, and
    Bill Bridges. *The Rhetoric of Laughter: The Best and
    Worst of Humor Night*. Fort Worth: Harcourt, 1996.
    Print.

Alternatively, you can name just the first author given on the title page and use the Latin abbreviation *et al.*, which means "and others."

IN-TEXT NOTE: (Guth et al. 95)

Works Cited

Guth, Hans P., et al. *The Rhetoric of Laughter: The
    Best and Worst of Humor Night*. Fort Worth:
    Harcourt, 1996. Print.

4. Book, Edited—Focus on the Original Author—MLA

IN-TEXT NOTE: (Cor. 3.3.119-35)

Work Cited

Shakespeare, William. *The Tragedy of Coriolanus*. Ed.
    Reuben Brower. New York: Signet, 1966. Print.

Coriolanus is a play by Shakespeare, so the note provides act, scene, and line numbers—not author and page numbers. It must be clear in the paper that the note refers to the Shakespeare play.

5. Book, Edited—Focus on the Editor—MLA

IN-TEXT NOTE: (Brower xxiii-1)

Works Cited

Brower, Reuben, ed. *The Tragedy of Coriolanus*. By
    William Shakespeare. New York: Signet, 1966. Print.

6. Book, Edited—Focus on the Editor, More than One Editor—MLA

IN-TEXT NOTE: (Kittredge and Smith xvi-xvii)

Works Cited

Kittredge, William, and Annick Smith, eds. *The Last Best*
    Place: A Montana Anthology. Seattle: U of
    Washington P, 1988. Print.

7. Book, Written by a Group—MLA
Treat the group as the author of the work. But to avoid an awkward note, identify the group author in the body of your paper and place only the relevant page numbers in parentheses.

IN-TEXT NOTE: The Reader's Digest *Fix-It-Yourself Manual*
explains the importance of a UL label (123). Print.

Works Cited

Reader's Digest. *Fix-It-Yourself Manual*. Pleasantville:
    Reader's Digest, 1977. Print.

8. Book with No Author—MLA
Cite the book by its title, alphabetized by the first major word (excluding *The*, *A*, or *An*). Use a shortened title in any note.

IN-TEXT NOTE: (*Kodak* 56-58)

Works Cited

Kodak Guide to 35 mm Photography. 6th ed. Rochester:
    Eastman, 1989. Print.

9. Book, Focus on a Foreword, Introduction, Preface, or Afterword—MLA
The note below refers to information in O'Rourke's introduction, not to material in the anthology itself.

IN-TEXT NOTE: (O'Rourke 5)

Works Cited

O'Rourke, P. J. Introduction. *Road Trips, Head Trips,*
    and Other Car-Crazed Writings. Ed. Jean Lindamood.
    New York: Atlantic, 1996. 1-8. Print.

10. Work of More than One Volume—MLA When you use only one volume of a multivolume set, identify both the volume you have used and the total number of volumes in the set.

IN-TEXT NOTE: (Spindler 17-18)

Works Cited

Spindler, Karlheinz. *Abstract Algebra with Applications*.

Vol. 1. New York: Dekker, 1994. 2 vols. Print.

When you use more than one volume of a set, identify the specific volumes in the notes as you cite them. Then, in the Works Cited entry, list the total number of volumes in that set.

IN-TEXT NOTES: (Spindler 1: 17-18); (Spindler 2: 369)

Works Cited

Spindler, Karlheinz. *Abstract Algebra with Applications*.

2 vols. New York: Dekker, 1994. Print.

11. Book, Translation—Focus on the Original Author—MLA

IN-TEXT NOTE: (Freire 137-38)

Works Cited

Freire, Paulo. *Learning to Question: A Pedagogy of*

Liberation. Trans. Tony Coates. New York:

Continuum, 1989. Print.

12. Book, Translation—Focus on the Translator—MLA

IN-TEXT NOTE: (Swanton 17-18)

Works Cited

Swanton, Michael, trans. *Beowulf*. New York: Barnes, 1978.

Print.

13. Book in a Foreign Language—MLA Copy the title of the foreign

work exactly as it appears on the title page, paying special attention to both accent marks and capitalization.

IN-TEXT NOTE: (Bablet and Jacquot 59)

Works Cited

Bablet, Denis, and Jean Jacquot. *Les Voies de la
création théâtrale*. Paris: Editions du Centre
National de la Recherche Scientifique, 1977. Print.

14. Book, Republished—MLA Give original publication dates for works of fiction that have been through many editions and reprints.

IN-TEXT NOTE: (Herbert 146)

Works Cited

Herbert, Frank. *Dune*. 1965. New York: Berkeley, 1977.
Print.

15. Book, Part of a Series—MLA Give the series name just before the publishing information. Do not underline or italicize a series name.

IN-TEXT NOTE: (Pemberton xii)

Works Cited

Pemberton, Michael, ed. *The Ethics of Writing
Instruction: Issues in Theory and Practice*.
Perspectives on Writing: Theory, Research, Practice
4. Stamford: Ablex, 2000. Print.

16. Book, a Reader or Anthology (or Other Compilation)—MLA
When you quote from the front matter of the collection, the page numbers for a note may sometimes be Roman numerals. (To cite a selection from within an anthology, see model 28.)

IN-TEXT NOTE: (Crane, Kawashima, and Kawasaki iv-v)

Works Cited

Crane, Diana, Nobuko Kawashima, and Ken'ichi Kawasaki,
eds. *Global Culture: Media, Arts, Policy, and
Globalization*. New York: Routledge, 2002. Print.

17. Book, a Second, Third, or Later Edition—MLA

IN-TEXT NOTE: (Rombauer 480-81)

Works Cited

Rombauer, Marjorie Dick. *Legal Problem Solving:*
Analysis, Research, and Writing. 5th ed. St. Paul:
West, 1991. Print.

18. Chapter in a Book—MLA When using only one chapter from a book, create an entry for the book, inserting the title of the chapter just before the title of the book.

IN-TEXT NOTE: (Shalit 144-60)

Works Cited

Shalit, Wendy. "Male Character." *A Return to Modesty:*
Discovering the Lost Virtue. New York: Free, 1999:
144-60. Print.

19. Book Published Before 1900—MLA Omit the name of the publisher in citations of works published prior to 1900.

IN-TEXT NOTE: (Bowdler 2: 47)

Works Cited

Bowdler, Thomas, ed. *The Family Shakespeare.* 10 vols.
London, 1818. Print.

20. Book Issued by a Division of a Publisher—a Special Imprint—MLA Attach the special imprint (Vintage in this case) to the publisher's name with a hyphen.

IN-TEXT NOTE: (Hofstader 192-93)

Works Cited

Hofstader, Douglas. *Gödel, Escher, Bach: An Eternal*
Golden Braid. New York: Vintage-Random, 1980. Print.

21. Book Review/Movie Review—Titled or Untitled—MLA Not all book, film, and arts reviews have titles, so the Works Cited form for a review may vary slightly.

IN-TEXT NOTE: (Keen 39)

Works Cited

Keen, Maurice. "The Knight of Knights." Rev. of *William
    Marshall: The Flower of Chivalry*, by Georges Duby.
    New York Review of Books 16 Jan. 1986: 39-40. Print.

A book title (*Uncle Tom's Cabin*) within a book title is not italicized
(Uncle Tom's Cabin *and American Culture*).

IN-TEXT NOTE: (Baym 691-92)

Works Cited

Baym, Nina. Rev. of Uncle Tom's Cabin *and American
    Culture*, by Thomas F. Gossett. *Journal of American
    History* 72 (1985): 691-92. Print.

Here's the form for a film review found online, in this case on the Web
site *The Flick Filosopher*. The citation includes the date of the review
itself, the date it was accessed online, and the medium of publication.

IN-TEXT NOTE: (Johanson)

Works Cited

Johanson, Mary Ann. "Sounds of Silence." Rev. of
    Apollo 13, dir. Ron Howard. *FlickFilosopher.com*.
    Flick Filosopher. 13 Mar. 2000. Web. 13 Aug. 2006.

22. Sacred Text—MLA Cite the source as an anonymous work, beginning with the title of the edition (underlined); then list the date the particular edition was originally published, secondary acknowledgments
from the edition's title page or byline, and print or electronic publication
details.

IN-TEXT NOTE: (Matt. 19.24)

Works Cited

The Bible: Authorized King James Version. 1611. Ed.
    Robert Carroll and Stephen Pricket. Oxford: Oxford
    UP, 1997. Print.

2 MLA: Scholarly journals checklist

BASIC INFORMATION	EXAMPLE (SEE MODEL 23)
Name of author(s) or editors(s)	Smith, Laurajane.
Title of article (between " ")	"Heritage Management . . . "
Name of journal (italicized)	*Antiquity*
Volume number	64
Issue number	259
Year/date of publication	(1994):
Pages	300–09.
Medium of publication	Print.

23. Article in a Scholarly Journal—MLA Scholarly journals may be paginated by volume (with multiple issues treated as a single volume) or the pages may be numbered separately within each issue. Both types of journals now require the same works cited format. Provide author, title of article, title of journal, volume number, issue number, year of publication, page numbers, and medium of publication. For an online journal article, see model 43.

IN-TEXT NOTE: (Smith 301)

Works Cited

Smith, Laurajane. "Heritage Management as Postprocessual
    Archaeology?" *Antiquity* 64.259 (1994): 300–09.
    Print.

24. Article in a Scholarly Journal—Paged by Issue—MLA

IN-TEXT NOTE: (Whalen 99)

Works Cited

Whalen, Tom. "Romancing Film: Images of Dracula."
    Literature-Film Quarterly 23.2 (1995): 99–101.
    Print.

3 MLA: Magazine/Newspaper checklist

BASIC INFORMATION	EXAMPLE (SEE MODEL 25)
Name of author(s) or editors(s)	Murray, Spencer.
Title of article (between " ")	"Roaming Wyoming."
Name of publication (italicized)	*Open Road*
Date of publication	Spring 1999:
Pages/sections	60-65.
Medium of publication	Print.

25. Article in a Popular Magazine, Generic—MLA Magazines are paginated issue by issue and identified by the seasonal, monthly, or weekly date of publication (not by volume number). Provide author, title of article, title of magazine, date of publication, page numbers, and medium of publication. Months are abbreviated in MLA style.

IN-TEXT NOTE: (Murray 63)

Works Cited

Murray, Spencer. "Roaming Wyoming." *Open Road* Spring

1999: 60-65. Print.

Articles in magazines often don't appear on consecutive pages. When that's the case, list the relevant page number(s) in the note. In the Works Cited entry give the first page on which the article appears, followed by a plus sign.

IN-TEXT NOTE: (Mackay 170)

Works Cited

Mackay, Jordan. "A Murder on Campus." *Texas Monthly* Jan.

2000: 112+. Print.

26. Article in a Weekly or Biweekly Magazine—MLA Give both the day and the month of publication as listed on the issue. Note that in MLA form the day precedes the month and no comma is used: *18 July 1994*. Months are abbreviated in MLA style.

IN-TEXT NOTE: (Klein)

Works Cited

Klein, David. "Emmy-worthy *Buffy* Musical Slays This

Critic." *Television Weekly* 8 July 2002: 6. Print.

27. Article in a Monthly Magazine—MLA Months are abbreviated in MLA style.

IN-TEXT NOTE: (Olders and Del Genio)

Works Cited

Olders, Henry G., and Anthony D. Del Genio. "What Causes
  Insomnia?" *Scientific American* Oct. 2003: 103. Print.

28. Article or Selection from a Reader or Anthology—MLA List the item on the Works Cited page by the author of the piece you are actually citing, not the editor(s) of the collection. Then provide the title of the particular selection, the title of the overall collection, the editor(s) of the collection, and publication information. Conclude with the page numbers of the selection and medium of publication.

IN-TEXT NOTE: (Tschumi 382)

Works Cited

Tschumi, Benard. "Architecture and the City." *The
  Unknown City: Contesting Architecture and Social
  Space.* Ed. Iain Borden, et al. Cambridge: MIT P,
  2001. 370-385. Print.

When you cite two or more selections from a reader or an anthology, list that collection fully on the Works Cited page.

Works Cited

Lunsford, Andrea, and John Ruszkiewicz, eds. *The
  Presence of Others: Voices and Images That Call for
  Response.* 3rd ed. New York: Bedford, 2000. Print.

Then, still in the Works Cited list, identify the authors and titles of all articles you cite from that reader or anthology, followed by the names of the editors and the page numbers of your selections.

IN-TEXT NOTES: (King 417-20); (Turkle 453)

Works Cited

King, Robert. "Should English Be the Law?" Lunsford and
  Ruszkiewicz 409-21. Print.
Turkle, Shirley. "Who Am We?" Lunsford and Ruszkiewicz
  442-58. Print.

For a scholarly article reprinted in a collection, you should usually give more detail about its original place of publication (when known) and then give the facts about the collection.

IN-TEXT NOTE: (Hartman 101)

Works Cited

Hartman, Geoffrey. "Milton's Counterplot." *ELH* 25

  (1958): 1–12. Rpt. in *Milton: A Collection of*

  Critical Essays. Ed. Louis L. Martz. Twentieth

  Century Views. Englewood Cliffs: Prentice-Spectrum,

  1966. 100–08. Print.

29. Article in a Newspaper—MLA Provide author, title of article, name of newspaper, date of article, edition, page numbers, and medium of publication. For page numbers, use the form in the newspaper you are citing; many papers are paginated according to sections. For an online newspaper, see model 45.

IN-TEXT NOTE: ("Despite")

Works Cited

"Despite Recent Appeals, Blood Supplies Are Low." *New*

  York Times 3 Aug. 1998, late ed.: B4. Print.

A plus sign following the page number (for example, 7+) indicates that an article continues beyond the designated page, but not necessarily on consecutive pages.

IN-TEXT NOTE: (Peterson 2A)

Works Cited

Peterson, Karen S. "Turns Out We Are 'Sexually

  Conventional.'" *USA Today* 7 Oct. 1994: 1A+. Print.

30. Editorial, Signed by Author—MLA After the title, insert the word "Editorial."

IN-TEXT NOTE: (Goett)

Works Cited

Goett, Pamela. "Houston, We Have a Problem." Editorial.

  Journal of Business Strategy 23.1 (2002): 2. Print.

31. Editorial—Author Not Named—MLA A shortened title is used in the note.

IN-TEXT NOTE: ("Negro College" 28)

Works Cited

"Negro College Fund: Mission Is Still Important on 50th
　　Anniversary." Editorial. *Dallas Morning News* 8 Oct.
　　1994: A28. Print.

32. Letter to the Editor—MLA

IN-TEXT NOTE: (Ceniceros)

Works Cited

Ceniceros, Claudia. Letter. *New York Times* 20 Aug. 2002,
　　late ed.: A18. Print.

33. Cartoon—MLA To avoid a confusing note, describe a cartoon in the text of your essay.

IN-TEXT NOTE: In the cartoon "Squib" by Miles Mathis . . .

Works Cited

Mathis, Miles. "Squib." Cartoon. *Daily Texan* 15 Jan.
　　1986: 19. Print.

34. Reference Work or Encyclopedia (Well-known Source)—MLA
With familiar reference works, especially those revised regularly, identify the edition you are using by its date. You may omit the names of editors and most publishing information. No page number is given in the parenthetical note when a work is arranged alphabetically.

IN-TEXT NOTE: ("Ypsilanti")

Works Cited

"Ypsilanti." *The New Encyclopaedia Britannica:*
　　Macropaedia. 15th ed. 1987. Print.

A citation for an online encyclopedia article would include a date of access and *Web* as the medium of publication.

Works Cited

"Northwest Passage." *Britannica Online*. Encyclopaedia
Britannica. Web. 8 Feb. 2000.

35. Reference Work (Specialized or Less Familiar)—MLA With
less familiar reference tools, a full entry is required. (See model 34 for a
comparison with familiar reference works.)

IN-TEXT NOTE: ("Polixenes")

Works Cited

"Polixenes." *The Oxford Companion to English Literature*.
Ed. M. Drabble. Oxford: Oxford UP, 1998. Print.

36. Bulletin, Brochure, or Pamphlet—MLA Treat these items as if
they were books.

IN-TEXT NOTE: (Morgan 8-9)

Works Cited

Morgan, Martha G., ed. *Campus Guide to Computer and Web
Services*. Austin: U of Texas, 1999. Print.

37. Government Document—MLA Give the name of the government
(national, state, or local) and the agency issuing the report, the title of
the document, and publishing information. If it is a congressional document other than the *Congressional Record*, identify the Congress and,
when important, the session (for example, *99th Cong., 1st sess.*) after the
title of the document. Avoid a lengthy note by naming the document in
the body of your essay and placing only the relevant page numbers
between parentheses. To cite information on a government Web site, see
model 46.

IN-TEXT NOTE: This information is from the *1985-86 Official
Congressional Directory* (182-84).

Works Cited

United States. Cong. Joint Committee on Printing.
1985-86 Official Congressional Directory. 99th
Cong., 1st sess. Washington: GPO, 1985. Print.

To cite the *Congressional Record*, give the date, page number, and medium of publication.

> Cong. Rec. 8 Feb. 1974: 3942-43. Print.

38. Computer Software—MLA Give the author if known, the title, the version number if any (for example: *Microsoft Word.* Vers. 7.0), and publication details for the installation media.

> IN-TEXT NOTE: With software such as Apple's *iTunes* . . .

Works Cited

> *iTunes.* Vers. 5. Apple, 2005. Software.

4 MLA: Web publications checklist

BASIC INFORMATION	EXAMPLE (SEE MODEL 39)
Creator or author of the site	
Title of the page (between " ")	"A New Lease on Life . . ."
Title of site (italicized)	*Parknet.*
Version or edition of site	
Sponsor of site (use *N.p.* if not available)	National Park Service.
Date of electronic publication	7 Dec. 1999.
Medium of publication	Web.
Date you examined the site	10 May 2009.

39. WWW Site—Generic—MLA The variety among Web pages is staggering, so you will have to adapt your documentation to particular sources. Quite often you will be citing Web pages without authors or creators named. Here, for example, is a citation to an entire Web site.

IN-TEXT NOTE: More information on National Parks in the United States can be found at *Parknet* . . .

Works Cited

Parknet. National Park Service. 8 May 2009. Web. 10 May 2009.

A citation to a particular page on that Web site would look like the following.

IN-TEXT NOTE: ("New Lease")

Works Cited

"A New Lease on Life: Museum Conservation in the National Park Service." *Parknet.* National Park Service. 7 Dec. 1999. Web. 10 May 2009.

Because most readers can easily locate Web sources by searching for titles and authors' names, MLA no longer requires you to include in citations the uniform resource locator (URL), the Web address usually beginning <http://www>. Now, include the URL as supplemental information in a citation *only* if readers need it to find the source. If you do include a URL in a works cited entry, place it after the date of access. Include the complete URL in angle brackets, followed by a period: <http://www.law.umkc.edu/faculty/projects/ftrials/salem/salem.htm>.

40. Web Page, Signed by Author—MLA

IN-TEXT NOTE: (Linder)

Works Cited

Linder, Douglas. "Salem Witchcraft Trials of 1692."

    Famous American Trials. Univ. of MO, Kansas City

    School of Law. Mar. 2007. Web. 11 May 2009.

41. Web Page, on Edited and Versioned Site—MLA The version or edition is listed after the title of the overall Web site. The abbreviation *N.p.* indicates that no sponsor or publisher is listed.

IN-TEXT NOTE: (Gray)

Works Cited

Gray, Terry A. "A Shakespeare Timeline: Birth and

    Early Years." *Mr. William Shakespeare and the*

    Internet. Ver. 4.0. N.p. 25 Feb. 2009. Web.

    11 May 2009.

42. WWW—Online Book—MLA Since some online books do not have page numbers, avoid parenthetical notes for those titles by identifying the book in your paper itself. Provide print publication information, followed by the name of the Web site, the medium of publication (*Web*), and the date you accessed the information.

IN-TEXT NOTE: In the final chapter of *Thinking Through the Body*, . . .

Works Cited

Gallop, Jane. *Thinking Through the Body*. New York: Columbia UP, 1988. *Google Book Search*. Web. 11 May 2009.

43. WWW—Online Scholarly Journal—MLA Since some online articles do not have page numbers, avoid parenthetical notes for those without page numbers by identifying the site in your paper itself.

IN-TEXT NOTE: (Castello et al.)

Works Cited

Castello, Ana, et al. "Long-Lasting Lipstick and Latent Prints." *Forensic Science Communications* 4.2 (2002): n. pag. Web. 11 May 2009.

44. WWW—Online Popular Magazine—MLA Since some online articles do not have page numbers, avoid parenthetical notes for those without page numbers by identifying the site in your paper itself.

IN-TEXT NOTE: "In 'Dial Miami for Murder,' Virginia Heffernan describes . . ."

Works Cited

Heffernan, Virginia. "Dial Miami for Murder: *CSI's* Florida Sojourn." *Slate*. Washington Post.Newsweek Interactive. 3 Oct. 2002. Web. 10 Oct. 2003.

45. WWW—Online News Source or Newspaper—MLA Provide all
the basic publication information, including the name of the newspaper,
the sponsor of the site, and the medium of publication (*Web*) between
the date of publication and the date you looked at the article. Provide
both the original date of the article and date of access, even when the
dates are the same.

IN-TEXT NOTE: (Olson)

Works Cited

Olson, Elizabeth. "Peer Support Cited in Black Students'

Success." *New York Times on the Web*. New York

Times, 17 May 2006. Web. 17 May 2006.

46. Online Government Publication—MLA Although these works
have traditionally appeared in print, they now are regularly accessed
online. When they are available, include original print publication
details before the site name. For information on citing government documents published in printed form, see model 37.

IN-TEXT NOTE: (Vermont)

Works Cited

Vermont. Agency of Natural Resources. "Introduction and

Greeting." *VTANR*. 2003. Web. 5 Oct. 2003.

47. Online Posting—Listserv—MLA List the subject line of the
posting after the author's name. Insert the name of the discussion
forum (neither underlined nor in quotation marks) before the date of
access.

IN-TEXT NOTE: (Cook)

Works Cited

Cook, Janice. "Re: What New Day Is Dawning?" Online

posting. Alliance for Computers and Writing

Listserv. 19 June 1997. Web. 4 Feb 1998.

48. Online Posting—Usenet—MLA

IN-TEXT NOTE: (Heady)

Works Cited

Heady, Christy. "Buy or Lease? Depends on How Long

    You'll Keep the Car." Online posting. N.p. 7 July

    1997. Web. 14 July 1997.

49. Online Posting—Blog—MLA Blog items with obvious authors and titles for daily entries can be cited without much difficulty, but many blog entries won't have conventional titles or pagination.

IN-TEXT NOTE: (Johnson)

Works Cited

Johnson, Scott. "God and Juan at Yale." Blog posting.

    Powerline. 26 Mar. 2006. Web. 11 May 2006.

50. Online Posting—Archived—MLA Many online discussions are archived and published in a fixed form.

IN-TEXT NOTE: (Knight)

Works Cited

Knight. "Will BMW Let ME Test Drive?" Online posting.

    4 Mar. 2000. *Bimmer*. Forums: E 46. 6 Mar. 2000.

51. PDF or Word-processing Document—Downloaded—MLA
Identify the type of source and include relevant publication information.
For the medium of publication, give the type of file.

IN-TEXT NOTE: (Belanus and Hunt 25)

Works Cited

Belanus, Betty, and Marjorie Hunt. "Building with Adobe."

Masters of the Building Arts. (2001):24-27.

Smithsonian Center for Folklife and Cultural

Heritage. PDF file.

52. Photograph—Downloaded from Internet—MLA For images
and recordings distributed over the Internet, use the guidelines for
typical audio/video works (see models 59–68, pp. 443–446), but replace
the standard publication details with electronic publication and
access information for the downloaded file (JPEGs, MP3s, etc.). For
information on citing images published in print form, see models 71
and 73.

IN-TEXT NOTE: (Nohl)

Works Cited

Nohl, Mark. "Taos Pueblo Pottery." NewMexico.org. New

Mexico Dept. of Tourism. 2002. Web. 13 Aug. 2003.

53. Audio Recording—Downloaded from Internet—MLA For
information on citing audio recordings not downloaded from the Web,
see model 59.

IN-TEXT NOTE: (Hanks)

Works Cited

Hanks, Tom, and Ron Howard. Interview with Larry King.

"Hanks Talks Angels Controversy." CNN.com. Cable

News Network. 13 May 2009. Web. 14 May 2009.

54. Article—on CD-ROM Reference—MLA Some electronic sources are found on recorded media, not the public Internet. Instead of typical online publication details, list the version being used, the city of publication and vendor, the year of production, and the medium of publication (CD-ROM).

IN-TEXT NOTE: ("Gallup")

Works Cited

"Gallup." *Microsoft Bookshelf 2000*. Redmond: Microsoft,

2000. CD-ROM.

55. Library Subscription Service—Journal Article—MLA Many writers now gain access to materials from information services to which their local or school libraries subscribe, such as LexisNexis, Gale, or EBSCO. Such services typically offer a full menu of databases.

To cite an article you find in a library subscription database, use the same guidelines for citing print periodicals, but omit *Print* as the medium of publication and include the title of the database in italics, the medium of publication (*Web*), and the date of access. Include page numbers if provided; if page numbers are not continuous, provide the first page number and a plus sign (*35+*). For articles without pagination, use *n.pag.* to indicate no page numbers are provided.

IN-TEXT NOTE: (Lewis et al.)

Works Cited

Lewis, Richard D., et al. "Prevalence and Degree of

Childhood and Adolescent Overweight in Rural,

Urban, and Suburban Georgia." *Journal of School*

Health 76.4 (2006): 126-32. *Expanded Academic*

ASAP. Web. 15 Sept. 2006.

56. Library Subscription Service—Magazine Article—MLA Treat the magazine as you would a print item. But also identify the database, medium of publication (*Web*), and access date.

IN-TEXT NOTE: (Harrison 18)

Works Cited

Harrison, Bobby R. "Phantom of the Bayou." *Natural
     History* Sept. 2005: 18-52. *Academic Search
     Premier*. Web. 15 Sept. 2006.

57. Library Subscription Service—Newspaper Article—MLA Pay

attention to any information used to identify the section number of the article as it appeared in print.

IN-TEXT NOTE: (Toner)

Works Cited

Toner, Mike. "Back to the Moon." *Atlanta Journal-
     Constitution* 13 Oct. 2005: A1. *LexisNexis*. Web.
     11 May 2006.

58. Library Subscription Service—Encyclopedia Article—MLA

Cite the entry you have consulted and provide the medium of publication and a date of access.

IN-TEXT NOTE: ("Schnauzer")

Works Cited

"Schnauzer." *Encyclopaedia Britannica Online*. 2006.
     Encyclopaedia Britannica. Web. 29 May 2006.

59. Audio Recording—MLA Begin with the artist(s) or composer(s),

unless it makes sense to focus on a different contributor (a producer, for example). Next list the title and other contributors. Then list the vendor, year, and medium of publication (*CD*, *Podcast*, *MP3*, etc.). To cite an audio recording distributed online, see model 53.

IN-TEXT NOTE: (Mayer)

Works Cited

Mayer, John. *Heavier Things*. Prod. Jack Joseph Puig.

Sony, 2003. CD.

60. Song—Podcast—MLA When you want to focus on a single song or track, list its title before the title of the recording.

IN-TEXT NOTE: (Funkadelic)

Works Cited

Funkadelic. "Biological Speculation." *America Eats Its*

Young. Perf. George Clinton. Westbound, 1972. LP.

61. Video Recording—MLA Begin with the title, unless you wish to foreground a particular contributor (the director, scriptwriters, etc.).

IN-TEXT NOTE: (*Species*)

Works Cited

Species. Dir. Roger Donaldson. Perf. Ben Kingsley, Forest

Whitaker, and Natasha Henstridge. MGM, 1995. DVD.

62. Film—Viewed in Theater—MLA

IN-TEXT NOTE: In the opening scene of *The Matrix*, . . .

Works Cited

The Matrix. Perf. Keanu Reeves and Laurence Fishburne.

Warner, 1999. Film.

63. Film—Focus on Director—MLA

IN-TEXT NOTE: (Spielberg)

Works Cited

Spielberg, Stephen, dir. *Jurassic Park*. Perf. Jeff

Goldblum, Wayne Knight, and Sam Neill. Universal,

1993. DVD.

64. Liner Notes/Bonus Material—MLA To cite supplementary material, list the author(s) of the supplement first; then describe the mate-

rial (*Liner notes, Director's audio commentary, Documentary*, etc.); finally, provide basic production details for the recording.

IN-TEXT NOTE: (Maguire)

Works Cited

Maguire, Tobey. Actor's audio commentary. *Spider-Man 2*.

Columbia, 2004. DVD.

65. Speech/Lecture—MLA To cite a live speech or lecture, list the speaker and the title of the talk. Then list the name of the event and its sponsoring group (if applicable), the venue, city, date, and medium. For information about citing a recording of a talk, see model 59.

IN-TEXT NOTE: (Kelly)

Works Cited

Kelly, Randy. "The Future of Saint Paul: Progress

through Partnerships." U of Minnesota Student

Center Theatre, St. Paul. 10 Apr. 2003. Address.

66. TV Show—MLA Begin with the title of the program, unless you wish to foreground a particular contributor (an actor, for example). Then list secondary contributors, the broadcasting network, the station, city, date of viewing, and medium of publication (*Television*).

IN-TEXT NOTE: (*Buena Vista*)

Works Cited

Buena Vista Social Club. PBS. KBYU, Provo, 19 July 2000.

Television.

67. TV Show—Particular Episode—MLA If you are citing a specific episode, insert the title of the episode (in quotation marks) before the title of the program.

IN-TEXT NOTE: In the episode "No Surrender, No Retreat" . . .

Works Cited

"No Surrender, No Retreat." Dir. Mike Vehar. Writ.

Michael Straczynksdi. Perf. Bruce Boxleitner,

Claudia Christian, and Mira Furlan. *Babylon 5*.

KEYE-42, Austin, 28 July 1997. Television.

68. Radio Broadcast—MLA

IN-TEXT NOTE: ("L.A. Votes")

Works Cited

"L.A. Votes to Break Up Its Landmark—Hollywood." *Which
Way L.A.?* Host Warren Olney. Natl. Public Radio.
KCRW, Santa Monica, 5 June 2002. Radio.

69. Drama or Play—Published Text—MLA Citing a printed text of a play differs from a live performance. For printed texts, provide the usual Works Cited information. In parenthetical notes, give the act, scene, and line numbers when the work is so divided; give page numbers when it is not.

IN-TEXT NOTE: (*Ham.* 5.2.219-24)

Works Cited

Shakespeare, William. *The Tragedy of Hamlet, Prince of
Denmark.* Ed. Frank Kermode. *The Riverside
Shakespeare.* 2nd ed. Ed. G. Blakemore Evans and
J.J.M. Tobin. Boston: Houghton, 1997. Print.

70. Drama or Play—Live Performance—MLA Give the title of the work, the author, and then any specific information that seems relevant—director, performers, producers, theater company, and so on. Conclude the entry with a theater, location, date, and medium of publication (*Performance*).

IN-TEXT NOTE: (*Producers*)

Works Cited

The Producers. By Mel Brooks. Perf. Jason Alexander and
Martin Short. Dir. and chor. Susan Stroman.
Pantages Theatre, Los Angeles. 25 June 2003.
Performance.

71. Artwork—MLA To cite a painting, photograph, or sculpture, list the artist and the title (italicized), the date of completion (if known), the medium of the work, the owner (a person or institution), and the city where the work is housed. If using a published image or reproduction of the work, attach standard publication details for that source at the end of your entry.

IN-TEXT NOTE: (Cassatt)

Works Cited

Cassatt, Mary. *In the Omnibus*. Ca. 1891. Oil on canvas.

　　　Chester Dale Collection. Natl. Gallery of Art,

　　　Washington.

72. Map/Chart/Diagram—Published Separately—MLA When
published separately, list artist (if known), title (underlined), a description (*Map, Chart*, etc.), and publication details (place, publisher, year, and medium of publication).

IN-TEXT NOTE: (*Arches*)

Works Cited

Arches National Park. Map. U.S. Natl. Park Service,

　　　2001. Print.

73. Map/Chart/Diagram—Published within Another Source—
MLA Place the title in quotes and provide publication details including sponsoring organization, date of publication, medium of publication (*Web*), and date of access.

IN-TEXT NOTE: (Evans)

Works Cited

Evans, James. "Dancing Feet." Photograph. 1993.

　　　Alterimage Gallery. Alterimage Gallery, 1993. Web.

　　　11 May 2009.

74. Musical Composition—MLA If citing a published score, format
the entry like a book or online book, depending on how published. If not using a particular recording or published score, simply list the artist, title, and year.

IN-TEXT NOTE: (Vivaldi)

Works Cited

Vivaldi, Antonio. *The Contest Between Harmony and*

　　　Invention. 1725.

75. Interview—Published—MLA Cite a published or recorded interview as you would any other book part, article, online document, recording, or broadcast—but list the interviewee first. Then insert the title (if given) and a descriptive phrase, *Interview with*. . . .

IN-TEXT NOTE: (Didion 2)

Works Cited

Didion, Joan. Interview with David Eggers. *Salon*. Salon

Media Group, 28 Oct. 1996. Web. 15 May 2009.

76. Interview—by Researcher—MLA If the interview is one that you conducted, list the interviewee, a description (*Personal interview, Telephone interview*, etc.) and the date(s).

IN-TEXT NOTE: (Halsam)

Works Cited

Halsam, Gerald. Personal interview. 23-24 Apr. 2003.

77. Email/Letter—Unpublished—MLA List the author(s), the subject line in quotation marks (for emails, memos), a description of the format and audience (*Letter to . . . , E-mail to the author*, etc.), the date sent, and medium of publication. For the medium of publication, use the abbreviation *TS* (typescript) for a typed letter and the abbreviation *MS* (manuscript) for a handwritten letter.

IN-TEXT NOTE: (Schwarz)

Works Cited

Schwarz, Sigmar. "Who's Going to Sacramento?" Message to

the author. 8 Oct. 2003. E-mail.

78. Memo—Unpublished—MLA

IN-TEXT NOTE: (Seward)

Works Cited

Seward, Daniel. "Proposal for Forum on Richard

Rodriguez's *Hunger of Memory*." Memo to English

Dept. fac., California Lutheran U. 1 May 2003. TS.

79. Letter—Published—MLA Cite a published letter, memo, or email as you would any other book part, periodical entry, or online document, depending upon the form of publication. After the title of the letter, insert the date of the correspondence and any identifying number added by the editor.

IN-TEXT NOTE: (Steinbeck)

Works Cited

Steinbeck, John. "To Lyndon B. Johnson." 24 Nov. 1963.
  Steinbeck: A Life in Letters. Ed. Elaine Steinbeck
  and Robert Wallsten. New York: Viking, 1975: 787-88.
  Print.

80. Advertisement—Published in a Magazine—MLA Begin with the name of the product or the company (if no product is mentioned). Then insert the phrase *Advertisement*.

IN-TEXT NOTE: (PeopleSoft)

Works Cited

PeopleSoft's Real-Time Enterprise. Advertisement.
  Business Week 9 June 2003: 17. Print.

81. Cartoon/Comic Strip—MLA

IN-TEXT NOTE: (Mckee)

Works Cited

Mckee, Rick. Cartoon. *Slate*. Washington Post.Newsweek
  Interactive, 23 July 2003. Web. 6 Mar. 2003.

44d Sample Research Paper—MLA

Nelson Rivera, a first-year student at the University of South Carolina, wrote "Taking a Closer Look at the Motorcycle Boom" in Spring 2005 while a student in "English 101: Rhetoric and Composition." The assignment sheet for the paper asked students to write a causal argument, which is a paper that tries to explain a phenomenon—in this case, the growing popularity of motorcycles. The paper appears here substantially as Rivera wrote it, though with some modifications to highlight additional features of MLA style. It is accompanied by annotations and checklists designed to help you set up a paper correctly in MLA style.

modifications to highlight additional features of MLA style. It is accompanied by annotations and checklists designed to help you set up a paper correctly in MLA style.

checklist 44.1

Formatting the Paper—MLA

Use the following general settings in your word processor for an MLA paper, but adjust them to match any special preferences set by your instructor. Subsequent checklists provide details for the title page, special items (quotations, tables, and figures), and the Works Cited page.

a. **Use white, 8 1/2-by-11-in. paper.** For a traditional academic assignment, never use color or lined paper. Handwrite a paper only with an instructor's permission.

b. **Insert your last name and page numbers 1/2 in. from the top of** *every* **page, aligned with the right-hand margin.** The best way to achieve this is to insert a running page header. (See the View or Insert menus.)

c. **Use the same readable font face throughout your paper.** Avoid fonts with too much decoration, since they can be hard on the eyes. Also be sure to use a moderate text size, 10 to 12 points depending upon the font face.

d. **Double-space the entire document.** This includes the *works cited* page and *title* page. (Use your word processor's Format or Paragraph menus to select line spacing.)

e. **Left-align the body of the paper and do not hyphenate words at the end of the line.** You may need to turn off your word processor's automatic hyphenation tool.

f. **Indent the first word of each paragraph 1/2 in.** Most word processors have a way to auto set an indent for the first line of paragraphs.

1/2 inch

Rivera 1

1 inch

Nelson Rivera

Ms. Melissa Jantz

English 101: Rhetoric and Composition

March 25, 2005

Double-space all elements on the title page. No special spacing or enlarged or enhanced fonts.

Taking a Closer Look at the Motorcycle Boom

In 1969 the film *Easy Rider* revolutionized the

1/2 inch

motorcycle world by creating the bad boy biker image

that is familiar to most people today (see fig. 1).

Fig. 1. Peter Fonda and Dennis Hopper growling down the

highway in *Easy Rider* (1969), representing bikers as

rebels.

1 inch

Bikers were renegades, counterculture road warriors who,

1 inch

according to scholars Jeremy Packer and Mary K. Coffey,

were "violent, heteronormative, and (for the most part)

masculine as they may be" (641). Though they weren't

typical heroes, Peter Fonda and Dennis Hopper portrayed

life on the road as life on their own terms, and after

the release of this movie, the motorcycle industry

experienced a 98% increase in motorcycle sales between

1970 and 1980. This increase diminished, however, soon

after it peaked. It wasn't until 1992 that the industry

experienced a rebirth with increases in motorcycle sales

1 inch

(Proportions shown in this paper are adjusted to fit space limitations of this book. Follow actual dimensions discussed in this book and your instructor's directions.)

checklist 44.2 ⌐ Formatting the Title Page—MLA

MLA does not require a separate cover sheet or title page—instead, at the *top of the first page* list the following items on a *separate* line. All these items are double-spaced. In particular, do not insert extra spaces above or below the title.

a. **List your full name on the first line of the first page, aligned to the left.**

b. **List your instructor's name with appropriate title, aligned to the left.** When uncertain about academic rank, use *Mr.*, *Ms.*, or *Prof.* Better, look up the title in a campus directory or simply ask your instructor.

c. **List the course title, aligned to the left.**

d. **List the date you submit the assignment, aligned to the left.**

e. **Give the title of your paper, capitalized and centered.** Capitalize the first and last words of the title, and all words in between *except* articles (*a, an,* and *the*), prepositions (including *to* when part of an infinitive), and coordinating conjunctions. Do not end the title with a period, but use a question mark when appropriate. Do not bold, underline, italicize, or specially format your title *except* for specific words and phrases that generally require special formatting.

> Taking a Closer Look at the Motorcycle Boom
>
> Nelson Rivera
>
>
>
> Ms. Melissa Jantz
> English 101: Rhetoric and Composition
> 25 March 2005

Note: If your instructor does ask for a title page, center the title of your paper and your name in the upper third of the paper. Center the course title, your instructor's name, and the date on the lower third of the sheet, double-spacing each item.

"not seen since the 1970's" ("Annual"). Today the industry has reached the one million mark in motorcycle sales. Up from just 278,000 motorcycles sold in 1992, these sales numbers represent an increase of over 270%, as seen in Table 1.

Table 1

Estimated New Motorcycle Sales from 1992-2004

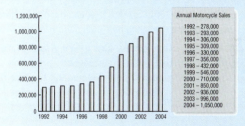

Source: *2003 Motorcycle Statistical Annual Report. Free Student Kit*. Motorcycle Industry Council 2004. Web. 16 Mar. 2008.

This trend has continued into what is now a twelfth consecutive year of record-breaking motorcycle sales. Unlike those involved in the first motorcycle craze in the 1970s, today's motorcycle enthusiasts do not have a box office hit movie to fuel their interest, and they do not dream of giving up the social responsibilities of work and family in the vein of *Easy Rider*'s free-living protagonists. Instead, this sales increase is likely due to several interrelated social and economic causes, especially including the rise in expendable income now enjoyed by the Baby Boom generation. Generally speaking, the counterculture biker image

checklist 44.3 — **Quotations, Tables, and Figures—MLA**

a. **Format quotations correctly.** MLA requires that you present long quotations—more than four lines—in block format. *Block quotations* are *not* enclosed by quotation marks. The entire quotation is indented one inch from the left margin. Use the same double-spacing as the rest of the document.

b. **Label and number tables, placing them as close as possible to related text.** Before the table, provide the label *Table*, an identifying number, and a caption, capitalized according to the standard rules for titles. Double-space the table (assuming you're not using an image of a table, as Rivera does), citing the source (if you didn't create it yourself) in a caption at the bottom. The caption should use the same one-inch margin as the rest of the paper.

c. **Label and number illustrations and other visual material.** Place the item as close as possible to the related text, providing underneath the label *Figure* (or *Fig.*), an identifying number, and the title (or a descriptive label or caption). For more on figures and tables, see Section 43b-2.

Rivera 3

appeals to this group of aging activists, and the biker
lifestyle is now much more accessible to those with the
social responsibilities of work and family.

Indeed, the stereotyped image of the average biker
has dramatically changed over the last 20 years. Today's
bikers are a new breed. No longer are they simply
leather-clad, beer-drinking Hell's Angels, as described
in 1966 by Hunter S. Thompson.

1 inch

> running fast and loud on the early morning free-
> way, low in the saddle, nobody smiles, jamming
> crazy through traffic and ninety miles an hour
> down the center stripe, missing by inches . . .
> like Genghis Khan on an iron horse, a monster
> steed . . . long hair in the wind, beards and
> bandanas flapping, earrings, armpits, chain
> whips . . . and stripped-down Harleys flashing
> chrome as traffic on 101 moves over, nervous, to
> let the formation pass like a burst of dirty
> thunder. (3)

Even though much of this rebellious style remains,
today's biker lifestyle does not necessarily exclude the
demands of a more traditional lifestyle. In fact, many
of today's bikers are law firm partners, accountants,
and doctors—a lifestyle still frowned upon in the early
1980s, when for example a cycle-riding metropolitan
court judge from New Mexico admitted in the *American Bar
Association Journal* that "people think you're crazy
riding a motorcycle, period" (Winter 527). Now, however,
the biker you see growling down the highway might even
be your boss.

Rivera 4

This change in image has made the biker lifestyle seem more accessible to professionals who might have otherwise felt too mainstream to take part in a counterculture.

In the 1970s it would have been unimaginable for television to advertise and promote the biker lifestyle because such an existence was seen as taboo. One need only turn on cable television to see that today's biker has not given up work and family in favor of the open road. The Discovery Channel, for example, is currently running two commercials advertising the network's upcoming bike-week, a programming theme that itself points to just how popular the biker lifestyle has become. One of these commercials shows a family man preparing his breakfast before leaving for work. Instead of pouring cereal into his bowl, he pours nuts and bolts, and instead of adding milk, he tops his breakfast off with motor oil. The man crunches away on his substantive breakfast as the message "getting ready for bike-week" is displayed on-screen. By juxtaposing garage staples like motor oil, nuts, and bolts, with images from a more traditional life that includes family and work, this ad seems to suggest that the two worlds need not be mutually exclusive. It says that men can have 9–5 jobs and still—figuratively at least—eat nuts and bolts for breakfast. This message of accessibility is not limited to men.

Another "getting ready for bike-week" commercial features a businesswoman with a notepad in her office, but instead of taking notes, she is practicing tattoo

artistry on her arm. By suggesting that the biker
lifestyle—still rebellious and *avant-garde*—is compatible
with family and professional life, these two commercials
suggest a new, more accessible ethos for the modern
biker. As the cable networks spotlight the biker world
with programs such as *World Biker Build-off*, *American
Steel*, and *American Choppers*, "the bikes that once
invoked images of greasy leathers and snarling gangs are
now just as likely to turn up in executives' garages"
(Hopkins G5). This attention by the media has lured
names such as Jay Leno, Dennis Rodman, and Shaquille
O'Neil to join the biker lifestyle. And the increase in
media coverage has in turn sparked the interest of a
wider range of Americans, creating a greater market
field and expanding the buyer segments.

Fig. 2. Biking goes mainstream with Paul Teutul Sr. and
Paul Teutul Jr. of *American Chopper*.

Rivera 6

Perhaps it is not that surprising, then, that women make up a significant new addition to the motorcycle market. In fact, women are the fastest growing segment in the market and, as Steve Pilkington succinctly notes, they "are no longer taking a back seat to men" (9). According to the Motorcycle Industry Council, female ridership increased from 2% in 1985 to 10% in 2003. An article in *Working Woman* reports that "[t]oday 1 out of every 11 American motorcycle owners is a woman, compared with 1 out of 100 in 1960" (Aronson 18). The overall increase in motorcycle sales can be attributed, in part, to this increase in female riders. Because many women have experienced a growth in disposable income, they can now make motorcycle purchases on their own, without the help of their male partners. Social factors surrounding the character and acceptance of the biker lifestyle by mainstream America may have also played a role in the increase of female motorcycle sales. The biker image now seems more accessible and acceptable, and women can more comfortably fit into this lifestyle.

This new gentler image is in large part created by a return to the saddle by the Baby Boomers who had previously abandoned their riding days in exchange for families and careers. During the last motorcycle boom, the average rate of increase in motorcycle sales matched that of the annual increase in the number of Baby Boom males reaching their 18th birthday. Ken Kurson, who points out these facts in *Motorcycles for Grown-Ups*, adds that "30 years later, much of this round of expansion comes from the fact that Baby Boomers are rediscovering their love of motorcycles" (112). In the last twelve years the motorcycling lifestyle has attracted wealthier older owners, both male and female, and this is largely due to the fact that the Baby Boom generation is now entering into a stage of financial stability with no dependents. The results of a 2003 consumer research report show the average age of bikers to be 41 with a median household income of $55,850 annually (see table 2).

Because of the Baby Boomers' large numbers and their inclination towards free spending, it was just a matter of time before the tourist industry jumped onto the motorcycle bandwagon ("Baby Boomers"). This increase in tourism, in turn, prompted some major cities to sponsor weeklong celebrations geared towards welcoming motorcycle enthusiasts and creating a $774-million-a-year tourist industry in Daytona Beach alone. A 2001 study conducted by the University of Central Florida shows that "this is significantly more than the $561 million generated by the Daytona 500 . . . or the $196 million from spring break" (Schneider 14). Not only is the motorcycle industry now more accessible to individuals who might have been reluctant or unable to take part before, but it is also more lucrative for the tourist industry, which now has financial incentive to sponsor biker events.

Celebrations such as these have brought about another factor that adds to the increase in motorcycle sales: Motorcycles provide the time-pressed rider with a short-term form of recreation. Vacations such as Bike-Week at Daytona Beach, Florida, weekend trips to the

Rivera 8

Table 2

Owner Profile by Age, Marital Status, Education,
Occupation and Income: 1985-2003

	% OF TOTAL OWNERS			
	2003	**1998**	**1990**	**1985**
AGE				
Under 18	3.7%	4.1%	8.3%	14.9%
18 – 24	10.8%	10.6%	15.5%	20.7%
25 – 29	7.6%	10.9%	17.1%	18.7%
30 – 34	8.9%	11.5%	16.4%	13.8%
35 – 39	10.4%	16.0%	14.3%	8.7%
40 – 49	27.9%	24.6%	16.3%	13.2%
50 and Over	25.1%	19.1%	10.1%	8.1%
Not Stated	5.6%	3.2%	2.0%	1.9%
Median Age	41.0 yrs.	38.0 yrs.	32.0 yrs.	27.1 yrs.
Mean Age	40.2 yrs.	38.1 yrs.	33.1 yrs.	28.5 yrs.
HOUSEHOLD INCOME FOR PRIOR YEAR				
Under $20,000	5.9%	9.3%	15.6%	31.8%
$20,000–$34,999	13.1%	19.4%	32.2%	26.7%
$35,000–$49,999	18.1%	19.1%	19.6%	14.4%
$50,000–$74,999	19.3%	18.8%	13.1%	** 6.1%
$75,000–$99,999	13.7%	8.3%	4.1%	
$100,000–$149,999	8.4%	3.8%	* 2.7%	
$150,000 and Over	4.8%	2.3%		
Not Stated	16.7%	19.0%	12.7%	21.0%
Median	$55,850	$44,250	$33,100	$25,600
* $100,000 and Over				
** $50,000 and Over				
MARITAL STATUS				
Single	41.1%	40.0%	41.1%	47.6%
Married	55.5%	58.8%	56.6%	50.3%
Not Stated	3.4%	1.2%	2.3%	2.1%
HIGHEST LEVEL OF EDUCATION				
Grade School	3.1%	3.3%	5.9%	7.5%
Some High School	6.9%	9.6%	9.5%	15.3%
High School Graduate	30.2%	36.0%	39.4%	36.5%
Some College/Technical	25.9%	26.5%	25.2%	21.6%
College Graduate	18.6%	16.0%	12.4%	12.2%
Post Graduate	10.5%	6.9%	5.2%	5.2%
Not Stated	4.8%	1.7%	2.4%	1.7%
OCCUPATION OF OWNER				
Professional/Technical	31.2%	31.3%	20.3%	19.0%
Mechanic/Craftsman	11.7%	15.3%	13.1%	15.1%
Manager/Proprietor	10.8%	7.5%	9.3%	8.9%
Laborer/Semi-Skilled	6.9%	12.7%	24.1%	23.2%
Service Worker	6.0%	7.5%	6.6%	6.4%
Clerical/Sales	4.4%	3.6%	6.8%	7.8%
Farmer/Farm Laborer	1.9%	2.8%	2.1%	5.1%
Military	1.3%	2.6%	1.5%	1.6%
Other	18.3%	13.5%	13.1%	4.6%
Not Stated	7.5%	3.2%	3.1%	8.3%
Note: Percentages based on owners employed				

Source: *2004 Motorcycle Statistical Annual Report. Free
Student Kit.* Motorcycle Industry Council 2005. Web. 16
Mar. 2008.

Rivera 9

mountains, and even local Sunday rides provide riders
with the opportunity to take trips that do not require a
huge investment in time. With a motorcycle, even the
ride to work can now be considered recreation.

Though the Baby Boomers are known for their capacity
for free spending, some research suggests that sales are
up in part because motorcycles provide the rider with an
economical and environmentally friendly method of
transportation. At a time when gas prices are soaring,
more people are becoming aware of the economic benefits
of owning a motorcycle. According to the U.S. Department
of Transportation, the average cost of self-serve
gasoline has risen from $1.12 in 1992 to $2.20 per gallon
in 2004 ("Table 3-8"). These figures reflect an increase
of 96%. With motorcycles averaging 50 miles per gallon of
gasoline versus 22 miles per gallon of gasoline for cars
and small trucks (U.S. Department of Transportation,
"Table 4-11"), one can either ride back and forth to work
all week or go joyriding for an entire weekend on just
$20 worth of fuel. Some motorcycle dealers have
attributed the sharp increase in motorcycle sales to the
higher cost of fuel, claiming that when faced with higher
prices at the pump "traditionally [. . .] people put
motorcycles into the mode of transportation versus the
mode it is usually in and that is recreation" (Kenny 1D).

Though it might seem odd that the very Baby Boomers
who can now enter the biker life because of their
expendable income are also attracted by the cost-saving
elements of owning a bike, the two causes are not
contradictory. According to the Strategic Edge, a market

research company that predicts the buying patterns of various target groups, many Baby Boomers were concerned with environmental issues when they came of age ("Baby Boomers"). In addition to the promise of the open road, then, the economic and environmentally responsible elements of the biker lifestyle also appeal to the Baby Boomer.

For both social and economic reasons, motorcycling is now enjoying a greater role in mainstream American culture. The changing of the biker image can be, in large part, credited to the return of the Baby Boomers who have opened up the motorcycle world to a wider range of Americans, expanding buyer segments and creating a greater market field, one that now includes a larger percentage of women riders. Add to this the media attention the motorcycle world has received in the last twelve years, and motorcycling has become an accepted and almost mainstream form of alternative American life. Another factor that has helped fuel the motorcycle boom is higher gasoline prices, which have led buyers to search for alternate and more economical methods of transportation. Of course, Peter Fonda's and Dennis Hopper's characters would never have considered the cost of fuel as they took to the road, and they certainly wouldn't have returned to the office after a weekend ride. But today's easy riders do not have to trade in their conventional lives for the chance to live and ride free. The new, more accessible and acceptable biker lifestyle has afforded them a taste of the open road, even if only for the weekend.

Works Cited

"Annual Motorcycle Sales Roar Through the One Million

Mark: Upward Trend Continues for 12th Consecutive

Year." *Business Wire* 21 Jan. 2005: n. pag.

InfoTrac. Web. 17 Mar. 2005.

Aronson, Amy. "A Vroom of One's Own: Women Riders are

Fueling a Motorcycling Boom." *Working Woman* June

1999: 18. Print.

"Baby Boomers Grow Up." *The Strategic Solution.* The

Strategic Edge. Fall 1996. Web. 15 Mar. 2005.

Easy Rider. Dir. Dennis Hopper. Perf. Peter Fonda and

Dennis Hopper. Columbia/TriStar Studios, 1969. DVD.

Easy Rider. Image. *40 Years of Easy Rider.* n.d. Web.

14 Mar. 2005.

"Estimated New Units Retail Sales." *2003 Motorcycle

Statistical Annual Report. Free Student Kit.*

Motorcycle Industry Council. 2004. Web. 16 Mar.

2008.

Hopkins, Brent. "Mid-Life Executives Help Alter Bike

Rider's Image." *Emotional Journal* 24 Dec. 2004:

G5. *LexisNexis.* Web. 15 Mar. 2005.

Kenny, Megan. "Husbands: Another Reason to Get a Bike.

Some Say Rising Prices at the Pump Are Leading

to a Spike in Motorcycle Sales." *Charleston Daily

Mail* 20 Sept. 2004: 1D. Print.

Kurson, Ken. "Motorcycles for Grown-Ups: Bikes Aren't

Just for Teenagers and Hell's Angels Anymore."

Money May 2001: 112-13. Print.

Rivera 12

"Owner Profile by Age, Marital Status, Education,
    Occupation, and Income: 1985–2003." *2004 Motorcycle
    Statistical Annual Report. Free Student Kit.*
    Motorcycle Industry Council. 2005. Web. 16 Mar.
    2008.

Packer, Jeremy, and Mark K. Coffey. "Hogging the
    Road: Cultural Governance and the Citizen
    Cyclist." *Cultural Studies* 18 (2004): 641-74.
    Print.

Paul Teutul, Sr. and Paul Teutul, Jr. Photograph. *The
    Discovery Channel: American Chopper.* n.d. Web. 10
    Mar. 2005.

Pilkington, Steve. "Women Roll into House of Harley."
    Alaska Business Monthly Feb. 2005:9. Print.

Schneider, Mike. "Daytona Revs Up Welcome for Bikers."
    The State. 10 Oct. 2004: E14. Print.

Thompson, Hunter S. *Hell's Angels: A Strange and
    Terrible Saga.* New York: Ballantine, 1966. Print.

United States Dept. of Transportation. "Table 3-8: Sales
    Price of Transportation Fuel to End-Users." *NTS
    Report 2004.* Bureau of Transportation Statistics.
    17 Nov. 2004. Web. 15 Mar. 2005.

---. "Table 4-11: Passenger Car and Motorcycle Fuel
    Consumption and Travel." *NTS Report 2004.* Bureau of
    Transportation Statistics. 17 Nov. 2004. Web. 15
    Mar. 2005.

Rivera 13

"U.S. Motorcycle Sales Set to Top One Million Units This
    Year." *Motorcyclist*. Source Interlink Media, 18
    Nov. 2004. Web.

Winter, Bill. "Biker-Judges and Lawyers Rev Up Their
    Image." *American Bar Association Journal* 68 (1982):
    527-28. Print.

checklist 44.4 ⌐ **Formatting the Works Cited Page—MLA**

Works Cited pages use the same double-spacing, one-inch margins, and running headers (including your last name and page number) as all other sections of an MLA document, so you can easily insert this page at the end of the electronic file you use to store your paper. But use these additional guidelines:

a. **Insert a page break before your Works Cited page.** The Works Cited list should start at the top of the first full page following the body of the paper.

b. **Center the title "Works Cited" on the first line.** If the list of Works Cited entries overflows this page, *do not* repeat this title on subsequent pages.

c. **Provide Works Cited entries for every source you mention in the paper.** Do not list materials you examined but do not cite in the body of the paper. (If you do include such items, the list can be retitled *Works Consulted*.)

d. **Arrange the entries alphabetically.** Use the first words of each entry (excluding *A, An,* and *The*) to alphabetize the list.

e. **Use a hanging indentation of 1/2 inch for each entry.** Unlike paragraphs in the body of the paper, the first line of each works-cited entry is not indented, but subsequent lines are. To adjust the indentation, use your word processor's paragraph formatting feature or, if provided, its indentation and tabbing ruler.

f. **When more than one entry begins with the same person's name,** replace the repeated information with three hyphens followed by a period. This helps readers see easily that the same person is responsible for more than one source on your list:

van der Plas, Rob. *The Mountain Bike Book: Choosing, Riding and Maintaining the Off-Road Bicycle.* 3rd ed. San Francisco: Bicycle, 1993. Print.

---. *Mountain Bike Magic.* Mill Valley: Bicycle, 1991. Print.

g. **Use cross references to shorten entries.** If citing multiple selections from the same book, you don't need to repeat all information about the book for each works-cited entry. Instead, create a separate, full entry for the book itself, referring to this entry as you create entries for individual selections. Insert the cross reference after the selection's title, where you would normally put the book's title and publication details, using the same guidelines for identifying sources here that you do for identifying them with in-text notes. (See Section 44a-1. An example follows.)

Behrens, Laurence, and Leonard F. Rosen. *Writing and*
Reading Across the Curriculum. 8th ed. New York:
Longman, 2003. Print.

Koplan, Jeffrey P., and William H. Dietz. "Caloric
Imbalance and Public Health Policy." Behrens and
Rosen. 440-47.

Morrison, Toni. "Cinderella's Stepsisters." Behrens and
Rosen. 590-92.

checklist 44.5  Formatting Footnotes and Endnotes—MLA

In some fields and majors, an instructor may ask for MLA-style endnotes or footnotes to document sources, rather than the in-text notes explained in Sections 44a and 44b. When that's the case, use the following models as examples for your notes. For endnotes and footnotes, place a raised number in your text after every sentence or passage you wish to document. This number is keyed to a specific endnote or footnote. Both endnotes and footnotes in MLA style are numbered consecutively throughout a project. On a computer you can create the raised numbers for notes by selecting *superscript* as the font type.

If you use endnotes, list them all on a separate, numbered page at the end of your project. Center the title Notes one inch from the top of this page. The notes are double-spaced, with the first lines indented 1/2 inch or five spaces.

If you use footnotes, place them two double spaces (that is, four lines) below the text on the same page where the citation occurs. Footnotes are single-spaced, but leave a double space between notes when you have more than one on a page.

Notice that endnotes and footnotes differ in indention, arrangement, and punctuation from the style of items on a Works Cited page.

- **Book—MLA endnote/footnote**

    [1]James Prosek, *The Complete Angler: A Connecticut*
Yankee Follows in the Footsteps of Walton (New York:
Harper, 1999) 246-47. Print.

continued on page 468

continued from page 467

- **Book, Edited—MLA endnote/footnote**

    [2]Reuben Brower, ed., *The Tragedy of Coriolanus*, by William Shakespeare (New York: Signet, 1966). Print.

- **Article in a Scholarly Journal—MLA endnote/footnote**

    [3]Laurajane Smith, "Heritage Management as Postprocessual Archaeology?" *Antiquity* 64.259 (1994): 300-09. Print.

- **Article in a Popular Magazine—MLA endnote/footnote**

    [4]Jordan Mackay, "A Murder on Campus," *Texas Monthly* Jan. 2000: 112. Print.

- **Article in a Newspaper—MLA endnote/footnote**

    [5]Richard Rorty, "The Unpatriotic Academy," *New York Times* 13 Feb. 1994: E15. Print.

- **Electronic Source—MLA endnote/footnote**

    [6]Bob Sandberg, *Jackie Robinson in Dodgers Uniform*, *American Memory*, Lib. of Congress, Washington, 1954, Web. 30 Jan. 2000.

How Do You Use APA Documentatin?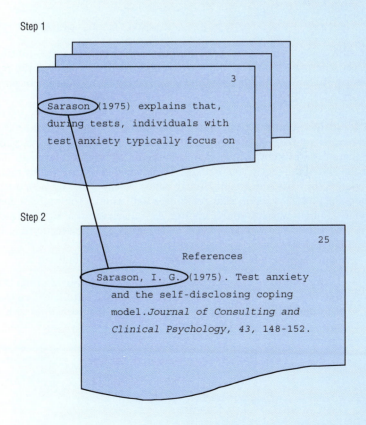

45

APA (American Psychological Association) documentation involves just two basic steps: inserting an in-text note at each point where a paper or project needs documentation (Section 45a) and then recording all sources used in these notes in a References list (Section 45b). A full explanation of APA procedures is provided by the *Publication Manual of the American Psychological Association*, fifth edition (2001). See also <http://www.apa.org/students>.

Step 1

3

Sarason (1975) explains that, during tests, individuals with test anxiety typically focus on

Step 2

25

References

Sarason, I. G. (1975). Test anxiety and the self-disclosing coping model. *Journal of Consulting and Clinical Psychology, 43,* 148-152.

45a Step 1: In the body of your paper, create a note for each source you use.

Each time you introduce material from an outside source into an APA paper, you insert a note to tell readers what your source is and when it was published. You create such notes by using a combination of *parenthetical citations*, which put information about a source between parentheses, and *signal phrases*, which name sources within the normal flow of the sentence. The following example shows how you can combine the two devices when quoting source material in APA documentation style:

Identifies outside source material   Locates source

Zuboff (1988) observes, "While it is true that computer-based automation continues to displace the human body and its know-how (a process . . . known as deskilling), the information power of the technology simultaneously creates pressure for a profound reskilling" **(p. 57)**.

In APA style, you need a page number only when you are quoting directly or citing material you have paraphrased. As you read the following guidelines, you'll see other patterns for citing sources in your paper.

1 Identify sources clearly each time you use them. Whether you introduce sources with parenthetical notes or signal phrases, your readers need to know which source you're using on the references list at the end of the paper you're using. Establish that connection by making sure that the note itself clearly refers to the word by which the source is alphabetized in that references list (usually the author's last name). To help identify sources better, APA also requires that you give the year the source was published, which is always the second item in the reference list entry.

Here are some guidelines to help you create clear in-text notes.

- **Citing a source listed under one person's name.** Mention the individual's *last name*. Provide first and middle initials before the last name when another entry on your reference list begins with an individual having the same last name.

  "Any institution that is going to keep its shape needs to gain legitimacy by distinctive grounding in nature and in reason" (**Douglas, 1986**, p. 112).

Nightingale (1858) reveals that a major cause of deaths in the Crimean War was unsanitary living conditions, not conflict on the battlefield.

- **Citing a source listed under two individuals' names.** Mention the *last names of both individuals*, separated by *and* (or & for parenthetical notes).

  Tarr and Pinker (1990) define *object constancy* as "the ability to recognize an object despite changes in its retinal image" (p. 253).

  Previous research **(Hazelhurst & Hutchins, 1998)** has shown that logical propositions are not so much the product of an innate ability to reason, but rather the result of trying to communicate in a shared world.

- **Citing a source listed under three to five individuals' names.** The first time you cite the source, list the *last name of every person*, separated by commas. Precede the last name in the list with *and* (or & for parenthetical notes). Shorten subsequent notes by naming only the first author followed by the abbreviation *et al.* (Latin for "and others").

  Human experience is somewhat of a conundrum: "Minds awaken in a world. We did not design our world. We simply found ourselves with it" **(Varela, Thompson, & Rosch, 1991**, p. 3) . . . *[later in same paper]* . . . **Varela et al. (1991)** reconcile the Eastern and Western views of human experience in order to . . .

- **Citing a source listed under six or more individuals' names.** Mention only the *last name of the first person*, followed by *et al.*

  Youth who are unsatisfied with their outside obligations have a greater tendency towards risky behavior **(Donohue et al., 2003**).

- **Citing a source listed under the name of a corporation or group.** Give the full name of the organization. If you need to mention the source again, you may use a well-known abbreviation or acronym, providing it in parentheses (or brackets if already in parentheses) after the first citation; use only this short version in subsequent notes.

> In 1999 over 350,000 were home-schooled for religious
> reasons, 38.4% of all home-schooled students (**National**
> **Center for Education Statistics [NCES], 2001**) . . .
> *[later in same paper]* . . . According to the **NCES (2001)**
> . . .

- **Citing a source listed by title.** For sources without authors, the title will appear first in the reference list entry—so in corresponding in-text citations, give a shortened version of the title (including always the first alphabetized word). Italicize titles that are italicized on the References page; place other titles in quotation marks when citing them in in-text notes.

> A tight labor market does not necessarily result in
> greater job satisfaction for those who are already
> employed (**"Job Satisfaction," 2003**).

- **Citing a source that is one of many listed under an author or title.** Do nothing special for most sources, because the year can be used to distinguish the entries. But when two sources are listed under the same name(s) in the same year, distinguish between them by attaching an identifying lowercase letter to the year (*1991a, 1991b*, etc.). The same letter should appear in the date of the corresponding reference list entry.

> The charge is raised by **Rosner (2004a)**, quickly
> answered by **Anderson (2004)**, and then raised again by
> **Rosner (2004b)**.

- **Citing multiple sources in one in-text note.** For multiple works all by one author, provide the years for each source after the name, separating each by a comma. When listing multiple sources by different authors, separate the references by a semicolon when using a parenthetical note; separate them by commas when using a signal phrase. Notice that authors who work with different coauthors are listed separately for each group of collaborators, even when their names appear first in all entries.

> Similar results have been observed in previous studies of the therapeutic effects of music on children with special developmental needs (**Murphy, 1957, 1958; Goldstein, 1964; Goldstein, Lingas & Sheafor, 1965**).

- **Citing sacred texts, classical works, entire Web sites, and unpublished correspondence.** None of these sources needs to be listed on your References page, but they do need to be cited in the body of your paper when used. For sacred texts and classical works (those that are widely available in commonly accepted versions), simply identify the source, naming the version in parentheses after the first reference.

> **Exodus** 22:33-37 (**New American Bible**) provides a basis for assessing and compensating damages in private torts. **Deuteronomy** 25:1-4 further . . .

When referring to an entire Web site (rather than just a page or section), give the name of the site in your signal phrase followed by its Internet address in parentheses (for the first reference only).

> The **U.S. Census Bureau** regularly publishes statistics on homeownership (http://www.census.gov), along with other demographic data.

For unpublished correspondence, name the person who wrote the letter or email in the signal phrase, followed in parentheses by the words *personal correspondence*, a comma, and the date the piece was written.

> According to **Rice (personal correspondence, August 28, 2002)**, . . .

2 Provide page numbers to locate quotations and paraphrased passages.

When you reference a specific passage from a source, you need to provide page numbers—or other kinds of specific reference—in addition to identifying the source and its publication year. Page numbers appear in parentheses just after quoted or paraphrased material. If presented in a parenthetical note with author and year, the page reference follows a comma.

SOURCES WITH STANDARD PAGINATION
Use *p.* or *pp.* before the reference. Use a hyphen to separate page ranges, for example, when a quote runs onto the next page.

(**p. 42**)

(Tannen, 1990, **pp. 130–131**)

(Man, Tam, & Li, 2003, **p. 778**)

SOURCES WITH NO PAGINATION
Indicate the numbering scheme used (¶ for paragraphs, *chap.* for chapter, etc.), and provide a reference number. If no numbering is available, state the heading of the nearest subsection, and identify the paragraph within the section.

(TEA, 1998, **chap. 110.c-d**)

(**¶ 4**)

(Green Day, 2004, **track 2**)

(Cheadle, 2001, **"Methods," ¶ 2-3**)

WORKS WITH TRADITIONAL NUMBERING
Classic works that are divided into precise hierarchical sections need no page references. Instead identify the relevant sections using the standard numbering.

(Aristotle, *Prior Analytics*, **68b.9-15**)

(Mark **10:25**)

3 Place and punctuate parenthetical notes appropriately. Insert citations immediately after the relevant quoted or paraphrased material.

> Predictions that the future would be uniform and sterile are proving to be wrong (**Postrel, 2003**).

If the citation occurs in the middle of a sentence, add no extra punctuation after the closing parentheses, except what may be needed to resume the normal flow of the sentence.

> Statistical analyses (**Levitt & Dubner, 2005**) suggest that what candidates spend on political campaigns matters much less than who they are and how much the public likes them.

When the citation occurs at the end of the sentence, place the parenthetical note before the ending period and after the end quotation mark.

```
Schlosser (2001) claims that fast food is a "revolutionary
force in American life" (p. 3).
```

Step 2: On a separate page at the end of your project, list alphabetically every source you have cited.

This list of sources, titled "References," provides readers with bibliographical information on all the materials you used in composing an article or project. A typical APA References entry includes the following basic information, with many variations.

- **Author(s)**, last name first, followed by a period. Use initials instead of first and middle names.
- **Date** of the work in parentheses, followed by a period. For books and journal articles, provide just the year of publication.
- **Title** of the work, followed by a period. Capitalize only the first word of the title, the first word of a subtitle (if any), and all proper nouns (e.g., *Italy*) or proper adjectives (e.g., *Italian*). Book titles are italicized, but titles of articles are neither italicized nor placed between quotation marks.
- **Publication information.** For books, provide place of publication (followed by a colon) and publisher (followed by a period). For articles, give the title of the journal and the volume number (italicizing both items), followed by relevant page numbers and a period.
- **Online retrieval information.** For online sources, state the date you last viewed the source, the site name, and the online address (URL) or database containing the source. Do not add a period at the end of an entry that concludes with a URL.

```
Retrieved July 27, 2007, from http://
www.drc.utexas.edu
```

The References page itself appears on its own page following the body of the essay (and an endnotes page if there is one). For a full sample References list, see page 508–509. See page 510 for a checklist on setting up a References page. The first entries on a typical References page might look like this.

Subsequent lines indented five spaces | "References" centered | All items double spaced

References

Hawkes, N. (2003, October 13). Monkeys' mind games. *The Times* (London), p. H9.

O'Ehley, J. (2002). Just what do you think you're doing, Dave? [Review of the movie *2001: A Space Odyssey*]. Retrieved August 3, 2003, from http://www.sciflicks.com/2001/ review.html

Suchman, L. A. (1987). *Plans and situated actions: The problem of human-machine communication.* Cambridge, England: Cambridge University Press.

45c APA Models

APA Models Index

(See the inside back cover of this book for an alphabetical index of APA model entries.)

1 APA: Books checklist

BASIC INFORMATION	EXAMPLE (SEE MODEL 1)
Name of author(s) or editor(s)	Pearson, G.
Year of publication	(1949).
Title (italicized)	*Emotional disorders of children.*
Publisher's location	Annapolis, MD:
Publisher	Naval Institute Press.

OTHER INFORMATION:	
Edition number	
Volume number	
Translator's name	
Series name	

1. Book, One Author—APA Cite books by providing author, date, title of book, place of publication, and publisher.

```
IN-TEXT NOTES:

Pearson (1949) found . . .

(Pearson, 1949)

(Pearson, 1949, p. 49)
```

References

```
Pearson, G. (1949). Emotional disorders of children.

        Annapolis, MD: Naval Institute Press.
```

2. Book, Two Authors—APA Notice the ampersand (&) between authors' names in the References list and in parenthetical notes. Note, however, that *and* is used when the authors are identified in the text itself.

IN-TEXT NOTES:

Lasswell and Kaplan (1950) found . . .

(Lasswell & Kaplan, 1950)

(Lasswell & Kaplan, 1950, pp. 210-213)

References

Lasswell, H. D., & Kaplan, A. (1950). *Power and society:*
  A framework for political inquiry. New York: Yale
  University Press.

3. Book, Three or More Authors—APA

IN-TEXT NOTES:

FIRST NOTE. Rosenberg, Gerver, and Howton (1971) found . . .

SUBSEQUENT NOTES. Rosenberg et al. (1971) found . . .

FIRST NOTE. (Rosenberg, Gerver, & Howton, 1971)

SUBSEQUENT NOTES. (Rosenberg et al., 1971)

References

Rosenberg, B., Gerver, I., & Howton, F. W. (1971). *Mass*
  society in crisis: Social problems and social
  pathology (2nd ed.). New York: Macmillan.

If a work has six or more authors, use the first author's name followed by *et al.* for all in-text references, including the first. In the References list, however, identify all the authors.

4. Book, Revised or New Edition—APA

IN-TEXT NOTES:

Philips (1996) found . . .

(Philips, 1996)

(Philips, 1996, p. 62)

References

```
Philips, E. B. (1996). City light: Urban-suburban life
        in the global society (2nd ed.). New York: Oxford
        University Press.
```

5. Book, Edited—APA Notice that APA uses an ampersand (&) to join the names of two editors or authors except when the names are mentioned in the body of a paper.

IN-TEXT NOTES:

```
Journet and Kling (1984) observe . . .
(Journet & Kling, 1984)
```

References

```
Journet, D., & Kling, J. (Eds.). (1984). Readings for
        technical writers. Glenview, IL: Scott, Foresman.
```

6. Book, No Author—APA

IN-TEXT NOTES:

```
In Illustrated Atlas (1985) . . .
(Illustrated Atlas, 1985, pp. 88-89)
```

References

```
Illustrated atlas of the world. (1985). Chicago: Rand
        McNally.
```

When the author of a work is actually listed as "Anonymous," cite the work that way in the References list and parenthetical note.

```
(Anonymous, 1995)
```

7. Work Within a Collection, Anthology, or Reader—APA List the item on the References page by the author of the piece you are actually citing, not the editor(s) of the collection. Then provide the title of the particular selection, its date, the editor(s) of the collection, the title of the collection, the pages on which the selection appears, and publication information.

IN-TEXT NOTES:

Williams, Herman, Liebman, and Dye (1988) find . . .

(Williams, Herman, Liebman, & Dye, 1988)

References

Williams, O. P., Herman, H., Liebman, C. S., & Dye,
T. R. (1988). Suburban differences and metropolitan
policies. In R. L. Warren & L. Lyon (Eds.), *New
perspectives on the American community* (pp.
214-219). Chicago: Dorsey.

8. Brochure or Pamphlet—APA. Describe the work in brackets following the title. Such items may lack authors or publication information. Provide all the details you can find on the document.

IN-TEXT NOTES:

According to the brochure *Welcome to Mac OS X* . . .

(Apple Computer, 2002)

References

Apple Computer. (2002). *Welcome to Mac OS X* [Brochure].

9. Book Chapter or Excerpt—APA List the author(s) of the part first, then the book's date, and the selection's title. Next, list standard book details, inserting pages for the selection in parentheses after the title (and any edition or volume info). List names in normal order when not in the first part of the entry.

IN-TEXT NOTES:

Putnam (2000) concludes . . .

(Putnam, 2000)

References

Putnam, R. D. (2000). Mobility and sprawl. In *Bowling
alone: The collapse and revival of American
community* (pp. 204-215). New York: Simon &
Schuster.

10. Book Review—APA Brackets surround the description of the item reviewed.

IN-TEXT NOTES:

Max (1999) claims . . .

(Max, 1999)

References

Max, D. T. (1999, December 27). All the world's an I.P.O.:
Shakespeare the profiteer [Review of the book
*Shakespeare's 21st-century economics: The morality
of love and money*]. *The New York Observer*, p. 35.

If a review is untitled, identify the author and date and describe the
item in brackets.

IN-TEXT NOTES:

Farquhar (1987) observes . . .

(Farquhar, 1987)

References

Farquhar, J. (1987). [Review of the book *Medical power
and social knowledge*]. *American Journal of
Psychology, 94,* 256.

2 APA: Periodical Articles checklist

BASIC INFORMATION	EXAMPLE (SEE MODEL 11)
Name of author(s) or editor(s)	Tebeaux, E.
Year of publication	(1991).
Title (no " " or underscore)	Ramus, visual rhetoric, and . . .
Name of journal (italicized)	*Written Communication,*
Volume number (italicized)	*8,*
Pages	411–445.

11. Article in a Scholarly Journal—Paged by Volume or Year—
APA Cite articles from such scholarly journals by providing author,
date, title of article, journal, volume, and page numbers.

IN-TEXT NOTES:

Tebeaux (1991) observes . . .

(Tebeaux, 1991, p. 411)

References

Tebeaux, E. (1991). Ramus, visual rhetoric, and the
emergence of page design in medical writing of the
English Renaissance. *Written Communication, 8*,
411–445.

12. Journal Article—Paged by Issue—APA List only the year for the date. Omit the issue if page numbering does not restart at 1 with each issue.

IN-TEXT NOTES

Kennedy (2003) shows . . .

(Kennedy, 2003)

References

Kennedy, M. (2003). Building better schools. *American
School & University, 75*(5), 30–35.

3 APA: Magazine/Newspaper checklist

BASIC INFORMATION	EXAMPLE (SEE MODEL 13)
Name of author(s) or editor(s)	Morton, O.
Date of publication	(2002, August).
Title of article (no " " or italics)	The new air war in Europe.
Name of publication (italicize)	*Wired,*
Pages/sections	76–78.

13. Article in a Monthly Periodical—APA To cite a magazine published monthly, give the author's name, the date (including the month, which is not abbreviated), the title of the article, the name of the magazine and volume number if available (italicized), and the page numbers.

IN-TEXT NOTES:

Morton (2002) notes . . .

(Morton, 2002)

References

Morton, O. (2002, August). The new air war in Europe.
Wired, 76–78.

14. Article in a Weekly or Biweekly Periodical—APA To cite a
weekly or biweekly periodical or magazine, give the author's name,
the date (including month and day), the title of the article, the name
of the magazine, the volume number if available (italicized), and page
numbers.

IN-TEXT NOTES:

Lasch-Quinn (2000) observes . . .

(Lasch-Quinn, 2000)

(Lasch-Quinn, 2000, p. 37)

References

Lasch-Quinn, E. (2000, March 6). Mothers and markets.
The New Republic, 222, 37-44.

15. Newspaper Article, Author Named—APA If the article does not
appear on consecutive pages in the newspaper, give all the page numbers, separated by a comma. Note that abbreviations for *page* (*p.*) and
pages (*pp.*) are used with newspaper entries.

IN-TEXT NOTES:

Brown (2002) suggests . . .

(Brown, 2002, p. A08)

References

Brown, L. (2002, September 28). Funding formula broken,
panel told. *Toronto Star*, p. A08, A11.

16. Newspaper Article, No Author Named—APA

IN-TEXT NOTES:

In the article "Scientists Find" (1994) . . .

("Scientists Find," 1994)

References

Scientists find new dinosaur species in Africa. (1994,
October 14). *The Daily Texan*, p. 3.

4 APA: Web Page checklist

BASIC INFORMATION:	EXAMPLE (SEE MODEL 17)
Creator or author of the site	Johnson, C. W., Jr.
Date of publication in parentheses	(2000, January 31).
Title of page (no " " or italics)	How our laws are made.
Title of site (italicize)	*Thomas.*
Date you examined the site	July 8, 2006.
Web address (no period at end)	Retrieved from http://thomas.loc . . .

17. Web Page, Signed by Author—APA List the author(s), date of posting (or copyright date), the title of the page, and online retrieval information, including date viewed and address.

```
IN-TEXT NOTES:

Cracknell (2006) comments that . . .

(Cracknell, 2006)
```

References

```
Cracknell, R. (2006, March 16). [Review of the movie

        V for Vendetta]. Retrieved August 22, 2006, from

        http://www.theplaza.ca/movie/Films/V/

        v_for_vendetta.html
```

18. Web Page, Unsigned—APA When no author is given, begin the entry with the title of the page.

```
IN-TEXT NOTES:

The "History of Billings" describes . . .

("History of Billings," 2003)
```

References

```
History of Billings. (2003). Retrieved August 29, 2003,

        from Rocky Mountain College Web site: http://

        www.rocky.edu/campus/billings.shtml
```

19. Online Article—Internet-only Periodical—APA Cite like a Web page, but insert the name of the periodical, volume, and pages after the title.

IN-TEXT NOTES:

Allan (2002) found . . .

(Allan, 2002)

References

Allan, A. (2002, March 28). Buffalo soldiers. *Salon.com*,

    1-4. Retrieved October 15, 2003, from http://

    archive.salon.com/people/feature/2002/03/28/

    buffalo_soldiers/

20. Online Article—Same as Print—APA If older articles are organized by issue, cite the source like a print article, inserting *[Electronic
version]* after the title.

IN-TEXT NOTES:

Dittman (2003) concludes . . .

(Dittman, 2003)

References

Dittman, M. (2003, June). Maintaining ethics in a rural

    setting [Electronic version]. *Monitor on*

    Psychology, 34(6), 66.

21. Online Source—Database—APA Simply provide the name of the
database, rather than the online address. You can add an accession
number if one is given, but you do not have to provide the URL of the
online database. Also see Models 37–39.

IN-TEXT NOTES:

Walker, Deng, and Dieser examine . . .

(Walker, Deng, & Dieser, 2001, p. 263)

References

Walker, G. J., Deng, J., & Dieser, R. B. (2001, October).

    Ethnicity, acculturation, self-construal, and

    motivations for outdoor recreation. *Leisure*

    Sciences, 23, 263-283. Retrieved October 31, 2003,

    from Psychology and Behavioral Sciences Collection

    database.

22. Blog—APA Cite like a Web page article with current URL for the site. If the article has been archived, provide the URL for the archive.

IN-TEXT NOTES:

Postrel (2006) argues that . . .

(Postrel, 2006)

References

Postrel, V. (2006, March 26). The box that changed the

world. *Dynamist.com*. Retrieved August 15, 2006, from

http://www.vpostrel.com/weblog/archives/index.html

23. Government Document, Published Online—APA List author, title of the report, date, and online retrieval information.

IN-TEXT NOTES:

According to figures compiled by the Texas Department of

Transportation (2006) . . .

(Texas Department of Transportation [TDOT], 2003)

References

Texas Department of Transportation. (2003). *1-10 East*

corridor study-El Paso, Texas. Retrieved October

20, 2003, from http://www.dot.state.tx.us/

elp/mis/i10east/project.htm

24. Online Abstract, for Article—from Database/Library Subscription Service—APA Cite an online abstract like you would cite the document described in the abstract, but begin the retrieval statement with the phrase *Abstract retrieved from* . . . .

IN-TEXT NOTES:

Cox, Cox, and Cox (2000) found . . .

(Cox, Cox, & Cox, 2000)

References

Cox, B. S., Cox, A. B., & Cox, D. J. (2000). Motivating

signage prompts safety belt use. *Journal of Applied*

Behavior Analysis, 33, 635-638. Abstract retrieved

October 20, 2002, from Social Science Abstracts
database.

25. Online Abstract, for Book—from Database—APA

IN-TEXT NOTES:

Groegor (2000) contends . . .

(Groegor, 2000)

References

Groegor, J. A. (2000). *Understanding driving: Applying
cognitive psychology to a complex everyday task.*
Philadelphia: Psychology Press. Abstract retrieved
October 10, 2003, from PsycINFO database.

26. Online Posting—APA List author, posting date, and subject line, followed by the message identifier (the subject line, number, or other identifier) in brackets, and the URL of the forum (preceded by the phrase *Message posted to . . .*).

IN-TEXT NOTES:

As Olsen (2003) notes, . . .

(Olsen, 2003)

References

Olson, F. M., III. (2003, October 16). [Msg. 4]. Message
posted to http://yourturn.npr.org/cgi-bin/
WebX?230@112.UaIsajPkfPR.43901@.1dd0664c

27. Videotape—APA Recorded media should be cited by indicating the format of the source within brackets after the title. If you are citing a film, give directors, scriptwriters, and producers primary credit.

IN-TEXT NOTES:

Pennebaker (1967/1997) documents . . .

(Pennebaker, 1967/1997)

References

Pennebaker, D. A. (Director). (1997). *Monterey pop*
    [Videotape]. United States: Rhino. (Original date,
    1967)

28. Audio Recording, Generic—APA List first the name given on the byline of the recording. Indicate the format of the source (in brackets) after the title.

IN-TEXT NOTES:

On *Live in San Francisco 1966* (1966/2002), Big Brother and
the Holding Company includes . . .

(Big Brother and the Holding Company, 1966/2002)

References

Big Brother and the Holding Company. *Live in San*
    Francisco 1966 [CD]. Studio City, CA: Verèse
    Sarabande. (2002).

29. Audio Recording—Song—APA If citing a specific song, list the songwriter first, the song's copyright date, the song's title, and person recording the song in brackets (if not the songwriter), all before giving the details for the full recording.

IN-TEXT NOTES:

Cropper and Redding (1967) wrote . . .

(Cropper & Redding, 1967)

References

Cropper, S., & Redding, O. (1967). (Sittin' on) the dock
    of the bay [Recorded by M. Bolton]. *The hunger*
    [CD]. United States: Sony. (1987)

30. Film—Viewed in Theater—APA

IN-TEXT NOTES:

Crowe and Bryce (2000) produced . . .

(Crowe & Bryce, 2000)

References

Crowe, C. (Writer/Director/Producer), & Bryce, I.

    (Producer). (2000). *Almost famous* [Motion picture].

    United States: Dreamworks.

31. Radio Broadcast—APA List producers, directors, and scriptwriters first. If applicable, name a specific episode before the program title.

IN-TEXT NOTES:

King Biscuit Entertainment (2003) created . . .

(King Biscuit Entertainment, 2003)

References

King Biscuit Entertainment (Producer). (2003, July 6).

    King Biscuit flower hour [Radio program]. Santa

    Rosa, CA: KMGG.

32. TV Show, Specific Episode—APA

IN-TEXT NOTES:

In one episode, Kuhn and Fefernan (2003) highlight . . .

(Kuhn & Fefernan, 2003)

References

Kuhn, R. L. (Creater/Host), & Fefernan, L.

    (Director/Producer). (2003, May 13). What makes music

    so significant? [Television series episode]. In L.

    Fefernan, *Closer to the truth*. Los Angeles: KCET.

33. Research Report—APA When no individual authors are given, list the agency or institution as the author of the report. If the report is part of a series, identify the series within parentheses as it is given on the title page. If the agency responsible for the report also published it, give "Author" as the publisher.

IN-TEXT NOTES:

The National Endowment for the Arts [NEA] (2004) collected

data from . . .

(National Endowment for the Arts [NEA], 2004. p. 3)

References

National Endowment for the Arts. (2004). *Reading at
    risk: A survey of literary reading in America*
    (Research Division Report #46). Washington, DC:
    Author.

34. Conference Paper, Unpublished—APA Academic papers read at conferences but not subsequently published may be cited simply by identifying the meeting and location.

IN-TEXT NOTES:

Tebeaux (2005) explains . . .

(Tebeaux, 2005)

References

Tebeaux, E. (2005, March). The evolution of technical
    writing: From text to visual text in applied
    discourse. Paper presented at the annual meeting of
    the Conference on College Composition and
    Communication, San Francisco.

35. Conference Paper, Published—APA Identify the paper and then give the title of the proceedings or publication following "In." Identify the editor if one is given.

IN-TEXT NOTES:

Matthews, Fong, and Mankoff (2005) suggest that . . .

(Matthews, Fong, & Mankoff, 2005)

References

Matthews, T., Fong, J., & Mankoff, J. (2005).
    Visualizing non-speech sounds for the deaf.
    In *Assets 2005. The seventh international ACM
    SIGACCESS conference on computers and
    accessibility.* (pp. 52-59). New York: ACM
    Press.

36. Library Service—Journal Article—APA To cite an article you find in a library subscription database, provide author, date, title of the article, and complete publication information. Then explain when and where the information was found. You can provide additional information if helpful, inlcuding an item or accession number. But you need not supply a lengthy URL.

```
IN-TEXT NOTES:
Gosling et al. (2004) speculate that . . .
(Gosling, Vazire, Srivastava, & John, 2004, p. 97)
```

References

```
Gosling, S., Vazire, S., Srivastava, S., & John, O.P.
    (2004) Should we trust Web-based studies? A
    comparative analysis of six preconceptions about
    Internet questionnaires. American Psychologist, 59,
    93-104. Retrieved May 29, 2006, from PsycINFO
    database.
```

37. Library Service—Magazine Article—APA Treat the magazine as you would a print item. But also furnish the date of access and the name of the database used.

```
IN-TEXT NOTES:
Harrison (2005) reports . . .
(Harrison, 2005, p. 51)
```

References

```
Harrison, B. R. (2005, September 15). Phantom of the
    bayou. Natural History, 18-52. Retrieved
    March 15, 2006, from Academic Search Premier
    database.
```

38. Library Service—Newspaper Article—APA How you identify the database may vary. You can cite a general database such as LexisNexis or provide the URL of the newspaper you searched.

```
IN-TEXT NOTES:

Toner (2005) reports . . .

(Toner, 2005)
```

References

```
Toner, M. (2005, October 13). Back to the moon. Atlanta
    Journal-Constitution. Retrieved May 11, 2006, from
    LexisNexis database.
```

39. Library Service—Encyclopedia Entry—APA Many libraries subscribe to online encyclopedias or reference works. Cite the entry you have consulted and provide a date of access and URL. The *Britannica Online* usually provides a preferred URL.

```
IN-TEXT NOTES:

According to the Encyclopedia Britannica (2006),

Schnauzers typically . . .

("Schnauzer," 2006)
```

References

```
Schnauzer. (2006) In Encyclopedia Britannica. Retrieved
    May 29, 2006, from Encyclopedia Britannica Online
    at http://search.eb.com/eb/article-9066176
```

45d Sample Empirical Research Paper—APA

The following APA-style research report was written by Jessica Carfolite at the University of South Carolina. In structure and language, it represents the kind of essays routinely prepared in psychology courses: it includes a title page, an abstract, a statement of hypothesis, and sections explaining method and results, a formal discussion section, references, and two tables. Carfolite's paper assumes that readers will be familiar with many technical terms and statistical procedures, as well as various research conventions in the field. Not every part of the paper will be easily accessible to every reader, but that is often the case with research in various scientific disciplines.

checklist 45.1

Parts of a Research Report—APA

When presenting the results of an empirical study, divide your paper into the following sections. Provide a header at the beginning of each section. Each header should be centered on a separate line. You can also create subsections (see, for example, the Method section in the sample paper), which should begin with an italicized header (on a separate line) aligned to the left-hand margin. Note that some sections should start on a new page.

a. **Title page.** This page presents the title of the study, and identifies the researchers and their affiliations. (See also Checklist 45.2.)

b. **Abstract.** The abstract is a concise summary of the paper. Start the abstract on a separate page. (See also Checklist 45.3.)

c. **Introduction.** The introduction is the first section of the main text of the paper. In this section you present your hypothesis and a review of literature related to your study. Unlike the other sections, don't begin the introduction with a header—instead, repeat the title of the paper you placed on the title page. Start this section on a new page.

d. **Method.** This section provides a detailed description of the procedures used in the research. Because the validity of the research depends on how the data were gathered, this is a critical section for readers assessing the report. Don't start this section on a new page—start this section on the line immediately following the Introduction section.

e. **Results.** This section reports the data, often given through figures, charts, graphs, and so on. The reliability of the data is explained here, but little comment is made on the study's implications. Don't start this section on a new page—start this section on the line immediately following the Method section.

f. **Discussion/Conclusions.** Here you analyze and interpret the data presented in the Results section. Don't start this section on a new page—start this section on the line immediately following the Results section.

g. **References.** As covered in Section 45b, this section is an alphabetized list of research materials cited in the report. Begin this section on a new page. (See also Checklist 45.6.)

h. **Appendixes.** Provide, in consecutively lettered appendixes, materials germane to the study but too lengthy to include in the body of the paper. You might, for example, provide a copy of a questionnaire you presented to participants in Appendix A, provide a copy of your consent form in Appendix B, and so on.

Assessing Social Skills Measurements 1

1/2 inch

5 spaces

Assessing Social Skills Measurements in

Middle School Students

Jessica Carfolite

University of South Carolina

checklist 45.2

Formatting Title Pages—APA

APA style requires a separate title page; use the preceding page excerpt as a model and apply the following guidelines:

a. **Choose an effective title.** Don't state the obvious, that you're presenting the results of a study. Instead, state the key variables you're researching.

b. **Present the title of your paper, centered, on the upper half of the page.** Capitalize all words *except* articles (*a*, *an*, and *the*), prepositions and conjunctions that are shorter than four letters.

c. **List your first name, middle initial, and last name, centered under the title.**

d. **List your institutional affiliation under your name, centered on the page.**

e. **Make sure the title page is numbered like the rest of your paper.** The page header should include (aligned to the right) a shortened title of the paper (two or three words) and the page number *1*. Separate the page number and shortened title by five spaces.

f. **For an article that will be published**, indicate at the top of the page what the running head for the essay should be in all caps. Running heads should not exceed fifty characters.

g. **Repeat the title at the top of the first page of the body of the paper.** Center the title on the top line(s) of the first page of the body of the paper.

Assessing Social Skills Measurements   2

Abstract

This study investigates the validity of the newly developed Social Activities Questionnaire (SAQ) for measuring children's social skills relative to an established measure, the Social Skills Rating System (SSRS). Based on data from 34 middle school students and their parents who were participating in an after-school program for children with learning or behavior problems, the SAQ was found to have small-to-moderate correlations with the widely used SSRS. However, unlike the SSRS, the SAQ showed moderate correlations with children's grade point averages in school, which research suggests is an important predictor of children's social success. This study suggests the SAQ is a promising measurement tool that should be subjected to further development and validation studies with larger and more diverse samples.

checklist 45.3 ⌐ Creating an Abstract—APA

Abstracts are common in papers using APA style and are required for articles submitted for publication.

a. **Place the abstract on a separate page after the title page.** This page should have the same spacing and margins as the rest of the document.

b. **Make sure the running head and correct page number (2) appears at the top of the page.**

c. **Insert the heading *Abstract* on the first line of the body of the page.** Start the paragraph containing the abstract on the following line.

d. **Do not indent the first line of the abstract.** Present the paragraph containing the abstract in block form, unlike paragraphs in the body of your paper.

e. **Summarize the paper accurately and concisely (120 or fewer words).** To be accurate, avoid discussing material not treated in the body of the paper. Also, avoid using abbreviations or references that aren't clear within the abstract itself—which is usually intended to be read as a stand-alone description of the paper. Describe in the abstract the problem or issue treated, the type of research used, and conclusions drawn from the study.

Assessing Social Skills Measurements

in Middle School Students

Effective social functioning can be a protective factor for students struggling with successful middle school adjustment. Skills Training (SST) intervention to improve a child's functioning is often employed, but it repeatedly fails to attain generalization (Gresham, 1998). One of the limitations in prior research on SST programs is the lack of empirically valid tools to measure social functioning. To address this issue, this study investigates the validity of the newly developed Social Activities Questionnaire (SAQ). This paper begins by addressing the complex and often ambiguous definition of social skills. It then explains the importance of social competence to children in the middle school age group. It also describes problems with past measurement tools and the recently proposed development. Finally, the introduction states the hypotheses for this study.

Importance of Social Functioning

Repeatedly, researchers have found evidence that poor peer adjustment can put children at risk for later difficulties in life. Peer interactions affect the development of social competence, and, if children are not accepted by peers, they are more likely to lack key social competencies (Parker & Asher, 1987). Conversely, positive peer relations may buffer the other vulnerabilities children experience. For instance, research shows that peer acceptance, as well as the number and quality of friendships, relates to loneliness

checklist 45.4

Document Formatting—APA

a. **Use white, 8 1/2-by-11-inch bond paper with at least 1-inch margins.** You can easily set margins by adjusting the document's Page Setup.

b. **Use 12-point Times, American Typewriter, or Courier font faces** when available. If not available, use a readable font.

c. **Double-space the entire document.** This includes the References page and title page. In certain circumstances you may use single-spacing to improve readability, for example, with tables, captions, and extended block quotations.

d. **Indent the first word of each paragraph 1/2 inch.** Note that the Abstract and the Reference pages do not follow this standard indentation.

e. **Left-align the body of the paper and do not hyphenate words.**

f. **Insert a shortened title for your paper and consecutive page numbers 1/2 inch from the top of *every* page, aligned to the right.** The best way to achieve this is to insert a running page header.

and depression of children (Nagle & Erdley, 2001).
Research on social competence in schools has found lower
substance abuse and a decrease in aggression and
emotional distress among socially skilled students
(Hartup, 1996).

Because social skills lessen the day-to-day
frustrations adolescents face in schools, it is not
surprising that they might also enhance academic
performance. Social skills create a "social context" for
learning by providing rules and role expectations for
students. As a result, social skills can facilitate
academic success by working in tandem with learning
goals (Maleki & Elliott, 2002). But it is not
necessarily social competence that leads to academic
competence. It is possible that academic competence
leads to social competence. Welsh, Park, Widaman, and
O'Neil (2001) found that academic competence in first
grade influenced second grade social competence. Thus
there is probably a reciprocal relationship between
social competence and academic performance. Success in
one arena likely promotes success in the other.
Conversely, problems with teachers and peers might
obstruct learning, while difficulties in academics might
create a stigma that causes social problems.

Defining Social Skills

Despite the hundreds of published studies on the
topic, there is no general consensus on what constitutes
"social skills" and how they should be measured in
children. Several studies have defined social skills in
terms of peer acceptance or popularity (Asher, Oden, &

Assessing Social Skills Measurements   5

Gottman, 1977). These definitions do not actually target the social skills themselves, but the outcome of using them. Other studies define social skills by actual behavior, such as the ability to start a conversation, make a joke, or resist the urge to interrupt mid-conversation (Foster & Ritchey, 1979). Still others look at a combination of social behaviors and levels of peer acceptance (Asher, 1978).

Social validity, a term coined by Gresham (2001), defines social skills as socially significant behaviors exhibited in specific situations that predict important social outcomes. These outcomes might include friendships, teacher and parent acceptance, and even school adjustment. Gresham's emphasis on establishing the social validity of interpersonal behaviors helps to focus social skills measurement and intervention on specific behaviors and outcomes important for current and future functioning.

Development of the SAQ

The SAQ was designed to measure outcomes of social skills training. The SAQ questions are direct, short, and easy to answer. Parents complete a report of 12 items about the social activities of their child. Items were selected based on a combination of practical experiences, mostly social outcome-related treatment goals, in the Challenging Horizon's Program (CHP). The final version of the SAQ was refined by suggestions made by the research staff of faculty advisors, graduate students, CHP counselors and parents at James Madison University. This study is one of the first empirical tests of the SAQ.

Assessing Social Skills Measurements   6

Statement of Hypotheses

The purpose of this study is to explore the predictive validity of the Social Activities Questionnaire (SAQ). It is expected that the SAQ and the SSRS should moderately correlate and these scales should also predict grade point average (GPA) and disciplinary referrals among children.

Method

Participants

The participants of this study are the 34 middle school students and 34 parents who completed and returned the survey packet. The sample was taken from the Challenging Horizons Program, an after-school program for students with AD/HD at Hand Middle School and Crayton Middle School in Columbia, South Carolina. Approximately 47% of the students in the study had screened positive for AD/HD, based on rating scales completed by parents or due to a parent-report that the student had previously been clinically diagnosed with AD/HD.

Crayton Middle School has approximately 936 students in grades 6-8. The racial distribution is: 45% black, 50% white, and 5% other. Forty-six percent of the students live at or below poverty level. Hand Middle School has approximately 958 students in grades 6-8. The racial distribution is 50% black, 47% white, and 3% other. Nearly half of the students live at or below the poverty level. The gender distribution for the study was: 70.5% male and 29.5% female. For the study, the grade distribution was: 50% sixth grade, 44% seventh grade, and 6% eighth grade.

Assessing Social Skills Measurements   7

Measures

The measures in this study consisted of 1) the Social Activities Questionnaire, 2) the Social Skills Rating System for Parents, 3) the Social Skills Rating System for Students, 4) Grade Point Averages for the 2004-2005 school year, and 5) disciplinary referrals for the 2004-2005 school year.

SAQ. The Social Activities Questionnaire (SAQ) is designed to be an objective measure of adolescent social activities with peers. Question 1 asks the actual number of friends with the criteria that they be "within 2 years of the child's age, not related to the child and that they spend time with the child outside of school, at least once a month." Question 2 inquires how many children live within walking distance of the child's school; it is used for interpretive value. The following eight questions ask about specific activities and the rate of those activities, for example: "My child invites friends over _____ times in a typical month," or "My child participated in _____ organized activities over the past year."

Other SAQ questions describe the quality of interactions during these activities, for example: "the time my child spends with friends often ends with one or both children angry" or "some of my child's friends use alcohol, tobacco or other prohibited substances." The final item asks about the percentage of time the child spends alone, with friends, and with family. The SAQ is an experimental measure with no published reliability or validity studies.

SSRS. The Social Skills Rating System (Gresham & Elliot, 1990) provides components for teachers, parents, and students to evaluate student social behaviors. These components can be used separately or together. For practical reasons related to the challenges of getting teacher data, this study used only the parent and student versions. The questionnaire is broken into five subscales that make up the total social skills score. Both the SSRS-Parent and SSRS-Student measure cooperation, assertion, and self-control. The SSRS-Parent version also measures responsibility and the SSRS-Student version also measures empathy. Research supports the reliability (.77 to .84 for parents; .52 to .66 for students) and validity for this social skills rating system (Gresham & Elliot, 1990).

Procedures

Permission was granted through Richland One School District to administer the SSRS-Student version to the students of the Challenging Horizons Program. After the students completed the SSRS-Student version, they were given a packet to take home to be filled out by their parent or guardian. Each packet included a self-addressed stamped envelope, the SAQ, the EERE, and a letter explaining the forms within the packet. The participants were asked to mail the two forms back in the stamped envelope provided or send it back with their children. Each child that filled out an SSRS-Student version received a small candy, and each child that returned a completed packet received a large candy bar of his or her choice.

Data Analysis Plan

 The hypothesis, which asks whether there might be correlations between the social skills scores, GPA, and number of disciplinary referrals, was tested with bivariate correlations with a statistical significance level of $p = .05$ (see Tables 1 and 2). It is noteworthy that this study had low statistical power. Specifically, the power to find a small- to moderate-sized correlation (i.e., $r = 0.20$, according to Cohen's conventions) was only .30 (with a directional alpha of .05). Given this low power, these non-significant statistical findings might be a series of Type II errors. Therefore, it is worthwhile to examine effect sizes. Because correlations with an absolute value greater than .20 were considered large enough to be interesting, these correlations are highlighted in Tables 1 and 2.

Results

 While it was hypothesized that GPA and disciplinary records would correlate with both social skills scales, none were statistically significant. However, there were correlations greater than .20, which are highlighted in boldface type in Tables 1 and 2. When examining the predictive power of the SSRS and SAQ for grade point average and disciplinary referrals, it appears that the SAQ items 9 and 10 were correlated with grade point average correlations (see Table 1). In addition, the SAQ detects a positive correlation between question 10, "Some of my child's closest friends use alcohol, tobacco or other prohibited substances" and the number of disciplinary referrals (see Table 1). Table 2 shows that the SSRS does not have those same predictive features for GPA and disciplinary referrals.

Discussion

This is a preliminary investigation into the construct validity of the Social Activities Questionnaire (SAQ), which is designed to measure important social behaviors of middle-school aged children. While it was hypothesized that the SAQ and the SSRS rating scales would be moderately correlated, at first glance, the data supports little to no convergent validity between these scales. In addition, the failure to find statistically significant correlations between the GPA and disciplinary referrals raises questions about the concurrent validity of the SAQ and the SSRS.

It is important to note that, as stated in the data analysis plan, this study was limited by low statistical power and, therefore, it may be appropriate to examine effect sizes. Indeed, examining the effect size does show some interesting results. Most notable were the positive correlations between the GPA scores and the scores on the SAQ, especially since the SSRS did not show correlations between the two. This suggests that the SAQ may be more ecologically valid than the SSRS because it is a better predictive tool for a critically important variable, GPA.

This study was limited by a small sample size, and future research should have a larger sample and a much larger and more diverse population. Despite these weaknesses, the study does provide unique information

Assessing Social Skills Measurements   11

about a new social skills assessment tool. Although the
results of this study are modest, there are indications
this SAQ might be an even better tool for predictor
variables like GPA than are scales like the SSRS.

In future studies, it is recommended that the
users of the SAQ consider some modifications. For
instance, it would be helpful to have the parents
indicate their level of confidence in each question.
This type of question, and other questions, might be
used to create an index of parental monitoring, which
has been shown to be an important predictor of outcomes
in middle school students. It would also improve the
questionnaire to know about the availability of
activities for the student and to create indices that
look at the ratio of engagement in available
activities. These recommended additions might improve
the overall assessment of the SAQ.

1 inch 1/2 inch

Assessing Social Skills Measurements 12

References

Asher, S. (1978). Children's peer relations. In

M. Lamb (Ed.), *Social and personality development.*

New York: Holt, Rinehart, & Winston.

Asher, S. R., Oden, S. L., & Gottman, J. M. (1977).

Children's friendships in school settings. In

L. G. Katz (Ed.), *Current topics in early*

childhood education (Vol. 1, pp. 32-61). Norwood,

NJ: Ablex.

Cohen, J. (1992). A power primer. *Psychological*

Bulletin, 112, 155-159.

Foster, S. L., & Ritchey, W. L. (1979). Issues in

the assessment of social competence in children.

Journal of Applied Behavior Analysis, 12,

625-638.

Gresham, F. (1998). Social skills training: Should we

raze, remodel, or rebuild? *Behavioral Disorders,*

24, 19-25.

Gresham, F., & Elliott, S. (1990). *Social skills rating*

system manual. Circle Pines, MN: American Guidance

Service.

Gresham, F., Sugai, G., & Horner, R. (2001). Interpreting

outcomes of social skills training for students

with high-incidence disabilities. *Exceptional*

Children, 67, 331-344. [Electronic Version]

Hartup, W. W. (1996). The company they keep:

Friendships and their developmental significance.

Child Development, 67, 1-13.

double space

1/2 inch

1 inch

1 inch

1 inch

Maleki, Christine, & Elliott, S. (2002). Children's
    social behaviors as predictors of academic
    achievement: A longitudinal analysis. *School
    Psychology Quarterly, 17,* 1–23.

Nagle, D., & Erdley, C., (2001). The role of friendship
    in psychological adjustment. [Special issue].
    *New Directions for Child and Adolescent
    Development,* 91.

Parker, J., & Asher, S. (1987). Peer relations and later
    personal adjustment: Are low-accepted children at
    risk? *Psychological Bulletin, 102,* 357–389.

Welsh, M., Parke, R., Widaman, K., & O'Neil, R. (2001).
    Linkages between children's social and academic
    competence: A longitudinal analysis. *Journal of
    School Psychology, 39,* 463–481.

checklist 45.5

Formatting Reference Pages—APA

Begin the References list on a separate page. Use the same formatting you used for the rest of the document, including double-spaced paragraphs, headers at the top of the page (with numbers and a shortened version of the paper's title), and 1-inch margins. But make the following adjustments:

a. **Center the title (References) at the top of the page.** If the list of entries runs over to a new page, do not repeat this title at the top.

b. **Create a 1/2 inch or 5 to 7 space hanging indentation for each entry.** In other words, the first line should be aligned with the left margin, while subsequent lines in an individual entry should be indented. (You can create hanging indentations easily by adjusting the paragraph settings for this page.)

c. **List all sources referenced in the body of the paper.** See Section 45b-1 for a list of sources that don't need to appear on the References page. Don't list sources you viewed, but don't reference in the body of your paper.

d. **Alphabetize the list according to the first word in each entry**—excluding articles (*a, an,* and *the*). When an individual appears first for entries as both single author and coauthor, place the single-author entries first, alphabetizing subsequent entries by the second (or third, or fourth, if necessary) coauthor.

e. **Proof carefully your punctuation and capitalization for each entry.** Review the guidelines for formatting individual entries. Pay close attention to the punctuation and capitalization used in the models in Section 45c.

Table 1

Grade Point Average and Disciplinary Referrals and
Social Activities Questionnaire

SAQ Questions	GPA	Disciplinary Referrals
1-friends not related, within 2 years, spends time once a month	**0.20**	−0.06
2-# of children within 2 years of age, within walking distance	0.03	−0.06
3-Invites friends over X times in a month	−0.08	0.12
4-Spends time with friends X times in a month	0.11	0.10
5-Participates in X activities in the past year	**0.30**	−0.02
6-Number of leadership roles in these activities	0.11	0.08
7-Amount of time on the phone	**−0.23**	0.15
8-Amount of time instant messaging (ICQ, AOL)	−0.10	0.12
9-Frequency of time spent with friends with one or both children angry	**−0.25**	0.01
10-Frequency of friends who use alcohol, tobacco, or like substances	**−0.34**	**0.27**
11-frequency of friends who are in trouble with authority	−0.32	0.16
Free Time Alone	**0.38**	**−0.34**
Free Time Friends	−0.08	0.11
Free Time Family	−0.16	−0.03

Note: Values are Pearson Product Moment Correlation Coefficients. All *p* values were greater than .05 (df=33). Correlations with an absolute value greater than .20 are printed in boldface type.

Table 2

Parent and Student Social Skills Rating System and GPA and Disciplinary Referrals

	Parent Cooperation	Parent Assertion	Parent Self-Control	Parent Responsibility	Parent Standard Score
DR	0.16	0.00	0.13	−0.15	0.01
GPA	0.14	**0.20**	0.07	0.17	0.12

	Student Cooperation	Student Assertion	Student Empathy	Student Self-Control	Student Standard Score
DR	0.14	0.04	0.10	**0.25**	0.01
GPA	0.15	**0.24**	0.17	0.04	0.18

Note: Values are Pearson product moment correlation coefficients. All *p* values were greater than .05 (*df*=33). Correlations with an absolute value greater than .20 are printed in boldface type.

checklist 45.6

Formatting Quotations, Tables, and Figures—APA

a. **Format long and short quotations correctly.** APA uses standard guidelines for presenting short quotations. (See Chapter 42.) Format long quotations—40 words or more—in block format. A *block quotation* is *not* enclosed by quotation marks, and it starts on a new line after the sentence introducing it. The entire quotation is indented 1/2 inch. Place a parenthetical citation for a block quotation after the final punctuation mark for the entire quote.

b. **Label and number tables.** Tables may be placed within the text in student theses, but ordinarily they appear at the end of a manuscript, one table per page. Provide the label *Table*, an identifying number, and a caption, italicized and capitalized. (Use the rules for paper titles in Checklist 45.2b.) Present any necessary explanatory or analytical information below the table, double-spaced. Keep such information brief.

c. **Label and number graphs and other visual material.** Place the item as close as possible to the related text or at the end of the paper, providing underneath the label *Figure*, an identifying number, and (optionally) a label.

d. **Insert footnotes to display copyright information.** Insert any footnotes (numbered consecutively) documenting all permissions information needed for quoted material not covered by academic fair use.

How Do You Use CMS Documentati⦿n?

46

Writers who prefer full footnotes or endnotes rather than in-text notes often use the humanities style of documentation recommended in *The Chicago Manual of Style* (15th ed., 2003) now also available in an online version. Basic procedures for this CMS documentary-note system are spelled out in the following sections. If you encounter documentation problems not discussed below or prefer the author-date style of CMS documentation, refer to the full manual or to *A Manual for Writers of Term Papers, Theses, and Dissertations* (6th ed., 1996), by Kate L. Turabian. (Although the latter is not updated to reflect the latest CMS citation guidelines, it is still used by many colleges to set formatting requirements for formal papers.)

e·t·i·p·s

Do you have specific questions about Chicago style or more general queries about editing? Check out the lively Q & A page supported by the manuscript editing department at the University of Chicago Press. Go to <http://www.press.uchicago.edu/> and link to the *Chicago Manual of Style* site.

Because notes in CMS humanities style include full publishing information, separate bibliographies are optional in CMS-style papers. However, both notes and bibliographies are covered below.

46a How does CMS documentation work?

Whereas MLA and APA styles use *in-text notes* together with *works cited* or *references* lists to document outside sources (see Chapters 44 and 45), CMS style uses *footnotes* or *endnotes*. Footnotes offer a fairly simple and traditional method of citation. A raised, or *superscript*, reference number (like this[2]) appears in the body of the paper where a writer quotes from, borrows from, or refers to another's work. These superscript numbers in the body of the paper correspond to numbered notes that appear at the bottom of a page. The notes include all bibliographic information necessary to identify outside sources, as well as page numbers to direct readers to specific locations in these items. No separate bibliography page is necessary—though one may be included (see Section 46d).

Writers using CMS style may have the option of using *endnotes*. Endnotes appear at the end of the paper rather than in the footer of each page. Footnotes work better for longer papers because endnotes require readers to flip to the end of the document to view details for each source. We provide guidelines that apply to both endnotes and footnotes, but Chicago style discourages endnotes. Consult with your instructor to determine which type of note he or she prefers.

46b How do you use CMS footnotes and endnotes?

There are two kinds of notes: *reference notes* that acknowledge the use of outside sources and *content notes* that add supplementary material and commentary to the paper. This chapter focuses on *reference notes*, which are necessary for proper citation. (Use content notes to include information you regard as important, but that might derail the train of thought if included in the main text.) Whether using reference notes, content notes, or both, number them all consecutively according to their order of appearance in the body of the paper.

1 Insert a raised note number after each passage you cite. To insert the number, use your word processor's footnote or endnote feature, which will format the raised number correctly (in *superscript* typestyle) and automatically number and order the notes. Place the note number after the material being documented, either at the end of the sentence or at the first natural pause after the borrowed material. Note numbers appear outside end quotation marks:

```
Ralph Bunche never wavered in his belief that the races in
America had to learn to live together: "In all of his
experience of racial discrimination Bunche never allowed
himself to become bitter."[3] . . .
```

You may also briefly identify sources in the body of your paper, especially as you introduce quotations, paraphrased passages, or borrowed ideas. Consult Section 42a for more on how to introduce quotations effectively.

2 Document a source fully in the first note it is mentioned. Whether you use endnotes or footnotes, provide full bibliographic details for a source the first time you cite it. After the full citation, give a page reference (preceded by a comma) to the relevant passage in the source:

> 3. Brian Urquart, *Ralph Bunche: An American Life*
>
> (New York: Norton, 1993), 435.

Note: You don't need a page reference in your note when you simply mention a source, rather than a specific passage within it. But *always* provide specific location references (as specific as possible) when you quote from or paraphrase another person's writing.

3 Shorten subsequent notes for sources you've already fully documented. Simply mention the last name of the author, a shortened title (four or fewer words), and a page reference.

> 4. Helen Wilkinson, "It's Just a Matter of Time,"
>
> *Utne Reader*, May/June 1995, 67.
>
> 5. Urquhart, *Ralph Bunche*, 177.
>
> 6. Wilkinson, "Matter of Time," 66.

This shortened format is sometimes used when a full bibliography is provided at the end of the paper. (See Section 46d.) Readers can use the last name and title to look up a works-cited entry that contains full citation details for a source. Consult the requirements of your paper to determine whether a bibliography is required and whether shortened notes are accepted.

Finally, you can shorten references to the same source in consecutive notes by using the Latin abbreviation *Ibid.* ("from the same place"):

> 7. Simon Singh, *The Code Book: The Science of Secrecy*
>
> *from Ancient Egypt to Quantum Cryptography* (New York:
>
> Anchor Books, 1999), 293.
>
> 8. Ibid., 303-304.

4 Use in-text parenthetical notes for numerous citations of one source. To cite multiple passages from one source, you may use a string of *Ibid.* notes. But consider using in-text parenthetical notes instead, especially when repeatedly citing well-known works (sacred texts, etc.) that are identified by standard abbreviations and numbering schemes. Simply provide full bibliographic details for the edition you're using in the first note, along with the abbreviation you will use in-text.

> 7. William Shakespeare, *Measure for Measure*, in
> *The Complete Works of Shakespeare*, 4th ed., ed. David
> Bevington (New York: Longman, 1997), act 1, sc. 3, ll.
> 39-43 (hereafter cited in-text as *MM* by act, scene, and
> line).

A subsequent parenthetical citation would look like this: The Duke exclaims, "O heavens, what stuff is here?" (*MM* 3.2.4).

46c   How do you format CMS footnotes and endnotes?

Both footnotes and endnotes are indented, beginning with the number of the note formatted in regular typestyle (not *superscript*). Footnotes appear at the bottom of a page preceded by a 1½-inch horizontal rule (usually inserted automatically by your word processor).

> 11. Karl P. Wentersdorf, "Hamlet's Encounter with the
> Pirates," *Shakespeare Quarterly* 34 (1983): 434-35.
> 12. Don Graham, "Wayne's World," *Texas Monthly*,
> March 2000, 110-11.

Endnotes begin on a separate page titled *Notes*. Single-space each note, double-spacing between them. As for the content of the note, follow the guidelines given here.

Basic Parts of CMS Footnotes and Endnotes

CMS notes have five basic parts. All items within a note are separated by commas and the entire citation ends with a period.

- **Author.** Each entry usually begins with the names of the author(s) or artist(s), but some begin with the names of other contributors (a book's editor, a movie's director, etc.). List all names in normal order: first name/last name. When four or more individuals are given for the source, list only the first person and the phrase *and others*. When giving primary acknowledgment to those not identified as the source's main author, provide an abbreviation to indicate their contribution (Dan Seward, ed.).

- **Title.** Capitalize the first word and all other words in the title, except articles (*a, an,* and *the*), prepositions, and coordinating conjunctions. Place the titles of longer works in italics and enclose the titles of shorter works in quotation marks. Place all titles that appear within titles in quotation marks.

- **Secondary Acknowledgments.** Some works are the result of many types of contributor: authors, editors, and translators for books; directors, performers, and scriptwriters for films; and so on. After the title of the source, list the names (in normal order) of those (besides the primary author) given credit for creating the work. Precede the names with an abbreviation indicating the form of contribution.

- **Publication or Production Information.** This part of a footnote can be the most complicated—especially when dealing with electronic documents—but you're always providing three key details: who published the source, where, and when. The models on the following pages provide examples of the types of publication information you should list for various kinds of sources.

- **Location Reference.** List the page number (or chapter, or section title, etc.) where the material you are citing appears in the source. This reference should be as specific as possible when citing quotations or paraphrased passages. It can be less specific or omitted when referring to the source as a whole.

> 1. Sandra Cisneros, *The House on Mango Street* (Houston: Arte Público Press, 1983), 89.
>
> 2. Gregory Nava, prod., "La Casa," *American Family*, perf. Raquel Welch and others, PBS, November 23, 2003.

46d CMS bibliographies

At the end of your paper, list alphabetically every source cited or used in the paper. This list is usually titled "Works Cited" when it includes only works actually mentioned in the essay; it is titled "Bibliography" if it also includes works consulted in preparing the paper but not actually cited. Because CMS notes are quite thorough, a Works Cited or Bibliography page may be optional, depending on the assignment: check with your instructor or editor about including such a page. Individual items on a Works Cited or Bibliography page are single-spaced, with a double space between each item.

When an author has more than one work on the list, those works are listed alphabetically under the author's name using this form.

```
Altick, Richard D. The Shows of London. Cambridge:
     Belknap-Harvard University Press, 1978.

——. Victorian People and Ideas. New York: Norton, 1973.

——. Victorian Studies in Scarlet. New York: Norton, 1977.
```

46e CMS models

In this section you will find the CMS notes and bibliography forms for a variety of sources. The numbered items in the list are the sample note forms, often showing specific page numbers as would be the case when you were preparing actual notes; the matching bibliography entries appear immediately after.

1. Book, One Author—CMS Provide author(s), title of the work (underlined or italicized), place of publication, publisher, and date of publication.

> 1. Steven Weinberg, *Dreams of a Final Theory* (New York: Pantheon Books, 1992), 38.

Weinberg, Steven. *Dreams of a Final Theory*. New York: Pantheon Books, 1992.

2. Book, Two or Three Authors or Editors—CMS

> 2. Peter Collier and David Horowitz. *Destructive Generation: Second Thoughts about the '60s*. (New York: Summit, 1989), 24.

Collier, Peter, and David Horowitz. *Destructive Generation: Second Thoughts about the '60s*. New York: Summit, 1989.

3. Book, Four or More Authors or Editors—CMS Use *and others* after naming the first author in the notes, but list all authors in the bibliography when that is convenient.

> 3. Philip Curtin and others, eds., *African History* (Boston: Little, Brown, 1978), 77.

Curtin, Philip, Steve Feierman, Leonard Thompson, and Jan Vansina, eds. *African History*. Boston: Little, Brown, 1978.

4. Book, Edited—Focus on the Editor—CMS If you cite an edited work by the editor's name, identify the original author after the title of the work.

> 4. Scott Elledge, ed., *Paradise Lost*, by John Milton (New York: Norton, 1975).

Elledge, Scott, ed. *Paradise Lost*, by John Milton. New York: Norton, 1975.

5. Book, Edited—Focus on the Original Author—CMS

5. William Shakespeare, *The Complete Works of Shakespeare*, 4th ed., ed. David Bevington (New York: Longman, 1997).

Shakespeare, William. *The Complete Works of Shakespeare*. 4th ed. Edited by David Bevington. New York: Longman, 1997.

6. Book Written by a Group—CMS

6. Council of Biology Editors, *Scientific Style and Format: The CBE Manual for Authors, Editors, and Publishers*, 6th ed. (Cambridge: Cambridge University Press, 1994).

Council of Biology Editors. *Scientific Style and Format: The CBE Manual for Authors, Editors, and Publishers*. 6th ed. Cambridge: Cambridge University Press, 1994.

7. Book with No Author—CMS List it by its title, alphabetized by the first major word (excluding *The, A,* or *An*).

7. *Webster's Collegiate Thesaurus* (Springfield: Merriam, 1976).

Webster's Collegiate Thesaurus. Springfield: Merriam, 1976.

8. Work of More Than One Volume—CMS

1. Ernest Jones, *The Last Phase*, vol. 3, *The Life and Work of Sigmund Freud* (New York: Basic Books, 1957), 97.

Jones, Ernest. *The Last Phase*. Vol. 3 of *The Life and Work of Sigmund Freud*. New York: Basic Books, 1957.

9. Work in a Series—CMS Do not underline or italicize a series name.

9. Grayson Kirk and Nils H. Wessell, eds., *The Soviet Threat: Myths and Realities*, Proceedings of the Academy of Political Science, no. 33 (New York: Academy of Political Science, 1978), 62.

Kirk, Grayson, and Nils H. Wessell, eds. *The Soviet Threat: Myths and Realities*. Proceedings of the Academy of Political Science, no. 33. New York: Academy of Political Science, 1978.

10. Chapter in a Book—CMS

10. Delia Owens and Mark Owens, "Home to the Dunes," in *The Eye of the Elephant: An Epic Adventure in the African Wilderness* (Boston: Houghton Mifflin, 1992), 11.

Owens, Delia, and Mark Owens. "Home to the Dunes." In *The Eye of the Elephant: An Epic Adventure in the African Wilderness*. Boston: Houghton Mifflin, 1992.

11. Article in a Scholarly Journal—CMS Provide author(s), title of the work (between quotation marks), name of periodical (underlined or italicized), volume number, date of publication, and page numbers.
If the journal restarts pagination with each issue, list the issue number (preceded by a comma and *no.*) before the year.

11. Kerri N. Boutelle and others, "Using Signs, Artwork, and Music to Promote Stair Use in a Public Building," *American Journal of Public Health* 91 (2001): 2005–6.

Boutelle, Kerri N., and others. "Using Signs, Artwork, and Music to Promote Stair Use in a Public Building." *American Journal of Public Health* 91 (2001): 2005–6.

12. Article in a Popular Magazine—CMS Provide author(s), title of the work (between quotation marks), name of magazine (underlined or italicized), date of publication, and page numbers. When an article does not appear on consecutive pages (as in the example below), omit page

numbers in the bibliography entry. Otherwise, include page numbers following the date (separated by a comma).

> 12. Don Graham, "Wayne's World," *Texas Monthly*, March 2000, 110–11.

> Graham, Don. "Wayne's World." *Texas Monthly*, March 2000, 110–11.

13. Article or Selection from a Reader or Anthology—CMS

> 13. Pamela Samuelson, "The Digital Rights War," in *The Presence of Others*, 3rd ed., ed. Andrea Lunsford and John Ruszkiewicz (New York: St. Martin's Press, 2000), 315–20.

> Samuelson, Pamela. "The Digital Rights War." In *The Presence of Others*. 3rd ed., edited by Andrea Lunsford and John Ruszkiewicz. New York: St. Martin's Press, 2000.

14. Article in a Newspaper—CMS Identify the issue by its publication date. Page references are usually omitted for newspapers, but you may list the section containing the article (before the issue date) and identify the edition used (after the date). Individual news stories are not usually listed in the bibliography.

> 14. Celestine Bohlen, "A Stunned Venice Surveys the Ruins of a Beloved Hall," *New York Times*, January 31, 1995, Sec. B, National edition.

15. Encyclopedia—CMS When a reference work is familiar (encyclopedias, dictionaries, thesauruses), omit the names of authors and editors and most publishing information. No page number is given when a work is arranged alphabetically; instead the item ref-erenced is named, following the abbreviation *s.v.* (*sub verbo*, mean-ing "under the word"). Familiar reference works are not listed in the bibliography.

> 15. *The Oxford Companion to English Literature*, 4th ed., s.v. "Locke, John."

16. Biblical Citation—CMS Biblical citations appear in notes but not in the bibliography. If important, you may mention the version of the Bible cited.

```
16. John 18: 37-38 (Jerusalem Bible.)
```

17. Web Page—CMS List the author (or site's sponsor if unsigned), the title of the page, site name, the site's sponsor (if not already mentioned), the address of the page, and date you last viewed the source.

```
16. Pat Schneider, "Your Boat, Your Words,"
Our Words Archive, Amherst Writers & Artists,
http://www.amherstwriters.com/Poems/BoatWord.html
(accessed November 19, 2003).

Schneider, Pat. "Your Boat, Your Words." Our Words
    Archive. Amherst Writers & Artists.
    http://www.amherstwriters.com/Poems/
    BoatWord.html (accessed November 19, 2003).
```

18. Online Article—from Internet Periodical—CMS Cite like a print periodical article, using the name of the Web site when no other periodical is named. Insert location references (if any) before the address. If the address of the article is long and cryptic, list the address of a search page.

```
18. Paul Skowronek, "Left and Right for
Rights," Trincoll Journal, March 13, 1997, http://
www.trincoll.edu/zines/ (accessed November 22, 2005).

Skowronek, Paul. "Left and Right for Rights."
    Trincoll Journal, March 13, 1997. http://
    www.trincoll.edu/zines/ (accessed November 22, 2005).
```

19. Online Article—From Database/Library Subscription Service—CMS Insert the location reference of the database before the address. If the address of the article is long and cryptic, list the address of a search page.

```
19. Mary Loeffelholz, "The Religion of Art in a City
at War: Boston's Public Poetry and the Great Organ, 1863,"
```

American Literary History 13 (2001): 221, http://

muse.jhu.edu/search/search.pl.

Loeffelholz, Mary. "The Religion of Art in a City at War:

　Boston's Public Poetry and the Great Organ, 1863."

　American Literary History 13 (2001): 221.

　http://muse.jhu.edu/search/search.pl.

20. Online Book—CMS Cite typical publication or production details for the original source, then list the address of the online version.

　20. Emily Dickinson, *The Complete Poems of Emily

Dickinson* (Boston: Little, Brown, and Company, 1924),

pt. 1, poem 89, http://www.bartleby.com/113 (accessed

October 31, 2003).

Dickinson, Emily. *The Complete Poems of Emily Dickinson.*

　Boston: Little, Brown and Company, 1924, pt. 1,

　poem 89. http://www.bartleby.com/113 (accessed

　October 31, 2003).

21. Online Video or Audio Recording—CMS Cite typical publication or production details for the original source, then identify the format and list the address of the online version.

　21. Derek Walcott, reading of *Omeros* (Sackler Lecture

Hall, Harvard University, MA, April 14, 2003), from WGBH,

Forum Network, RAM. http://streams.wgbh.org/forum/

ram.php?id=1147&size=hi (accessed November 19, 2003).

Walcott, Derek. Reading of *Omeros* (Sackler Lecture Hall,

　Harvard University, Cambridge, MA, April 14, 2003).

　WGBH, *Forum Network*, RAM. http://streams.wgbh.org/

　forum/ram.php?id=1147&size=hi (accessed November 19,

　2003).

22. Speech—CMS List the speaker, the title of the talk, and in parentheses the type of talk, the venue, city, and date.

22. Vera Katz, "Let's Get Portland Back to Work,"
(mayoral address, Governor Hotel, Portland, OR, October
28, 2002).

Katz, Vera. "Let's Get Portland Back to Work." Mayoral
address, Governor Hotel, Portland, OR, October 28,
2002.

23. Government Document—Print—CMS Name the government agency, the title of the document, and basic publication information. For congressional documents, begin by identifying the house, committee, and session; then list the type of document, an identifying number, and other publication details.

23. U.S. Census Bureau, *Statistical Abstracts of the
United States: The National Data Book*, 120th ed.
(Washington, DC: GPO, 2000), table no. 643.

U.S. Census Bureau. *Statistical Abstracts of the United
States: The National Data Book*, 120th ed. Washington,
DC: GPO, 2000.

24. Government Document—Online—CMS After listing traditional publication information, provide online access information.

24. U.S. Department of Labor, "Minimum Wage and
Overtime Pay," *Employment Law Guide*. "Who is covered."
http://www.labor.gov/asp/programs/guide/minwage.htm
(accessed May 1, 2006).

U.S. Department of Labor, "Minimum Wage and Overtime Pay,"
Employment Law Guide. "Who is covered." http://
www.labor.gov/asp/programs/guide/minwage.htm
(accessed May 1, 2006).

25. Video Recording—CMS List the writer or director, the title of the recording, and production details. List secondary acknowledgments where appropriate.

25. Nunnally Johnson, dir. and adapt., *The Man in the Gray Flannel Suit*, VHS, prod. Darryl F. Zanuck, perf. Gregory Peck and others (1956; US: 20th Century Fox, 1997).

Johnson, Nunnally, dir. and adapt. *The Man in the Gray Flannel Suit*. VHS. Produced by Darryl F. Zanuck. Performed by Gregory Peck and others. US: 20th Century Fox, 1997.

26. Audio Recording—Song—CMS If citing a specific track or song, list its title in quotes, before the title of the full recording.

29. Sting [Gordon Sumner], "Synchronicity II," perf. by The Police, *Synchronicity*, CD (1983; US: A&M SP-3735, 2003).

Sting [Gordon Sumner]. "Synchronicity II." Perf. The Police. *Synchronicity*. CD. 1983. US: A&M SP-3735, 2003.

Glossary of Terms nd Usage

This glossary includes words that often cause problems for writers.

a, an. **A** and **an** are **indefinite articles** because they point to objects in a general way (**a** book, **a** church), while the **definite article the** refers to specific things (**the** book, **the** church). **A** is used when the word following it begins with a consonant sound: **a** *house*, **a** *year*, **a** *boat*, **a** *unique* experience. **An** is used when the word following it begins with a vowel sound: **an** *hour*, **an** *interest*, **an** *annoyance*, **an** *illusory* image.

Notice that you choose the article by the *sound* of the word following it. Not all words that begin with vowels actually begin with vowel sounds, and not all words that begin with consonants have initial consonant sounds.

accept/except. **Accept** means "to take, receive, or approve of something." **Except** means "to exclude, or not including": *I **accepted** all the apologies **except** George's.*

adverse/averse. **Adverse** describes something hostile, unfavorable, or difficult. **Averse** indicates the opposition someone has to something; it is ordinarily followed by *to*: *Travis was **averse** to playing soccer under **adverse** field conditions.*

advice/advise. These words aren't interchangeable. **Advice** is a noun meaning "an opinion" or "counsel." **Advise** is a verb meaning "to give counsel or advice": *I'd **advise** you not to give Maggie **advice** about running her business.*

affect/effect. Each word can be either a noun or a verb, although **affect** is ordinarily a verb and **effect** a noun. In its usual sense, **affect** is a verb meaning "to influence" or "to give the appearance of ": *How will the stormy weather **affect** the plans for the outdoor concert? The meteorologist **affected** ignorance when we asked her for a forecast.*

Only rarely is **affect** a noun—as a term in psychology meaning "feeling" or "emotion." On the other hand, **effect** is usually a noun, meaning "consequence" or "result": *The **effect** of the weather may be serious.*

Effect may, however, also be a verb, meaning "to cause" or "to bring about": *The funnel cloud **effected** a change in our plans.* (Compare with: The funnel cloud **affected** our plans.)

aggravate/irritate. Many people use both of these verbs to mean "to annoy" or "to make angry." **Irritate** means "to annoy" whereas **aggravate** means "to make something worse": *It **irritated** Greta when her husband **aggravated** his allergies by smoking.*

ain't. The word isn't appropriate in academic or professional writing.

all ready/already. **All ready**, an adjective phrase, means "prepared and set to go": *Rita signaled that the camera was **all ready** for shooting.*

528

Already, an adverb, means "before" or "previously": *Rita had **already** loaded the film.*

all right. **All right** is the only acceptable spelling. **Alright** is not acceptable in standard English.

allude/elude. **Allude** means "to refer to." **Elude** means "to escape": *Kyle's joke **alluded** to the fact that it was easy to **elude** the portly security guard.*

allude/refer. To **allude** is to mention something indirectly; to **refer** is to mention something directly: *Carter **alluded** to rituals the new students didn't understand. Carter did, however, **refer** to ancient undergraduate traditions and the honor of the college.*

allusion/illusion. An **allusion** is an indirect reference to something. An **illusion** is a false impression or a misleading appearance: *The entire class missed Professor Sweno's **allusion** to the ghost in Hamlet. Professor Sweno entertained the **illusion** that everyone read Shakespeare as often as he did.*

a lot. Often misspelled as one word. It is two. Many readers consider **a lot** inappropriate in academic writing, preferring **many, much,** or some comparable expression.

already. See **all ready/already.**

alright. See **all right.**

among/between. Use **between** with two objects, **among** with three or more: *Francie had to choose **between** Richard and Kyle. Francie had to choose from **among** a dozen actors.*

amount/number. Use **amount** for quantities that can be measured but not counted. Use **number** for things that can be counted, not measured: the **amount** of water in the ocean; the **number** of fish in the sea. Remember that **amount of** is followed by a singular noun, while **number of** is followed by a plural noun.

an. See **a, an.**

and etc. A redundant expression. Use **etc.** alone or **and so on**. See **etc.**

and/or. Can be a useful form in some situations, especially in business and technical writing. Work around it if you can, especially in academic writing. **And/or** is typed with no space before or after the slash.

angry/mad. One should use **angry** to describe displeasure, **mad** to describe insanity.

anyone/any one. These expressions have different meanings. Notice the difference highlighted in these sentences: ***Any one** of those problems could develop into a crisis. I doubt that **anyone** will be able to find a solution to **any one** of the equations.*

anyways. A nonstandard form. Use **anyway**.

as being. A wordy expression. You can usually cut **being**: *In most cases, telephone solicitors are regarded **as (being)** a nuisance.*

averse/adverse.   See **adverse/averse.**

awful.   **Awful** is inappropriate as a synonym for *very: The findings of the two research teams were* **very** *(not* **awful***) close.*

awhile/a while.   **Awhile** is an adverb; **a while** is a noun phrase. After prepositions, always use **a while:** *Bud stood* **awhile** *looking at the grass. Bud decided that the lawn would not have to be cut for* **a while.**

bad/badly.   Remember that **bad** is an adjective describing what something is like; **badly** is an adverb explaining how something is done: *Stanley's taste in music wasn't* **bad.** *Unfortunately, he treated his musicians* **badly.** Problems usually crop up with verbs that explain how something feels, tastes, smells, or looks. In such cases, use **bad:** *The situation looked* **bad.**

because of/due to.   Careful writers usually prefer **because of** to **due to** in many situations: *The investigation into Bud's sudden disappearance stalled* **because of** *(not* **due to***) Officer Bricker's concern for correct procedure.* However, **due to** is often the better choice when it serves as a **subject complement** after a **linking verb:** *Bricker's discretion seemed* **due to cowardice.**

being as/being that.   Both of these expressions sound wordy and awkward when used in place of **because** or **since.** Use **because** and **since** in formal and academic writing.

beside/besides.   **Beside** is a preposition meaning "next to" or "alongside"; **besides** is a preposition meaning "in addition to" or "other than": ***Besides** a sworn confession, the detectives also had the suspect's fingerprints on a gun found* **beside** *the body.* **Besides** can also be an adverb meaning "in addition" or "moreover": *Professor Bellona didn't mind assisting the athletic department, and* **besides,** *she actually liked coaching volleyball.*

between.   See **among/between.**

can/may.   Use **can** to express an ability to do something: *Charnelle* **can** *work differential equations.* Use **may** to express either permission or possibility: *You* **may** *want to compare my solution to the problem to Charnelle's.*

can't hardly.   A colloquial expression that is, technically, a double negative. Use **can hardly** instead when you write.

censor/censure.   As verbs, **censor** means "to cut," "to repress," or "to remove"; **censure** means "to disapprove" and "to condemn": *The student editorial board voted to* **censor** *the four-letter words from Connie Lim's editorial and to* **censure** *her for attempting to publish the controversial piece.*

complement/complementary, compliment/complimentary.   **Complement** and **complementary** describe things completed or compatible. **Compliment** and **complimentary** refer to things praised or given away free: *Travis's sweater* **complemented** *his green eyes. The two parts of Greta's essay were* **complementary,** *examining the same subject from dif-*

*fering perspectives. Travis **complimented** Greta on her successful paper. Greta found his **compliment** sincere. She rewarded him with a **complimentary** sack of rice cakes from her health food store.*

conscience/conscious. **Conscience** is a noun referring to an inner ethical sense; **conscious** is an adjective describing a state of awareness or wakefulness: *The linebacker felt a twinge of **conscience** after knocking the quarterback **unconscious**.*

consensus. This expression is redundant when followed by **of opinion; consensus** by itself implies an opinion. Use **consensus** alone.

could of/would of/should of. Nonstandard forms when used instead of **could have, would have**, or **should have**.

couple of. Casual. Avoid it in formal or academic writing: *The article accused the admissions office of several (not **a couple of**) major blunders.*

credible/credulous. **Credible** means "believable"; **credulous** means "willing to believe on slim evidence." See *also* **incredible/incredulous:** *Officer Bricker found Mr. Hutton's excuse for his speeding **credible**. However, Bricker was known to be a **credulous** police officer, liable to believe any story.*

criteria, criterion. **Criteria**, the plural form, is more familiar, but the word does have a singular form—**criterion**: *John Maynard, age sixty-four, complained that he was often judged according to a single **criterion**, his age. Other **criteria** ought to matter in hiring.*

data/datum. **Data** is the plural form of *datum*. But in informal writing and speech, you will typically see *data* treated as if it were singular: *The **data** is not convincing.* In academic writing use **datum** when a singular form is expected. If **datum** seems awkward, rewrite the sentence to avoid the singular: *The most intriguing **datum** in the study was the rate of population decline. In all the **data**, no figure was more intriguing than the rate of population decline.*

different from/different than. In formal writing, **different from** is usually preferred to **different than**.

discreet/discrete. **Discreet** means "tactful" or "sensitive to appearances" (*discreet* behavior); **discrete** means "individual" or "separate" (*discrete* objects): *Joel was **discreet** about the money spent on his project. He had several **discrete** funds at his disposal.*

disinterested/uninterested. **Disinterested** means "neutral" or "uninvolved"; **uninterested** means "not interested" or "bored": *Alyce and Richard sought a **disinterested** party to arbitrate their dispute. Stanley was **uninterested** in the club's management.*

don't. Writers sometimes forget the apostrophe in this contraction and others like it: **can't, won't.**

due to/because of. See **because of/due to**.

due to the fact that. Wordy. Replace it with **because** when possible.

effect/affect. See **affect/effect**.

elicit/illicit. **Elicit** means to "draw out" or "bring forth"; **illicit** describes something illegal or prohibited: *The detective tried to* ***elicit*** *an admission of* ***illicit*** *behavior from Bud.*

elude/allude. See **allude/elude**.

eminent/imminent. **Eminent** means "distinguished" and "prominent"; **imminent** describes something about to happen: *The arrival of the* ***eminent*** *scholar is* ***imminent***.

enthused. A colloquial expression that should not appear in academic or professional writing. Use **enthusiastic** instead: *Francie was* ***enthusiastic*** *(not* ***enthused***) *about Wilco's latest album.* Never use **enthused** as a verb.

equally as. Redundant. Use either **equally** or **as** to express a comparison—whichever works in a particular sentence.

etc. This common abbreviation for *et cetera* should be avoided in most academic and formal writing. Instead, use **and so on** or **and so forth**. Never use **and etc**.

even though. **Even though** is two words, not one.

everyone/every one. **Everyone** describes a group collectively. **Every one** focuses on the individual elements within a group or collective term. Notice the difference highlighted in these sentences: ***Every one*** *of those problems could develop into an international crisis* ***everyone*** *would regret. I doubt that* ***everyone*** *will be able to attend* ***every one*** *of the sessions.*

except/accept. See **accept/except**.

fact that, the. Wordy. You can usually replace the entire expression with **that**.

farther/further. Use **farther** to refer to distances that can be measured: *It is* ***farther*** *from El Paso to Houston than from New York to Detroit.* Use **further**, meaning "more" or "additional," when physical distance or separation is not involved: *The detective decided that the crime warranted* ***further*** *investigation.*

fewer than/less than. Use **fewer than** with things you can count; use **less than** with quantities that must be measured or can be considered as a whole: *The express lane was reserved for customers buying* ***fewer than*** *ten items. Matthew had* ***less than*** *half a gallon of gasoline.*

flaunt/flout. **Flaunt** means "to show off "; **flout** means "to disregard" or "to show contempt for": *To* ***flaunt*** *his wealth, Mr. Lin bought a Van Gogh landscape.* ***Flouting*** *a gag order, the newspaper published its exposé of corruption in the city council.*

fun, funner, funnest. Used as an adjective, **fun** is not appropriate in academic writing; replace it with a more formal expression. The comparative and superlative forms, **funner** and **funnest**, while increasingly common in spoken English, are inappropriate in writing. In writing, use **more fun** or **most fun**.

get/got/gotten. Both forms are acceptable: *Aretha **has gotten** an* A *average in microbiology. Aretha **has got** an* A *average in microbiology.* Many expressions, formal and informal, rely on **get**. Use the less formal ones only with appropriate audiences: ***get** it together; **get** straight; **get** real.*

good and. Informal. Avoid it in academic writing. *The lake was **icy** (not **good and**) cold when the sailors threw Sean in.*

good/well. As a modifier, **good** is an adjective only; **well** can be either an adjective or an adverb: ***Katy is good. Katy is well.*** **Good** is often mistakenly used as an adverb: *Juin conducts the orchestra well (not **good**).*

hanged, hung. **Hanged** has been the past participle conventionally reserved for executions; **hung** is used on other occasions. The distinction is a nice one, probably worth observing: *Connie was miffed when her disgruntled editorial staff decided she should be **hanged** in effigy. Portraits of the faculty were **hung** in the student union.*

he/she. Using **he/she** (or *his/her* or *s/he*) is a way to avoid a sexist pronoun reference.

hisself. A nonstandard form. Don't use it.

hopefully. Some readers object to using the adverb *hopefully* as a sentence modifier. *Hopefully*, they argue, should be used to mean only "with hope": *Traders watched **hopefully** as stock prices approached yet another record.* However, English includes many adverbs like *hopefully* that function as sentence modifiers, including words such as *understandably, mercifully, predictably*, and *honestly*. By precedent and general usage, *hopefully* seems entrenched as a sentence modifier.

illicit/elicit. See **elicit/illicit**.

illusion/allusion. See **allusion/illusion**.

imminent/eminent. See **eminent/imminent**.

imply/infer. **Imply** means "to suggest" or "to convey an idea without stating it." **Infer** is what you might do to figure out what someone else has implied; you examine evidence and draw conclusions from it: *By joking calmly, the pilot sought to **imply** that the aircraft was out of danger. But from the crack that had opened in the wing, the passengers **inferred** that the landing would be harrowing.*

incredible/incredulous. **Incredible** means "unbelievable"; **incredulous** means "unwilling to believe" and "doubting." See also **credible/credulous**. *The press found the governor's explanation for his wealth* *incredible*. *You could hardly blame them for being* **incredulous** *when he attributed his vast holdings to coupon savings.*

infer/imply.   See **imply/infer**.

irregardless.   A nonstandard form. Use **regardless** instead.

irritate/aggravate.   See **aggravate/irritate**.

its/it's.   **It's** is a contraction for *it is*. **Its** is a possessive pronoun meaning "belonging to it."

judgment/judgement.   The British spell this word with two *e*'s. Americans spell it with just one: **judgment**.

kind of.   This expression is colloquial when used to mean "rather." Avoid *kind of* in formal writing.

less than.   See **fewer than/less than**.

lie/lay.   **Lie** means "recline" and doesn't take an object: *Travis **lies** under the cottonwood tree. He **lay** there all afternoon.* Its principal parts are **lie, lay, lain**. **Lay** means "place" or "put" and takes an object: *Jenny **lays** a book on Travis's desk. Yesterday, she **laid** a memo on his desk.* Its principal parts are **lay, laid, laid**.

like/as.   **As, as if,** or **as though** are preferred in situations where a comparison involves a subject and verb. *Mr. Butcher is self-disciplined,* **as** (*not* **like**) *you would expect a champion weightlifter to be.* **Like** is acceptable when it introduces a prepositional phrase, not a clause: *Yvonne looks **like** her mother.*

literally.   When you write that something is **literally** true, you mean that it is exactly as you have stated. The following sentence means that Bernice emitted heated water vapor: *Bernice **literally** steamed when Ike ordered her to marry him.* If you want to keep the image (*steamed*), omit **literally**: *Bernice steamed when Ike ordered her to marry him.*

lose/loose.   **Lose** is a verb, meaning "to misplace," "to be deprived of," or "to be defeated." **Loose** can be either an adjective or a verb. As an adjective, **loose** means "not tight"; as a verb, **loose** means "to let go" or "to untighten": *Without Martin as quarterback, the team might **lose** its first game of the season. The strap on Martin's helmet had worked **loose**. It **loosened** so much that Martin **lost** his helmet.*

mad, angry.   See **angry/mad**.

majority/plurality.   A **majority** is more than half of a group; a **plurality** is the largest part of a group when there is *less than a majority*. In an election, for example, a candidate who wins 50.1 percent of the vote can claim a **majority**. One who wins a race with 40 percent of the vote may claim a **plurality**, but not a majority.

many times.   Wordy. Use **often** instead.

may/can.   See **can/may**.

media/medium. **Medium** is the singular of **media**: *Connie believed that the press could be as powerful a **medium** as television. The visual **media** are discussed in the textbook.* The term **media** is commonly used to refer to newspapers and magazines, as well as television and radio.

might of. A nonstandard form. Use **might have** instead.

moral, morale. As a noun, **moral** is a lesson. **Morale** is a state of mind: *The **moral** of the fable was to avoid temptation. The **morale** of the team was destroyed by the accident.*

must of. Nonstandard. Use **must have** instead.

nice. This adjective has little impact when used to mean "pleasant": *It was a **nice** day; Sally is a **nice** person.* Find a more specific word or expression. **Nice** can be used effectively to mean "precise" or "fine": *There was a **nice** distinction between the two positions.*

nowheres. Nonstandard version of **nowhere** or **anywhere**.

number/amount. See **amount/number**.

off of. A wordy expression. **Off** is enough: *Arthur drove his Jeep **off** the road.*

O.K., OK, okay. Not the best choice for formal writing; but give the expression respect. It's an internationally recognized expression of approval. OK?

persecute/prosecute. **Persecute** means "to oppress" or "to torment"; **prosecute** is a legal term meaning "to bring charges or legal proceedings" against someone or something: *Connie felt **persecuted** by criticisms of her political activism. She threatened to **prosecute** anyone who interfered with her First Amendment rights.*

personal/personnel. **Personal** refers to what is private, belonging to an individual. **Personnel** are the people staffing an office or institution: *Drug testing all airline **personnel** might infringe on **personal** freedom.*

phenomena/phenomenon. **Phenomenon** is singular; **phenomena** is plural: *The astral **phenomenon** of meteor showers is common in August. Many other astral **phenomena** are linked to particular seasons.*

plurality/majority. See **majority/plurality**.

plus. Don't use **plus** as a conjunction or conjunctive adverb meaning "and," "moreover," "besides," or "in addition to": *Mr. Burton admitted to cheating on his income taxes this year. **Moreover** (not **Plus**), he acknowledged that he had filed false returns for the last three years.*

prejudice/prejudiced. **Prejudice** is a noun; **prejudiced** is a verb form. Do not drop the **-d** from **prejudiced**: *Joe Kamakura is **prejudiced** (not **prejudice**) against liberals.*

principal/principle. **Principal** means "chief" or "most important." It also names the head of an elementary or secondary school (remember "The

principal is your pal"?). Finally, it can be a sum of money lent or borrowed. A **principle**, on the other hand, is a guiding rule or fundamental truth: *Ike intended to be the **principal** breadwinner of the household. Ike declared it was against his **principles** to have his wife work.*

proceed to.   A wordy and redundant construction when it merely delays the real action of a sentence: *We **opened** (**not proceeded to**) the strongbox.*

real.   Often used as a colloquial version of **very**: "I was **real** scared." This usage is inappropriate in academic writing.

really.   An adverb too vague to make much of an impression in many sentences: *It was **really** hot; I am **really** sorry.* Replace **really** with a more precise expression or delete it.

reason is . . . because.   The expression is redundant. Use one half of the expression or the other—not both: *The reason the cat is ferocious is that (not **because**) she is protecting her kittens.* Or: *The cat is ferocious **because** she is protecting her kittens.*

refer/allude.   See **allude/refer**.

set/sit.   **To sit** means "to take a seat" and doesn't take an object. Its main forms are **sit, sat, sat**: *Haskell **sits** under the cottonwood tree. He **sat** there all afternoon.* **To set** means "to place" or "to put" and takes a direct object. Its main forms are **set, set, set**: *Jenny **set** a plate on the table. At Christmas, we **set** a star atop the tree.*

should of.   Mistaken form of **should have**. Also incorrect are **could of** and **would of**.

sit/set.   See **set/sit**.

so.   Vague when used as an intensifier, especially when no explanation follows **so**: *Sue Ellen was **so** sad.* **So** used this way can sound trite (*how sad is **so** sad?*) or juvenile: *Professor Sweno's play was **so** bad.* If you use **so**, complete your statement: *Sue Ellen was **so** sad she cried for an hour.*

stationary/stationery.   **Stationary**, an adjective, means "immovable, fixed in place." **Stationery** is a noun meaning "writing material."

supposed to.   Many writers forget the *d* at the end of **suppose** when the word is used with auxiliary verbs: *Calina was **supposed** (not suppose) **to** check her inventory.*

than/then.   **Than** is a conjunction expressing difference or comparison; **then** is an adverb expressing time: *If the film is playing tomorrow, Shannon would rather go **then** than today.*

theirselves.   A nonstandard form. Use **themselves** instead.

then/than.   See **than/then**.

thusly.   A fussy, nonstandard form. Don't use it. **Thus** is stuffy enough without the *-ly*.

till/until. **Until** is used more often in school and business writing, though the words are usually interchangeable. No apostrophe is used with **till**. You may occasionally see the poetic form **'til**, but don't use it in academic or business writing.

to/too. Most people know the difference between these words. But a writer in a hurry can easily put down the preposition **to** when the adverb **too** is intended. *Coach Rhoades was **too** (not **to**) surprised to speak after his team won its first game in four years.*

toward/towards. **Toward** is preferred, though either form is fine.

try and. An informal expression. In writing, use **try to** instead.

type. You can usually delete this word: *Hector was polite.* Not: *Hector was a polite **type** of guy.*

uninterested/disinterested. See **disinterested/uninterested**.

unique. Something **unique** is one of a kind. It can't be compared with anything else, so expressions such as *most unique, more unique*, or *very unique* don't make sense. The word **unique**, when used properly, should stand alone. Quite often **unique** appears where another, more specific adjective is appropriate: *The **most inventive** (not **unique**) merchant on the block was Tong-chai.*

until/till. See **till/until**.

used to. Many writers forget the **d** at the end of **use**.

utilize. Many readers prefer the simpler term **use**: *Mr. Ringling **used** (not **utilized**) his gavel to regain the crowd's attention.*

well/good. See **good/well**.

who/whom. Use **who** when the pronoun is a subject; use **whom** when it is an object: ***Who** wrote the ticket? **To whom** was the ticket given?*

with regards to. Drop the **s** in regards. The correct expression is **with regard to**.

won't. Writers sometimes forget the apostrophe in this contraction and in others like it: **can't, don't**.

would of. Mistaken form of **would have**. Also incorrect are **could of** and **should of**.

you all. Southern expression for *you*, usually plural. Not used in academic writing.

your/you're. **You're** is the contraction for *you are*; **your** is a possessive form: ***You're** certain Maxine has been to Iran? **Your** certainty on this matter may be important.*

Credits

Text Credits

Angier, Natalie, "Mating for Life?" in *The Beauty and the Beastly*. New York: Houghton Mifflin Company, 1995.

Anzaldúa, Gloria, From "How to Tame a Wild Tongue" in *Borderlands/La Frontera: The New Mestiza*. Copyright © 1987, 1999 by Gloria Anzaldúa. Reprinted by permission of Aunt Lute Books.

Barnett, Lincoln, *The Universe and Dr. Einstein*. Copyright © 1948 by Harper & Brothers. Copyright © 1948 by Lincoln Barnett. Revised editions copyright © 1950 by Lincoln Barnett.

Barnett, Rosalind Shait and Caryl Rivers. "The Persistence of Gender Myths in Math." Originally appeared in *Education Week*, October 13, 2004. Reprinted by permission of the authors.

Bilger, Burkhard. "The Egg Men: How Breakfast Gets Served at the Flamingo Hotel in Las Vegas," *The New Yorker*, September 5, 2005. Reprinted by permission of the author.

Blake, William, "The Tyger," 1794.

Broache, Anne. "Oh Deer!" Originally published in *Smithsonian*, October, 2005.

Costas, Bob. "Eulogy for Mickey Mantle," August 15, 1995.

Crouch, Stanley. "Blues for Jackie." *All American Skin Game, or the Decoy of Race: The Long and the Short of It, 1990–1994*. New York: Pantheon Books, 1995.

Deng, Alephonsion. "I Have Had to Learn to Live With Peace." From *Newsweek*, October 2005. © 2005 Newsweek, Inc. All rights reserved. Reprinted by permission.

Didion, Joan. "Georgia O'Keefe," originally published in *The White Album*. Reprinted by permission of the author.

Edge, John T. From "I'm Not Leaving Until I Eat This Thing." *Oxford American Magazine*, September/October 1999. Reprinted by permission of the author.

Engle, Gary. "What Makes Superman So Darned American?" Excerpt from *Superman at Fifty*. Ed. Gary Engle and Dennis Dooley. © 1987 Octavia Books.

Gerstner, Louis Jr. "High Marks for Standardized Tests," *Prism Online*, February 2001. <http://prismonline.com>.

Hamilton, Joan C. "Journey to the Center of the Mind." Reprinted from *Business Week*, April 19, 2004. © 2004 The McGraw-Hill Companies, Inc.

Hoberman, Barry. "Translating the Bible," as originally published in the February 1985 issue of *The Atlantic Monthly*, Vol. 255, No. 2. Copyright © 1985 Atlantic Monthly.

Hughes, Robert. *Culture of Complaint: The Fraying of America*. © 1993 Oxford University Press. By permission of Oxford University Press, Inc.

Johnson, Steve. "Watching TV Makes You Smarter." From *Everything Bad is Good for You: How Today's Popular Culture is Actually Making Us Smarter*. Copyright © 2005 Riverhead Trade Publishing. Reprinted by permission of the Penguin Group. Originally appeared in *The New York Times Magazine*, April 24, 2005.

Kennedy, John F. *Inaugural Address*. January 20, 1961.

Kerouac, Jack. *On the Road*. New York: Penguin Books. © 1955, 1957 by Jack Kerouac; Copyright renewed © 1983 by Stella Kerouac, renewed © 1985 by Stella Kerouac and Jan Kerouac. Used by permission of Viking, a division of Penguin Group (USA) Inc.

Lewon, Dennis. From "Malaria's Not So Magic Bullet," *Escape*, July 1999. Reprinted by permission of the author.

McGrath, Charles. "Not Funnies," by Charles McGrath. Originally appeared in *The New York Times Magazine*, July 11, 2004 © 2004 The New York Times. Reprinted by permission.

Olds, Sharon. "The One Girl at the Boy's Party" from *The Dead and the Living* by Sharon Olds. Copyright © 1987 by Sharon Olds. Used by permission of Alfred A. Knopf, a division of Random House, Inc.

Ravitch, Diane. "Educational Insensitivity." Originally published in *The New York Times*, March 24, 1998. Copyright The New York Times. Reprinted by permission.

Santiago, Chiori. "The Fine and Friendly Art of Luis Jiménez," *Smithsonian*, 1993. Reprinted by permission of the author.

Schor, Juliet. *The Overworked American.* New York: Basic Books, 1991. Reprinted by permission of the Perseus Books Group.

Sigma Tau Delta Newsletter. From the Spring 2000 issue of the *Sigma Tau Delta Newsletter*, © 2000 by Sigma Tau Delta International English Honor Society. Reprinted by permission.

Stateman, Alison. "Postcards from the Edge," *New York Times*, June 15, 2003. © 2003 The New York Times. Reprinted by permission.

Stern, Barbara Lang. "Tears Can be Crucial to Your Physical and Emotional Health," *Vogue*, June 1979. Reprinted by permission of the author.

Sternbergh, Adam. "Got Bud All Up in the Hizzle, Yo! If it weren't for rap, our only new words would be 'ideate' and 'synergy.'" First appeared in the *National Post*, March 15, 2003. Reprinted by permission of the author.

Student Work: Jessica Carfolite's APA essay.

Student Work: Conclusion paragraph by Jeremy Christiansen.

Student Work: Thesis from Tallon Harding's paper "Overwhelmed and Overlooked."

Student Work: Nelson Rivera's MLA essay.

Student Work: Literary Analysis by Sally Shelton.

Walzer, Michael. "Feed the Face," *The New Republic*, June 9, 1997, v. 21, p. 29. Reprinted by permission of the author.

The Weekly Standard. "homepage." <http://weeklystandard.com>.

West, Cornel. *Race Matters.* Copyright © 1993, 2001 by Cornel West. Reprinted by permission of Beacon Press, Boston.

Wright, Richard. *Native Son.* New York: Harper & Brothers, 1940.

Yahoo! Web page. Reproduced with permission of Yahoo! Inc. Copyright 2000 by Yahoo! Inc. Yahoo! and the Yahoo! logo are trademarks of Yahoo! Inc.

Yankelovich, Daniel. "The Work Ethic is Underemployed." *Psychology Today.* May 1983. Ziff-Davis Publishing.

Zinsser, William. "American Places." From *Willie and Drake: An American Profile*. New York: HarperCollins, 1992.

Photo Credits

In**d**ex

540

Editing And Proofreading Symbols

The boldface chapter and section numbers to the right of each symbol and explanation direct you to relevant places in this book.

abbr	Problem with an **abbr**eviation.	**37a**
adj	Problem with an **adj**ective.	**25b–d**
adv	Problem with an **adv**erb.	**25e–f**
agr	Problem with subject-verb or pronoun-antecedent **agr**eement.	**17, 22**
apos	An **apos**trophe is missing or misused.	**20b**
art	An **art**icle is misused.	**20d, 28b**
awk	**Awk**ward. Sentence reads poorly, but problem is difficult to identify.	**15f–i, 16a–c**
cap	A word needs to be **cap**italized.	**36b, 36c**
case	A pronoun is in the wrong **case**.	**23**
coh	A sentence or paragraph lacks **coh**erence.	**12a, 12b**
cs	Sentence contains a **c**omma **s**plice.	**30c**
div	Word **div**ided in the wrong place.	**35b**
dm (or dang)	**D**angling **m**odifier. A modifying phrase without a specific term to modify.	**25a**
frag	Sentence **frag**ment.	**30a**
ital	**Ital**ics needed.	**36a**
lc	Use a **l**ower**c**ase instead of a capital letter.	**36b, 36c**
mm	A **m**odifier is **m**isplaced.	**25a**
num	Problem with the use of **num**bers.	**37b**
p	Error in **p**unctuation.	**27, 29–33, 35**
pass	A **pass**ive verb is used ineffectively.	**16, 18e**

pl	**Pl**ural form is faulty.	**20a**
pron	**Pron**oun is faulty in some way.	**24**
ref	Not clear what a pronoun **ref**ers to.	**21**
rep	Word or phrase is **rep**eated ineffectively.	**16c**
run-on (or fs)	A **run-on** sentence or **f**used **s**entence.	**30d**
sp	A word is mis**sp**elled.	**5b**
sub	**Sub**ordination is faulty.	**15g**
trans	A **trans**ition is weak or absent.	**14**
vb	Problem with **vb** form.	**18, 27**
ww	**W**rong **w**ord in this situation.	**00**
¶	Begin a new paragraph.	**12**
no ¶	Do not begin a new paragraph.	**12**
⊙	Insert a period.	**29a**
∧	Insert a comma.	**31a–31c, 31e**
no ∧	No comma needed.	**31d**
∨	Insert an apostrophe.	**20b**
⦙	Insert a colon.	**32b**
⦙	Insert a semicolon.	**32a**
∨	Insert quotation marks.	**33a**
//	Make these items parallel.	**15h**
∧	Insert.	
ↄ	Cut this word or phrase.	
#	Leave a space.	
⌒	Close up a space.	
✕	Problem here; find it.	
∼	Reverse these items.	